D1598527

JUDAISM AND HOMOSEXUALITY

JUDAISM AND HOMOSEXUALITY

An Authentic Orthodox View

RABBI CHAIM RAPOPORT

Foreword by
Chief Rabbi Professor Jonathan Sacks

Preface by Dayan Berkovits

VALLENTINE MITCHELL
LONDON • PORTLAND, OR

First Published in 2004 in Great Britain by
VALLENTINE MITCHELL
Crown House, 47 Chase Side
Southgate, London N14 5BP

and in the United States of America by
VALLENTINE MITCHELL
c/o ISBS, 920 N.E. 58th Avenue, Suite 300
Portland, Oregon 97213-3786

Website: http://www.vmbooks.com

British Library Cataloguing in Publication Data

Rapoport, Chaim, Rabbi
    Judaism and homosexuality: an authentic orthodox view
    1. Homosexuality – Religious aspects – Judaism
    I. Title
    296.3'66

ISBN 0-85303-452-4 (Paper)
ISBN 0-85303-501-6 (Cloth)

Library of Congress Cataloging-in-Publication Data

Rapoport, Hayim.
    Judaism and homosexuality: an authentic orthodox view/Chaim Rapoport; with a
foreword by Jonathan Sacks.
    p. cm.
    Includes bibliographical references and index.
    ISBN 0-85303-452-4 (cloth)
    1. Homosexuality–Religious aspects–Judaism. 2. Orthodox Judaism–Doctrines. 3.
Pastoral psychology (Judaism) I. Title.

BM729.H65R37 2003
296'.086'64–dc21
                                                                    2003057164

Typeset in 11/13pt Sabon by Vitaset, Paddock Wood, Kent
Printed in Great Britain by
MPG Books Ltd, Bodmin, Cornwall

Contents

Foreword

At the heart of Judaism is a remarkable idea, that first an individual, then a family, a tribe, a collection of tribes and then a nation entered into a covenant with God to live a life faithful to His word. It would become, in the biblical phrase, a 'kingdom of priests and a holy nation'. Its collective existence would be devoted to 'righteousness and justice' on the one hand, 'holiness' on the other, and by its dedication to these ideals it would become a living witness to God's presence in the world.

Needless to say, these were high standards to live up to, and much of Jewish literature is marked by candid acknowledgement of Israel's shortcomings. Yet in no small measure that is what the people became. Few in numbers, insignificant in power, dispersed and all too often persecuted, they kept faith with the covenant and took immense care to hand on their values to future generations. The chapter they wrote in the history of mankind is a moving testament to the fidelity of the human spirit in response to the call of God.

One of Judaism's fundamental beliefs is that the God of revelation is also the God of creation. There is, in other words, a deep congruence between the life we are called on to lead (revelation) and the universe in which we are called on to live it (creation). Judaism is neither an abandonment *of* the world nor an abandonment *to* the world but a struggle to establish God's presence within it. To put it another way, Judaism is neither a renunciation of pleasure (asceticism) nor an amoral pursuit of it (hedonism) but a way of life that *sanctifies* pleasure by dedicating it to God and to the wider values of the covenant as a whole.

Nowhere is this more apparent than in Judaism's understanding of sexuality. There have been cultures marked by a profound distrust of sexuality, seeing it as a shameful acknowledgement of the physicality of human existence, to be foregone in pursuit of a more spiritual, otherworldly life. From this came the concept of a monastic existence and the adoption of celibacy as an ideal. At the opposite extreme are cultures that embrace sexuality as the celebration of the physical, in contradistinction to the spiritual, divesting it of any higher purpose than transitory pleasure, unaccompanied by lasting commitment or responsibility. The secular West is passing through such a phase today. Judaism rejects both alternatives, for each contains only half the truth of the human situation. We are physical beings, embodied selves, part of nature, or as the Torah puts it, 'dust of the earth'. But we are not only physical beings. We are self-conscious, reflective persons, capable of moral choice. There is within us the 'breath of God'. In a bold and original challenge to humanity, the Torah invites those who heed its call to combine sexuality with spirituality.

Hence the unusual significance of sexual ethics within the Jewish way of life. Judaism is not puritanical. It does not condemn sexual pleasure; it values it. But Judaism is not hedonistic either. It does not believe that, in a covenantal life, one can divorce pleasure from the moral framework in which it takes place. The institution which the Torah sets forth as its ideal is marriage – not marriage as a social convention but as the human counterpart of Israel's covenant with God. In marriage, man and woman pledge themselves to one another in a bond of love, and in and through that love bring new lives into existence. The prophets – Hosea, Isaiah, Jeremiah and Ezekiel – saw marriage as the supreme metaphor for God's relationship with His people. The I-and-Thou between man and wife mirrors the I-and-Thou of God and mankind.

It need hardly be said that there are few aspects of Judaism more out-of-step with today's radically individualistic culture than its view of sexual ethics. That, however, has always been the fate of one or other element of Jewish life. To be a Jew has always involved being willing to challenge the idols of the age, whatever the idols, whichever the age. One of the idols of our time is the idea of the sovereign self, navigating the world with no binding commitments beyond personal inclination and private desire. Today's secular culture resists the idea that there may be boundaries to the life we may legitimately pursue. It finds it difficult to understand that the logic of 'I ought' is quite different to that of 'I feel' or 'I want'. At such times, Judaism's ethics become counter-cultural. To live by the call of Torah is not an easy undertaking. At times, it is little short of heroic.

This is particularly so for those with a homosexual orientation. The

Torah forbids homosexual activity as such: that much is clear from the testimony of both biblical and post-biblical literature. It does not condemn a homosexual disposition, because the Torah does not speak about what we are, but about what we do. It does, however, ask of one who has such a disposition to suppress or sublimate it and act within the Torah's constraints. What this might involve requires case-by-case counselling: homosexuality is not a single phenomenon but a spectrum of conditions and existential circumstances, and sensitive advice is needed for each individual. Whatever the counsel, however, none of us should under-estimate the difficult journey he or she may have to make. For most, it will be fraught with immense pain.

Just as the Torah asks of the homosexual to wrestle with his or her sexual desires, however, so too it asks of the rest of us to understand his or her plight, caught between two identities and two cultures. I, for one, can never forget the fact that lesbians, gay men and bisexuals as well as Jews, were the victims of Nazi Germany and remain the object of prejudice and misunderstanding today. As Jews, therefore, we have special reason to be on our guard against attitudes, words and behaviour that give needless offence or in any other way add to the trauma of those already fraught with great internal conflict. Stereotyping, homophobia and verbal or other abuse are absolutely forbidden. Jewish law and teaching condemn in the strongest possible terms those who shame others. 'One should rather throw oneself into a fiery furnace', said the sages, 'than humiliate someone else in public.'

It is not enough to know that something is forbidden. Our full humanity requires of us that we understand the difficulty – physical, psychological, even existential – that individuals may experience as they engage in inner struggle between instinct and obligation, desire and duty, personal emotion and religious imperative. Compassion, sympathy, empathy, understanding – these are essential elements of Judaism. They are what homosexual Jews who care about Judaism need from us today. That is what lies behind Rabbi Chaim Rapoport's book.

It is a sensitive, thoughtful work on a subject too often either ignored or treated superficially. Although it contains an impressive array of halachic sources, its subject is less *halachah* than pastoral psychology; not, what is permitted and what forbidden, but how shall an individual cope with profound dissonance between what he feels himself to be and what Judaism calls on us to be. No one should under-estimate the depth of that conflict. It is real and painful, sometimes to the point of depression and despair. There are homosexual Jews who care deeply about Judaism, who seek to live by its laws and ideals, but at the same time need counsel from someone who has made the effort to listen, enter into their struggle, and find the words which, while not dissolving the problem, ease some of its loneliness and emotional confusion.

What makes Rabbi Rapoport's book invaluable is that he has understood this. He is a courageous figure who has written on a difficult subject that many would rather avoid. Parts of the book will be controversial. As he himself indicates at various points, there are halachic authorities who take a view different from his own. Nonetheless, this is a work of genuine psychological depth and insight. We pray, in the *kaddish de-rabbanan*, for rabbis to be blessed with 'grace, loving kindness and compassion'. In Rabbi Rapoport we have such a man.

Judaism can rarely be internalised without prolonged inner struggle. Many of the Psalms speak directly from this tempestuous emotional realm. According to the Torah, the Jewish people acquired its name only when Jacob, alone and afraid, wrestled at night with the angel that had no name. 'Israel', the name he was given after that contest, means 'one who struggles with God and with mankind and prevails'. The great thinkers of Judaism have always known that it is not a faith that brings serenity or peace of mind. The religions that promise these things purchase them at great price: a withdrawal from engagement with the conflicts and challenges of a life that seeks to refashion the physical in response to the spiritual. Judaism never lets us rest because it holds before us two conflicting realities – the world that is and the world we are called on to make, the 'I' of human desire and the 'Thou' of God's call. From that cognitive dissonance comes the 'strife of the spirit' in which true greatness is born.

Those who read this book will not discover that this strife can suddenly be resolved. They will, however, know that in Rabbi Chaim Rapoport they have found a sensitive and sympathetic spirit, prepared to address a real and painful conflict with honesty and the best available guidance; that, in short, they are not alone. This is an important and courageous book, urgently needed, well written, thoroughly researched, and graciously conceived. I congratulate its author. May it bring understanding and insight to all who read it.

Jonathan Sacks
Chief Rabbi of the United Hebrew Congregations
of the Commonwealth

Preface

This is an important and challenging book: probably the first meaningful attempt to articulate a strictly Orthodox perspective on the question of homosexuality. It is written *be'safah berurah u'vin'imah* – in a manner which is clear and uncompromising as to halachic values and norms, yet at the same time compassionate and sensitive to the needs of those who find themselves in a religious predicament because of their sexual proclivities.

Rabbi Rapoport is to be congratulated for his courage in tackling a topic which is so unenviable in its complexities.

The book is a valuable academic study, with a multitude of references and wealth of information. Simultaneously it serves as a practical guide to help rabbis, and others, relate to the homosexual in our midst. Rabbi Rapoport does not shrink from facing up to the difficult issues.

The flavour of the book can perhaps best be gleaned from the chapter entitled 'Questions and Responses'. This chapter, responding as it does to input from the general community, gives us a wide insight as to the complexities of the issues, and the nature of the concerns which need to be addressed.

Not everybody will agree, of course, with all of Rabbi Rapoport's conclusions, or even with the direction of his arguments. There will also be some, no doubt, who are uncomfortable with the book as a whole, or who may think that it should not have been written and publicly disseminated. We grew up, after all, in an age (or so it seemed), of comparative innocence, in which sexual matters were not openly discussed. And even if some topics were not beyond the pale, one recoiled, instinctively, from talking about homosexuality.

We can, however, no longer afford the luxury of avoiding the unpalatable. The book is important, because it is timely and challenging, because the issues are contemporary. *Halachah* is there to deal with real-life problems and situations, rather than to dabble in abstractions.

The phenomenon of homosexuality has, of course, always been with us – as evidenced by the Torah's unequivocal and unambiguous prohibition of all forms of male homosexual practice. And halachic literature deals comprehensively, as Rabbi Rapoport shows, with all aspects of the phenomenon, as well as with lesbian behaviour.

As a practical halachic issue, however, it has only become significant in recent years, with the increased awareness of homosexual behaviour in our society, and its increased acceptance in Western society.

The fact, however, that these issues are now out in the open means that it is a subject from which we cannot escape. We have to deal with today's issues, rather than those of yesterday, and we have to articulate clearly, and in a balanced manner, what the Torah has to say about these issues.

They will not go away simply by ignoring them, or wishing that they would not be here. Whether we like it or not, we do not live in a vacuum, and (other than a few fortunate few) cannot simply retreat to a cocoon.

And there is also another consideration. The attitudes of the society in which we live, whether excessively intolerant, or excessively liberal, are bound to influence us. If we take our *yiddishkeit* seriously, we have to constantly examine our beliefs and perspectives, and ask ourselves whether or not they are those of the Torah. Have we, perhaps, allowed ourselves, even if only subconsciously, to be affected either by extraneous prejudices or by contemporary norms?

The effect of the world outside upon our *weltanschauung* is specifically emphasised by Rambam in his *Hilchot De'ot*. It is neatly illustrated by the well-known anecdote about the man who declared – when homosexual practices between consenting adults was decriminalised – that he was emigrating. 'Is that not a somewhat excessive response', he was asked, 'to a change in legislation?' 'Well,' came the answer, 'a hundred years ago they put you to death for such behaviour. Fifty years ago it was hard labour for life. Until now it has been a criminal offence. I have decided to emigrate before they make it compulsory.'

There is a germ of truth in this anecdote. As legal norms become more liberal, people's attitudes to what is morally acceptable become increasingly more tolerant. What was previously unthinkable eventually becomes quite acceptable.

This kind of gradual moral relativism is clearly rejected by the Torah. It is definitely unacceptable for an Orthodox Jew to whittle down or ameliorate the perspectives of *halachah*, simply to accommodate contemporary political correctness.

In an original exercise of lateral thinking, Rabbi Rapoport suggests that the very liberalism of the secular world (with its undoubted challenge for the Torah-true Jew) may provide something of a 'solution' to the problem of how to treat Jewish homosexuals. Many such people nowadays, he suggests, can be classified as a *tinok shenishbah* – someone who bears a kind of 'diminished responsibility', by virtue of the pervasive secular influences of the outside world on their beliefs and values.

Opinions may differ as to the halachic viability of this approach, as well as the extent to which it can provide a general formula for our dealings with Jewish homosexuals. But it does have the merit of providing specific halachic parameters as a basis for consideration. Needless to say, as Rabbi Rapoport emphasises, it is only meant to be a *bedi'avad* rationale (dealing with the reality of the phenomenon), and should not be taken as a *hechsher* for people seeking to engage in homosexual conduct.

Rabbi Rapoport's book shows true compassion for the confused Orthodox homosexual. He does, however, not adequately deal with a disturbing aspect of the contemporary attitude to homosexuality – which might best be described as the ideological underpinnings of the gay movement. This lobby seeks – often in an openly militant fashion – to legitimise and validate homosexuality as an alternative life-style, and to assert the 'rights' of homosexuals as against those of the heterosexual community.

The word 'gay', itself, is in fact an acronym for the phrase 'good as you'. Thus, the term seeks to promote the general proposition that all forms of sexual behaviour are equally acceptable. Specifically, it implies that there is moral equivalence between heterosexual and homosexual conduct.

From a Jewish standpoint, however, such a proposition is totally unacceptable. However much sympathy we may have for the individual homosexual, this should not be translated into ambivalence in terms of our moral perspectives. Helping individual homosexuals, as human beings, should not conflict with our duty to counter philosophies which fundamentally conflict with the Torah.

Two thousand years ago, in a different context, the great *tanna*

Rabbi Yochanan ben Zakai expressed an ineluctable ethical dilemma: 'Woe to me if I speak, and woe to me if I desist.' What should be the position of a leader of Judaism faced with behaviour which is clearly antithetical to *halachah*? Should he say nothing about it, for fear that public discussion may encourage further transgression? Or should he speak out, precisely *because of* the problematic nature of the issue, so as to demonstrate that rabbis are not unaware of what happens in the outside world?

Rabbi Rapoport has clearly asked himself the same wrenching question, and has answered it in the spirit of Rabbi Yochanan ben Zakai. '*Ki yesharim darchei Hashem: tzadikim yelchu vam, u'foshim yikashlu vam*'. Torah is eternal truth, of eternal relevance, and must at all times be articulated. Those who wish to learn, and follow the path of the Torah, will find the necessary guidance. Those who wish to distort the Torah's message, must bear their own responsibility.

To the extent that Rabbi Rapoport's book opens up the debate, and helps people to come closer to *Hakadosh Baruch Hu*, it will have amply justified its composition. Knowing him as I do, and knowing that his intentions are entirely *l'shem Shamayim*, I am honoured to have been asked to write this Preface to his work.

Dayan Berel Berkovits
Beth Din, Federation of Synagogues, London

Author's Preface

A rather unexpected set of circumstances brought me to confront the challenges of Jewish homosexuals and their families in a manner that I had never anticipated. Divine Providence had evidently ordained that, in my destiny as a community Rabbi, I should be sought to help, counsel and endeavour to alleviate the suffering of fellow Jews. A phone call that I received a few years ago from Rabbi Jonathan Dove, then senior Chaplain to Jewish students in London, served as a catalyst in this regard. Rabbi Dove told me that he was searching for an Orthodox Rabbi and religious counsellor who would agree to meet students, some of them Orthodox Jews, who were homosexuals. These students sought guidance and enlightenment on a broad variety of issues: what exactly does Jewish law say about homosexuality? Are gays and lesbians supposed to marry and raise families or are they commanded to remain celibate? If the former, is it conceivable that the Benevolent God would dictate that such individuals embark upon a relationship which was so unnatural for them? If the latter, why would an All-Merciful God create innocent human beings with a homosexual disposition and then condemn them to lifelong celibacy or inevitable sin, stigma and suffering? Why are fellow Jews, sometimes even the strictly observant, so unkind to those with a minority sexual orientation? Why do some families disown their loved ones when they discover that their psychological chemistry is so radically different from what they expected? I listened, researched, discussed, consulted expert religious and psychological authority, advised and tried to help.

... And then, here in Britain, came the tumultuous controversy about homosexuality that pervaded the national Media, the Jewish

Press and preoccupied the minds of religious theologians and secular moralists.[1]

The Chief Rabbi Professor Jonathan Sacks, in a statement issued on 26 January 2000, gave clear expression to the Jewish view on this matter. Commenting from Sweden, where he was attending an international Holocaust conference, Rabbi Sacks said he could 'never forget as a Jew that homosexuals were sent to Auschwitz just as Jews were'. But while it was 'right to fight against prejudice', it was 'quite wrong to suppose that this means abandoning a moral code shared by virtually all the world's greatest religions. In Judaism, homosexual practice is forbidden. This teaching should go hand in hand with sensitivity to those with homosexual feelings and a sympathetic understanding of the challenges they face.'

Public response to the Chief Rabbi's statement varied. The debate that ensued raised vociferous voices from across the spectrum of society as to the attitude one should espouse towards homosexuals and homosexuality. A host of questions surfaced regarding the Chief Rabbi's measured stance, that seeks to create a delicate balance between compassion, understanding and 'inclusivism' on the one hand and an unambiguous condemnation of homosexual practices on the other.

As a member of the Chief Rabbi's Cabinet, a number of these queries were forwarded to me. A variety of questions, posed by a wide range of people, from Rabbinic and lay leaders of the Jewish community to members of non-Jewish communities, as well as individual gays and lesbians, have had to be considered. These include many sensitive and painful issues which some would rather avoid confronting. Yet feigning oblivion to any problem does not make it disappear. On the contrary it often compounds and exacerbates the issue. The same is true regarding the issue of homosexuality. The fact must be faced that as we stand on the threshold of the twenty-first century, there is almost no Jewish community that does not have to contend with the challenges faced by

---

1   The storm in the secular world, and amongst the religious denominations, was fuelled by an attempt to repeal 'Section 28', a clause in an Act of Parliament which was passed by the Conservative Government in 1988. The clause reads as follows: 'A local authority shall not – (a) intentionally promote homosexuality or publish material with the intention of promoting homosexuality; (b) promote the teaching in any maintained school of the acceptability of homosexuality as a pretended family relationship.'

   Some Church leaders expressed grave concern about the ramifications of any changes to such legislation. The Chief Rabbi expressed his opinion that the abolition of Section 28 would 'confuse many young people whose sexual identities are still fluid. It will frustrate any attempt to educate children in the importance of marriage as the basis of a stable and caring society.'

homosexuals and their families. The issues are many and far-reaching. To turn a blind eye would be foolish at best and cruel escapism at worst.

It is with this realisation in mind that I responded to the communal quest for religious advice and guidance in an article published in the *Jewish Chronicle* (which is reproduced in Chapter 8). This article – which represented an initial response to this most controversial issue – received enthusiastic support from the Chief Rabbi, Professor Jonathan Sacks, and members of his ecclesiastical Court, the London Beth Din. I am still receiving a wide-ranging correspondence generated by this article. Rabbis and lay leaders as well as congregational members from across the board of Anglo-Jewry seek clarification of certain concepts, and advice regarding the details of this controversy-laden issue.

It is in the wake of all the above that I decided to write the following chapters, with the hope that Jewish leaders and thinkers will draw ideas and information when forming their own policies and attitudes. In a reciprocal manner I also hope that colleagues in the Rabbinate will share with this author from their own knowledge and experience. This will enable us to work collectively towards the formation of a community that represents the letter and spirit of Jewish law, and reflects the Divine Attributes of justice and benevolence.

This book is not intended to provide answers to all the questions and solutions to all the problems. Rather, it is presented as a humble attempt to address the issues raised from the perspective of our holy Torah. Especially with regard to matters of Jewish law, where a complexity of issues must be considered, the views expressed in this book should not be seen as 'halachic-verdicts'. They are presented as a basis for consultation, discussion and – under the authority of a competent Rabbi – ultimately, decision-making.

I pray to God Almighty that I should not err. No one, however, is immune to error. It is for this reason that our Sages tell us 'Do not make unilateral judgements'. Despite extensive consultation of Rabbinic authority and the review of this book by professional Orthodox counsellors, some mistakes or inaccuracies may have been incorporated. I appeal to readers and scholars to share their constructive criticism with this author. Such co-operation will enable me to ensure that future publications of this volume will be rendered free of the inadequacies of this first publication.

I pray to God Almighty on behalf of all those facing the challenges of homosexuality, whether in person or in an advisory capacity, that they should be given the strength, stamina and courage that they will invariably need in order to rise to their challenges. I pray to God Almighty that the Jewish community should have the fortitude to remain loyal to the teachings of the Torah, even in such time when they are axiomatically opposed to the ideas of modern society. I pray to God Almighty that the Jewish community, collectively and individually, should provide home and hope, support and solicitude for all Jewish people whatever their challenges, achievements, failings and successes may be. If this book will have contributed to these goals in any small way, it will have made this endeavour worthwhile.

Rabbi Chaim Rapoport
Ilford Synagogue
Nissan/April 5762/2002

Acknowledgements

I would like to express my gratitude and appreciation to those whose help has been invaluable in the completion of this work.

Firstly, I would like to thank the Chairmen, Honorary Officers and members of the Ilford Synagogue, whose support and encouragement for all my endeavours has been a great source of strength. The staff of the Synagogue Office has been particularly accommodating in helping me with the writing of this book.

I am also grateful to the many rabbis, counsellors and psychologists who have so willingly discussed and given advice to me on this subject. Their wealth of knowledge has been an important contribution towards the final product.

I received considerable assistance in typing, and proof-reading from Andrew Barnett, Dr Ben Bradley, Harry Marin and Anne Martin. I am indebted to all of them for their hard work, supportive attitude and feedback. I also appreciate the efforts of the librarians of the London School of Jewish Studies – Esra Kahn and his assistants Aaron Prys, Erla Zimmels and Kayla Roberg – who have been of immense help with the research for this book.

My heartfelt thanks go to Rachel Schenker for her painstaking and meticulous editorial work. She has managed to maintain a cheerful and helpful attitude in the face of all my demands and literary idiosyncrasies; her assistance has been indispensable. Any mistakes in the final version should be attributed to me.

Finally, my dear wife, Rachel Clara, and our wonderful children have been a constant source of joy, inspiration and support to me. May they all be blessed with good health, happiness and continued success, both materially and spiritually.

Approbations

'I am pleased to write [these words of] approbation for a very thoughtful and sensitively written book on a subject that has, until now, avoided the depth of approach included in Rabbi Chaim Rapoport's treatment of the subject of Orthodox Judaism and homosexuality.

By means of introduction, I am an Orthodox Jewish, Board-certified psychiatrist who has been practicing psychiatry for over thirty years, specializing in the treatment of the Orthodox Jewish psychiatric patient. I am also the founding president of the Mesorah Society for Traditional Judaism and Psychiatry, the only Jewish society affiliated with the American Psychiatric Association. (Further biographical information, including awards and honors, available upon request.)

Among the thousands of patients I have treated, Orthodox Jewish homosexuals are well represented. Those who wish to remain faithful to their tradition are severely tested. Orthodox doctrine is clearly unaccepting of the ultimate homosexual act and many homosexuals feel rejected by God as well. Resulting suicidal feelings and self-loathing are exceedingly common. I have witnessed some changes in orientation of some homosexuals but not in any reliable and predictable manner and have also seen some homosexuals revert to their homosexual orientation even after fifteen years of practicing heterosexuality, accompanied by disastrous results.

There are many controversies that are tackled head-on in this courageous and sensitive book. What is the proper Orthodox approach to the homosexual? Is there a difference in the religious approach to the male homosexual and the lesbian? Are there distinctions to be drawn between the act and the actor? Are there differences in approach to the various manifestations of homosexual actions? What is the most felicitous halachic appreciation of the homosexual orientation? Can one accept that God has challenged an individual in a manner that he feels incapable of resisting? Should the Orthodox advisor or clergyman demand that the homosexual fulfill the God-given *mitzvah* of procreation? Should the homosexual be advised to marry even if he has no heterosexual inclination? Should the homosexual be directed to the so-called "reparative" therapies that promise a heterosexual re-orientation even though adequate scientific data are remarkably lacking to back that contention?

Rabbi Rapoport deals with all these issues in both a scholarly and very humane manner. One clearly appreciates that Rabbi Rapoport has truly met these suffering human beings at great emotional depth. He has not been merely preaching to them. He has been carefully listening to them and *following them over time*. He understands the intensity of their pain and deeply respects their trials.
He reviews the halachic literature carefully and with painstaking annotation. He explores various halachic categories and their possible application to homosexuals. His chapter on the concept of the *tinok shenishbah* as an exculpatory theory provides a novel and convincing argument, one that appears to this reviewer to be most felicitous from a psychological perspective. It, however, is not universally applicable and other approaches will also be needed.

My favorite section of the book is the chapter which details his compassionate responses to letters addressed to him by suffering Orthodox homosexuals and lesbians. It makes for emotionally wrenching but, ultimately, uplifting reading.

I strongly recommend this courageous and humane book for all those who will be dealing with the Orthodox homosexual patient.

Sincerely,

Abba E. Borowich, MD
Founding President, Mesorah Society for Traditional Judaism
and Psychiatry'

'It is with great pleasure that I offer my humble opinion about Rabbi Rapoport's latest book, *Judaism and Homosexuality*.

It cannot be emphasized enough that this book towers heads and shoulders above many other books and articles which have been published on the subject.

Equipped with an unusual knowledge of Jewish Law, Rabbi Rapoport cuts with his razor fine mind through all the available literature. Showing great courage, he is not afraid to state his opinion even in the face of great halachic and secular authorities. Sometimes he explains the depths of their arguments; at other times he shows, with great dignity and due respect, their inconsistencies and dubious arguments.

The book is enriched with many footnotes which take the reader far beyond the issue of homosexuality. Halachic observations on totally different matters suddenly become relevant to the topic and new light is shed on an old problem.

Besides the wealth of halachic material, Rabbi Rapoport provides sound psychological insight into the problem and above all a great amount of compassion.

At this time in Jewish history, in which so many young people, including those who try to live religious lives, have been confronted with the issue of homosexuality, Rabbi Rapoport's book is refreshing and enlightening.

I have no doubt that it will become a classic.

Rabbi Dr Nathan Lopes Cardozo
The David Cardozo Academy, Machon Ohr Aaron'

'This letter is written as an enthusiastic endorsement of *Judaism and Homosexuality: An Authentic Orthodox View*. I write these words from three distinct perspectives.

First, this is a work of a dear friend and revered colleague, Rabbi Chaim Rapoport. Rabbi Rapoport is an outstanding Torah scholar, and a most compassionate Jewish leader. He is deeply concerned with the problems which face our community at this era of great social change. He is committed to the purest ideals of Jewish tradition, especially as the tradition confronts the challenges of modernity. This book is but one example of his commitment to cope with the serious problems of our time.

Secondly, this is a work of impeccable Torah scholarship. Rabbi Rapoport has made use of his keen and broad-ranging expertise, and has written a volume which is extensive and comprehensive while at the same time profoundly analytical. His copious footnotes support his arguments meticulously.

Thirdly, while never compromising the highest standards of *halachah*, the author demonstrates his familiarity with the condition of those who struggle with homosexuality, as well as an empathy and concern for their humanness and their Jewishness. Rabbi Rapoport also demonstrates expert knowledge of the secular professional literature on this subject.

Those who work with individuals who identify themselves as homosexual, be they clergy or mental health professionals, need to study this book thoroughly, and then keep it handy as a desk reference.

I recommend this book to all serious students of our tradition, because of its ability to constructively relate to the social conditions of the early twenty-first century.

Tzvi Hersh Weinreb, Ph.D.
Executive Vice President, Union of Orthodox Jewish
Congregations of America
(formerly Rabbi, Shomrei Emunah Congregation, Baltimore, Maryland)
Rabbinic Liaison, NEFESH, International Network of Orthodox
Mental Health Professionals
Member of the Executive Committee of the Rabbinical Council of America

1

The Prohibition of Homosexual Practices

MALE HOMOSEXUAL BEHAVIOUR

The Book of Leviticus contains two chapters[1] that enumerate various forms of forbidden sexual intercourse. Broadly speaking, the categories of incestuous relationships, adulterous unions, intercourse with a woman before purification after menstruation, male to male intercourse and bestiality are all subsumed under the title of *arayot*, namely illicit sexual contacts. Underscoring the severity of these commandments is the fact that they entail either some form of capital punishment or the Divine penalty of *karet*, which refers to either premature death[2] or spiritual annihilation.[3] Whilst these penalties are rarely, if ever, meted out,[4] the fact that – in theory at least – these transgressions are severely penalised serves to emphasise the serious nature of such prohibitions.

These sexual prohibitions also have an additional burden of severity as they fall under the category of *giluy arayot*.[5] This is one of three categories of transgression where a person is obliged to forfeit his life rather than sin. Generally speaking where human life is at risk, the commandments of the Torah are over-ridden. Thus, one may desecrate the Sabbath, eat pork – or leaven on Passover – if life-threatening situations warrant. *Avodah zarah* (idolatry), *giluy arayot*, and *shefichut damim* (murder) are the three cardinal sins of Judaism, which a person may not transgress even in order to save his or her life (*yehareg ve-al ya'avor*).[6]

In the above-mentioned section of Leviticus, the Bible unequivocally proscribes male-to-male intercourse. In Leviticus 18:22, Scripture states: 'You shall not lie with a man as one lies with a woman; it is a *to'evah* (an abomination).' A second verse, Leviticus 20:13, further underscores the severity of this prohibition and states: 'A man who lies with a man as one lies with a woman, they have both done an abomination; they shall be put to death, their blood is upon themselves.' On the basis of unanimous opinion in the Mishnah and the Talmud, Maimonides codifies:

> One who [actively] copulates with a male or one who brings a male upon himself [i.e. submits himself to the male copulative act]: as soon as the penetrative act has begun if they were both adults they are to be stoned [according to the prescribed manner] ...[7]

The biblical prohibition of 'a man lying with a man', in common with other prohibited sexual liaisons, refers primarily to penetrative intercourse. In the case of *mishkav zachar*, this refers specifically to anal penetrative intercourse. As with other *arayot*, any form of sexual intimacy is also forbidden, and falls under the rubric of the negative commandment '*lo tikrevu*' ('do not approach').[8] As such, they are included in the area of *giluy arayot* as described above.[9]

In addition to the ban on active homosexual practices, *wilfully* engaging oneself in homosexual fantasy, self-stimulation and masturbation, or voluntary exposure to provocative material would be a violation of Jewish Law.[10] These prohibitions are not unique to homosexuality. Indeed any form of auto-eroticism or sexual provocation is forbidden outside of the immediate environment of marital intercourse.[11] It is only in the realm of marriage that sexual activity is not only permitted, but may become a desirable, sacred and Godly act, one in which there is a manifestation of the Divine Presence.

FEMALE HOMOSEXUALITY

Lesbianism is not mentioned explicitly in the Bible. However, a proscription against such behaviour is derived from another biblical passage: 'According to the deeds of the Land of Egypt, in which you dwelt, you shall not do; and according to the doings of the Land of Canaan, where I bring you, you shall not do; and in their statutes you shall not walk.'[12]

Our sages[13] elaborate upon this passage, emphasising the last phrase

'… and in their statutes'. What were these statutes? 'A man would marry a man, and a woman would marry a woman, and a woman would marry two men, and a man would marry a woman and her daughter. Therefore the Torah states: "*And in their statutes you shall not walk*".'

Whilst the above-mentioned quotation refers to women who 'marry' each other, the Talmud[14] and subsequent Codes declare (on the basis of the verse in Leviticus) that the prohibition includes all lesbian activity. Maimonides,[15] followed by the *Shulchan Aruch*[16] states:

> It is forbidden for women to enmesh (play around)[17] with one another and this belongs to the 'practices of the Egyptians' concerning which we have been warned: 'you shall not copy the practices of the Land of Egypt' … although such conduct is forbidden, it is not punishable with lashes since there is no specific prohibition against it and no sexual intercourse takes place at all. Consequently, such women are not forbidden to marry *Cohanim* on account of promiscuity, nor is a woman prohibited to her husband because of it, since this does not constitute adultery. It is, however, appropriate to subject such women to *makat mardut* (disciplinary lashes) since they committed a prohibited act. A man should be particular with his wife concerning this matter and he should prevent women who are known for their lesbian practices from visiting her or from having her visit them.

The halachic authorities disagree about the status of this prohibition. According to Rabbi Yehoshua Falk (c.1555–1614), in his commentary to the classical code the *Tur*,[18] the prohibition of female homosexuality is 'merely rabbinic' and the biblical prohibition 'and in their statutes you shall not walk' refers only to the perversity of 'one woman marrying two men'. On the other hand, Rabbi Moshe di Trani (1500–1580) and Rabbi Mordechai Jaffe (1535–1612), maintain that Maimonides considers female homosexual practices to be forbidden on biblical grounds. The fact that the punishment of *malkut* (whip lashes) is not prescribed for violation of this prohibition is due to the fact that it is a *lav shebichlalut* (a prohibition which is merely a sub-category of the all-embracing condemnation of 'According to the deeds of the Land of Egypt … you shall not do').[19] Rabbi Yosef Rozin (1858–1936), in his *Tzofnat Pa'aneach*,[20] likewise holds that Maimonides considers lesbian practices to be proscribed on biblical grounds.[21]

Since rabbinical injunctions must be adhered to with the same commitment as biblical law, this dispute does not give rise to much practical difference. However, there is a substantial difference between female and male homosexuality. As mentioned, the prohibition of the latter is subsumed under the class of illicit sexual relations known as *arayot*, hence its violation is subject to the grave stricture of *yehareg ve'al ya-avor*; namely that in most circumstances one must choose death over any alternative which involves committing homosexual acts. In contrast, female homosexuality is described as *peritzuta* (obscenity) rather than *arayot* and as such would not ordinarily warrant the same degree of sacrifice as would abstention from male homosexual intercourse.[22]

UNIVERSAL RESPONSIBILITY

Judaism, generally speaking, refers to 613 commandments that are binding for Jews,[23] and seven categories of commandment that God revealed to all mankind, which are referred to as the Noachide Laws.[24] Generally speaking, these laws form the bedrock of a stable and ethically orientated society. They include prohibitions against religious aberrations such as idolatry and blasphemy. They condemn the practices of homicide, theft and cruelty to animals. They insist on the institution of a legislative and governing body that will enforce and uphold the rule of law, thus preventing the moral degeneration of society. The Noachide Code also contains a clause that prohibits certain sexual practices under the title of *giluy arayot*. Under this heading, male homosexual practices are forbidden for all of mankind.[25]

In addition to the biblical ban on male homosexual activity, which relates directly to the individual, there is also an obligation upon the Jewish people to encourage and inspire all members of the Jewish fraternity to behave in accordance with Jewish Law.[26] Hence the issue of homosexual practices is relevant to all who are able, whether individually or collectively, to influence members of the faith to live in accordance with the dictates of the Torah's sexual code.

Furthermore, Maimonides, writing in the last section of his *magnum opus* the *Yad ha-Chazakah*,[27] declares that at the Revelation at Sinai, the Jewish people were charged with a mission: to serve as a 'light unto the nations'. In this capacity, the Jewish people are called upon to bring to realisation the observance of the Noachide Code amongst the nations of the world. Rabbi Yom Tov Lipmann Heller, the sixteenth-century author of a classical commentary on the Mishnah, paraphrases and adopts the Maimonidean perspective.[28] He writes that all the inhabitants of the world are beloved of God and have the capacity to obey the Divine Will. Jews, who have an obligation to spread the word of God to all humans, are 'commanded to influence the Gentiles with persuasive dialogue, to draw their heart to the will of their Master and the desire of their Rock'. These teachings clearly convey the message that the Jewish people have been given the additional vocation as ambassadors of the Torah. Where possible, Jews – as the recipients and custodians of the Torah – have the responsibility to communicate the ideals of religious morality and ethics to all members of the brotherhood of man.[29]

All the above provides the answer to the oft-asked question, 'Does the Almighty "belong" in the bedroom?' The answer is, unequivocally, yes. The believing person accepts that his or her Creator has expressed His immutable will in His Torah. God Almighty has summoned His subjects to conduct their intimate lives in accordance with His design. He has also given us the challenge of communicating this ideal to anyone upon whom we may have positive influence. In our context, it must be stated categorically that whether or not the Torah's teachings about homosexual behaviour are in vogue, the faithful will remain loyal to the Divine message and calling.[30]

THE NATURE OF THE PROHIBITION

Categories of Divine Commandments

Rabbinic literature tends to divide the commandments of the Torah into three categories: *eidot, chukkim* and *mishpatim*.[31] The last, *mishpatim*, refers to those commandments that may be described as logical or moral imperatives. Commandments such as honouring one's parents, being honest, having concern for the property of others, all fall under this rubric. These laws may well have been mandated by the intelligent and sensitive human being, as part of a non-divine logical structure. A conglomeration of pragmatism, consequentialism, and utilitarianism, coupled with the dictates of human conscience, would have in all probability brought man to implement such laws.[32]

The first category, *chukkim*, refers to those commandments which transcend human understanding. Examples of *chukkim* include the prohibitions against forbidden admixtures in agriculture and garments; the exclusion of pork and other specific foodstuffs from the Jewish diet, and

– the *chok par excellence* – the Law of the Red Heifer, which features in the process of purification from ritual defilement as a result of contact with the dead. These commandments may be perceived by the human mind as totally irrational, yet the believer accepts them by virtue of their Divinity, even though he knows he may never understand them.[33]

Finally, *eidot* refers to those commandments which are by no means logical or ethical imperatives, yet possess a meaning that can be appreciated by the rational person. This category includes those commandments that serve in a commemorative or symbolic capacity. The Sabbath and the Festivals, whose purpose is to help us to recall and reflect upon events such as the Creation and the Exodus, may be described as *eidot*. Commandments such as *tefillin* (phylacteries), *tzitzit* (fringes attached to four-cornered garments), and *mezuzah* (a scroll containing core biblical teachings, affixed to the doorpost of every room in a Jewish home) are also examples of *eidot*. These symbols serve to remind us of our mission in life. They assist us in the endeavour of walking on the correct path. All such commandments have a rational component, namely to help us inculcate and internalise certain fundamental truths or to provide some benefit for society.[34]

The truth is, however, that this 'neat' categorisation of the commandments is an oversimplification of a much more complex dynamic. Whilst in general terms one may speak of rational commandments, supra-rational commandments, and symbolic commandments, it would be inappropriate to speak about these in absolute terms. For even a neophyte in the study of Torah will recognise that the so-called 'rational' commandments also contain elements that defy the human mind. Conversely, one may also be able to discover symbolism and rationalism in certain aspects of the 'irrational' commandments. Thus, when we use the traditional terminology, '*eidot, chukkim* and *mishpatim*', the reference is to the *predominant* characteristic of that particular commandment.[35]

ILLICIT SEXUAL RELATIONSHIPS – DIVINE DECREES OR LOGICAL IMPERATIVES?

It is with this awareness in mind that we approach the issue of the nature of those commandments that govern humankind's sexual practices. Mediaeval Jewish classics do offer reasons for at least some of the sexual prohibitions in the Torah.[36] This has led many people to believe that these commandments are strictly predicated on rational considerations. Consequently, some have concluded that if the rationales that have been provided for a particular sexual prohibition do not appear to be relevant (for whatever reason), then the commandment loses its binding force. This is a grave error. For, even those Jewish thinkers who sought to underscore the Divine commandments with reasons never assumed that they had plumbed the depths of God's wisdom.

A clear example is the classic ascribed to Rabbi Aharon ha-Levi of Barcelona (c.1230–c.1300),[37] the *Sefer ha-Chinnuch*, in which he enumerates the 613 commandments of the Torah. For each commandment, the author presents an outline of the parameters of the law in question, in addition to an exposition on the ethical and religious 'root-ideas' underlying each *mitzvah*. As he states in the Introduction to his work, he makes no claim to offer an exhaustive treatment of the reason for any given *mitzvah*. He clearly states: 'I recount in the ears of my son and his friends *what I understand* of the excellencies of the commandments.' Nor were the reasons he gave for the respective commandments intended to be accepted as certainties. He considered his ideas as tentative and suggestive. The reasons that he provided for the *mitzvot* were designed to help the reader 'appreciate *some* of the profundity of the Torah's teachings, so that he may be inspired to observe all the commandments *irrespective of the particular reason and purpose assigned to them individually'*. In light of this, we may say that those who endeavour to elicit support for their revolutionary qualifications of commandments, based on the rationale provided in the *Sefer ha-Chinnuch* or similar works, are misusing, or even abusing, the very works they seek to base their novel ideas on.

RATIONALISM TAKEN TO ITS EXTREME

A particular focus for this kind of revisionist thinking is the prohibition against male homosexual behaviour. Rabbinic works have offered several approaches to this prohibition. They tend to dwell on the biblical appellation for male homosexual behaviour as a *to'evah* – an abomination – as well as the talmudic interpretation of this term as it is used in this specific context. One Progressive thinker presents a résumé of the various reasons for the Torah's objection to homosexual conduct, and its designation as a *to'evah*. Mark Solomon[38] explored various reasons for the prohibition termed an abomination, and came to the conclusion that these reasons do not hold water when applied to people with a homosexual disposition. This intellectual adventure seems to have contributed to Solomon's subsequent rejection of the Torah's commandments and ultimate dismissal of the fundamental tenet of Judaism that the Torah is totally Divine and free from error.[39]

Had Solomon realised that the Word of God may not always appeal to our minds – even the most rational of commandments may appear to be irrational and unjust in certain circumstances – he may have remained loyal to the faith of his ancestors. His over-indulgence in rationalising the commandments proved to be a fatal exercise, for when rationale became unconvincing, the commandment had to become obsolete.[40] This scenario lends substantial support for the contention of contemporary Rabbi Dr Nathan Lopez Cardozo that over-preoccupation with rationalising the biblical interdicts on sexual conduct may prove to be counter-productive.[41] A commandment that makes sense and appeals in certain places and in certain times may be viewed with suspicion in a different environment.

It is nevertheless perfectly legitimate and even advisable to inquire into the reasons for the respective commandments. This endeavour ought to help us appreciate – in our own terms – the 'value' of the commandment and its contribution to the refinement of our personalities and enhancement of our spirituality.

It is in this context that we provide a summary of the reasons for the prohibition of homosexual conduct. So long as this is tempered with the knowledge that ultimately the commandments represent the infinite will of God, which must be honoured, irrespective of whether or not they appear to contribute to any edifying or sanctifying agenda, this inquiry will only enhance our human appreciation of the Divine Law.

As mentioned above, the springboard for the discussion about the prohibition on male homosexual conduct is rooted in the designation of such conduct as a *to'evah*. Whilst it is true that the Torah also employs this term regarding adultery, incest and other forms of sexual practices, the Talmud makes much of the fact that the Torah places special emphasis on homosexual intercourse as an abomination.[42] For the term 'abomination' is used only collectively with regard to other sexual aberrations, whereas homosexual intercourse is singled out as a *to'evah*, in addition to being described as such in conjunction with other proscribed acts.

The talmudic comment on the word *to'evah* is based on the homiletical technique known as *notarikon,* according to which the word *to'evah* is understood as a conflation of the words '*to'eh atah bah –* you go astray in it'.[43] This interpretation itself demands explanation and several ideas have been advanced in classical Jewish sources.

HOMOSEXUALITY – THE ANTITHESIS OF PROCREATION

The midrashic work, *Pesikta Zutrata,* more familiar as *Midrash Lekach Tov,* explains that the undesirable element inherent in homosexual practices is due to the fact that 'from it [homosexual relations] one can have no offspring'.[44] One of the major functions – if not *the* major function – of sexual intercourse is reproduction, and this reason for the human being's sexual capacity is frustrated when one invests this energy in homosexual intercourse. This approach is adopted by the *Sefer ha-Chinnuch,* which describes such intercourse as in contravention of God's will to populate the world and simply a barren exercise in libidinal pleasure. He writes:

> At the root of the precept lies the reason that the Holy One Blessed is He desires that the world that He created be inhabited and settled. Therefore He commanded us not to destroy human seed by sexual relations with males. For this is indeed a destructive act since there can be no fruitful benefit of offspring from it, nor the fulfilment of the *mitzvah* to honour the conjugal rights [due one's wife].[45]

Likewise Nachmanides, in his commentary on Leviticus, also speaks of the aberration of homosexual practices in reference to the fact that they frustrate the mission of man to be fruitful and multiply and fill the earth with inhabitants.[46]

In Judaism, the family occupies a central position. 'Be fruitful and multiply' is not only the first command in the Torah; it is the fundamental imperative of Jewish existence. As Chief Rabbi Dr Jonathan Sacks has put it: 'in choosing to have children, to take responsibility for their welfare and education, and to work for a world fit for them to live in, we find the root and fount of our entire ethical enterprise'. In light of this, 'the ideals of heterosexuality … are written into the entire fabric of the biblical vision', and hence, 'traditional sexual ethics become … the only persuasive way of life for those who want to engage in the ethical undertaking'.[47]

DESTRUCTIVE FOR MARRIAGE

The fourteenth-century commentator on the Talmud, Rabbi Nissim ben Reuven of Gerona, explains the above-mentioned terse phrase 'you go astray in it'. He writes: 'one abandons heterosexual intercourse (*mishkevei ishah*) and seeks sexual relationships with males'. Once again, this 'explanation' leaves room for ambiguity. The mediaeval commentaries *Tosafot* and *Rosh*[48] explain that 'you go astray in it' means that 'men leave *their wives* and pursue homosexual intercourse'. In other words, the abomination consists of the danger that a married man with homosexual tendencies may disrupt his family life in order to pursue his desire. That homosexuality can have a disruptive effect on married life is currently evident by the fact that many cases have been known where couples who separate or divorce, often accompanied with great acrimony, do so because of the homosexual adventures of one of the partners in marriage. This understanding of the *Tosafot* and the *Rosh* is accepted by, amongst others,[49] Rabbi J. David Bleich, who writes: '*Tosafot* and *Rosh* ... indicate that the homosexual goes astray in the sense that he abandons his family. According to this interpretation, the abomination associated with such conduct lies in the destruction of the family unit.'[50]

INTRINSICALLY REPULSIVE

A completely different understanding of the view of the *Tosafot* emerges from the writings of one of the great halachic authorities of our generation, Rabbi Moshe Feinstein (1895–1986). R. Feinstein understands the mediaeval commentaries to be saying that the *to'evah* inherent in homosexual relationships is due to the fact that those who engage in such practices desert normal, natural, understandable sexual practices in favour of abnormal, unnatural and irrational ones. This, he says, is the purport of the phrase 'men leave their wives and pursue homosexual intercourse'. R. Feinstein claims that the words 'their wives' should be understood as 'female sexual relationships' in general. The perversity of homosexual behaviour according to R. Feinstein is the very notion of deviating from the 'natural' act of heterosexual intercourse and pursuing homosexual relationships for which there cannot possibly be, he says, any natural desire.[51]

Consistent with his extremely harsh view (which we will elaborate on in Chapter 2), R. Feinstein argues that the very search for a reason for the prohibition of homosexual behaviour is in itself an aberration. He castigates those who dare ask 'why the Torah forbids homosexual relations', for in doing so, 'they undermine the severity of the prohibition in the eyes of the evildoers who lust for this repugnant indulgence, which is one of the greatest abominations. Even the nations of the world consider that homosexual conduct is unparalleled in its loathsomeness.' The truth is, says R. Feinstein, 'that no reason at all is required to explain the abominable nature of homosexual activity, which is considered repugnant by the entire world who consider practising homosexuals to be despicable and uncivilised'.[52] In another letter, R. Feinsten offers guidance to someone who had to contend with homosexual desires. R. Feinstein suggests that, among other things, the knowledge that 'the entire world – even the wicked – ridicule those who commit homosexual transgressions, and he even disgraces himself in the eyes of the wicked accomplice in the homosexual act' will provide strong fortification in his battle with the 'evil inclination'.[53]

R. Feinstein concludes that the sin of homosexual activity, in addition to being a severe violation of the Torah, is 'an affront to humanity', and causes the sinner 'to become degraded and disgraced with the utmost depravity'. Here and elsewhere, R. Feinstein adds that the disgrace is not only for the individual concerned, but also for his entire family.[54]

Rabbi Levi ben Gershom (1288–1344), commonly referred to as the *Ralbag*, interprets the word *to'evah* in his commentary on Leviticus. He states categorically that this means that homosexual intercourse is a *to'evah b'atzmuto* – intrinsically abominable.[55] At the risk of second guessing the *Ralbag*, it is possible that he had in mind something along the lines of what contemporary Rabbi Dr Norman Lamm has described as 'an abomination *prima facie*'.[56] Rabbi Dr Lamm, in a manner not too dissimilar to R. Feinstein, presents an argument whereby the very search for a reason for the prohibition on homosexual intercourse is unnecessary. As he expresses it in his landmark 1974 essay entitled 'Judaism and the Modern Attitude to Homosexuality': 'an act characterised as an "abomination" is *prima facie* disgusting and cannot be further defined or explained … it is, as it were, a visceral reaction, an intuitive disqualification of the act, and we run the risk of distorting the biblical judgement if we rationalise it. *To'evah* constitutes a category of objectionableness *sui generis*: it is a primary phenomenon.'

It is also possible that this idea is encapsulated in the words of the

Sefer ha- Chinnuch who objects to homosexuality on the grounds that it yields no offspring, and then states:

> This is in addition to the fact that the nature of this unclean act is extremely repulsive and repugnant in the eyes of every intelligent human being. It is simply not fitting that a man, created to serve his maker, should become perverted by these ugly deeds.[57]

THE ARGUMENT FROM NATURE

Another interpretation of the *to'evah* aspect of homosexuality has been extrapolated from the writings of Rabbi Baruch Ha-Levi Epstein (1860–1942), in his well-known commentary on the Pentateuch, *Torah Temimah*.[58] However, this idea is more explicit in the above-mentioned *Pesikta Zutrata*. In a second interpretation on the word *to'evah*, the Midrash says: 'Scripture has considered him more abominable than the ass. For the he-ass does not cohabit with [another] he-ass, but with the she-ass. Yet this man has perverted his way more than the ass and all other animals and birds.' It is difficult to know *exactly* what the Midrash wishes to convey. I believe that the idea suggested in this Midrash is something analogous to the concept of 'a crime against nature'. It appears to emphasise the 'unnaturalness' of the homosexual act as the reason for its being designated as *to'evah*. Consistent with other rabbinic teachings, the Midrash alludes to the fact that the norms of nature can, and should, be observed from the animal kingdom, who act instinctively and naturally. The fact that, according to the Midrash, animals only engage in heterosexual mating, indicates the naturalness of this form of co-habitation and *ipso facto* the unnaturalness of homosexual co-habitation.[59]

It is possible that a comment of Maimonides also supports this notion.[60] Much has been made of the observation that the human anatomy facilitates heterosexual intercourse rather than homosexual anal intercourse.[61] Once again, the argument goes, this indicates the unnaturalness of homosexual intercourse. Whilst it is definitely possible for both homosexual and heterosexual people to engage in non-vaginal intercourse, the fact that the human genitalia suggest the 'naturalness' of vaginal intercourse is due to the fact that the Creator of Nature intended – as He states in His Torah – human beings to engage in heterosexual rather than homosexual intercourse.

This explanation does not offer a reason as to *why* the Creator wished to proscribe homosexual intercourse; rather, it argues that homosexual intercourse is 'a crime against' the nature that God Almighty – for reasons known to Him – designed. Hence the talmudic statement *'to'eh atah bah* – you go astray in it'. According to this idea, homosexual intercourse is a deviation from the Laws of Nature that God has decreed.

It may be argued that anal heterosexual intercourse is likewise unnatural. Indeed, in talmudic terminology, it is described as such. This does not necessarily negate the above-mentioned argument. For indeed, the only recommended form of intercourse, in the Jewish tradition, is heterosexual vaginal intercourse. It is true that some authorities condone anal intercourse within the confines of a heterosexual marriage; however, such conduct is frowned upon and, even when permitted, subjected to certain qualifications. Suffice to say that nowhere is anal intercourse – even within a marriage – attributed any intrinsic worth. It is evident that those authorities who sanction the occasional dalliance in anal intercourse do so by way of concession to human weakness. Provided that such 'unnatural' acts remain the exception, rather than the rule, and are performed within – and in order to enhance – marriage, they are tolerated.[62] In contradistinction, homosexual penetrative intercourse does by definition not conform to the 'natural' heterosexual norm.

CONTEMPORARY CONTRIBUTIONS

In recent times, many theologians have argued that a number of rational objections to homosexual conduct can be found in the consequences often resulting from homosexual relationships. This approach was given particular emphasis in the first decades of the outbreak of the AIDS epidemic in the West. Lord Immanuel Jakobovits (1921–1999), then the Chief Rabbi of the British Commonwealth, and considered by many as the pioneer of 'Jewish Medical Ethics' in the modern sense of the phrase,[63] often expressed the view that AIDS should be seen as a consequence – albeit not a punishment – of indulgence in homosexual activities that violate the Word of God. Lord Jakobovits takes great pains to emphasise that 'it is not part of the Jewish doctrine of reward and punishment to so identify individual cases with the individual experiences of great anguish. I therefore do not go along with, but on the contrary, *strongly reject* and oppose those preachers, or would-be preachers, who declare that it is Divine vengeance that the wrath of God is being visited on those who deserve it because they live in the cesspools of evil. On the contrary, we should seek to stretch out a hand of help, of understanding, of solace, of compassion one can to sufferers, not to inflict, in addition to the agony through which they go, the additional humiliation and indignity and reproof of saying "you deserve it". *This is utterly un-Jewish, and is utterly to be rejected.*'[64] Having said that, Jakobovits suggests the adoption of the notion that AIDS 'is the price we pay for the "benefits" of the permissive society' in which we live. He states:

> I think we should declare in very plain and explicit terms indicating that our society violated some of the norms of the Divine Law, and of the natural law, and that as a consequence, we pay a price and an exceedingly heavy price. This certainly is Jewish Doctrine. So there is a clear line of demarcation between punishment and consequence to be drawn. I need hardly spell out to an informed audience, certainly one that is likely to know the rudiments of Jewish teaching, that any form of sexual gratification outside marriage cannot be condoned by Jewish Law. Whether this is pre-marital or extra-marital, or whether this is altogether unnatural in the form of homosexuality – we utterly disapprove of this as an abomination. It is treated by biblical law as a moral aberration that we cannot come to terms with.[65]

Lord Jakobovits, in this article and in many other statements, appeals for universal recognition that promiscuous, licentious behaviour, coupled with the type of liberal legislation which has allowed for the more widespread phenomenon of homosexual intercourse, has lead to 'a collapse of nature's self-defence against degeneracy'.

Some have also argued that male homosexuals are more promiscuous than male heterosexuals. This may be due to a variety of reasons. All would agree, however, that promiscuity does not enhance family life, or emotional and social stability. If homosexuality is perceived as a synonym for promiscuity, then we have a very good reason to reject homosexuality.[66]

It is beyond the scope of this book to explore in detail every possible rational or dogmatic rejection of homosexual behaviour. It is the opinion of this author that all these objections may be reasonably entertained in certain circumstances and situations. It is likewise *possible* that even all the reasons, when taken together, do not provide sufficient premise for objection to homosexual conduct in *all* circumstances. For example, the arguments that homosexuality undermines procreation or fidelity are relevant primarily in the case of a heterosexual or bisexual who ought to get married and procreate. These reasons are inadequate when dealing with people who have an *exclusively* homosexual disposition. For as we shall argue in Chapter 7, those with such orientation would be generally speaking best advised to avoid marriage. The arguments that homosexual activities invite disease and engender promiscuity are subjective. Such ideas would be unlikely to convince deeply loyal partners in gay and lesbian relationships, who would be more immune to sexually transmitted diseases, and the harmful results of promiscuous behaviour, than many of their 'sexually liberated' heterosexual counterparts. The so-called arguments from nature may be perceived as inadequate for those who do not engage in anal intercourse and who may well argue that their homosexuality is also 'natural' and, as such, must be taken into consideration. R. Feinstein's contention that no reason is needed to proscribe homosexuality, since it is universally recognised as an abomination *par excellence*, is also subject to the conditioning of society. In an age of ever-increasing acceptance of homosexuality, the appeal of R. Feinstein's argument is reduced. The same could be said regarding the interpretation of the *Ralbag* and its paraphrase in the modern terminology of Dr Lamm.

Yet as argued earlier in this chapter, it has never been suggested or implied in traditional sources that the prohibition of homosexuality be limited to those cases where it impinges on one value or another. It is undeniably the case that homosexual practices when fostered by a married man or explored by a heterosexual single stand in the way of the realisation of the primary values of the family unit and procreation that the Torah seeks to promote. Hence, the ideas advanced above may be seen as substantial factors in the ban on homosexual activity. Likewise, the other reasons for objection to homosexuality may also provide plausible rationale and basis for the prohibition it entails. Where applicable, they may also be considered component factors of the Jewish stance regarding homosexuality. They are significant *factors* of an all-embracing commandment, but they should not be misconstrued as providing an exhaustive explanation – hence limitation – of the commandment.[67]

To couch this in the above-mentioned category terms, we may say

that homosexuality may be perceived as a rationally compelling commandment – a *mishpat* – in certain cases, whilst in others it may well
be perceived – rightly or wrongly – as a commandment that transcends
human logic, a *chok*. In this, homosexuality does not differ from other
illicit sexual practices which in certain cases may be seen as moral
imperatives, whilst in others may seem to belong to the supra-rational
category of *chukkim*.

R. Bleich has tentatively read this sort of idea into the above-cited
talmudic teaching that the word *to'evah*, in the context of the scriptural
ban on homosexual behaviour, alludes to the phrase '*to'eh atah bah* –
you go astray in it'. He writes:

> For the *vast majority of humanity*, homosexual activity is deviant
> behaviour; it is unnatural and repugnant – an abomination. To speak of
> such conduct as losing one's way – 'going astray' – is almost to minimise
> the infraction. It may not be reading too much into the rabbinic text if
> it is understood as *directed to homosexuals who feel no repugnance
> regarding their conduct. A person burdened by homosexual orientation
> 'goes astray' if he believes such activity to be acceptable because it does
> not appear to him as an abomination.* Countenancing a homosexual
> lifestyle as morally or socially acceptable *constitutes deviation from
> divinely established norms* and hence social institutions legitimising
> such arrangements cannot be accepted with approbation.[68]

In other words, religious morality is not contingent upon the same
criteria as secular morality. The fact that a person with an exclusive
homosexual orientation has no outlet through which to express what
R. Bleich describes as 'natural' for man – who 'is a sensual and sexual
being' – compels the homosexual to fight a lifelong battle against his
nature. It is debatable whether a system of secular morality would have
sufficient grounds on which to base a prohibition on homosexual
behaviour for homosexuals of exclusive orientation. It is for this reason
that many irreligious moderns have discarded the claim that law-
abiding, faithful and honest homosexual partners are violating any
moral norms.[69]

Indeed, R. Bleich argues that the homosexual desires in gays and
lesbians are no different from the desire for pre-marital sex amongst
heterosexuals – except for the fact that the former are confronted with
a more difficult trial than the latter. Extrapolating upon this analogy,
we may point to the fact that pre-marital sexual relationships – at least

when practised in the context of a stable, long-term and mutually loving relationship – are rarely condemned today on the grounds of purely secular principles of ethical conduct. To be sure, religious theologians will draw our attention to the dangers inherent in fornication, but ultimately, the irrefutable claim for the condemnation of such practices remains the fact that they deviate from what R. Bleich describes as 'divinely established norms'. By the same token, we ought to emphasise that the major objection to homosexual behaviour on behalf of confirmed homosexuals does not lie in any subjective moral argument, but is anchored in the word of God, as revealed in the Bible.

In layman's terms, we postulate the notion that the Torah's objection to homosexual activities makes perfect sense in relation to heterosexual or even bisexual people. It may, however, not always make sense for the confirmed homosexual person, who generally speaking would not be encouraged to embark upon marriage and procreation, but nevertheless – like most human beings – seeks companionship, love and intimacy. Moreover, a person of homosexual disposition, who craves for affection and intimacy with a member of the same sex, would by definition be unlikely to share the attitude to homosexual desires voiced by R. Feinstein. Rather, the observant homosexual would acknowledge: 'My Creator has instilled in me (or has allowed me to develop) a homosexual disposition. I have an intense desire to develop a meaningful and mutually beneficial loving relationship with another person. As a homosexual, I feel unable to accomplish this with a woman. I desire the warmth, security, and intimacy that most human beings long for. My Creator has effectively deprived me of these blessings. I do not understand why He has presented me with this predicament. The rational and emotional objections expressed by our sages make little sense to me, at least as far as I personally am concerned. However, I accept that God has forbidden homosexual practices and – without seeking to second guess His wisdom – I accept I have to subordinate myself to the Will of my Creator and do my best to overcome the temptations I confront.'

2

The Nature of Homosexuality –
A Jewish Perspective

CONTEMPORARY UNDERSTANDING OF SEXUAL ORIENTATION[1]

In contemporary psychological parlance, the term 'sexual orientation' generally refers to an enduring emotional, sexual-affectional attraction that a person feels towards other people. If this attraction is manifest towards members of the opposite gender, it is described as a heterosexual orientation. If it is manifest towards members of one's own gender, it is described as a homosexual orientation. It is widely accepted, however, that sexual orientation falls along a continuum. In other words, one's orientation does not have to be exclusive. It is possible to feel varying degrees of attraction for both genders. (One who is attracted to both members of his own gender and to members of the opposite gender is referred to as someone with a bisexual orientation. 'Bisexual' people are also not all equally orientated. There are those who have a stronger inclination towards heterosexual relationships, although they may be quite comfortable with homosexual relationships, and there are those who are 'predominantly' attracted to members of their own gender but may also have a less passionate – but quite spontaneous – attraction to members of the opposite gender.)

Furthermore, it is possible that a person who has essentially a heterosexual orientation could be sexually attracted to members of his own gender in certain circumstances, for example when restricted in a close-knit same-gender environment for a lengthy period of time or deprived, for some other reason, of any heterosexual outlet. Teenagers going through the process of emotional development, and indulging in social or sexual experimental experiences, may erroneously conclude that the homosexual desires they have felt, or tendencies they have developed, are indicative of a confirmed, exclusive homosexual orientation, when in reality it may either be a temporary and transient stage or, even if 'permanent', it is possible that a bisexual orientation (with or without a predominant homosexual leaning) is being confused with and perceived as an exclusive disposition.

However, there are – according to the studies in contemporary human psychology – a significant number of people who have a confirmed and exclusive homosexual orientation, as indeed it is universally accepted that the majority of human beings have an exclusive heterosexual orientation. People who have an exclusive (or almost exclusive) homosexual orientation are generally referred to as 'homosexuals' or 'gay' (a modern term for the homosexual). Given the complexity of human nature and sexual chemistry, it may be better to define the term 'exclusive homosexual' in our context as referring to the homosexual whose lack of sexual attraction to members of the opposite gender does not reasonably enable them to sustain a healthy heterosexual relationship. (For an understanding of the concept of a 'healthy' heterosexual relationship, see the elaboration in Chapter 7 of this book.)

Furthermore, whilst there are a variety of theories as to the origins ('aetiology') of a homosexual orientation (biological and genetic influences, early life experiences, family dynamics, social experiences and others), it is generally accepted that people do not ordinarily 'select' their orientation (as, for example, people 'choose' their practices). Hence, the homosexual is someone whose sexual-affectional chemistry is directed, through no choice of his own, towards members of his own gender, in the same way that the heterosexual is someone whose sexual-affectional chemistry is directed, through no choice of his own, towards members of the opposite gender.

To be sure, it may be possible for homosexuals to engage in heterosexual intimacy, as indeed it may be possible for heterosexuals to engage in homosexual intimacy. However, such experiences go against the grain of one's orientation and would, generally speaking, have to be performed in a mechanical, emotionally detached manner. Also, such relationships do not usually have any staying power, as they do not provide the emotional fulfilment for the partners in such a relationship. At any rate, from the psychological perspective, a person would be classified as a homosexual – if that is his orientation – even if he had never engaged in any homosexual activity (or even if he had engaged in heterosexual activity). Likewise, a person would be classified as a heterosexual – if that is his orientation – even if he had never engaged in heterosexual activity (or even if he had engaged in homosexual activity).

In writing this book, I have also adopted the contemporary terminology. Throughout this book, unless otherwise stated, reference to homosexuals (or gays and lesbians) is to those whose sexual inclination, at least at the stage of their life under consideration, is exclusively directed towards members of their own gender. In contrast to homosexual behaviour, practice, conduct etc., these terms are not indicative of engagement in prohibited behaviour by the homosexual individual. Where the reference is to homosexuals who engage in homosexual activity, this is stated explicitly, or the terms 'practising homosexual', 'sexually active homosexual' and the like are employed.

As we have explained in Chapter 1, the Torah forbids homosexual activity. There are also several accounts in the Written Torah and in rabbinic literature in which homosexual activity features.[2] There does not seem to be, however, any reference in Torah literature to the phenomenon of a 'homosexual orientation' as described above. Consequently, there is no discussion in rabbinic writings about whether or not it is possible for a person to 'choose' or 'select' his sexual orientation. In the absence of any contrary teachings, it is reasonable to believe that a faithful Jew has no cause to reject the current appreciation of an exclusive homosexual orientation – developed by nature or nurture – as indicated by so much empirical, scientific and psychological evidence.

However, the idea that some people are exclusive homosexuals and do not have a choice with regard to their orientation does present us with a somewhat novel appreciation of the Torah's commandments against homosexual relationships. For if homosexuality were either an elective orientation, or there was no such thing as a homosexual orientation, the proscription would create no 'problem' for the believing Jew. On such an understanding the prohibition against *mishkav zachar* and lesbian activity allows for temptation for heterosexual people or bisexual people to engage in homosexual practices. The Torah can be understood to recognise that heterosexuals may be willing to broaden the spectrum of their sexual experience, or may possibly even wish to acquire a novel sexual direction. The purport of the negative commandment proscribing such adventures would be: God has created us with sexual desires; these may be appreciated in the heterosexual marriage but must be disciplined and curbed in any other context. Thus the Torah does not deny the human being sexual fulfilment, and in the case of a woman, even makes it a mandate in the marriage laws, and a *mitzvah* that her conjugal rights are honoured.[3]

It is not unreasonable for one to accept that the heterosexual, or even bisexual, person should live in accordance with these commandments. It would be impossible for mankind to exist and thrive without sexual intimacy[4] and it would likewise lead to social chaos and degeneration if man's desires were not harnessed and focused. Thus, in a world where heterosexuality, or even bisexuality, were assumed as being universal, the biblical and rabbinical prohibitions against *mishkav zachar* and lesbian activity would present no unique concept.

However, in light of the contemporary understanding of human psychology and sexual orientation as described above, the unqualified ban on *mishkav zachar* and lesbian practices assumes a new dimension. Today, the homosexual individual is perceived as a person desiring love and companionship, affection and the bliss of intimacy, just like the heterosexual. Yet unlike the heterosexual (who, in certain circumstances, may be tempted to engage in situational or opportunistic homosexual exchanges) or the bisexual (who has the option of entering into a heterosexual relationship), the *confirmed* homosexual is capable of appreciating such a union only with someone of the same sex. Moreover, he or she will not be able to engage in a heterosexual relationship without enduring – and often inflicting on the partner – considerable emotional trauma. In some extreme cases, heterosex is literally physically impossible.

Consequently, the unqualified and all-embracing ban on homosexual activities in Jewish Law now must be understood to mean that, for some people, the Torah has forbidden all plausible sexual activity. In other words, for homosexuals, the purport of the commandments of the Torah is: God has created us with sexual desires; these must be completely suppressed and never expressed. The commandment against homosexual practices for exclusive homosexuals is in essence a commandment to live a life of total celibacy and sexual abstention. The perceived 'unreasonableness' of such a commandment has led some contemporary rabbis to argue that homosexuality as an orientation *must* be 'treatable'. In their opinion, Judaism cannot accept the idea that the homosexual cannot be 're-orientated' so that he is able to find expression for his natural desires for intimacy in a heterosexual marriage. According to this school of thought, the purport of the Torah's commandment – insofar as homosexuals are concerned – is: God has created us with, or allowed us to develop (through no fault of our own), a homosexual orientation; we are obliged to re-orientate ourselves and develop a heterosexual orientation, or at least the capacity to engage in a healthy heterosexual relationship. In brief, the commandment of the Torah – according to this understanding – includes the mandate for homosexuals to embark upon some form of reparative therapy, thus enabling them to express their sexuality in a heterosexual context.[5]

Yet this does not really solve the problem. If it were indeed possible for all homosexuals to 're-orientate' themselves, this understanding of the Divine commandments may be tenable. However, as we shall see, even the most optimistic and highly controversial views with regard to the so-called conversion or reparative therapies acknowledge that there exist a substantial number of people (the exact percentage is, for our purposes, not really relevant) who – for one reason or another – cannot be 'enabled' to embark upon a heterosexual relationship even through therapy. This leads us to a brief discussion on the issue of reparative therapy and the current 'state of the art' with regard to psychological techniques for change in sexual orientation. The main function of the following section is to demonstrate that, even according to the optimistic enthusiasts, the possibility of therapy does not remove the above-mentioned, perceived 'unreasonableness' in the commandments against homosexual practices.

'CURING' HOMOSEXUALITY?

It is clear that, from the perspective of Jewish teachings, if sexual orientation can be changed, then homosexuals ought to re-orientate themselves and 'become' heterosexuals. The reason for this claim is that, since Jewish Law prohibits homosexual activities, and since Jews are commanded (and in the case of women, are strongly encouraged) to get married, it would be wrong for a person to voluntarily 'retain' a sexual orientation that (a) burdens him or her with an almost impossible challenge (total celibacy), and (b) serves as an impediment to entering a healthy marital relationship. Furthermore, inasmuch as homosexuality 'undermines the natural order of creation', and to the extent that homosexual behaviour may contribute to the prevalence of promiscuity and its consequences, it is only logical that, if a person can 'convert' to heterosexuality (thereby circumventing the temptations that may increase one's propensity to indulge in 'multiple' sexual partners and may make one more vulnerable to the sometimes unfortunate consequences of such relationships), he or she ought to do so.

Even if we are to accept the notion that homosexuality is biologically or genetically determined, and, consequently, one could argue that 'it is God Almighty Who has made a certain percentage of people *naturally* homosexual', this would not constitute reason for avoiding change. Whatever the reason may be, many of us were created with natural 'imperfections' and – given the chance – it is our responsibility to become 'partners in the dynamics of creation' by working towards perfection. By way of analogy, a person may be created with biological infertility. Yet it would not be considered wrong for such a person to endeavour, through medical procedures, to become fertile. Far from being an intrusion into God's domain, those who attempt to mend nature's deficiencies are actually responding to the Divine calling on mankind. We are enjoined by the Creator to bring 'perfection' (or *tikkun*) to those elements of creation which we find 'wanting'.

Thus, in contrast to many secular, and religious, thinkers who are *in principle* opposed to sexual re-orientation, on the grounds that 'if it ain't broke, don't fix it', the Jewish view is that if a homosexual can become a heterosexual, or even can develop the capacity for a healthy heterosexual relationship, he would be obliged to do so.

However, the crux of the issue is not whether or not a person *should* change, but whether or not *it is possible* for a person to change his or her sexual orientation. If it is not possible to change, then there cannot conceivably be any religious requirement to do so. Moreover, if it is not possible to change, then it would be most unfair, if not cruel, to persist with the demand that someone achieves that which is not possible. To insist that a person perform an impossible task is surely illogical, if not sadistic.

Furthermore, when contemplating the possibility of change, it is also necessary to take into consideration the 'price' that will have to be paid for such change. To revert to the above analogy of infertility treatment, if an infertile person could become fertile, but as a result he would contract a debilitating disease, or the therapy to induce fertility would entail a violation of Torah Law, such treatment would, needless to say, not be recommended. By the same token, if the endeavours to change sexual orientation would induce, say, a nervous breakdown, or would lead to severe depression or even suicide, there would be more than reason to oppose such therapies.

It is fair to say that, insofar as exclusive homosexuals – namely men or women who have never experienced sexual attraction to members of the opposite gender – are concerned, there is a predominant view in the vast majority of medical and psychological schools that re-orientation is not ordinarily possible. Many practising professionals, amongst them a number of observant Jews, have confirmed – based on years of experience – the rectitude of this view.

Furthermore, many psychologists are concerned about the dangers of reparative or re-orientation therapies. According to the President of the American Psychiatric Association (APA): 'There is no scientific evidence that reparative or conversion therapy is effective in changing a person's sexual orientation. There is, however, evidence that this type of therapy can be destructive.' According to this 'school of thought', reparative therapy runs the risk of harming patients by causing severe clinical depression and self-destructive behaviour.[6]

There is, however, a minority opinion that some people may be able to benefit from therapy.[7] Advocates of conversion therapy have argued that the above-mentioned statement of the APA, as well as other statements made by the formal body of that association, did not reflect a balanced view of its professional constituents and was heavily influenced and severely manipulated by the politically militant 'gay lobby'. Moreover, recently, Dr Robert Spitzer – who spearheaded the 1973 removal of homosexuality from the APA's list of psychiatric disorders – presented a study that demonstrated that some homosexual men and women had experienced a shift from homosexual to heterosexual attraction and had sustained that shift for more than five years. He concluded: 'contrary to conventional wisdom, some highly motivated individuals, using a variety of change efforts, can make substantial change in multiple indicators of sexual orientation'. However, even proponents of conversion and reparative therapy acknowledge that in many cases such therapy can, at the very most, help the individual in his pursuit of celibacy, but would not enable him to embark upon a potentially viable marital union. Furthermore, even one of the greatest optimists about the success of sexual re-orientation therapies (Orthodox) Dr Joseph Berger, acknowledges that *even under the best of circumstances, with highly motivated, suitable patients, the success rate is between 30 and 50 per cent*[8] (emphasis added). Consequently, we may conclude that it is almost universally recognised that people of exclusive and apparently unalterable orientation do exist in a significant number.[9]

In addition to the still persisting controversy in academic and professional circles as to the value and credibility of 'reparative' therapies, there are substantial halachic questions. Psychotherapy and related therapies in general are not disciplines that never cause a clash with halachic values. When attempting to deal with issues related to sexuality and intimacy, there are numerous issues in which even an ultra-Orthodox psychoanalyst will confront tension between psychotherapeutic and halachic norms. Some of these areas have been explored and discussed, others await treatment.[10] It is not possible for me to predict what the ultimate answers to these complexities will be. The answer may well vary from case to case and from situation to situation. As Rabbi Moshe Spero has observed, we still await a thorough treatment of the halachic complexities from a halachically renowned authority.

In addition, there are pragmatic concerns. For example, the Council of the British Association of Psychotherapists confirmed (in personal correspondence dated 27 September 2000) to this author: 'if a person wished to attempt to achieve any deep change in sexual orientation, it would involve attendance [at psychoanalytic therapy] four or five times weekly at a cost of thirty to forty pounds per session, for some years, *without any guarantee of achieving their desired change*' (emphasis added). Financial and other 'logistical' difficulties often make therapy inaccessible, even for a person who otherwise may benefit from such therapy.

It is not my intention to express an authoritative view on the credits or discredits of reparative, conversion therapies. However, the above 'survey' should make it abundantly clear that, even as these lines are being written, and for the foreseeable future, there will be those who have to contend with the challenges thrown up by their unchanged or unchangeable homosexual orientation. This conclusion is not based on the acceptance of any one school of thought with regard to the effectiveness of reparative therapy. Rather, it has been demonstrated that this conclusion would be inevitable even if we were to ignore some of the currently predominant professional views and espouse some of the most controversially optimistic views about the successes of conversion therapies. It is based on this awareness that I believe that the debate around the feasibility or otherwise of methods of amelioration or change cannot serve as a substitute for a considered and realistic response to the very tangible challenges faced by gays and lesbians.[11]

THE HARD LINE

Another attitude that has been adopted in certain circles with regard to homosexuals is simply to deny their existence. Whilst the above-mentioned rabbis (who see psychological therapy as the ultimate answer to their problem) allow for the possibility of a homosexual orientation, but understand the Torah's commandments to entail a mandate for those with such an orientation to re-orientate themselves, this 'school of thought' argues that the commandments against homosexual activities indicate that there is no such thing as a person who does not have the capacity for a healthy and sustainable heterosexual relationship. Based on the idea that the Torah does not demand the impossible, and 'according to the camel is the burden', some rabbis have felt compelled to dismiss the modern understanding of homosexuality. If there is no such thing as a homosexual orientation, there is no reason to be troubled by the Torah's proscription of homosexual activities. For these commandments do not contain a mandate for perpetual celibacy for anyone. Consequently, the purport of the commandments against homosexual activity is: God has created mankind with sexual desires. Everyone has the ability to express these desires in a heterosexual relationship. Some people may, in addition to their heterosexual desires, be tempted to express their sexuality in a homosexual relationship. This desire must be disciplined. Period.

Some theologians have based their thinking on the writings of a great twentieth-century halachic authority. The renowned Rabbi Moshe Feinstein, adopts an extremely harsh position regarding *male* homosexuals. In a responsum dated 1976, addressed to a young man who had asked for help in dealing with his homosexual impulses, R. Feinstein offers his interlocutor three reflections to help him resist succumbing to the temptations of his evil inclination. One of these contemplations is that it is inconceivable for anyone to have any natural desire whatsoever for homosexual liaison. Such relationships are in total contradiction to the physical and psychological chemistry of mankind. Ordinary sinners, who merely seek self-gratification, do not indulge in homosexual practices, which have no root in the human sex drive. Rather, they are performed simply *because* they are forbidden; an expression of a desire to annoy the Almighty. Hence the severity of the sin of *mishkav zachar*, which is tantamount to a wanton rebellion against the Master of the Universe. In other words, not only does R. Feinstein seem to rule out the possibility of a homosexual orientation, but he seems to rule out the possibility of any intrinsic desire on the part of anyone for the pleasure afforded by male homosexual congress. An extensive quotation[12] from R. Feinstein's 'Letters' is deemed appropriate:

... [the employment of the word *to'evah*[13] in reference to homosexual conduct reflects] God's remonstration with the wicked. [The Almighty says] according to the laws of nature that I have created there can be no desire for homosexual relations. This is in contrast to the natural desire for physical intimacy with women, which is indispensable for the perpetuation of the human species. Hence the desire for illicit relationships with women is part of natural creation. For, as the Talmud[14] says, it would not be possible for a man to be possessed with desire for a woman who is permitted to him and at the same time not desire the woman who is forbidden to him. In contrast, the desire for homosexual relations [which are not necessary for the perpetuation of the species] is not natural, it is verily a deviation from nature, even the wicked who would not be deterred from lustful indulgence in sinful relationships, do not engage in homosexual intimacy. The desire for such relations is, in essence, a desire to do something forbidden, *because it is forbidden*. This is analogous to the one who sins 'in order to annoy', Heaven Forfend. [Consequently, homosexual transgressions are much more reprehensible than heterosexual transgressions.] The Gemara[15] says that when the wicked are summoned to Justice, they will be challenged for not having immersed themselves in Torah study (an antidote for lustful sins). If the sinner will say, 'I was handsome', and therefore had ample opportunity to sin, or 'I was possessed by my passionate desires', his justification will be dismissed by proof from Joseph. [The seduction and enticement to sin, that Joseph confronted in the house of his Egyptian mistress, was immense, and yet, ultimately, Joseph overcame temptation.[16] It is evident from this talmudic teaching that those who succumb to sexual temptation may have some *argument* – although no *justification* – in their favour.] For the sin of homosexual intercourse, however, the wicked transgressor has no room for excuse, because *it would not have been possible for him to even desire to perform this transgression* ... The verse [that describes homosexual conduct as a *to'evah* does not just refer to one who also indulges in other illicit sexual liaisons, rather it] also refers to one who is not suspected to behave licentiously with regard to other categories of sexual sin. *The verse is [also] addressing one who may be beyond suspicion with regard to other proscribed relationships, [but requires a forewarning] with regard to homosexual relationships.*

Even such a person is described by our verse as deviating from the naturally inherent desires, in favour of the forbidden. The Gemara says that a Jew who eats a gnat or a fly may be doing so to satisfy his desire. This is because of the desire for the unknown. The Jew may never have tasted these abominable creatures, and may think that there is indeed some tasty delight to be gained from eating them.[17] *This is not the case with those who engage in homosexual relationships.*

To speak of a desire for homosexual intimacy is a contradiction in terms. In essence, the wicked also have no desire for this, rather *the desire is only to do something which is forbidden, because it is forbidden.* The evil inclination entices the person to rebel against the will of the Holy One Blessed Be He. This awareness should serve you in good stead in your struggle with your evil inclination. For essentially you have already vanquished it, inasmuch as you believe in the Holy One Blessed Be He, and in all the Thirteen Principles of Faith, and in all of the Torah [and therefore you would surely not want to annoy the God you trust in. Your belief in God is your ammunition] to be victorious over your evil inclination that seeks to entice you to rebel against the Will of God, and to anger Him.

This is also the meaning of the verse in Deuteronomy:[18] 'They anger him with their abominations'. *Rashi* comments that the reference in 'abominations' is to sins such as homosexual relations.[19] This clearly demonstrates that homosexual sins are performed [only] in order to anger the Almighty.[20]

The responsa of R. Feinstein certainly do not reflect an awareness or an acceptance of the distinction between homosexual acts performed by heterosexuals, and the existence of a homosexual disposition, which – whatever its origin – does not stem from a desire to anger God. According to R. Feinstein's views, the purport of the Torah's commandments against homosexual activities is: God has created human beings with sexual desires. These may be expressed within the context of a heterosexual relationship. No man has any innate or essential yearnings for homosexual intimacy. Some people may have a desire to rebel against God and indulge in homosexual activities in order to annoy Him. (It is possible that the motivation to anger the Almighty, and subsequent indulgence in homosexual activity, may – even according to R. Feinstein – lead such a person to 'acquire a taste' for homosexual relationships. Essentially, however, the motivation is to rebel against the Creator.) This understanding of homosexuality not only seems to fly in the face of much empirical evidence to the contrary, but also goes against a number of Jewish sources that seem to indicate that men may experience powerful sexual urges and desires for homosexual relationships, which are not based on the motivation to anger God.[21]

If the words of R. Feinstein are to be taken at face value, it would be baffling to discover the phenomenon of many trustworthy men who claim never to have experienced any attraction towards women and always to have experienced passionate desires for intimacy with men. It would be astonishing to encounter many fine, God-fearing and pious people – who may have never engaged in *mishkav zachar* – who, despite their Herculean efforts to develop the capacity for heterosexual relationships, have not been able to do so and according to their own understanding (as well as the understanding of the God-fearing professionals they have consulted) have either an inborn or deeply ingrained desire for homosexual intimacy. Homosexuals who are *ba'alei teshuvah*, and extremely devout and committed Orthodox people who struggle with very powerful and passionate desires to experience the warmth and pleasure of intimacy exclusively with members of their own gender, would all be something of an enigma. I do not understand R. Feinstein's views on this matter. However, R. Feinstein is not the only Orthodox voice on this subject. Others have taken a different position, which reflects a more favourable assessment of homosexual people.

RABBINIC RECOGNITION OF THE HOMOSEXUAL DISPOSITION

Rabbi Menachem Schneerson (1902–1994), the Lubavitcher Rebbe, acknowledges that desires for homosexual congress may be very deeply rooted in a person and even 'inborn and part of his nature'. In a landmark address delivered at a public gathering in 1986, the Rebbe focused on 'the problem of individuals who express an inclination towards a particular form of physical relationship in which the libidinal gratification is sought with members of one's own gender'. The Rebbe based his approach on the teachings of Maimonides. He declared:

> Maimonides teaches (*Hilchot Teshuvah* ch. 5): Free Will is bestowed on every human being. If one desires to turn towards the good way and be righteous he has the power to do so. If one wishes to turn toward the evil way and be wicked, he is at liberty to do so. Consequently this true, free will, described by Maimonides, is decisively all-powerful. Yet, in the

laws relating to Moral Disposition and Ethical Conduct, Maimonides admits that:

> Every human being is characterised by moral dispositions ... exceedingly divergent. One man is choleric, always hot tempered; another sedate, never angry ... one is a sensualist whose lusts are never gratified; another is so pure that he does not even long for the few things that our physical nature needs ... stingy, generous, cruel, merciful, and so forth.[22]

Maimonides adds: 'Of all the various dispositions, some belong to one from the beginning of his existence and correspond to his physical constitution.'[23]

Accordingly, the faithful Jew need not discard the modern appreciation of the nature of homosexuality. Homosexuality, like the temperaments and dispositions Maimonides speaks of, may have little or no appeal to one individual. For another, it may not even be sufficient to describe it as a strong desire or propensity, rather it may 'belong' to him 'from the beginning of his existence and correspond to his physical constitution'. This school of thought recognises the possibility of homosexuality as an intrinsic constituent of the nature of the individual, in contrast to its being an acquired disposition, or worse still, a perverse form of religious rebellion.

According to Rabbi Schneerson, the homosexual, despite his in-built nature, is not compelled 'to act in a particular way. He still has an absolutely free will!'

Rabbi J. David Bleich has also elaborated upon this approach, likewise taking his cue from Maimonidean teachings. The following segment of his essay is most illuminating:

> The validity or non-validity of the claim that homosexuality is natural rather than aberrant, or a normal state rather than an illness, is irrelevant to Jewish teaching regarding this matter. Not everything that is normal and natural is also licit and morally acceptable. Monogamy, for example, is probably not natural to the human species ... yet Western Society has commonly maintained that ... monogamy represents a moral value despite the fact that a monogamous lifestyle is not dictated by emotional, physiological, or sexual impulses. Divine commandments, by their very nature, are designed to curb and channel human desires. They are not necessarily reflective of that which comes naturally to man.[24]

Another prominent contemporary thinker and Rosh Yeshivah takes a similar line. In 'A Personal Correspondence' with a homosexual, Rabbi Aharon Feldman writes to an individual who had experienced much anguish as a result of his homosexuality and for whom the situation had become 'especially tortuous' since he became a *ba'al teshuvah*. Rabbi Feldman says:[25]

> ... I believe that the course you have taken is correct: *you refuse to deny your nature as a homosexual* while at the same time refuse to deny your Jewishness. There is no contradiction between the two if they are viewed in their proper perspective.
>
> *Judaism looks negatively at homosexual activity, but not at the homosexual.* Whatever the source of his nature, whether it is genetic or acquired (*the Torah does not express any view on the matter*), is immaterial. The nature in no way diminishes or affects the Jewishness of a homosexual. He is as beloved in God's eyes as any other Jew, and is as responsible as any Jew in all the *mitzvos*. He is obligated to achieve life's goals by directing his life towards spiritual growth, sanctity and perfection of his character no less than is any other Jew. He will merit the same share in the world to come, which every Jew merits, minimally by being the descendant of *Avraham Avinu* and maximally by totally devoting his life towards the service of God.[26]

DENIAL OR ACKNOWLEDGEMENT

In light of the above, it may be argued that it is not only acceptable for people to acknowledge their homosexual tendencies, but moreover it is the correct and advisable thing to do. However a person chooses to confront the challenges presented by his or her dispositions or character traits, honesty to oneself is a prerequisite. The same is true regarding sexuality; denial of reality is spiritually and emotionally counter-productive. A heterosexual who is uncomfortable with the fact that he is 'plagued' with carnal desire, would be acting irresponsibly if he were to simply deny the very existence of his sexual yearnings. Rather he ought to be aware of his physical and psychological chemistry, and endeavour to harness, foster and discipline his instincts. The same is true for the homosexual individual who tries to feign oblivion to his nature. He will not be able to manage the challenges of his particular life unless he is able to confront them. This may be in sharp contrast to some 'ecclesiastical advice' that is in vogue in certain communities. Yet experience has demonstrated that ignoring reality does not solve any problems. It usually exacerbates them. Consequently, the homosexual ought to be advised to confront what may be an extremely painful realisation with the hope that he or she will then have an opportunity to meet the challenges of Jewish life with bravery and integrity.

A similar idea has been expressed with regard to homosexuality by Rabbi Bleich. Resorting to an analogy from the kosher dietary laws, and basing himself on a landmark statement made by Maimonides in this context, Rabbi Bleich eloquently writes:

> ... Among modern philosophers it was Kant, in his *Groundwork of the Metaphysics of Morals*, who grapples with the question of whether, ideally, one should act in a virtuous manner out of a desire to do so, or whether it is a greater virtue to behave morally in defiance of natural desire. Rambam [Maimonides], in addressing essentially the same question, distinguishes between various categories of commandments and points out that while the Torah does, of course, proscribe certain forms of behaviour, that are unnatural and instinctively abhorrent, there are also many commandments that serve to forbid conduct that is entirely normal and natural.[27] There is no natural repugnance associated with eating the flesh of swine; nor is there any reason to regard carnivorous birds as naturally repulsive. The prohibitions contained within the dietary code are not designed to condition us to react negatively to forbidden foods ... *the appropriate response is* [rather] *a frank and candid recognition that in the absence of a divine command, one would naturally be inclined to enjoy such delicacies* (emphasis added).[28]

Thus, neither Rabbi Bleich nor Rabbi Feldman sees anything wrong in describing (in a relevant context) a person whose sexual orientation is directed towards members of his own gender as a homosexual. They do not see this as a breach of any Torah values. Yet, some Orthodox thinkers seem to have taken exception to the use of the term 'homosexual' other than as an adjective for behaviour, or as a descriptive term for people who engage in homosexual liaisons. They claim that according to Judaism, there is no such thing as a 'homosexual' who does not engage in homosexual activity. Whatever this semantic play is supposed to achieve, the fact is that all evidence goes to show that there are many people, among them a substantial number of Jews, who are exclusively attracted to members of the same sex. I believe that it is perfectly appropriate to describe such people as 'homosexual' or 'gay', inasmuch as it is appropriate to describe the majority of the word's population as 'heterosexual' or 'straight', by virtue of their exclusive attraction to members of the opposite sex.[29]

A UNIQUE ARGUMENT

At this juncture, it is proposed to examine an interesting theory advanced by Rabbi Barry Freundel.[30] Rabbi Freundel, an Orthodox thinker, trying to make sense of the homosexual orientation and the commandment against homosexual activity, proposes the following idea. According to Rabbi Freundel, homosexuality may be a natural orientation in general society, but in the Orthodox Jewish community, there are, he claims, very few manifestations of this nature. He mentions 'the anomalous fact that the one community in which the percentage of homosexual preference is significantly lower than in the general population is the Orthodox Jewish community'.[31] He then argues that the biblical proscription of homosexual activity actually influences the psyche of those loyal to the Divine Commandments, and makes them somewhat immune to the homosexual drive. He states:

> ... It is almost as if Halacha rejects the notion of an individual called a homosexual, rejects the necessity of the homosexual act for any individual, rejects the idea of an irrevocable homosexual orientation, and thus creates a society in which these ideals can, apparently quite successfully, be lived.[32]

Serious questions can be asked of Rabbi Freundel on a number of points. Most relevant to the crux of his argument is the fact that it would be almost impossible to demonstrate with any degree of accuracy the prevalence of matters relating to the intimate details of people's idiosyncratic sexual lives within the Orthodox community. In the unlikely circumstances whereby a reliable statistical study regarding homosexuality were available, Rabbi Freundel's thesis would still not be substantiated. It is more than likely that people of Orthodox persuasion, when confronted with their homosexual orientation, may feel compelled to either attempt to deny, or otherwise conceal their particular struggles in this regard. Furthermore, as has often been the case, they may feel – albeit based on erroneous assumptions – that there is no room for them within Orthodoxy. Given these and other obscuring factors, it appears to this writer that we are not able to empirically ascertain the level of homosexual desires within the contemporary Orthodox community.

The fact that many pastoral rabbis, Orthodox counsellors and advisors (both within the so-called 'yeshivah community' and outside of it) are seemingly aware of the not-infrequent appeal from amongst their charges for guidance regarding homosexual impulses, surely demonstrates that the halachic community has not achieved immunity to the homosexual orientation.

Rabbi Freundel, like other rabbis whose views were mentioned earlier in this chapter, was apparently troubled by the talmudic teaching that God does not demand the impossible of his creations.[33] He writes: 'Particularly as the area of sexuality is an area of such deeply personal implications to any individual, it is difficult to imagine God creating a situation wherein those who feel themselves to possess a homosexual orientation cannot change and are consequently locked in a living prison with no exit and no key.' This argument from reason leads him to reject the authenticity of the homosexual drive, at least as a permanent state. However, even R. Freundel is compelled to admit that there is no universal guarantee for change. Thus, to whatever degree change is not possible, the conundrum posed by Rabbi Freundel remains.

One must also bear in mind that the above-mentioned considerations that discussion of possibility for change, when approached from a religious perspective, cannot limit itself to theoretical or even experiential professional viewpoints. Even if change is possible, it is not always accessible or available within certain social, financial and halachic contexts. In a community where psychological expertise is viewed with suspicion – particularly when it seeks to deal with sexual matters – many homosexuals would still remain in the 'living prison' that R. Freundel so poignantly describes. Therapy often demands extraordinary stamina and financial backing. It may only be successful with a compatible therapist, and may often only be accomplished over many years, if at all. Particularly in the event of partial amelioration of exclusive homosexual desires, it may be impossible for the Orthodox Jew to find a spouse. Hence it is incorrect to say that even the most optimistic theories regarding therapy have provided the 'key' to the exit from the unenviable situation the homosexual is 'locked in'.

CONCLUSION

We can only conclude by reiterating the principles enunciated in this chapter. Homosexual desires may be as natural for a minority of society (Orthodox or otherwise) as heterosexual desires are for the majority. Given the right circumstances, the homosexual may be able to develop the capacity for, and embark upon, a healthy heterosexual relationship. However, the reality of life confirms that there are hundreds, if not thousands, of people who strive to live in accordance with God's will, yet find themselves trapped in their exclusively homosexual orientation, without key or exit. We are thus compelled to accept that God Almighty has indeed confronted many of His creatures with this formidable challenge.

3

The Formidable Challenge

FREEDOM OF CHOICE

In the previous chapter we presented the view that, whether inborn or developed ('nature or nurture'), the homosexual disposition is not ordinarily acquired as a matter of conscious choice. The homosexual may have never elected to be of this disposition, had he been given any say in the matter. As stated categorically in the first chapter of this book, all people, including homosexuals, are charged with a Divine command to discipline their urges. The fact that this can be achieved is based on a maxim that is central to the Jewish creed. Every individual has the ability to choose right from wrong. Deuteronomy 35:7 declares, 'Behold I have placed before you this day life and good, death and evil. *And you shall choose life.*' In contrast to some other faith denominations that espouse a determinist view on the human condition, Judaism insists that every person has the ability to choose his or her course of action.[1]

In general terms, human activity can be divided into three categories: thought, speech and action. The Torah, which consists of biblical and rabbinic law, gives specific instructions as to which thoughts may be entertained, which words may or should be spoken, and which actions are constructive, destructive or 'neutral'. We may be tempted to violate the laws of the Torah, and this is only natural. It is, however, our duty to exercise self-discipline and restraint so that our lives should be lived in accordance with the Divine will as expressed in the Torah.

If a person were a 'programmed robot' whereby he or she was compelled to behave in a certain manner, the Jewish religion would make no sense. Judaism is to a large degree a religion of practice, consisting of 248 positive categories of commandment and 365 negative categories of commandment.[2] If our actions were determined by our instincts, as are those of animals, it would be a futile exercise to issue commandments to creatures of instinct.[3]

Another major tenet of our faith is the belief that God rewards the righteous and punishes the wicked.[4] As the *Yigdal* hymn phrases it: 'He rewards the good man according to his deeds; He metes out punishment to the wicked man according to his wickedness'. Once again, this principle is contingent upon the parallel belief in man's ability to choose right from wrong. The terms 'righteous' and 'wicked' – and consequently 'reward' and 'punishment' – would all be rendered meaningless in a society consisting of pre-programmed beings.[5]

'EVERYTHING IS IN THE HANDS OF HEAVEN'

The doctrine of the freedom of choice refers, as the Talmud[6] puts it, to our 'Fear of Heaven'. We may be visited by a variety of thoughts. The human mind is open and vulnerable. We do not have a choice in *this* matter. We are able, however, to choose whether or not we wish to 'entertain' certain thoughts that occur in our minds, rather than brush them aside. It may be enormously difficult to expel a persistent thought, but it is not normally in the realm of the *impossible.*[7] Instinctively, we are prone to contemplate ideas, fantasies and wishes, but we are not necessarily compelled to do so. The fact that we may have an urge to say certain forbidden things may not be within the remit of our choice, but whether in actuality we say them or not *is* our decision. We are sometimes unable to circumvent our *desires* and temptations to do certain forbidden things. We do have the ability to refrain from *realising* our desires.

All of us are born with many instinctive desires and nurture many powerful and seductive temptations. It is a lifetime's task to struggle with our individual inclinations.[8] Indeed, as we have argued in the previous chapter, a mature and realistic approach to life entails the recognition that we will have to constantly battle with our lusts and passions, and this is assuredly no cause for guilt feelings. The challenge of life is not to annihilate our desires, but to control them.

UNEQUAL TRIALS

Whether we like it or not, the fact is that life is – or at least appears to be – easier for some people and harder for others. The same is true regarding mankind's life-long struggle with his 'evil inclination'. Some people may have a relatively mild battle on their hands, whilst others are engaged in awesome struggles on a daily basis.[9] However intense the struggle is, it may still vary from person to person. As we explained in the previous chapter, some people may be born with or develop a stronger propensity for one type of desire or another. Some people may have an insatiable appetite for food, others for money, and yet others may have an 'overactive' libido. Naturally, every person's challenges are different. One may have to exercise great self-restraint in order not to lose his temper, whereas another may be quite passive and docile by nature. One person may be able to share his wealth easily, and as such the *mitzvah* of donating to charity will not require much effort from him or her. Another may require a Herculean effort to overcome his miserly nature in order to practice kindness and benevolence. The only common factor is that everyone is confronted with tests and trials and that ultimately all people normally have the ability to conquer their passions and rise to the challenge of their duties.

The same is true for people who have a strong desire for homosexual intercourse. The fact that the Torah forbids homosexual practices implies that the Creator of all beings knows that some people may be desirous of engaging in homosexual activity. Moses, when he stood on Mount Sinai, was challenged by the angels as to why he felt that the Torah's rightful place was on the lowly earth, and not in Heaven. His reply was that the commandments as found in the Torah do not relate to the angels. 'Do you have parents [that you need a commandment to honour them]?; Do you conduct business with one another [that you need commandments about honesty and ethics in commerce]?; Do you have an evil inclination [that requires Divine commandments to keep in check]?'[10]. In other words, the very existence of a commandment pre-supposes that an inclination to violate it may naturally occur.

The same may be said with regard to homosexuality. The fact that human beings were given a Torah in which there is a commandment against engaging in homosexual conduct is in itself a testimony to the fact that urges of this type may be manifest in human beings. Whilst it is acceptable to have feelings and desires, it does not follow that responding to those urges in practice is also acceptable.

THE UNIQUE CHALLENGE OF HOMOSEXUALITY

It is true that, as we discussed in the previous chapter, the Torah does *not* discuss the subject of homosexual orientation. Nevertheless, the fact that the Torah – the Eternal Law given by the Eternal God – issues a blanket prohibition against homosexual activity demonstrates that this prohibition is unqualified and applies to all people, irrespective of personal sexual orientation.

This notwithstanding, it is specifically the modern appreciation of the concept of 'sexual orientation' that makes the commandment against homosexual practices 'unique' – at least insofar as homosexuals are concerned. For, if those who are homosexually orientated do not have the capacity for heterosexual relationships, they are consigned by the Torah's commandments to a life of celibacy and considerable loneliness. Considering the fact that – as stated in *Meshech Chochmah* – 'the Torah did not deprive sexual pleasure from any creature with the exception of Moses', since the Torah does not demand that people should commit themselves to 'unfair' and 'unrealistic' expectations,[11] one would have to accept that homosexuals are an (example of an) exception to the rule. The commandments that effectively demand that homosexuals commit themselves to single and lonely lives certainly do not fit in with the framework of what the *Meshech Chochmah* describes as a 'pleasant' and 'amenable' Torah, that makes various allowances and concessions out of consideration for the human condition.

Furthermore, Jewish sources emphasise that sexual intercourse is a necessary component of healthy living. Rabbi Ya'akov Emden (1697–1776), for example, speaks of the crucial role sexual intercourse plays in the maintenance of a person's psychological and physiological health.[12] Once again, granted that confirmed homosexuals do not have the capacity for (marriage, and hence) heterosexual intercourse, one would have to assume that the Torah does 'impose' upon homosexuals the unhealthy consequences of a sexless life. Likewise, the fact that homosexuals who are unable to marry are destined to live without 'partners' and soul-mates effectively means that they are deprived of all the benefits of companionship and mutual support as described in the Talmud and subsequent rabbinic literature.[13] The commandments of the Torah, if not the homosexual orientation itself, certainly do not provide a similar framework for human fulfilment in the case of homosexuals.

All this may not appeal to the reasonable human mind. Given the perceived 'unreasonableness' of such a predicament for a significant number of people (albeit a small minority), a number of contemporary rabbis have made various suggestions designed to 'overcome' this difficulty and to re-assert the 'reasonableness' of the Torah's commandments. A survey and critique of these ideas has been presented in the previous chapter.

Our conclusion was that these positions do not really solve the problem. We were therefore compelled to accept that, notwithstanding the perceived 'unreasonableness' of the commandments – from the human perspective – such is the will of God. He has indeed presented those of a homosexual orientation with a formidable challenge.

Our sages have taught us 'that God does not demand the impossible from his creatures', and 'according to the camel's ability is the load'.[14] Yet, sometimes this load is extremely difficult to bear. It imposes an awesome burden on the one confronted with such challenges. This is certainly true for any person who finds himself constrained in a situation whereby, just like the heterosexual, he desires love and companionship, but unlike the heterosexual, he can only find this with someone of the same gender. It would seem that the Almighty has invested extraordinary qualities in all such people and, therefore, challenges them with the awesome tests that they ordinarily confront.

Yet, this does not mean that the homosexual is necessarily compelled by his instincts to engage in a sexually active relationship, or even in auto-erotic indulgences. In this regard the homosexual is in a similar situation to a healthy heterosexual who, for one reason or another, cannot envisage ever getting married and as a consequence faces the prospect of perpetual sexual frustration and untold loneliness. Such a heterosexual person also faces a tremendous 'test' (*nisayon*).

A FATAL EQUATION

However, the fact that some people are constrained within a homosexual disposition and, at the same time, are subjected to the Divine ban on homosexual behaviour, has led some theologians – both Jewish and non-Jewish – to 'reconsider' the Divine commandment in this respect. One Conservative thinker has even concluded that the Orthodox position regarding those that cannot change their sexual orientation – namely that they should remain celibate all their lives – 'is downright cruel'. Dr Elliot Dorff writes:

I find such a position theologically untenable. I, for one, cannot believe that the God who created us all produced a certain percentage of us to have sexual drives that cannot be legally expressed under any circumstances. That is simply mind-boggling – and, frankly, un-Jewish. Jewish sources see human beings as having conflicting urges that can be controlled and directed by obedience to the wise words of the Torah. It is Christian to see human beings as being endowed with urges that should ideally be forever suppressed. To hold that God created homosexuals to be sexually frustrated all their lives, makes of God a cruel playwright and director in this drama we call life, and our tradition knew better. It called God not only merciful but good. God's law, then, must surely be interpreted to take those root beliefs of our tradition into account. Jewish theology and law are not two disparate realms; here, as always, they must be interpreted to reflect each other.[15]

Dr Dorff is correct in his assertions that God is merciful and good,[16] but it is his subsequent arithmetic that does not add up. For if we were to follow his line of thinking, we would be compelled to concede that, in certain circumstances, pre-marital sex and extra-marital sex are also permissible. We would then have to 'interpret' the biblical and rabbinical laws that proscribe such sexual activities in a manner that they reflect the compassion and goodness of God which are so central to Jewish theology. Consider the plight of someone trapped in a marriage in which he cannot hope for sexual fulfilment, and which cannot be terminated by divorce. The frustration of someone who has no reasonable hope to find a compatible partner should also be considered. Surely, it is Divine Providence that has placed all such people in the unenviable circumstances in which they find themselves. Would Dr Dorff suggest that these people, who are equally innocent victims of their circumstances, be permitted to engage in sexual activity that Jewish Law proscribes?

Furthermore, if we were to proceed down Dr Dorff's line of thinking, we would have to 're-interpret', namely abolish, a number of cognate laws. Take the case of a man whose testes are perforated.[17] Here, the 'problem' is physical, and clearly defined, unlike the more complex psychological or genetic problem posed by homosexuality. Biblical Law forbids such a person from 'entering into the Congregation of Israel'. A person whose testicles have been damaged may have the same desires as any other person for intimate relations, and thus his suffering and his lifelong sexual frustration is to be likened to that of the homosexual.

Whilst this law has existed and been studied for thousands of years, no authority has ever suggested 're-interpreting' it in light of the sexual frustration that results from its application.

There is another case in Jewish Law where the result is similar – but the cause is not psychological or physical. According to the Law, a Jewish person who is the offspring of certain adulterous or incestuous unions may only marry another such person, or a convert.[18] Even such relationships are only remotely possible and are often discouraged.[19] Thus, such an individual finds that his or her chance of meeting a permitted spouse is severely circumscribed to the degree that, in effect, marriage for such a person is normally a theoretical possibility only.

Rabbinic literature records the sympathy and compassion that rabbis throughout the ages had on the offspring of the above-mentioned forbidden unions, whom Jewish Law effectively deprived of the opportunity to marry into the 'mainstream' of the Jewish People. The Midrash teaches that God is 'attentive to the tears of those who are oppressed' by the constraints of Jewish Law in this manner.[20] God acknowledges that the offspring of illicit unions are not themselves guilty of any crime, but suffer the consequences of their personal status, which is a result of the actions of their parents. God promises that such people will be compensated 'in the world to come' for the hardships that they endured in this world, yet nowhere do traditional Jewish sources advocate the re-interpretation of the Law in these cases.[21]

Even if one were to accept Dr Dorff's hypothesis, and, furthermore, be ready to apply it to premarital and extra-marital sex, one would still be faced with the question of why so many lonely and pious people have never been able to find their partner in life. Answers for theological questions may be sought, but they must never be placed as a pre-requisite to the acceptance of God's commandments.

I concede to Dr Dorff that it is indeed often theologically challenging to accept that God Almighty and All-Merciful has placed His creatures into *near* impossible situations. The pain, the suffering and the misery that homosexuals have to endure, raise the ancient question: 'Why do bad things happen to good people?' Notwithstanding the fact that Jewish Law explicitly forbids the practice of homosexual intimacy, the believing Jew accepts that God has some good reason for creating people who can find no other sexual outlet in their lives. He also accepts that, whilst not necessarily fathomable to us, there exists in the scheme of our Creator a reason and purpose for such a phenomenon. It is a reason that may transcend human understanding, but the faithfully devout does not expect his mortal mind to appreciate every aspect of God's plans.

Yet, I still refer to this phenomenon as 'challenging', because Jewish theology insists that God is not only omniscient but also omnipotent. Any positive purpose that God had in mind when placing people in circumstances where perpetual loneliness, celibacy and – consequently – childlessness is necessarily mandated could, it would seem to the true believer, have been achieved in a less painful manner. God surely could have brought about whatever Divine purpose there is in the emotional trauma, depression, despair and even suicidal feelings that homosexuals – especially those who are trying to avoid temptation and transgression – may be subject to, without 'suffering and evil malaise'. Ultimately, therefore, the fact that human beings have to endure intense misery, even if it is in order to receive the subsequent good, remains – at a certain level – an enigma.[22]

Yet the range of theological complexities that emerges from the dilemma of the homosexual is not essentially connected with that state of being. These questions belong to the broad spectrum of questions as to why painful things happen to people. Philosophers have forever grappled with this problem, and various reasons for the suffering of the righteous have been delineated in the Holy Scriptures and rabbinic writings. The Jewish mind may find meaning in such rationalisation, but would ultimately echo the words of our sages: 'We do not have the ability to comprehend the ... suffering of the righteous.'[23]

Dr Dorff's error is that he has allowed a theological question to be answered by changing the Law.[24] This is untenable for the Jew who believes in the immutability of Jewish Law. For one who accepts that the laws of the Torah are an expression of the will of the Eternal God, it is inconceivable that the laws will be altered or substituted.[25]

The Talmud[26] relates that God showed Moses all the future generations and their rabbis and leaders. Moses stood in awe of the great Rabbi Akiva who expounded the finest nuances of the Torah, thereby yielding a multitude of new teachings and insights, all of which were based on the Torah that Moses himself had delivered to the Jewish people many generations previously. As the vision continued, Moses then saw Rabbi Akiva being tortured by the Romans and his skin being scraped off with iron combs. Shocked by this scene, Moses exclaimed: 'This is the Torah, and this is its reward!?' On hearing this, God replied: 'Keep silent! This is what arose in [my Divine] thought.'

This narrative demonstrates that no matter how great the teacher

may be, and how brilliant the student, the human mind is not conditioned to plumbing the depths of God's scheme. Although the
Almighty Himself was the 'teacher' and the greatest of prophets was
the pupil in this talmudic anecdote, we find that the gap could still not
be bridged, 'For my thoughts are not like your thoughts, nor are your
ways like my ways, says the Lord'.[27]

To be sure, Judaism affirms that 'The Lord is righteous in all His
ways, and pious in all his deeds'.[28] When Jews throughout the ages
experienced unbelievable suffering as a result of their commitment
to Jewish Law, they did not advance a Dorff-like argument. They
remained loyal to God's commandments, even in circumstances where
the ordeals incurred by their commitment involved great hardship.
They believed that every aspect of their daily lives was governed by
Divine Providence, and that their suffering was directly a result of
God's will. Yet they still believed that God's commandments were
immutable and that the God who commanded them to observe these
commandments, even when doing so led to privation and difficulties,
is good and benevolent.

UNIQUE ASPECTS OF THE HOMOSEXUAL CHALLENGE

We have compared – in a theological context – the difficulty of a person
with a homosexual orientation to that of any single person who has
not married or is not able to marry (who may also suffer from loneliness
and sexual celibacy). However, it must be acknowledged that there
exist substantial differences between the two situations. These differences may make the challenge of the homosexual significantly harder
and ever more trying than the challenge of the single heterosexual.

The additional burden that may be the plight of the homosexual
does not detract from our dismissal of Dr Dorff's views. For once it
has been established that God's Commandments and Providence do
seem to put people in extremely difficult, and from our perspective
'unfair', positions, the exact degree of difficulty and unfairness is not
relevant to the theological debate. From our perspective it may seem
inconceivable that the Almighty should have reason to cause unbearable pain to His children. Once, however, we have conceded that the
Almighty does cause us to endure painful experiences – for reasons that
transcend our comprehension – the exact quality or quantity of the
pain does not really change the overall 'picture'.

Nevertheless, in terms of our own, human, response to homosexuals, it is necessary that we endeavour to appreciate the unique aspects of the challenges they are likely to face. To be sure, there are many religious leaders who have expressed sensitivity in this area. Rabbi Aharon Feldman, for example, has shown great empathy for practising homosexuals who are trying to live their lives in accordance with the Torah. He states for example that:

> ... It is not necessary that he [the practising homosexual] change his sexual orientation (if this is at all possible), but that he cease this activity. *It is obvious that for many people this will be difficult, and will have to be accomplished over a period of time.* But it must be done, and it can be done (emphasis added).[29]

Likewise, Rabbi Bleich acknowledges that homosexuals are confronted with an additional aspect of human nature in which natural tendencies must be subdued. This, he says, constitutes 'an additional – and perhaps more difficult – trial. *The challenge may be onerous in the extreme* ... for some the challenge is undoubtedly greater than for others' (emphasis added).[30]

I believe, however, that the exact nature of this 'onerous' challenge has not received sufficient emphasis. Such emphasis is necessary for many reasons. These include the need for empathy. As R. Bleich[31] puts it: 'Others, more fortunate in not having been burdened in this manner, are duty-bound to exhibit compassion and solicitude and to provide all possible support to those endeavouring to overcome' the unique challenges they face. True understanding is a pre-requisite for compassion, and it is with this in mind that I endeavour to help the reader of this book to appreciate the hardships confronted by their homosexual brothers and sisters. It is hoped that this will contribute to the prevalence of a more understanding attitude in society.

Let us take for example the case of a heterosexual person who has a healthy and powerful emotional and sexual chemistry, but, for one reason or another, is unable to get married. This person who does not wish to, or cannot, get married, even if he has a passionate desire for physical intimacy, may be able to avoid constant temptation and frustration. The Jewish tradition encourages men and women who are unrelated to mingle with members of their own gender and avoid unnecessary exposure to temptation through social intercourse with members of the opposite gender. This is especially true in the case of unmarried people.[32] Thus, the great academies and centres of Jewish learning and education cater for boys and girls, men and women, separately. This is based on an understanding of human psychology. 'The eyes see, and the heart desires,' our sages tell us, and 'the organs of the body implement the transgression.'[33] The culpability of the transgressor is not so much for his final succumbing to temptation, as it is for his or her voluntary and wilful experience of situations likely to accentuate the desire to transgress. It is for this reason that the Jewish Code of Law and subsequent authorities advocate a reasonable separation between the sexes. In this way, both males and females, particularly those who are not married, can avoid putting themselves in situations where they will be most vulnerable to straying after their eyes and hearts.

In Orthodox circles, there are ample opportunities for people to study, pray, work and socialise without having to come into close contact with a member of the opposite sex. Consequently, the heterosexual single may be able to immerse himself in an academic or working occupation in which he can avoid excessive frustration. In this way he will be able to escape from the awesome challenge and considerable trauma presented by constant exposure to temptation.

This is not the case for a gay man or a lesbian woman. Unless the gay man, for example, is going to become a hermit, he will ordinarily be confronted with constant temptation and unwanted stimulation of desire in a manner that it is almost impossible to escape from. For the heterosexual to appreciate the unique challenge of the homosexual, he need only envisage a situation where he would be compelled to remain single but conduct his affairs in the company of girls and women. The Orthodox homosexual man does not usually have the option of immersing himself in an all-female environment and, as such, will, ordinarily speaking, find himself almost constantly in a same-sex environment. This may be no less difficult a situation for the confirmed homosexual as the analogous situation described for the heterosexual.

Moreover, the heterosexual single man who finds himself in a female-dominated environment can more easily avoid the type of contact that leads to stimulation and transgression of the Torah's sexual code of behaviour. Both male and female are aware of the potential for the natural heterosexual desire to become manifest, and therefore – in the Orthodox community – will behave accordingly. On the other hand, the homosexual will more often than not confront members of the same sex who are not sensitive to his particular situation, and as such it will be incredibly difficult for him to avoid the type of stimulus that even casual contact can bring.[34] This problem assumes a greater dimension if the homosexual is still deeply 'closeted'.

These difficulties assume a greater proportion for those homosexuals who are trying to change their sexual orientation through therapy. For, whilst therapy may – according to some psychologists – be an advisable option for certain manifestations of homosexuality, it may also serve to exacerbate the above-mentioned problem, at least during the earlier stages of therapy. For, in certain prevalent models of therapy it is necessary for the homosexual to forge a close, even intimate – albeit not physical or erotic – relationship with a member of the same gender. During this process, the homosexual may experience more intense and overwhelming desire for sexual gratification.[35] Even if he avoids a homosexual liaison, he would be compromising on his Jewish lifestyle if he were to indulge in fantasy and auto-eroticism, which are forbidden in the context of all proscribed sexual practices.

Taking all the above into consideration, it becomes amply clear that the challenge of the homosexual may be incomparably more daunting and taxing than the challenge confronted by the heterosexual single. Notwithstanding the useful analogy of the heterosexual single that we employed in our rejection of Dr Dorff's hypothesis, it must therefore be emphasised that this analogy has its limitations. When assessing the awesome trials and tribulations of the homosexual who endeavours to live in accordance with the Word of God, the reality of day to day life must be taken into consideration. It is proposed that those who reflect upon the unique aspects of the homosexual challenge will be less prone to express the type of knee-jerk, if not flippant, dismissals of the very real issues confronted by homosexuals that are sometimes heard even in religious society.

Gay men and women *cannot be blamed or censored for having the feelings and desires that they naturally have.* To do so would be a violation of basic morality and would be antithetical to Jewish values. The True and Fair Judge of the Universe would not possibly want us to penalise people whom He has either invested with, or allowed to develop – through no fault of their own – a homosexual orientation. For, to paraphrase Genesis:[36] 'Shall He Who judges the entire world not do justice?' An appreciation of what the 'other' endures and an appropriate measure of compassion will surely enable people to engage in mutually beneficial communication. It will also help achieve a more healthy equilibrium between moral judgement and humane understanding. This will be further elaborated upon in Chapter 5.

4

Attitudes to the Practising Homosexual

TWO TYPES OF TRANSGRESSORS

In the previous chapters of this book, several principles have been established. Firstly, that homosexual practices are forbidden by Jewish law for both men and women. Secondly, that it is not antithetical to Jewish teaching to accept that there are people who are exclusively homosexual in their orientation. Thirdly, irrespective of whether or not the rationales suggested by classical authorities for this prohibition seem to be applicable in any given case, the prohibitions remain in force. Finally, those who find themselves constrained within the boundaries of an exclusive homosexual disposition face a formidable and unenviable challenge.

Taking all these factors into consideration, it is not surprising to learn that in our day and age, there are many homosexuals who do not feel able to abide by the dictates of the *halachah*. Even homosexuals who may be totally committed to all other areas of Jewish Law – in letter and in spirit – may succumb to the persistent and powerful pressure brought upon them by their all-too-human desire for emotional intimacy and sexual love.[1]

The question that must therefore be confronted is: what attitude should the religious Jew, or for that matter the religious non-Jew, espouse in relation to homosexuals who are not celibate, and engage in one form or another of same-sex intimacy? Needless to say, this matter has been the subject of many heated debates, and highly divergent opinions have emerged over the last few decades.

It is, parenthetically, of interest to note that some otherwise Liberal

and 'broad-minded' theologians have expressed some extremely condemnatory attitudes which do not reflect their overall attitude towards
Jewish Law. It is possible that, at least in some cases, the reason for this
is that such theologians are merely projecting their own personal prejudice onto the teachings of the Jewish tradition.[2] This would explain the
inconsistency of their tolerance of other illicit sexual relationships,
with their extremely harsh attitude towards homosexual prohibitions.
Such manipulation of religious teaching to serve as 'an axe with which
to grind' one's own personal ideas is surely deplorable. Nor do such
acrobatics work. For those who reject the Divine nature of the Torah;
disregard the laws of family purity (*taharat hamishpachah*); do not
condemn masturbation, fornication and numerous other biblical and
rabbinic prohibitions, cannot truly appeal to biblical or rabbinic texts
as a justification for their absolute condemnation of illicit homosexual
behaviour. It appears to this author that to do so smacks of sheer
hypocrisy.

In a religious system that is highly selective in its commitment to
biblical law, and facilitates radical changes in its beliefs and practices
in the light of modern ideas, what lasting meaning can a verse in
Leviticus have when dealing with the proscription of homosexual
activities?[3] Thus, it is towards those who accept the binding nature of
Jewish Law that I direct my words in this chapter.

The Talmud differentiates between two kinds of sinner: someone
who sins out of spite – the 'defiant rebel (*mumar le-hachis*)' – and one
who does not conform to Jewish Law because of his desire for self-
gratification – the 'lusting renegade (*mumar le-tei'avon*)'. In the Talmud
and subsequent halachic literature, the difference between these two
kinds of sinners is demonstrated by the circumstances in which they
are prepared to commit transgressions. The 'lusting renegade' would
ideally prefer to refrain from sinning. In a situation where, for example,
kosher food is available, he will not eat forbidden food, for, as the
Talmud puts it: 'He will not abandon the permitted, and eat the forbidden'. In contrast, the 'defiant rebel' refers to the arrogant and aggressive
sinner. He is a man of 'principles' – he will make a point of eating
forbidden food, despite the availability of a kosher alternative. His
spitefulness will propel him to indulge in the illicit, even in such circumstances where his desires could be satiated through permissible means.[4]

In the *halachah*, there is a clear and major distinction made between
these two categories of sinner. The 'defiant rebel' is treated as a religious
outcast. As such, he loses many of the rights and privileges that are

granted to a member of the Jewish fraternity. In contrast, the 'lusting renegade' – provided that he does not completely discard his allegiance to all aspects of Jewish Law – whilst censured for his non-compliance with the Law, is still treated as being within the pale of the Jewish Community. The 'defiant rebel' is deemed a religious outcast even if his rebellion is manifest in relation to only one particular law, for example, eating forbidden foods, or wearing forbidden garments. This is due to the fact that, by virtue of his spiteful motivation he, like the heretic and the idolater, has excluded himself from the Community of the faithful.[5]

When ascertaining the status of any violator of Jewish Law, it is necessary, therefore, to determine which of the above categories he may be said to belong to. It may be said with reasonable confidence that in contemporary times there are very few people who sin out of spite and would thus be defined as 'defiant rebels'. The majority of people, and I am talking of those who are familiar with the dictates of the Torah, fall into sin when their desire for gratification overwhelms them. This is true with regard to the majority of forbidden activities that are committed by contemporary Jews.[6]

It is even more so with regard to homosexuals. We have more than reason to believe that the only motivation that otherwise faithful Jewish homosexuals have for transgressing the prohibitions associated with homosexual activity is the fact that they have no other legitimate outlet for their sexual and emotional desires. Consequently, the status of the vast majority of knowledgeable Jewish practising homosexuals is – *at worst* – the talmudic category of the 'hedonistic renegade'. As such, the attitude towards practising homosexuals recommended by classical Jewish teachings is one whereby the severity of the prohibition notwithstanding, the individual committing the prohibited act is still within the ambit of the Jewish Fraternity. By way of analogy, he should be treated no differently than a Jew who, due to his intense desire, does not abide by the laws of family purity, *kashrut*, and those concerning pre- or extra-marital sexual relations.[7]

A CASE APART?

It has often been pointed out in this context that homosexual transgressions cannot be equated with the violation of any other Jewish Laws. Consequently, it is argued that practising homosexuals should be treated more 'harshly' than other transgressors. The argument goes thus: Leviticus forbids male anal intercourse under the ban of the death penalty. This is not the case with regard to the kosher dietary laws, for example, for the transgression of which the statutory punishment is lashes or, in some cases, 'divine excommunication (*karet*)'. These penalties represent a less severe castigation of the sinner.[8] Yet, this argument is not convincing. Some adulterous and incestuous relationships and the desecration of the Sabbath (even when not committed in public[9]) are also subject to the death penalty.[10] Nevertheless, those involved in such relationships may still be categorised as 'hedonistic' rather than 'defiant' renegades. The reason for this is that, despite the additional severity inherent in committing an act which is, at least in theory, punishable by death, so long as the motivation is lust rather than spite, the offender has not excluded him or herself from the Community of the faithful.

Another argument that has been advanced in favour of advocating a more 'exclusivist' attitude towards the practising male homosexual is based on the fact that his sin belongs to the category of *giluy arayot*.[11] The severity of such transgressions is underscored by the fact that a person ought to forfeit his or her life rather than transgress.[12] Once again, the argument is less than convincing. Firstly, other illicit sexual relationships, such as those which violate the code of family purity, are also in this category.[13] Nevertheless, Jewish Law would still be prepared to define one who violates these laws as a 'hedonistic renogade' rather than a 'defiant rebel'.[14] Secondly, even if this argument has any validity, it would only apply to practising male homosexuals, not to female homosexuals, for as mentioned, lesbian behaviour does not fall under the rubric of *giluy arayot*.[15]

It is not my intention, God forbid, to undermine the severity of any violation of Divine Law, relating to homosexual activity or otherwise. The main purpose of the above paragraphs is to demonstrate that, whether valid or not, recourse to the severe factors involved in the homosexual transgression are not helpful. The real issue in determining the status of the transgressor and one's attitude towards him is the *motivation* for transgression. If an individual violates a relatively 'lenient' transgression out of spite, he has become a 'defiant rebel', with all the attendant consequences of that status. If, on the other hand, one violates a 'serious' transgression – even one involving the death penalty – out of desire, he remains within the category of a 'hedonistic renegade', and as such has not excluded himself from the Community.[16]

UNFAIR PERSPECTIVES

At this juncture it is deemed appropriate to explore various contemporary attitudes to practising homosexuals and the flaws which I believe to be inherent in the reasoning of the proponents of these views. The views to be presented generally refer (although do not always say so) to male homosexuals as is evident from the arguments that they employ.

Rabbi Basil Herring cites, with seeming approval, the view of the eminent halachist Rabbi Moshe Feinstein, which I have elaborated upon in the second chapter of this book.[17] Rabbi Herring paraphrases Rabbi Feinstein's view that homosexual behaviour is 'a fundamental expression of rebellion ... a deliberate flaunting that is carried out *because* the act is forbidden. Accordingly, the homosexual act has no justification whatsoever; by its nature it is an act of defiance and it is therefore the abomination par excellence.'[18]

As has been explained in Chapter 2, this argument assumes an extremely condemnatory understanding of the motivations for homosexual intercourse, one which does not reflect the reality of the situation as we know it. There are many homosexuals who, evidently, do have an intense desire for homosexual intercourse and, if they engage in such, do so not – God forbid – *le-hachis*, but *le-tei'avon*.[19] To accuse all practising homosexuals of being 'defiant rebels' is unfair, unjustifiable and could be extremely devastating for a practising homosexual who is trying to keep the Torah.

In a slightly different vein, Rabbi Reuven P. Bulka also seems to label the homosexual as a 'defiant rebel'. Rabbi Bulka bases his argument on the premise that most homosexuals 'can consummate a heterosexual union' (although he acknowledges that 'there are some, very few to be sure, who are totally incapable of heterosex'). As a corollary to this, Rabbi Bulka writes:

> One who can achieve consummation with a member of the opposite sex, but instead opts for a same sex partner, has arguably committed a more serious breach since such a homosexual act comes at the expense of an available, achievable and permissible alternative. In such instance, *the homosexual act is simultaneously an act of rebellion against the Torah* [emphasis added].'[20]

The idea that one who 'can achieve consummation with a member of the opposite sex' automatically has 'an available, achievable and permissible alternative' is, in my opinion, a grave error. The ability to consummate a heterosexual relationship does not necessarily provide such an alternative. In view of the prohibition of sexual intercourse outside of marriage, the only 'alternative' the homosexual would have would be to marry a woman.[21] However, marriage, for the homosexual, is not ordinarily available and achievable, nor is it necessarily permissible in light of the considerations to be elaborated upon in this book.[22]

At any rate, the fact that a homosexual could feasibly consummate heterosexual intercourse does not necessarily mean that 'the homosexual act is simultaneously an act of rebellion against the Torah'. By way of analogy, the fact that a heterosexual person could engage in intercourse with his wife, but chooses to do so with someone else's, does not *necessarily* render him a 'defiant rebel'. The category of *mumar le-hachis* refers specifically to one who could satisfy his particular lust in a permissible manner but chooses to do so in a forbidden one. One who, for example, is possessed with a specific passion for pork is not considered a *mumar le-hachis* if he chooses to eat pork rather than kosher beef. Since he has no alternate avenue to satisfy his desire for pork, he would ordinarily be classified as a *mumar le-tei'avon*. By the same token, a person who has a passionate desire for a particular woman, and commits adultery with her, may still be a *mumar le-tei'avon* despite the fact that he could engage in intercourse with his wife. Since his specific lust would not be satisfied through marital intercourse, he does not become a *mumar le-hachis* by performing extra-marital intercourse.[23]

Likewise, a homosexual does not become a *mumar le-hachis* as a result of engaging in homosexual intercourse simply because he 'can achieve consummation with a member of the opposite sex'. Even if the homosexual has the capacity for a heterosexual relationship, it would not necessarily satisfy his intense craving for homosexual intercourse. Therefore, he may well not be pursuing 'an act of rebellion against the Torah', but a pleasurable experience for himself. This argument applies *a fortiori* to a confirmed homosexual, who, whilst possibly able to consummate a heterosexual relationship, may not derive much more pleasure or satisfaction from such a relationship than a heterosexual would from a homosexual relationship.[24]

Another attempt to put the practising homosexual in the more severe category of sinner has been made by Dr David Novak. He concludes that the distinction between what he calls the 'provocative sinner' (*mumar le-hachis*) and the 'sinner for appetite' (*mumar le-tei'avon*) is not actually contingent upon the motivation for sin. Rather, he says:

> ... the essential distinction between these two types of sinners is not seen to be the motivation behind their respective acts, that is, the former being motivated to rebel against the authority of God by violating what has been revealed in the Torah, the latter being motivated by the desire for instant gratification. Rather, Maimonides interprets the difference between the two types of sinners to be whether or not the sin is habitual and wilful. If one sins habitually and wilfully, then he or she is considered to be a *provocative* sinner. But if one sins occasionally and with guilt, that person is considered to be a sinner *for appetite*.[25]

Based on this criterion, Dr Novak argues that 'it would seem that active homosexuals and drug users do indeed fall into the category of provocative sinners. Their actions seem to be both habitual and wilful.' Novak therefore contends that active homosexuals, despite the fact that they are motivated by desire – 'their immediate gratification takes precedence over the observance of moral restraints' – are nevertheless subject (at least, in theory) to the strictures applied to the one who sins *le-hachis*. Parenthetically, one must assume that Dr Novak would apply the same judgement to people who regularly and habitually eat non-kosher food, wear garments containing *sha'atnez* (forbidden mixtures of wool and linen), or do not affix *mezuzot* to their door-posts.[26]

In support of his claim that Maimonides sees the difference between the transgressor *le-tei'avon* and the transgressor *le-hachis* not in terms of their respective motivation for transgression, but in terms of the regularity or habit of transgression, Dr Novak refers to two statements in Maimonides' *Yad HaChazakah*. The first is in *Hilchot Rotze'ach*, where Maimonides discusses various categories of sinners and the responsibility of society in their regard. There, Maimonides states that heretics, those who worship idols, as well as those who sin out of spite, ought – in ideal (albeit theoretical) circumstances – to be eliminated from society. There is nothing in this statement that supports Dr Novak's contention that, according to Maimonides, 'the essential distinction between these two types of sinners is not seen to be the motivation behind their respective acts'. On the contrary, Maimonides seems to assert that the term *mumar le-hachis* refers precisely to the sinner who – like the idolater and the heretic – transgresses the law 'out of spite'. However, Maimonides continues in a sequential paragraph to discuss another category of sinner, described (in the Talmud) as *ro'ei beheimah dakah*[27] (who – in contradistinction to the *mumar le-hachis* – ought not to be deliberately eliminated, but neither ought they to be saved when in peril). The *ro'ei beheimah dakah* were stereotypical shepherds of small livestock who were known to constantly pasture their flocks in other people's fields; henceforth, the 'shepherd of small livestock' became a synonym for a habitual thief. Maimonides writes:

> With regard to ... a Jewish shepherd of small livestock [*ro'ei beheimah dakah*] and the like – one should not try to cause their death. It is, however, forbidden to save their lives if their lives are in danger. For example, if such a person fell into the sea, one should not rescue him. Scripture states [Leviticus 19:16]: 'Do not stand idly by while your brother's blood is at stake'. [This does not apply with regard to such individuals, because] they are not 'your brothers'. When does the above apply? With regard to a Jew who commits transgressions, is persistent in his wickedness and constantly practises such evil, the likes of the *ro'ei beheimah dakah* who completely disregard the prohibition against theft and persevere with their perverse behaviour. However, with regard to a Jew who commits transgressions, but does not constantly persist and persevere with his wickedness, rather he commits transgressions for his own personal pleasure – for example, one who eats non-kosher food *le-tei'avon* – it is a *mitzvah* to save his life, and it is forbidden to stand idly by when his life is in danger.[28]

It is probably based on this statement, primarily,[29] that Dr Novak regards Maimonides as differentiating between the categories of *le-tei'avon* and *le-hachis* in terms of the frequency and regularity of transgression, rather than in terms of motivation. This codification of Maimonides is paraphrased by the two subsequent halachic codes of Rabbi Yaakov ben Asher (c.1275–c.1340) and R. Yosef Caro (1488–1575).[30] In this classification, the *mumar le-hachis* is described in contradistinction to the *ro'ei beheimah dakah*: the latter is a persistent sinner who totally disregards the laws of theft, whereas the former does not sin 'constantly' but only 'for his own personal pleasure'. This classification may seem to lend support to Dr Novak's thesis that, for Maimonides (and the Codes who adopt his ruling), the category of *mumar le-tei'avon* is reserved for those who sin 'occasionally and with guilt'. (However, it should be noted that, even if this were the correct

interpretation of Maimonides and the subsequent Codes, this would
not yield Dr Novak's conclusion that the 'habitual and wilful' sinner
is essentially a *mumar le-hachis*. It would only serve to place such a
sinner in the category of *ro'ei beheimah dakah*, which, whilst subjected
to more severe treatment that the *mumar le-tei'avon*, is not parallel to
the category of *mumar le-hachis*; we are not enjoined to seek the
elimination of *ro'ei beheimah dakah* as we are of the *mumar le-hachis*.)
Yet, this interpretation of Maimonides and the Codes does not reflect
the understanding of the classical halachic authorities. Given the
somewhat ambiguous nature of Maimonides' classification of *ro'ei
beheimah dakah*, two possible interpretations are provided for the
uniqueness of the archetypal category 'shepherd of small livestock' and
its attendant stringency.

Rabbi Caro, the author of the *Shulchan Aruch*, in his classical
commentary *Bet Yosef* on the *Tur*, poses the question:

> Why are *ro'ei beheimah dakah* different from all other 'hedonistic
> renogades'; after all, it is surely their desire for financial wealth that
> motivates them to pasture their animals on other people's fields?

He answers thus:

> these shepherds are different from other sinners, inasmuch as they
> transgress the law *all day, constantly*. In contrast, one who eats non-
> kosher food *le-tei'avon* does not do so [all day] but only for the duration
> of a certain amount of time in the day. Furthermore, [the one who eats
> non-kosher food to satisfy his lust] does not necessarily do so every single
> day [in contradistinction to the *ro'ei beheimah dakah*, who transgress the
> laws of theft all day, every day]. This is why the *Tur* [paraphrasing
> Maimonides] emphasises that the shepherds of small livestock have
> completely disregarded the prohibition against theft, and persevere with
> their perverseness. In contrast, when describing the individual who eats
> non-kosher food *le-tei'avon*, the *Tur* [as does Maimonides] emphasises
> that he does not constantly persevere with his evil behaviour.[31]

Rabbi Yehoshua Falk (c.1555–1614), in his *Derishah* on the *Tur* and in
his classical *Sefer Me'irat Enayim* on the *Shulchan Aruch*, responds to
the question of the *Bet Yosef* in a different manner. He writes:

> The one who eats non-kosher food *le-tei'avon* is different [from the
> 'shepherds'], for the consumer of non-kosher food is committing an evil

only against 'Heaven'. His sin is in the category of '*bein adam le-Makom* (between man and the Omnipresent)'. Therefore, provided that he does not commit such sins to anger God but merely to satisfy his lust, it is forbidden to stand idly by when he is in danger. In contrast, the 'shepherds', who steal other people's money and encroach on their livelihood – even though they do so to satisfy their desire for personal gain – since they are 'evil to their fellow beings', one is not obliged to rescue them when their lives are threatened.[32]

These distinctions are echoed in the writings of later halachic authorities, where the Maimonidean definition of *ro'ei beheimah dakah*, which serves as the basis for a unique category of sinner, is said to refer either to one who 'is completely entrenched in sin and his livelihood is derived from sin'[33] or to one who (habitually) exploits other people for the purpose of his own pleasure. Dr Novak's idea, whereby any habitual sinner is categorised as one who transgresses *le-hachis* (irrespective of his motivation), and its concomitants, is not reflected in the works of the normative halachists. Dr Novak himself does not suggest that *contemporary* homosexuals should be treated with the harsh treatment prescribed for 'rebellious renegades'. He acknowledges the ruling of Rabbi Avraham Yeshayah Karelitz, the *Chazon Ish* (1878–1953), who wrote that in 'contemporary' times it would be counterproductive for the Jewish People to respond to sinners in such a harsh manner. Rather, he says that the modern method is to encourage the sinners to repent.[34] Dr Novak, however, maintains that in principle, even if not in practice, the *halachah* would categorise practising homosexuals as 'provocative sinners'.

Yet, in light of the above, Dr Novak's attempt to classify homosexuals who habitually engage in homosexual activities as 'provocative sinners' is halachically untenable. In consideration of the fact that practising homosexuals, like regular consumers of non-kosher food, do not commit transgressions 'all day, every day', and given that indulgence in forbidden sexual practices usually comes under the category of *bein adam le-Makom* – a sin committed 'between man and the Omnipresent'[35] – the final halachic ruling would, as we have argued in this chapter, categorise such individuals as 'sinners for appetite' with the attendant 'lenience' of that category.

Furthermore, Maimonides' understanding of *ro'ei beheimah dakah* as an archetypal category for all sinners who share their characteristics is (and Dr Novak himself does not seem to be completely unaware of this) the subject of dispute. The Tosafists,[36] followed by a number of prominent halachic authorities,[37] are of the opinion that the special censure of *ro'ei beheimah dakah* is something of an anomaly, designed by the talmudic sages to serve as a precautionary measure against those who are lenient with regard to rabbinic transgressions.[38] The perceived leniency of rabbinic laws might lead people to be less than scrupulous with regard to practices forbidden by those laws and the rabbis, therefore, found it necessary to reassert the severity of such crimes by imposing a severe penalty on the *ro'ei beheimah dakah*. According to this view, it seems clear that other transgressors of biblical law (*le-tei'avon*) do not come under the parameters of *ro'ei beheimah dakah* provided that they sin out of lust, rather than out of spite. Once again, according to this criterion, practising homosexuals would come under the normative category of *mumar le-tei'avon*, 'hedonistic renogades', whose lives we must care for as we care for the lives of other Jews who transgress the laws *le-tei'avon*.

Another depiction of practising homosexuals as being worse than other sinners seems to emerge from the writings of Rabbi Dr Norman Lamm. In the midst of his landmark article on the subject,[39] Dr Lamm declares:

> Under no circumstances can Judaism suffer homosexuality to become respectable. Were society to give its open or even tacit approval to homosexuality, it would invite more aggressiveness on the part of adult pederasts toward young people.[40]

If Dr Lamm wishes to equate practising homosexuals with paedophiles or with predatory characters constantly waiting to assault or entice a naïve youth, his views must be rejected. There may be an untold number of homosexual paedophiles or practising homosexuals otherwise corrupted in their treatment of their fellow men. This, however, does not justify the automatic association of homosexuals with pederasts or other molesters.[41] There are undoubtedly an untold number of heterosexual paedophiles and heterosexual people who are guilty of all sorts of sex-related crimes and misdemeanours. This does not justify tarring all heterosexuals who do not live their private lives in accordance with the Torah with the same brush. By the same token, it is extremely unfair to incriminate all practising homosexuals as 'pederasts' lying in ambush to corrupt young people, just because there exist those homosexuals who do just that.[42]

A LEGITIMATE CONCERN

Dennis Prager, in his lengthy discussion on homosexuality,[43] advances an important argument about the particular dangers that practising homosexuals face. His ideas warrant serious consideration. Prager considers the stereotypical phenomenon of a 'homosexual lifestyle'. He writes:

> While it is possible for male homosexuals to live lives of fidelity comparable to those of heterosexual males, it is usually not the case. While the typical lesbian has had fewer than ten lovers, the typical male homosexual in America has had over 500.[44] In general, neither homosexuals nor heterosexuals confront the fact that it is this male homosexual lifestyle, more than the specific homosexual act, that disturbs most people.
>
> This is probably why less attention is paid to female homosexuality. When male sexuality is not controlled, the consequences are considerably more destructive than when female sexuality is not controlled. ... Men are more frequently consumed by their sex drive, and wander from sex partner to sex partner ...
>
> The indiscriminate sex that characterises much of male homosexual life represents the antithesis of Judaism's goal of elevating human life from the animal-like to the God-like.[45]

There are a variety of theories as to why many practising homosexuals do indulge in a heavily promiscuous and sexually 'casual' lifestyle. Some people suggest that, since society – by and large – does not accept single-sex marriages, and at any rate there is certainly very little sociological, cultural and governmental support for homosexual 'marriages', it is no wonder that many practising homosexuals resort to the stereotypical carefree and multiple sexual liaisons that characterise what Prager calls the 'homosexual lifestyle'. Prager himself, when discussing the possibility of 'homosexual marriages', dismisses this argument. He contends that, even if society were to condone and support homosexual marriages, promiscuity amongst gay men would probably not decrease:

> The male propensity to promiscuity would simply overwhelm most homosexual males' marital vows. It is women who keep most heterosexual men monogamous or at least far less likely to cruise, but gay men have no such break on their cruising natures. Male nature, not the

inability to marry, compels gay men to wander from man to man. This
is proven by the behaviour of lesbians, who, though also prevented from
marrying each other, are not at all promiscuous.[46]

Prager makes, in my opinion, a valid argument. Indeed, one may add
that it is not only women, but also the many responsibilities and
privileges inherent in married life, that serve to impede the natural
'cruising natures' of men. In the fortunate event that the marriage is
blessed with children, the 'family' provides a number of component
factors which contribute to the commitment of both spouses to a long-
term monogamous relationship. The earning of a livelihood to support
the family requires much time and energy; the mother and father do
not have an excess of 'surplus' time to indulge in 'pleasure-hunting'.[47]
The fact that both parents have a shared interest in the welfare of their
offspring serves to unite them even in circumstances where they may
otherwise have drifted apart. Couples who are committed to the family
values that Judaism cherishes so greatly will, therefore, be more
reluctant to sever their relationship in a time of crisis and will have a
stronger motivation to remain loyal to the other parent of their child
who – in this capacity – will remain their partner for life.

Whatever the reason may be for the fact that many gay men often
experience only ephemeral relationships with their partners, or indulge
in sexual liaisons with many partners during the same period, it is
certainly not a 'desirable' phenomenon. From a psychological, medical,
moral and religious perspective, there are many reasons for opposing
promiscuous or short-lived relationships. Consequently, whilst there
are many promiscuous heterosexuals, the awareness that (practising)
homosexuals have a stronger propensity to the instabilities and consequences of ephemeral and casual sexual encounters is certainly cause
for additional concern.

This, however, must not only propel religious leaders to denounce
promiscuity and its corollaries as a mistaken and destructive lifestyle,
but must also evoke rabbis and lay-leaders of the community to provide
extra solicitude for its members who are more likely to stumble in such
pitfalls. Recognising the dangers inherent in what Prager describes as
the 'homosexual lifestyle' surely provides a stronger motivation to
protect those of our brothers who have not exhibited the strength to
remain celibate and who are most vulnerable to the attractions of such
carefree and casual relationships.

Many college students, of a heterosexual disposition, also do not live celibate lives. For a variety of reasons, in their particular environment, they may also have a stronger tendency to engage in short-term and even promiscuous relationships. Even in the event that the single student was not committed to celibacy, it would be wrong to alienate him. The Student Chaplain ought rather to endeavour to educate and inspire his 'flock' to avoid un-Jewish, unhealthy and unethical lifestyles. No responsible mentor of contemporary college students would shun those of their single charges who was not living a celibate life because of the stronger propensity for promiscuity that prevails on many a student campus. On the contrary, his awareness of the dangers of promiscuity ought to motivate him to be even more 'protective' of those who are most vulnerable to the dangers of a liberal and carefree environment. The same applies to homosexuals.[48]

In simple terms, in an age when promiscuity is quite popular even amongst heterosexuals, the male homosexual – who may have a stronger propensity to be promiscuous – will require additional encouragement to ensure that he does not embark on a destructive path in life. Condemnation is unlikely to achieve this end. Understanding and compassion are surely the key to success in positive education.

THE DURESS HYPOTHESIS

In contrast to the above arguments that seek to depict the practising homosexual in an extremely harsh light, there have also been attempts to advocate a softer view. A number of Orthodox rabbis have advanced the notion that practising homosexuals may be exonerated for their transgression of Jewish Law on the grounds that they are *annusim*, namely subjects of compulsion. It is axiomatic to both Jewish Law and theology that the 'All Merciful One exempts one who is compelled'[49] to transgress His commandments. Consequently, it is argued, confirmed homosexuals who have no choice with regard to their sexual inclination must be released from culpability for violating the code in Leviticus that proscribes homosexual activities. Rabbi Shlomo Riskin, in his article on homosexuality, writes as follows:

> ... But, one might argue, how can we deny a human being the expression of his physical and psychic being? If there's a problem with the kettle, blame the manufacturer. Is it not cruel to condemn an individual from doing that which his biological and genetic make-up demand that he do?

The traditional Jewish response would be that if indeed the individual is acting out of compulsion, he would not be held culpable for his act.[50]

Rabbi Barry Freundel also cites (and *rejects* the view of) 'some Orthodox authorities' who 'regard the homosexual as *anoos* (compelled), thus removing moral culpability while condemning the act'.[51] One rabbi has engaged in speculation about the future in this regard. Rabbi Nachum Amsel writes:

> In fact, if it can be proven in the future that specific homosexual behavior is due to a sickness and is uncontrollable, rather than is a tendency, urge, and a lifestyle made by choice, then those who engage in this type of homosexual behavior would be in the Jewish category of *ones* and would not be morally responsible. Similarly, a shoplifter who is kleptomaniac and psychologically deemed not in control is not looked upon as a sinner unless the immoral act is made out of free choice. However, homosexuality has not yet been proven to be an illness.[52]

Rabbi Dr Norman Lamm has also suggested 'that Jews regard homosexual deviance as a pathology'. If we accept 'the notion of disease', opines Dr Lamm, one would have to conclude that 'genuine homosexuality experienced under duress most obviously lends itself to being termed pathological, especially where dysfunction appears in other aspects of the personality'.[53] Dr Lamm elaborates:

> An example of a criminal act that is treated with compassion by the *halakhah*, which in practice considers the act pathological rather than criminal, is suicide. Technically, the suicide or attempted suicide is in violation of the Law.[54] The *halakhah* denies to the suicide the honor of a eulogy, the rending of the garments by relatives or witnesses to the death,[55] and (according to Maimonides[56]) insists that the relatives are not to observe the normal mourning period for the suicide. Yet, in the course of time, the tendency has been to remove the stigma from the suicide on the basis of mental disease. Thus, halakhic scholars do not apply the technical category of intentional (*la-da'at*) suicide to one who did not clearly demonstrate, before performing the act, that he knew what he was doing, and was of sound mind, to the extent that there was no hiatus between the act of self destruction and actual death. If these conditions are not present, we assume that it was an insane act, or that between the act and death, he experienced pangs of contrition, and is therefore repentant, hence excused before the law …[57]

... Admittedly, there are differences between the two cases: pederasty[58] is clearly a severe violation of Biblical law, whereas the stricture against suicide is derived exegetically[59] from a verse in Genesis.[60] Nevertheless, the principle operative in the one is applicable to the other: where one can attribute an act to mental illness, it is done out of simple humanitarian considerations.

The suicide analogy should not, of course, lead one to conclude that there are grounds for a blanket exculpation of homosexuality as mental illness. Not all forms of homosexuality can be so termed ... and the act itself remains an 'abomination'. With few exceptions, most people do not ordinarily propose that suicide be considered an acceptable and legitimate alternative to the rigours of daily life. No sane and moral person sits passively and watches a fellow man attempt suicide because he 'understands' him and because it has been decided that suicide is a 'morally neutral' act. By the same token, in orienting ourselves to certain types of homosexuals as patients rather than criminals, we do not condone the act but attempt to help the homosexual.[61]

If I understand Dr Lamm correctly, he is suggesting that the homosexual act, like the suicidal act, is categorically wrong. However, employing the same analogy, one may say that the perpetrator of the homosexual act is not guilty – fully responsible and accountable – for his wrongdoing, just as one who commits suicide is not condemned for his action. In both cases – suicide and homosexuality – the exoneration of responsibility for the wrongdoing lies in the notion that suicidal activities, as homosexual relationships, take place under a certain degree of duress. In contradistinction to the heterosexual who would be held accountable for engaging in pre-marital or extra-marital sex, the homosexual who engages in homosexual intercourse is exculpated because of his 'pathological condition'. A healthy person, it is assumed, may be plagued with passions for the forbidden, but will undeniably be able to discipline his desires; if he does not do so, he is held responsible. Whereas a person infused with homosexual desire will, as a result of his 'illness', be treated like one who has committed suicide, who is 'exonerated' on 'compassionate grounds'. According to 'the standards of modern psychology' he 'may be regarded as acting under compulsion'.

The upshot of this hypothesis is that homosexual acts, like suicide, are morally objectionable, and one ought to exercise control to prevent people from committing such acts. However, in the event that an individual does commit suicide or engage in a homosexual liaison, one would be inclined to argue that the person committed his or her wrongdoing under the compelling influence of a 'pathological condition'.[62]

Similar ideas have been expressed by a number of Conservative thinkers. Hershel Matt, for example, states that, 'When forbidden acts are performed in the absence of voluntary choice ... or, in the absence of other options, the offenders are judged more leniently than otherwise'.[63] In light of this distinction, Matt argues that this very leniency should be applied to homosexuals who 'cannot change' and are therefore subjects of duress. Consequently, he advocates that we convey to those homosexuals who qualify as *annusim* (persons constrained due to circumstances beyond their control) that this very status 'removes from them ... all burden of blame and guilt – accepting them as they are'. Matt differs from Dr Lamm who considers homosexuality to be a pathology – but both these thinkers agree that those who have an unalterable homosexual orientation may, at least in certain circumstances, not be able to resist acting upon their desires.

Yet all the above argumentation appears to this author to be severely flawed. It is definitely plausible, as has been demonstrated in previous chapters of this book, that the homosexual orientation – namely the state of a person who can only engage in sexual intercourse with members of the same sex – may indeed be beyond an individual's ability to change. This does not mean that a person who experiences such orientation will be compelled to act upon his natural desires. As it is the action, *not* the orientation, that constitutes a violation of Divine Law, the fact that the orientation may not be alterable does not serve as an exoneration for the act of homosexual intercourse.[64]

To be sure, it is possible, at least theoretically, that there exist homosexuals who do not have the ability to control their actions. As Rabbi J. David Bleich puts it, this situation 'is analogous to that of a person who goes berserk and embarks upon a rampage of crime'.[65] This phenomenon has no intrinsic link with homosexual orientation. Heterosexual people suffering from mental or psychological disorders may well be diagnosed as deprived of the ability to exercise free will, by virtue of their pathological condition. Yet it borders on the absurd to suggest that the majority of sexual transgressions of any description – homosexual or heterosexual – are committed under the duress of a pathological condition.

Furthermore, according to some Jewish theologians, even completely healthy people may not always be able to control their actions. According to Rabbi Zadok ha-Kohen (1823–1900)[66] and other mystics,[67] the doctrine of free will, which is so central to Judaism, does not negate the possibility that God Almighty may choose to confiscate a person's free will – thus forcing him to commit a transgression – at any given time. Once again, this possibility represents the exception, rather than the rule. Generally speaking, one has to assume that the normative scheme of free will – the autonomy of choice that mankind is granted – and its attendant consequences, operate.

Dr Lamm's analogy with suicide is unfortunate and misleading. It is almost as incoherent as the suggestion that a frustrated *agunah* ('chained wife' who, for halachic reasons, cannot remarry) who engages in an illicit sexual liaison is not culpable because of her uncontrollable frustration. In the most extreme cases, perpetual frustration can lead to clinical depression, which in turn can lead to suicidal tendencies. But the suggestion that the generally accepted, lenient attitude towards a suicide has a similar bearing on sexual misdemeanours, is untenable.

Suicide in today's culture is almost inevitably linked with prolonged and advanced stages of clinically defined depression. The vast majority of suicides can be attributed to a level of depression that borders on insanity, thus exculpating the individual concerned.[68] If some of the contemporary suicides are not committed under duress of this nature, they most definitely represent an exception to the rule. Therefore, when in doubt, rabbinic authorities have, as Dr Lamm correctly points out, treated such cases with justified compassion 'on the basis of mental disease'.

There is, however, no evidence to suggest that a similar degree of duress compels the average homosexual person to engage in homosexual activities. All evidence goes to show that, notwithstanding the frustration involved in a celibate life and the most onerous challenges arising for those with a homosexual disposition, both heterosexual and homosexual singles possess the ability to curb their sexual expression.

Furthermore, the idea that homosexuals do not possess the ability to refrain from sexual intercourse may be perceived as extremely condescending towards them. As Dr Novak has correctly suggested, the assumption that 'homosexual activity is as consciously involuntary as homosexual feeling and desire', that all homosexuals have been deprived of free choice 'is hardly compassion, for it denies them their moral personality, an essential part of their full human functioning'.[69]

Therefore, even when considering Dr Lamm's qualifications that

(a) not all forms of homosexuality can be equated with suicide, and (b) homosexual activities remain beyond the pale of the acceptable, one cannot endorse the 'psychological attitude' he advocates as eminently reasonable. Whilst his claim that 'where one can attribute an act to mental illness it is done out of simple humanitarian considerations' is tenable as an abstract idea, it is irrelevant in our context. His recommendation that 'Jews regard homosexual deviance as a pathology, thus reconciling the insights of Jewish tradition with the exigencies of contemporary life and scientific information', must be disregarded.

All the above notwithstanding, I do accept that the 'tests' (nisyonot) confronted by homosexuals are, generally, far more severe than those of heterosexuals. This has been explained and elaborated upon in Chapter 3, but it is, I believe, necessary to re-iterate this point at this stage. For, whilst I have argued in this chapter that practising homosexuals are essentially no different from those who disregard the laws of family purity, kashrut and other mitzvot in order to satisfy their desires, this is only true in terms of the general halachic categorisation of transgressors. This categorisation divides violators of Jewish Law into the two, above-mentioned, classes: mumar le-tei'avon and mumar le-hachis. I maintained that the practising homosexual should be classified in the 'lenient' category of mumar le-tei'avon rather than in the more severe category of mumar le-hachis.

Yet, this does not really do adequate 'justice' to practising homosexuals, in as much as their desires are absolutely impossible to accommodate in a halachically permissible manner. Whilst it is true that a person who has a passion for pork could hardly satisfy that particular desire by eating chopped liver, he would nevertheless be able to indulge in other gastronomic delights. This would provide a certain outlet for his yearning for the pleasures of the palate. In contrast, the homosexual who has no alternative outlet for his sexual desires must be seen in a more favourable light. The more difficult the challenge is, the more God has compassion on the transgressor, and we should follow suit.

Rabbi Hillel Goldberg, in his discussion on homosexuality, expresses this idea eloquently:

> ... Ultimately, therefore, a person was responsible for his every violation of the norm, no matter how profound the drive to violate it. Ultimately. In the meantime, God measures each violation of the ritual, ethical, character, and attitudinal norm not only, and not even primarily, against

its objective magnitude, but *against the magnitude of the subjective struggle necessary to prevent it.* The stronger the inherent drive toward the violation, the greater the Divine mercy toward the violator. The weaker the inherent drive toward the violation, the more severe the Divine judgment of the violator [emphasis added].[70]

The necessity for understanding and compassion to operate alongside judgmentalism, will be further elaborated upon in the next chapter.

Furthermore, in our appraisal of contemporary practising gays and lesbians, it is necessary to consider the concept of *tinok she-nishbah*, a halachic category that has received great emphasis in the rabbinic literature of the last two centuries. This category and its attendant consequences, is the subject of Chapter 6.

5

Understanding and Judgmentalism – A Synthesis

Ours is an age of extremes. This is true in the realm of moral and ethical judgement. Some individuals, as well as some groups, espouse an extremely condemnatory attitude towards those who act in a manner that they perceive to be wrong. Others have adopted an extremely liberal approach where the very categories of right and wrong have become totally subjective and fluid, to the extent that there is almost no scope for moral judgement. The former attitude tends to see things in black or white, with little room for ambiguity or subtlety. The latter attitude assumes near impossibility of establishing any firm moral ground.

Amongst religious groups, the same sort of spectrum of opinion and belief can be found in connection with 'religious tolerance' or the lack of it. The religious dogmatist has no doubts about what is right and what is wrong in terms of man's obligations to God. Frequently, the religious extremist will readily condemn, lock stock and barrel, the 'other' – who does not live in accordance to his religious convictions. In contrast, the religious pluralist *par excellence* will have no problem in accepting the legitimacy and equality of the religious beliefs and practices of the 'other', even when they are axiomatically opposed to his own.

The appeal of either of these extreme *weltanschauungen* may lie in their universal clarity, as one who subscribes to such a viewpoint may have no internal philosophical conflict or tension. Everything is clear-cut. Yet, despite this advantage, such attitudes are inherently untenable for a number of reasons. The extreme dogmatist may rightfully claim that he possesses – or even monopolises – the truth, but more often than not, his judgement of the 'other' is, to say the least, less than fair. To condemn and reject one who has not had the opportunity to embrace the truth is frightfully cruel. To be insensitive to the struggles of those that have not exhibited the strength to live up to the ideals they know to be true is symptomatic of one who has not grasped the weakness and reality of the human condition.

Conversely, notwithstanding the current popularity of pluralistic trends, they remain inadequate for the religiously devout. If we were to take this philosophy to its extreme, it would border on the absurd. One would have to acquiesce, for example, that theft is only wrong for those who believe it to be so on religious, utilitarian or other grounds. Even in its milder forms, the pluralistic framework tends to exclude any absolute expression of right and wrong. In addition to the intrinsic problems inherent in such attitudes, the relativistic character of this persuasion puts parents and educators in an unenviable – moreover, an impossible – position.

The believing Jew is convinced that the Supreme Being, the Creator of Heaven and Earth, would not leave His universe and its population to grapple in total darkness. Certainly, He must have conveyed some clear and concrete directives to the people He has created and loves. He would not allow us to falter in a state of moral and religious chaos if He expects us to meet the challenges that He places in our paths. Therefore, He conveyed to us how to behave through the teachings of the Torah. Consequently, the faithful Jew declares unequivocally that conduct which contravenes the Laws of God is categorically wrong and those who indulge in such behaviour make the world into a darker place. Does this mean that there is no room for patience, tolerance, understanding and empathy for those who succumb to temptation and transgress the will of God?

The eighteenth-century Chasidic Master, Rabbi Schneur Zalman of Liady (1745–1813), the founder of the Chabad Dynasty, presents an alternative to the extreme positions outlined above. In his seminal work *Likkutei Amarim – Tanya*, he dwells on two rabbinic maxims found in the 'Ethics of the Fathers'. The first (*Avot* 4:10), 'And be humble of spirit before all men', and the second (ibid. 2:4), 'Judge not your fellow until you stand in his place', are discussed in Chapter 30. Rabbi Schneur Zalman sees these teachings as contingent upon each other. How is it possible for the refined and disciplined individual to experience humility 'even in the presence of the most worthless of worthless men'? Can it really be expected that the noble individual should be genuinely humble in relation to the lustful, self-indulgent person? The answer is:

> For it is his 'place' that causes him to sin, because his livelihood requires him to go to the market for the whole day, and to be one of those who 'sit at the [street] corners', where his eyes confront all the temptations; the eye sees, and the heart desires, and his passions are kindled like a baker's red-hot oven … it is different, however, with one who goes but little to the marketplace, and who remains in his house for the greater part of the day, or even if he spends the entire day in the market, it is possible that he is not so passionate by nature. People vary with regard to [the voracity and intensity of their lusts and] their nature.

So far, Rabbi Schneur Zalman has provided the would-be 'holier-than-thou', condescending extremist with sufficient reason to temper his perceived supremacy over those who have succumbed to temptations that he has not even had to wrestle with. So long as one has not stood, literally or figuratively, in one's fellow's position, it is impossible to appreciate the struggles that the other has had. This leads the self-righteous thinker to a sobering conclusion: if he had been placed in the circumstances of the sinner, how would he have fared? Such intro-spection may even lead him to the conclusion that he would have degenerated spiritually even more than the object of his judgement. If one internalises this analysis, it is indeed possible for every person to be extremely humble of spirit 'in the presence of any individual'.

Does this mean to say that the indulgent sinner is truly justified in his behaviour? Is the author of the *Tanya* advocating a deterministic philosophy as a vehicle for inculcating humility? In order to rule out any such notion, Rabbi Schneur Zalman continues:

> In truth, however, even he whose nature is extremely passionate and whose livelihood obliges him to sit all day at the street corners, has no excuse whatsoever for his sins. He is termed an unmitigated sinner, because [when he committed his sin] the Awe of God was not before his eyes. He should have controlled himself and restrained the impulse of his desire in his heart, because of God Who sees all his actions … [and such discipline is possible] for the mind has dominion over the heart by nature.
>
> It is indeed a great and fierce struggle to conquer one's passion, which burns like a fiery flame, through fear of God …

The upshot of these teachings is that there are moral absolutes. What is wrong is wrong, and what is right is right. This will not and cannot be changed. Moreover, the person that does wrong – or, for that matter, right – *is* responsible and accountable for his actions. Even if the temptation is overwhelming and the challenge (*nisayon*) seems nearly impossible to meet, every person has the ability to overrule his inclinations in favour of doing what is right. If a person is truly imbued with the awareness that God Almighty is looking down on him or her, this will provide the fortitude to avoid transgression in the presence of the Creator and Commander.

Yet there is still room and *need* for understanding and empathy. Empathising with the tremendous frustrations and enormous challenges of the 'other' is of paramount importance, not only for one's appreciation of the 'other', but also in order to develop a fair and modest perception of one's own standing in relation to others.

Here we have a unique hybrid of subjectivity and objectivity, of viewing the situation from the vantage point of the Torah, whilst appreciating the challenges of the mere mortal. I believe that such a balanced perspective ought to be preached and practised in the Jewish community with regard to people's attitudes towards practising homosexuals. A Jew who believes in the Divine origin and immutability of the Torah must profess that homosexual activities are categorically forbidden. This is no mere knee-jerk condemnation or 'homophobic' intolerance; it is intrinsic to the Jew's belief in the Revelation at Sinai, which serves as a basis for his entire religious framework.

Yet, when fostering attitudes to men or women who do not live up to the rules of the Torah in the realm of their private lives, it is critical that we apply the wisdom of Rabbi Schneur Zalman. In this context, the heterosexual Jew ought to ask himself questions such as: 'If I were to find myself in a situation whereby I would constantly be yearning to be in a loving relationship – of a type that includes physical intimacy – and the only sexual relationships I could reasonably have would be with a member of the same gender, would I live up to the Torah's demands?', or 'If I knew that there is never likely to be any way of experiencing sexual fulfilment in a halachically permissible manner, and at the same time, I would be almost constantly exposed to sexual temptation, would I have the fortitude to remain alone and celibate?'

I venture to say that many a heterosexual person who confronts himself honestly with such questions would indeed be humbled. The framework of the *Tanya*, where introspective analysis is a pre-requisite to judgmentalism, enables the conscientious person to develop an attitude of understanding and empathy without compromising one iota on his religious beliefs.

A critical ingredient in fostering a healthy and constructive relationship with people who are of homosexual orientation is that of understanding. By this I mean the ability for the majority of society to appreciate the intensity of the struggles confronted by a minority in our society (however small that minority may be). This may not be easily achieved. For, amongst other reasons, it is enormously difficult for a person to appreciate the struggles of someone who is confronted with desires that are so foreign to him. Most heterosexual people find the very idea of homosexual congress most distasteful. Consequently, it can be quite a challenge to relate to the fact that another person sees such activity as the only meaningful form of sexual intimacy. However, the ability to understand the other who is so different is of paramount importance.

Such understanding is required as an end in itself. It helps nurture the correct attitude towards one's fellow and oneself. It is also important if there is a sincere desire to communicate with homosexuals. It is axiomatic to any teacher or counsellor that understanding the challenges of their charge is critical in any endeavour to have positive influence. If rabbis and would-be mentors are to communicate the biblical message that homosexual intercourse is forbidden – even for homosexuals – it is essential that they at least understand the ordeals that this entails. As Rabbi Bleich puts it, the difficulties and trials they endure are 'onerous in the extreme' (*Bioethical Dilemmas*, p.136).

Homosexuals in the Jewish Community, for example, would benefit so much if their co-religionists were able to understand what they are compelled to endure. One sometimes gets the impression that some teachers think that if they acknowledge the homosexual orientation of their pupil, they are making a 'concession' in their religious beliefs. Even those who, in private, are ready to acknowledge the existence of a homosexual orientation, are sometimes reluctant to do so in public. It seems as if they think that such acknowledgement would not do justice to the biblical message, and would undermine the effect of their 'admonishment'. Yet the fact is that homosexuality is, in this context, no different from any other area of religious morality. If one would endeavour to convince teenagers to abstain from all pre-marital sexual activities – including any indulgence in sexual fantasy and masturbation – it would be a pre-requisite to acknowledge the sometimes overwhelming frustration that they endure. The passionate teenager may then be able to say: 'My mentor understands me. He knows what I'm going through. He appreciates my struggles and yet he has the confidence that I am able to meet the challenges I confront with bravery and success.' If, however, the teacher resorts to some sort of fanciful denial, in which the teenager is not even given acknowledgement of what he may be going through, the teacher's words are more likely than not to fall on deaf ears. This applies *a fortiori* to a religious mentor trying to offer help to a homosexual – who faces considerably harder challenges than the passionate teenager, who can more easily avoid temptation, and knows that ultimately, there is at least the possibility of sexual experience in a manner allowed by the Torah. I therefore contend that, rather than undermining the potency of one's words, understanding and relating to the complex and convoluted emotional and practical problems a homosexual may have would serve to enhance the effect of one's communication.

All of the above applies to sexually-active homosexuals. If a homosexual does not actually engage in prohibited activity, there is of course no room for being judgmental. This should be self-evident. Unfortunately, however, we often witness unwarranted prejudice and unfair discrimination against all homosexual people. To be sure, prejudices and paranoia, even 'irrational animosity' (*sin'at chinam*) are prevalent in society. Unjustifiable as it may be, this is a fact of contemporary life. What makes such hatred particularly deplorable is the fact that people seek to use the teachings of the Torah as an axe with which to grind their personal prejudices. The Torah does not express any hatred or intolerance for homosexuals. By definition, the Torah – which is described as *Torat Chesed*, 'a teaching of lovingkindness' – could not possibly condone intolerance for a person merely because of his or her disposition. On the contrary, Judaism insists that we exhibit greater tolerance and solicitude for those whom Divine Providence has presented such formidable challenges. To be intolerant of a person because of his or her disposition is no better than harbouring hatred to a person because of the colour of his or her skin. It must be stated unequivocally that hatred and prejudice leading to unfair discrimination and humiliation based on race, ethnicity, and by the same token, sexual orientation *per se*, are anathema to Judaism.

Even those homosexuals who do not have the fortitude to abstain from all sexual expression at all times – something which realistically speaking is most unique – may still not be stigmatised because of their orientation. It is the homosexual actions that the Torah prohibits, not the disposition. To harbour ill feeling towards a homosexual, practising or otherwise, simply on the grounds that his feelings work and respond in a radically different way from a heterosexual's, is a crime against one's fellow man and arguably a crime against one's Creator.

Why all these pedantics? Does it really make a difference to the homosexual, I hear some readers ask, whether we refer to the act or the actor? Whether we consider the transgression as abhorrent or the people with the disposition as an abomination? Is this not all a futile play on semantics or a trivial hair-splitting exercise?

Once again, such questions bespeak a severe moral failure on the part of the questioner. To paraphrase the above-quoted Mishnah: 'Judge not your fellow until you stand in his place'. For a homosexual who faces the lifelong challenges unique to his or her situation, these distinctions make a world of difference. Consider the plight of a person, say a friend of yours, who since puberty has only experienced sexual and romantic desires of a homosexual nature. He has lived for many years keeping this a secret, even from his nearest and dearest, out of fear or embarrassment. He has explored avenues of change and re-orientation, but without success. Over the years he has developed a low sense of self-esteem, even an extremely negative view of himself as a human being. He has been drawn to the brink of despair and often suffers from depression. (Parenthetically, it should be stated that such a scenario is unfortunately far from hypothetical.) After much thought and contemplation, your friend plucks up the courage to confide in you and share with you the burden that he carries. He knows that there are no magical solutions to his problems, but he is hoping for some understanding, some empathy. He reveals the secrets of his heart to you, and endures the embarrassment of baring his most intimate and private emotional dynamics to you. He looks expectantly towards you as he has finally managed to share his pain with a close friend and confidant.

At this juncture, you know that your every word counts, your body language is important, and that your friend is clever enough to read between the lines of the words you say to him. You are well aware that it could be a matter of life and death. If he finds you understanding and supportive, you will be able to provide encouragement, reassurance and uplift. If, however, at this critical moment in time, you turn to him with scorn: 'It is an abomination, it is perverse, you are abnormal', you may well have laid the final paving stones for your friend to walk towards suicidal despair. In such a situation, you will understand that there is a colossal difference between denouncing the transgression, and condemning the individual because of his orientation. At this crucial moment, you understand that your function is to help your friend overcome the destructive and negative self-perception he may have internalised, and begin a process of building self-esteem which is indispensable to the spiritual growth you would like him to experience.

Yet, one need not be in the centre of such a melodramatic scene to appreciate the power of words and the destruction caused by employing inaccurate terms of blame and derision. It could be a parenthetical comment in a sermon from the synagogue pulpit, or a casual conversation over the Sabbath meal. It could be the rabbi's choice of words at a lecture, or the nuances of an author in a publication. Whether it is the observations *en passant* of a college student, or facial expressions of a teacher in a classroom, the effects can be the same. Whilst hurting someone with words is in itself a terrible crime, the far-reaching effect of insensitive speech directed at homosexuals is even more reprehensible, because of the ripple effects that result from such comments. Furthermore, unlike many other cases, the victim of verbal persecution is likely to be 'invisible'. Whether observant or not, the homosexual will often be 'closeted', and therefore unidentifiable. The anonymous homosexual present may be just as vulnerable as in the above-mentioned scenario. This provides an even greater cause for caution. The employment of wrong terminology and pejorative words for homosexuals have the ability to drive the homosexual away from his peers, to alienate him from his religion, to inspire self-hatred, and to legitimise unfair and unethical prejudice and conduct towards homosexuals. The far-reaching consequences of erroneous expressions in this most sensitive area are often not envisaged by the glib speaker. In the language of the Mishnah (*Avot* 1:11): 'Wise men, be cautious with your words!'

6

The Child's Cry

THE *TINOK SHENISHBAH*

In Chapter 4, we explored a suggested 'solution' for an Orthodox or halachic attitude towards homosexuality and practising homosexuals. Some rabbis had advanced the argument that homosexuals may be acting under duress and, in comparison to a suicide, may be exonerated on the grounds that their 'mental illness' compelled them to engage in a forbidden act. We concluded that this application of the status of *annusim* or quasi-*annusim* to homosexuals is inherently problematic. If it does have any value, it would be in relation to a minority of situations, not to the average case. For, whilst a homosexual may be *annus* (compelled) insofar as his *orientation* is concerned, he is not ordinarily *annus* to engage in homosexual practices.

However, another consideration, also rooted in the halachic category of *onnes,* may be relevant when discussing the status of an individual homosexual who engages in homosexual activity. The reference is to the broad-ranging category of *tinok shenishbah* – 'a child taken into captivity' – which insists that we take into consideration the educational climate in which the individual was raised, before deeming him responsible and accountable for his or her religious failings.

The Talmud[1] discusses the case of a *tinok shenishbah bein ha-akum,* that is, a Jewish child raised from infancy amongst gentiles, who has no understanding of Judaism. Such a person is not held accountable for not living in accordance with the Torah because he cannot be blamed for his lack of belief and observance.

The Rambam (Maimonides) takes this a stage further. In his Code of Jewish Law, under 'The Laws of Rebels',[2] he codifies what amounts to a harsh and uncompromising stance with regards to the treatment of certain groups of free thinkers, heretics and apostates. He then proceeds to discuss the status of a particular sectarian group, the Karaites – whom he says were the theological descendants of Zadok and Boethus – who deny the authenticity of the Oral Tradition. The Rambam differentiates between the original Karaites who were once part of the community of believing Jews, but then broke away from it, and those of subsequent generations who were raised in that tradition. Regarding the latter, the Rambam writes:

> However, the children and grandchildren of these errants, whose parents have misled them, those who have been born among the Karaites, who have reared them in their views, are like children who have been taken captive among them, have been reared by them, and are therefore not alacritous in following the paths of the commandments. The status [of a second generation Karaite] is comparable to that of an individual who has been coerced. Even if he later learns that he is a Jew and becomes acquainted with Jews and their religion, he is nevertheless to be regarded as a victim of compulsion [by others], for he was reared in their erroneous ways.
>
> The same is true for those who follow in the footsteps of their misguided ancestors. Therefore it is proper to influence them to return in repentance and draw them near with words of peace until they return to the strength-giving Torah (*eitan haTorah*).[3]

Thus, the Rambam adds a new dimension to the talmudic concept of *tinok shenishbah* – an infant captured and raised by Gentiles – and uses it in the broader sense of the word, to determine the status of second generation non-believers and non-observant Jews. The basis of this concept is that, in order to determine the halachic status of the individual Jew, we must first enquire into the many different factors which might have influenced and moulded an individual's development and behaviour. If his rejection of belief or practice results neither from personal rebelliousness nor even from his reluctance to subjugate his natural desires to what *he knows and understands* to be the will of God – namely his desire to enjoy life without religious restraints – but simply from his conformity to the prevailing norms and values of the culture in which he lives, where the word of God is not taught and His commandments are not considered binding, he is exonerated from the charge of deliberate heresy or rebelliousness and is included amongst those whom we are commanded to love and care for.

The Rambam's ruling concerning the second-generation Karaites – based on his definition of *tinok shenishbah* – has been seen by rabbinic leaders and halachic authorities throughout the generations as applicable to many categories of irreligious and non-believing Jews. In recent times, this stance has been advocated by numerous authorities in relation to non-observant affiliates of Orthodox communities, in addition to Conservative, Reform and Reconstructionist Progressives. It has been applied systematically to Jews who publicly violate the Sabbath laws,[4] constantly ignore all the commandments of the Torah,[5] or marry out of the faith.[6] It has been cogently argued that Jews who were born and bred in an environment that did not enable them to internalise a wholly positive attitude to Judaism, and more often than not contained a certain degree of anti-religious bias, are to be classified as *tinokot shenishbu.*[7]

In the above-quoted paragraph, the Rambam makes it clear that a person does not lose his classification as a *tinok shenishbah* merely because he has become aware of his Jewish origins and has been informed of Jewish practice. In spite of his continued rejection of the Torah, both in theory and practice, he cannot possibly be compared to a wanton sinner or rebel. It is illogical to expect him to be able to abandon his previous ideas and behaviour simply because he may have been exposed to committed Jews or just discovered his true Jewish identity.

Rabbi Simcha Wasserman has eloquently paraphrased this teaching of Maimonides and its application to contemporary situations:

> If they have not been raised and trained with Torah, you cannot criticise them for not living up to its standards. He [Maimonides] goes even further and says that even if, later in life, they come into contact with Jewish communities where there are full Jewish standards and they are not diligent in adopting the standards of the community, do not blame them, because they were raised differently, and you cannot expect people in their adulthood to suddenly change their ways. He is saying that for many years they have seen other standards and have become part of those other standards. Do not expect them to jump and change. They were raised on those errors.[8]

Many authorities have amplified the concept of *tinok shenishbah* to include a wide range of estranged Jews in the modern era, including some who would not fit in with a minimalist reading of the *tinok shenishbah* doctrine. Rabbi Isaac Herzog, for example, argued that 'in our generation even those who did receive a proper *cheder* education have been so adversely influenced by modernism – which, at its root, is a Gentile influence – that they may be partially exonerated in the same manner as those who have not received any education at all'.[9]

In early nineteenth-century Germany, Rabbi Zvi Hirsch Chajes (1805–1855) declared that Reform was a heretical movement, and that its adherents were to be classified as heretics.[10] Yet, Rabbi Chajes qualified his opinions by stating that it is appropriate to denounce only the protagonists and leaders of the movement. It would be wrong, he said, to include the masses in his condemnation, for they have been 'misled by their teachers' and as a result are to be treated as *tinokot shenishbu*.[11] The novelty in this statement lies in the fact that the subjects of his discussion were first-generation Reformers. Many of these had been born and bred in Orthodox homes. Yet, their exposure to such skilled pedagogues, who espoused heretical views, rendered them *tinokot shenishbu*, and as such exonerated them from culpability. Rabbi Chajes maintained that Maimonides' ruling *vis-à-vis* the second-generation Karaites applied to such Jews who were under the impression that they had 'discovered a permissive Beth Din'.

In our own generation, Rabbi Shimon Schwab (1908–1995), the great leader of German Orthodoxy, maintained that even 'those who have been brought up in a Torah-true atmosphere' but have become disillusioned as a result of despair and nihilism, ought to be treated as 'children captured by heathens' (*tinokot shenishbu*). Their lack of faith and, consequently, their lack of practice must be attributed to the confusion caused by the 'total eclipse of the Divine Providence', which reigned during the Holocaust.[12]

These examples serve to demonstrate that even when a person does have free will to choose right from wrong, he is only considered guilty for choosing the latter if he was in a position to *know* right from wrong. Rabbinic leaders were sensitive to the fact that a host of personal and communal factors may contribute to or undermine a person's knowledge, understanding and appreciation of what is right and what is wrong. When Maimonides stated that the *tinok shenishbah* is acting under duress, he laid the foundation stone for the halachic procedure whereby the individual's upbringing, the experiences and the influences he was exposed to, must always be taken into the equation. If it can justifiably be said that a person's background conditioned his worldview to the extent that he or she is not personally responsible for the lack of faith or practice in a particular area of his or her life, he or she may halachically be considered a subject of duress.[13]

If we are to be consistent in our reasoning and judgement, it appears that one must be ready to evoke the principle of *tinok shenishbah where it applies* in relation to sexually active homosexuals. Jews – or for that matter gentiles[14] – who have been raised in a secular ambience or have been seduced by Westernised culture and value systems, may not be culpable for their homosexual behaviour. We currently live in a permissive society, where the predominant secular view tolerates homosexual conduct and – in the case of individuals with an exclusive homosexual orientation – even advocates 'self-realisation' in the sense of acting upon their sexual impulses. In these circumstances, it is arguable that the same mitigating factors that help to mould our response towards other transgressors of Jewish Law should be similarly applied to those who engage in homosexual activity. For, if a person's attitude to the Torah and its prohibitions can be attributed to the education he received from his forebears or to the intellectual climate of his society, this can and should be considered when judging any individual homosexual.[15]

Furthermore, whilst it is true that homosexual practices may not be as accepted in secular society as promiscuity, adultery and, needless to say, the desecration of the Sabbath, it is increasingly becoming legitimised by public consent. In the political hierarchy of Westernised countries it is becoming commonplace for prominent positions to be occupied by individuals who make no bones about declaring their homosexual relationships. Other religious denominations, such as the Church of England, are gradually mellowing their condemnation of homosexual conduct and homosexual relationships. In some cases, Christian clerics have openly declared their acceptance of homosexual lifestyles. Even the Jewish community has not been immune to the influence that emanates from this shift in public opinion. Progressive synagogues, in England for example, have appointed several clerics who are proud of their homosexual relationships. Some of these leaders are highly esteemed in the national community.[16]

In the caring professions, and in the multi-faceted disciplines of psychology and psychiatry, many institutions reject, or even cast scorn on, the Jewish attitude towards homosexual relationships. Such institutions will often guide parents and teachers in helping their homosexual children to realise their potential in physical intimacy with members of the same gender. In general, I think it is fair to say that the societal trend is most definitely one of acceptance of, if not encouragement to, emerging practising homosexuals.[17] All this makes it even more difficult for a person who has been predominantly influenced by secular society to accept the Jewish view on homosexuality.

As regrettable as this situation may be, it is the reality of today's day and age. Hence, it must be taken into account when determining the status of someone whose ideals have been strongly influenced, if not completely moulded, by current mores. The individual who was raised in a climate that did not enable him to internalise the belief in the infallibility and immutability of the commandments of the Torah, and at the same time exposed him to the inculcation of prevailing secular attitudes with regard to homosexuality, may not be held accountable for adopting a liberal, permissive view. A careful appraisal of the 'conditioning' of an individual sexually active homosexual may well lead to the conclusion that the person in question ought to be granted the status of a *tinok shenishbah*, with its attendant ramifications. In the event that a person is deemed a *tinok shenishbah*, we ought to apply to him the verdict of Maimonides, who declares that 'he is to be regarded as a victim of compulsion'.[18] Consequently, we are duty bound to befriend and reach out to the individual homosexual with 'words of peace' and with 'thick bonds of love'.[19]

All the above notwithstanding, it cannot be over-emphasised that the concept of *tinok shenishbah*, and the leniency it generates, is applicable to the person who is included within this category, not to the sin that they do. A *tinok shenishbah* may be exonerated for the sins he has committed, but this does not serve to neutralise the inherent negativity of the sin itself. Unfortunately, however, there are some who abuse this concept and cultivate an attitude of unbridled moral relativism. The *tinok shenishbah* should not be condemned, but those of his actions that undermine the word of God must be denounced. In simple terms, we relate to the *tinok shenishbah* as a sibling who has been led astray, through no fault of their own; this awareness, itself, motivates us to bring them back into the fold and – slowly, but surely – accept upon themselves the yoke of the heavenly kingdom, the commandments of God.

COMMUNAL INCLUSIVISM

Dr Fred Rosner, in an article entitled 'AIDS: A Jewish View',[20] discusses various questions with regard to Jewish homosexuals.

i.   'May patients with AIDS who are homosexuals and/or drug addicts
     be counted as part of a ... *minyan* [i.e. can they count towards the
     quorum of ten Jewish adult males, necessary for 'congregational
     prayer']?';

ii. May such a person 'lead services in the synagogue as a cantor
     (*shaliach tzibur*) or Torah reader?';

iii. 'Is it permissible for a *kohen* [a member of the priestly family] to
     offer the priestly benediction ... if he has AIDS related to homo-
     sexuality or drug addiction?';

iv. 'Should a patient with AIDS be honoured in the synagogue?';

v.   'Can a patient with AIDS serve as a witness?';

vi. 'Are the laws of mourning to be observed for a homosexual patient
     who dies of AIDS?'.

Dr Rosner seems to assume the premise that all (practising) homosexuals deserve the appellation of 'wicked sinner' and, in the ideal
halachic world, ought to be excommunicated. He then proceeds to
solve his problems by drawing on various prototypes of sinners mentioned in the halachic codes and responsa literature, and the stances
that were taken by the rabbis towards them. A summary of Dr Rosner's
position is as follows:

i.   Rosner presupposes that 'homosexuality is a sin for which the
     transgressor is worthy of being excommunicated'. Therefore, he
     contends that even though nowadays sinners are not usually placed
     under ban of excommunication, they ought to be excluded from
     the *minyan* according to the view that 'if a person is worthy of
     being excommunicated, by virtue of transgressions he has commit-
     ted, he cannot be counted as part of a *minyan*, even though he is
     not actually excommunicated';[21]

ii. Only if the homosexual has repented for his sins, 'including the sin
     of homosexuality' could he be entertained as a candidate for lead-
     ing congregational services;[22]

iii. The homosexual *kohen* is permitted to recite the priestly blessing,
     even if he has not repented.[23] 'Someone might ask: what good is
     his blessing if he is a sinner? The answer is that the *kohen* only
     recites the words, but the actual blessing comes from God, as it is
     written (Numbers 6:27): *and I will bless them*';[24]

iv. Dr Rosner is concerned that 'if a homosexual ... is honoured in the synagogue by being called up to the Torah, people may be misled into thinking that his behaviour is acceptable'. Regarding other honours, such as opening and closing the Holy Ark, and removing and subsequently returning the Torah to the Ark, Dr Rosner is more ambivalent;[25]

v. Somewhat inconsistently and, in my opinion erroneously, when it comes to bearing witness in a Jewish Court, Dr Rosner finds scope for legitimating the testimony of a practising homosexual, on the grounds of that such people 'can be considered to lack self-control over their strong desire: Jewish law states that a person who sins under compulsion is divinely exempted from punishment';[26]

vi. Finally, Dr Rosner contends that if the homosexual suffered from illness for a significant period of time before his death, he 'should probably be mourned on the assumption that' he had repented during his illness. Nevertheless, 'It is certainly not proper to honour an AIDS patient after death by naming a school or playground after him. ... If it is public knowledge that the AIDS patient was a sinner, he should not be honoured after death by having a person or thing named after him. It is also a punishment for the wicked not to honour them after death.'[27]

Given the date of original publication, Dr Rosner's almost synonymous association of AIDS and drug abuse with homosexuality must be considered as subjective thinking. At any rate, the questions he poses, although sometimes phrased poorly, are relevant with regard to sexually active homosexuals. Dr Rosner's conclusions must be subjected to criticism.

I believe that Dr Rosner's approach to these issues is unfortunate. I do not propose to respond in detail to all of his assumptions and conclusions. Suffice to say that halachic categorisations of those who transgress the Law are far more complex and subjective than Dr Rosner's article reflects.[28] The primary issue that is relevant to all the questions raised by Dr Rosner is the category of *tinok shenishbah* that we have discussed earlier in this chapter.

Strictly speaking, a person who desecrates the Sabbath publicly,[29] or does not believe in the Cardinal Principles of Faith,[30] may not be counted in a *minyan,* called up to the Torah, or lead the services in congregational prayer.[31] Such a person may not deliver the priestly benediction,[32] act as witness,[33] circumciser (*mohel*)[34] or ritual slaughterer (*shochet*).[35] He is not entitled to honour as a parent,[36] to be mourned on his death,[37] or to certain other privileges bestowed upon members of the Jewish Nation.[38] Some halachic authorities have applied the same rules to a Jew or Jewess who has married out of the faith,[39] or to a Jew who has, for no good reason, not been circumcised.[40] Yet, in practice, these laws are often treated as 'inapplicable'. Why? The circumstances of transgression must be taken into consideration.

In the last two centuries, halachic authorities have been increasingly of the opinion that the majority of 'contemporary' transgressors of Jewish Law, as 'non-believers' in Judaism, are not treated as deliberate sinners and, therefore, are not subject to the exclusivism advocated by the above laws. They are considered to be classical examples of the Maimonidean category of *tinok shenishbah* and are treated as inadvertent, if not involuntary, transgressors of the Law. This attitude has most definitely become the normative Jewish Orthodox approach. In synagogues, Jewish schools and colleges, organisations and establishments throughout the world, Jews who violate the laws of the Sabbath publicly or clearly do not accept all the dogmas of faith, are welcomed into the fold. In most synagogues they are counted as members of the *minyan,* called up to the Torah, and sometimes even allowed to lead the services. In Jewish families throughout the world, ultra-Orthodox people honour their non-observant parents, befriend and encourage their 'out-married' relatives, and observe the mourning rites for their religiously estranged relatives. To borrow Dr Rosner's example, schools and playgrounds are often named after philanthropists whose behaviour may have had them excommunicated in yesteryear's Jewish Community. Similarly, Progressives and modern 'heretics' are welcomed in our synagogues and are accepted as legitimate constituents of the necessary quorum for congregational prayers and the like.[41] The reason for this shift in attitude is based on the appreciation that today's non-observant and non-believing Jews are, generally speaking, not to be blamed for their transgressions. They are seen as products of the overwhelmingly secular environment. They are *tinokot shenishbu.*

In light of the above, it is clear that Dr Rosner's analysis of the halachic problems he poses seems to ignore the by-now normative halachic position that has emerged over the last 200 years. To be sure, there may be practising homosexuals who do not deserve the halachic classification of *tinok shenishbah*. But the same is true for non-believing Jews, desecrators of the Sabbath, and those who marry out of the faith. In any event, a particular community may be justified and sometimes even commended for setting certain standards for observance as a prerequisite to full participation in communal and synagogal life. Demarcation lines and recognition of religious excellence may be constructive within the framework of any given community.[42] However, consistency is of paramount importance. To accept that a person may mourn and even honour his deceased, non-believing, non-observant relative, but should not do so for his homosexual parents who did not 'suffer for variable periods of time before their death' – and, therefore, there is no reasonable 'assumption that they repented' – is logically implausible.[43] Likewise, for a synagogue to welcome open-handedly known Sabbath-breakers, non-believers, eaters of forbidden foods, and violators of other aspects of the sexual code in Leviticus, while at the same time treating a person who is known to be a practising gay or lesbian as an unwelcome intruder, smacks of sheer hypocrisy. It is of course possible that Dr Rosner would encourage families and synagogues to ostracise – albeit not excommunicate – their irreligious members. For those of us who follow the inclusivist attitude advocated by some of the greatest halachic authorities in recent and contemporary times, we would be guilty of unfair discrimination – if not the projection of our own prejudices onto the Torah – if we were to select gays and lesbians for alienation and disenfranchisement.

HUMBLE PIE FOR THE SELF-RIGHTEOUS

By taking into consideration the concept of *tinok shenishbah*, we have – in addition to the halachic ramifications – substantial basis for a humbling self-reflection, especially for the judgementally inclined. The truth is that no one is really in a position to calculate the relative merits and demerits of any one individual. In the words of Maimonides, the evaluation of any particular merit or demerit must take into consideration a number of objective and subjective considerations to which only the Omniscient God is privy.[44] Yet whilst it is ordinarily assumed that most people have accumulated a number of merits and demerits, this cannot be applied to the *tinok shenishbah*.

Rabbi Menachem Schneerson, the late Lubavitcher Rebbe, argued that the *tinok shenishbah* would almost invariably have many merits for which he could take credit, but no demerits for which he would be culpable. The *tinok shenishbah* is not accountable for his sins because, paraphrasing Maimonides, they are considered to be involuntary transgressions. It is axiomatic to Jewish Law and theology that 'the All-Merciful exempts the one who acts under duress'.[45] Consequently, the *tinok shenishbah*, who is not considered a 'free agent', cannot possibly be responsible for his religious failings. On the other hand, the *tinok shenishbah* does deserve the credit for the good deeds which he will have performed.[46] All Jewish people, including the *tinok shenishbah*, have willingly done many good deeds for which they deserve credit. Hence, in the 'absence' of demerits, the *tinok shenishbah* will necessarily be deserving of special endearment to God Almighty, in view of his 'untainted' record of merits.[47]

HOMOSEXUAL ORGANISATIONS

Yet one crucial caveat to this overall 'tolerant attitude' must be made. The reference is to the distinction between individuals and institutions. The analogy between homosexuals and other transgressors of the Law may be illustrative at this point. Say for example, a Jew who was possessed with an insatiable passion for forbidden food, was to come to my home or my synagogue. It would be incumbent upon me to endeavour to assist him to refrain from indulging in this form of self-gratification. However, even if the individual concerned did not exhibit the strength to curb his indulgence, it would be my responsibility and privilege to do whatever I am capable of in addressing and caring for his other physical and spiritual needs.

In contrast, if an organisation designed to foster or even encourage the practice of eating non-kosher food requested my patronage or input as a rabbi, it would be reprehensible for me to acquiesce to their request. A naïve thinker may challenge this distinction. True, he would argue, the organisation – say, the restaurant – provides a service for consumers of forbidden food. But why should they be deprived of the spiritual experience of a *Chanukah* or *Purim* service, for example? Yet the answer is obvious. An organisation that sanctions, encourages or supports the practice of anti-Torah behaviour is anathema to the religiously sensitive Jew.[48]

To be tolerant of non-halachic behaviour does not imply the sanction of such conduct. It is merely indicative of a humane and realistic approach to education, whether of children or of adults. To condone such behaviour is tantamount to denial of the authenticity of the Torah teachings that proscribe such behaviour. A rabbi or a synagogue that welcomes with open arms Jews who profane the Sabbath, or violate the laws of *kashrut*, are merely demonstrating a mature and Torah-oriented pragmatism. It is in full keeping with the letter and spirit of Jewish Law. If, on the other hand, one were to sanction the violation of the Sabbath or the eating of non-kosher food, it would be a tangible expression of heresy or defiance.

Moreover, if a synagogue or yeshivah were to open up its car park on the Sabbath, or host a non-kosher function on its premises, such public defiance of Torah law would be immeasurably more serious. To allow non-Godly behaviour to take place in the House of God is an audacity and *chillul hashem* (desecration of God's Name) of the first order.

By the same token, we say that understanding and sensitivity to an individual homosexual is not only commendable, but may even be a religious imperative. On the other hand, to lend active or passive support to institutions that officially condone or encourage homosexual activities is tantamount to a denial or defiance of the word of God.

Extending the analogy further, we conclude that a synagogue or 'religious' institution that officially endorses homosexual practices as 'kosher' is an 'unwelcome intrusion' into God's domain. Any institution that legitimises homosexual practices – or for that matter any anti-Torah practice – represents the embodiment of the sins it seeks to promote.[49] If it is purported to be a House of Worship to God Almighty, it constitutes a most perverse form of brazenness towards the Creator of All.

Consequently, it goes without saying that 'Gay Synagogues' and similar organisations and institutions are completely outside the pale of acceptability. The pioneers and leaders of such organisations are, whether knowingly or unwittingly, undermining the core values of Judaism in their endeavours to institutionalise the forbidden and to sanctify that which the Torah has proscribed.[50]

As individuals, we must sympathise with the plight of all our brothers and sisters. We must extend a welcoming embrace to those who often feel alienated from our communities. We must extend a hand of solicitude to all those who find themselves constrained in circumstances of tremendous challenge and theological turmoil. But, insofar as institutions and ideologies and autonomous movements are concerned, that is an entirely different matter. For the believing Jew may not and cannot compromise on his belief in God and in His commandments.

Quite aside from our intrinsic interest in befriending all Jewish people who wish to find expression for their Jewishness, the recent proliferation of 'Gay Temples' and even so-called 'Orthodox Gay Shuls' world-wide provides an additional dimension to this concern. For if people with a homosexual orientation or those who engage in homosexual activity feel disenfranchised or even are ostracised in Orthodox institutions, it can only serve to reinforce the erroneous notion, held by many gay and lesbian individuals, that there is 'no portion for them in the God of Israel'. This will almost inevitably direct them to seek a 'different type' of Judaism in which homosexual conduct is promoted and even sanctified. As Rabbi Reuven Bulka writes:

> Having a homosexual congregation makes as much sense as having a Shabbat desecrators' synagogue or a ham-eaters' congregation ... The homosexuals and their friends who have launched these groups, contend that they do not feel welcome in conventional congregations. I am not sure what is the precise source for this unwelcome feeling ... whatever the case, it is imperative that rabbis and their congregations make sure that everyone feels welcome in their environs, without in any way compromising the Torah-based integrity of their congregations.
>
> It is admittedly a delicate tightrope, welcoming without condoning. But, we do it with those who do not observe the Shabbat, we do it with ham-eaters. Why should we not be able to do it with so-called homosexuals? and, unlike the case with non-Shabbat observers or ham-eaters, failure to create a climate wherein self-declared homosexuals feel they can take part in congregational activity may drive them ...'[51]

As we have explained, one would not welcome any open display of alliance with anti-Torah gay organisations nor would one tolerate, in the environment of an Orthodox synagogue, overt displays of homosexual, or for that matter, heterosexual, sexually suggestive behaviour. Yet, in the absence of any such demonstrations, one ought to do whatever possible to befriend Jews who are experiencing strong pangs of estrangement from the faith of their ancestors. Our message to all such Jews must be unequivocal: 'Even if you have given up with Judaism, Judaism has not given up with you.' As Rabbi J. David Bleich writes, the attitude towards the practising homosexual must be as it is to 'any person who violates any of the Commandments of the Torah'. The practising homosexual, says Rabbi Bleich, 'remains a brother and our relationship with him must be the fraternal relationship one has with a brother who has strayed from the values and morays of the family, i.e. a brother to whom one's arms are always open and who will be warmly and affectionately welcomed at all times.'

A disclaimer may be necessary in this discussion. Our negative reference to homosexual institutions and organisations applies to such organisations that undermine the Jewish beliefs and halachic rulings regarding homosexuality. This is surely the case with synagogues and such support groups that clearly condone, sanction or even promote behaviour proscribed by the Torah. This does not apply to such organisations, institutions and support groups that are designed to help people with a homosexual disposition and active gays and lesbians through their respective and formidable challenges in life, which they will inevitably encounter. This includes various supportive structures for people who find themselves leaning towards depression or disillusionment with Judaism; alienated from their nearest and dearest, or suffering from the psychological trauma of an HIV+ diagnosis, or the debilitating effects of AIDS or other sexually transmitted diseases. Such organisations may be exemplary in their pursuit of kindness and benevolence and unconditional *ahavat Yisrael*.

7

Procreation and Parenthood

A number of years ago, Rev. Dr Alan Unterman of Manchester University, and Minister of the Yeshurun Synagogue in South Manchester, presented 'Some Orthodox Perspectives' on Judaism and homosexuality in *The Jewish Quarterly*.[1] His article, which was republished in a compendium entitled *Jewish Explorations of Sexuality*, summarises what he considers to be the Orthodox position as follows:

> It is not forbidden to be sexually attracted to members of one's own sex, but it is forbidden to act on such preferences. Similarly, it is not demanded that one should be sexually attracted to members of the opposite sex, but it is demanded that, attracted or not, one should still get married and have children.[2]

Dr Unterman presumably had in mind the biblical imperative of *p'ru u'rvu*, 'Be fruitful and multiply'.[3] This Divine commandment is the first in the chronological order of biblical commandments,[4] and is also assigned great importance in rabbinic teachings. In the *Shulchan Aruch*,[5] the rabbinical maxim 'He who [wilfully] abstains from procreation is as though he shed human blood'[6] is codified to underscore the paramount importance of this *mitzvah*. In other words, failure to respond positively to this Divine commandment is tantamount to negligence of the command to perpetuate the human species and cause it to proliferate. Thus, he who abstains from procreation is accountable for the consequences of his passivity. Hence, Dr Unterman's claim that a gay man (or a lesbian woman) must get married.

That procreation is contingent upon marriage ought to go without saying. Yet, given the increasing popularity of so-called 'alternative' family structures, it is deemed necessary to state categorically that such ideas and arrangements are not in keeping with the teachings of the Jewish tradition.

In the best of situations, the halachic authorities have never been comfortable with methods of procreation that are designed to produce offspring outside the traditional family nucleus. The various procedures undertaken in current arrangements for sperm donation, impregnation, and host mothering are all fraught with considerable halachic and ethical quandaries. Details of these are beyond the scope of this work, and may be found in the voluminous and ever-increasing literature on the subject of fertility treatment and Jewish Medical Ethics.[7]

I do, however, consider it my duty to emphasise that various modes of alternative family structure employed by homosexual or unmarried heterosexual people are antithetical to the spirit, if not the letter, of Jewish Law. No marriages have a guarantee for success, nor do lives for that matter. Consequently, there are many children who are brought up by single parents, through no fault of their own or of their parents. If a marriage was beyond redemption, or a parent dies young, one cannot usually point a finger of blame in any direction. This is, however, only the case if the marriage was entered into in good faith and with every intention to forge an everlasting bond. To embark, however, on single parenthood *ab initio* is, arguably, an act of injustice to the disadvantaged children brought into the world and, in my opinion, constitutes a wilful departure from the normative family structure and the ethos of Jewish teachings.

'There are three partners in the formation of a child' – our sages tell us – 'The Holy One, Blessed be He, the father, and the mother'.[8] God Almighty invested into the laws of nature that a child has a biological father and mother. He ingrained into the very fabric of mankind that a person develops an intrinsic and irrevocable bond with his genetic and blood parents and family.[9] God instilled in each of the parents the special qualities they require in order to foster the growth of a physically and emotionally healthy child. In order to facilitate the needs of mankind, God made one of the parents male and the other female, so that their respective attributes should complement each other to create the desired mixture of characteristics necessary for an ideal family.[10] Human beings may not realise their true potential, and may fall short of this ideal. What is lamentable, however, is that there are those who seek to frustrate this system intentionally, and endeavour to override the Divine plan.

'Alternative' family structures whereby the child is 'designed' to be taken away, at birth or later, from its father or mother – thus depriving both parent and child of their rightful and continuous bond with *and obligations towards* each other – inasmuch as they create such unnecessary disadvantages cannot, in my opinion, be justified. The fact that a child is 'designed' to be raised by a 'step-parent', instead of his or her authentic parent, is likewise unacceptable. To 'plan' to bring children into the world with the intention that they will be 'parented' by a parental team composed of anything other than a male (biological) father and female (biological) mother, who are married to each other, is not in keeping with the ideal that God implemented in His world for the benefit of His creatures. I believe that *to wilfully embark upon such an arrangement* is categorically wrong. (This, of course, is not intended to undermine the nobility of married couples – fertile or infertile – who adopt children who, for one reason or another, have lost their natural parents and have been deprived of the 'ideal'. Notwithstanding the various halachic and psychological concerns involved in the procedure of adoption,[11] such kindness is most praiseworthy. In such situations, couples have responded to the realistic circumstances – which were not of their making – and have created a place in their homes and hearts for a less fortunate person to find true care, love and security.)

The only acceptable option for one who wishes to respond to the Divine calling to 'be fruitful and multiply' is to marry. Thus, every male who is able to procreate is duty-bound to search for a wife, get married, and have children. The commandment is addressed to the male only, and whilst it is certainly a Jewish ideal that a woman should get married, and have children, it is – from the strict *legal* perspective of the *halachah* – an optional vocation for the female.[12]

Parenthetically, Rabbi Meir Simchah of Dvinsk (1843–1926) offers a rational interpretation of this perceived 'discrimination' against women. He says that the Torah – which is also called *'Torat Chesed'*, 'the teachings of kindness' – does not wish to enforce a law that would compel a woman to initiate a procedure whereby she would be inviting upon herself the trials and tribulations of pregnancy and childbirth.[13] Whilst it is considered a great privilege to have children, for a woman there is still a certain degree of mortal risk in childbirth. It is for this reason that the laws of the Sabbath may be desecrated when necessary for the wellbeing of a 'woman in travail'; she is considered to be in a situation of danger. Life-saving missions override the Sabbath laws.[14]

The Torah makes it compulsory for a man to seek a wife who is willing to get married and assume the responsibilities of childbirth. For the man, there is no danger involved. In contrast, the woman, for whom childbirth involves a much greater sacrifice, is invited to participate in this great *mitzvah*, but is not subjected to the compelling force of the Law.[15]

The paramount importance of *p'ru u'rvu* notwithstanding, there may be circumstances in which a person does not have to fulfil this commandment in practice. Despite the great importance attached to the *mitzvah* of procreation, it still falls under the parameters that govern the requisite effort and devotion demanded by Jewish Law for fulfilment of 'positive commandments'. The halachic guidelines for such requirements may be drawn from the limit Jewish Law places upon the financial burden that one must be ready to assume in order to fulfil a positive commandment. Classical halachic sources state that a person need not expend more than a fifth of his or her wealth in order to fulfil a positive commandment.[16] According to some authorities, a person is not required to spend more than ten per cent of his fortune on the fulfilment of such commandments.[17] Whilst these guidelines deal with financial expenditure, the principle has been established that a person does not need to give away everything in order to fulfil a positive commandment. This is in contrast to a negative commandment – such as the prohibition against profaning the Sabbath, eating forbidden foods, or wearing garments containing a mixture of wool and linen – for which a person is obliged to forfeit everything, except his life, rather than transgress the commandment.[18]

Halachic authorities have, therefore, extrapolated from this principle that a person need not, likewise, exhaust all possibilities – including health hazards (albeit *not* life-threatening) and considerable trauma – in order to be able to fulfil a positive commandment.[19] The halachic mandate to fulfil the positive commandment does not apply in circumstances where considerable, prolonged and inestimable suffering may be caused as a result. As some halachists have put it, an ordinary person would gladly spend a fifth of his financial resources in order to avoid acute suffering. Thus, it may be said that incurring such pain is actually tantamount to the expenditure of more than a fifth of one's possessions.[20] According to this argument, the limitations on heroic undertakings for the fulfilment of positive commandments are clearly anchored in the financial limitation delineated by the Law.

Whilst it is true that the positive commandment to procreate is treated more severely than many other positive commandments,[21] several contemporary authorities have suggested that, insofar as the above-mentioned parameters are concerned, the commandment to procreate is no different. The renowned Rabbi Shlomoh Zalman Auerbach (1910–1995) tentatively applied this ruling to a person whose children were likely to be burdened with the life-long constraints imposed by haemophilia. In line with the above, Rabbi Auerbach argued that the positive commandment to procreate does not engender an obligation for a person to embark upon a course of action that he would not be obliged to undertake in the performance of any other positive commandment.[22]

In view of the above, the unqualified stance attributed by Rev. Unterman to the *halachah* that it 'is demanded that, attracted or not, one should still get married and have children' must be rejected. On assessment of whether a *confirmed* homosexual is *obliged* to embark upon a marriage, in light of the above halachic parameters and the forthcoming considerations, it may, in many cases, be concluded that he is not required to do so. Furthermore, the considerations to be proposed in this chapter would, generally speaking, provide sufficient grounds to *dissuade* such a homosexual from drawing another person into a marital relationship.[23]

It is important to reiterate the difference between a person who, even if he or she predominantly experiences homosexual desires, has some interest in heterosexual relationships and – the subject of this chapter – a confirmed homosexual. The considerations proposed here are primarily (although not exclusively) relevant for the confirmed homosexual. Someone with even a small degree of heterosexual interest may have more reason to be optimistic about the possibility of marriage than the confirmed homosexual would. A competent psychologist may be able to provide critical assistance for a person who is somewhat ambiguous about his sexuality. A professional who is sensitive to the letter and spirit of Jewish Law may be able to help such a person determine – after consultation with a rabbinical authority – whether or not he or she should consider the option of marriage. For the confirmed homosexual, however, the following considerations assume even greater importance. Since the mandate to procreate falls primarily on the man (as explained above), the considerations are articulated in terms that pertain to the male homosexual. Implication and extrapolation will enable the reader to deduce those considerations that are also relevant to the female homosexual.

Firstly, a person with an exclusive gay disposition could experience much trauma and emotional agony, if not depression, when living with a lifelong heterosexual partner. (In some cases the predicament of a homosexual man living with a heterosexual woman may be analogous to the plight of a heterosexual man living in a homosexual relationship.) If someone lacks the drive, if not the capacity, for affectionate and meaningful intimacy with a woman, it would not ordinarily bode well for the psychological and emotional health of that person, and his partner in life. Furthermore, if the homosexual finds heterosexual intimacy positively repulsive – as some homosexuals do – in light of the above mentioned criteria for the obligation to fulfil positive commandments, the *halachah* would not ordinarily demand of him that he should embark upon a relationship that is likely to be fraught with suffering.

It must be emphasised that, upon marriage, a man undertakes the obligation to provide for his wife's material and emotional support.[24] The duty to provide the emotional security afforded by meaningful intimacy is written into the very marriage contract as an essential component. In the vast majority of cases it is unlikely that a confirmed gay husband will be able to honour his commitment to his wife's 'conjugal rights', even if he were able to have intercourse with her in a mechanical fashion. It would therefore be wrong for him to enter the institution of marriage with the knowledge that he could not 'gladden his wife' in the manner required by the Torah as an integral part of the marriage relationship.[25]

Thirdly and most significantly, even if a gay man were confident that he would be able to fulfil his duties towards his wife and was ready to undertake such a challenge, he would be obliged to be honest with his prospective spouse about his sexual orientation.[26] This would apply even if he had never acted upon it. It is unlikely that a woman would willingly and knowingly enter a marriage with a person whose sexual and affectionate sympathies lay exclusively with members of his own gender.[27] Even if he were to find a willing partner for such a marriage, it is arguable that, generally speaking, one ought to dissuade a woman who is unaware of the far-reaching implications of such a long-term relationship from embarking upon it.[28]

It is accepted that (after marriage) a woman may forgo her entitlement to the privileges of physical intimacy written into the marriage contract. However, a declaration on her part that she does not mind being sexually neglected – even when made upon entry into the marriage – may not be demonstrative of her true feelings. Halachic authorities have cautioned that, sometimes, statements of relinquishment of rights in this area may not reflect the genuine sentiments of a woman. A person may prefer to renounce her rights to conjugal pleasure precisely because she perceives that her spouse has, or will have, no desire to be intimate with her. Rather than being a wholehearted abnegation of her rights, it is but a way of avoiding further trauma and humiliation.[29]

Even if the abnegation were genuine and sincere, it may be insufficient to justify a marriage between a heterosexual woman and a homosexual man. Whilst a person may be able to forgo what is rightfully owed to her, this principle may only be relevant in our context when the relinquishing party is cognisant of the full implications of the renunciation of her rights. Arguably, a woman standing on the threshold of married life may not be able to appreciate the enormity of the sacrifice she is making when marrying a man who has no sexual desire for a woman. She would not be experientially informed of the consequences of a marriage where that ingredient is lacking. Hence, she would not be in a position to make a responsible decision and commitment by which she would waive her rights to marital intimacy for a lifetime *a priori*. There is a very real possibility that she will change her mind at a later stage.[30]

Jewish teachings on marital intimacy emphasise the importance of total harmony between husband and wife during intercourse. Intimacy must only take place with the total consent of both partners in the marriage, when their faculties are lucid and the atmosphere is tranquil. In the event that these conditions are lacking (even in the event that husband or wife are intoxicated with alcoholic beverages during intercourse), the sanctity and purity of marital intimacy are severely compromised.[31] If a man entertains erotic thoughts during intercourse that are disassociated from his wife, it is considered a perversion. Our sages tell us that the offspring of such a union may be adversely affected. It is hence unlikely that, in a marital union where one or both partners have an exclusive homosexual orientation, the halachic prerequisites for engaging in intimacy could be consistently met.

In addition to all the aforementioned, there is the very real concern that a homosexual partner in a marriage may have a stronger propensity towards sexual infidelity, given that his desires and urges remain totally repressed in a heterosexual relationship. If the scenario were to occur that the gay partner in the marriage succumbed, in a moment of 'desperation', to the forces of his impulse, it would be likely to wreak havoc on the marriage. Given the fact that homosexual partners in heterosexual relationships may, understandably, seek fulfilment of their desires in a clandestine setting (possibly – in a moment of 'uncontrol- lable' urge – with an anonymous partner) the possibility of contracting sexually transmitted diseases and transmitting them to the innocent (and unsuspecting) partner is increased. Likewise, in the event that the homosexual partner in the marriage does not satisfy the spouse's intimate needs, the neglected spouse may be, after a lengthy period of want and frustration, tempted to engage in extra-marital intimate activities, the consequences of which I need hardly spell out.

In light of all the above, and at the risk of generalising, I maintain that a confirmed homosexual may not be equipped for marriage. In the interest of saving himself and his potential partner from untold difficulties and misery, he may be best advised to invest his energies in areas other than raising a family. Every rule has an exception, but it seems clear that in the majority of contemporary cases, marriage for the confirmed homosexual would almost invariably entail a violation of (at least some of) the halachic and ethical principles enshrined in Torah Law.

Some readers may wonder why I have elaborated upon such an obvious matter. Surely the halachic minutiae are unnecessary to demonstrate the authenticity of a stance which is self-evident? How- ever, the fact that, as I am personally aware, some religious leaders have cavalierly advised homosexuals to get married, leads me to the con- clusion that it is necessary to expound upon this matter at some length. Some religious counsellors, apparently, naively believe that if a homosexual gets married his spouse will automatically 'cure' his homo- sexuality, and he will become, sooner or later, heterosexually orien- tated. It is hoped that the considerations delineated above will encourage greater caution on the part of homosexuals and their spiritual mentors before advocating involvement in a relationship in which they may be committing great injustice.

I realise that many homosexuals very much desire to build a family. They may crave the blessings inherent in a Jewish marriage and the *nachas* and posterity afforded by children. If there exist confirmed homosexuals who feel able to get married without violating any of the halachic or ethical principles discussed, there may be room for the endeavour of marriage, after appropriate consultation with a compe- tent rabbi and qualified psychologist. If, however, there is little reason to believe that this can be achieved, then the correct thing to do would be for the homosexual to abstain from getting married. Rather than castigating such people for 'selfishness' and 'egocentricity',[32] they should be commended as people who are noble and selfless in the acceptance of their position. In their awareness that marriage entails responsibility as well as privilege, they are resigned to forgo the many privileges, pleasures and joys of married life. Their readiness to accept the reality of their situation should be contrasted with the many recorded cases of homosexuals – active or otherwise – who have taken the liberty to draw another naïve and innocent person into a marriage, with the consequent violation of the above principles. It is regrettable that, due to sociological, familial or personal pressure, a homosexual man or woman will often feel compelled to enter into a marriage, with the knowledge that he or she will not be acting in accordance with the spirit or the letter of the law.

It is evident that acceptance of life as an unmarried person is difficult and may be demoralising. The knowledge that one is unable to build a 'faithful Jewish home' is undoubtedly painful for those men in this unenviable situation who desperately wish to have children. It could be hard and extremely painful for them and their families to come to terms with the fact that the Almighty has not given them the opportunity to father children, and the privileges and blessings that this entails. In this they share the inner torment and pain that so many heterosexual men and women endure, when discovering that they are unable to raise a family for whatever reason.

In this context, rabbis and counsellors can draw from the wisdom of Rabbi Aharon Feldman, Dean of *Yeshivas Be'er Hatorah* in Jerusalem, a noted authority in the field of Jewish values and ethics. He writes:

> Family and children are important in Jewish society, but one who does not have these need not feel that he is not a full-fledged member of the community. The verse in Isaiah 56 [verses 3–5], which is read by Jews all over the world on every public fast day, is addressed to the homosexual:
>
> '*Let not the* saris [who is physically unable to have children] *say, "I am a dried-up tree". For so saith God to the* sarisim *who keep My Sabbath, who choose what I desire, and who keep My covenant: I shall make them in My house and within My walls a monument, a shrine, superior to sons and daughters. I shall render their [lit., his] name everlasting, one which will never be forgotten.*'[33]

A homosexual who does not have a family can make serious contributions to Judaism which others cannot: for example, bringing Judaism to smaller communities where there are no facilities for raising a Jewish family.

Activities involving much travel, such as fundraising (a vital aspect of Jewish survival), are best accomplished by someone who is not tied down to a family. I know of a homosexual who helped establish several important institutions through his fundraising.

Even within one's community, devotion to public causes can more easily be done by someone who has no family obligations. Several individuals whom I know became respected, active members of their communities during their lifetimes, even though it was well known that they had no interest in marriage.

Notwithstanding the value of R. Feldman's proposals, they do admittedly seem to assume an over-simplistic solution to the problem. Firstly, society in general, especially the Orthodox Jewish community, has a long way to go in accepting people who are of a minority type disposition. Old prejudices die hard. Secondly, even if such persons are not alienated, they are at this point in time unlikely to be given equal opportunities in community life. Thirdly, it is unlikely that many homosexual individuals will remain totally celibate, a factor recognised by most realistic people. (As R. Feldman acknowledges in the above-mentioned correspondence to a homosexual *ba'al teshuvah* – whom he encourages to dedicate himself to causes such as 'bringing Judaism to smaller communities where there are no facilities for raising a Jewish family' – the (practising) homosexual will have to accomplish cessation of homosexual activity 'over a period of time'.) Finally, those 'gay militants' who advocate a highly promiscuous lifestyle have unfortunately created a negative stereotypical image of the homosexual person. In some communities, homosexuality has become a synonym for sexual 'libertarianism'. Consequently, all homosexuals, even *celibate* homosexuals may, unfortunately, often not be trusted, and will, therefore, find their avenues of opportunity for teaching Torah and participating in communal work etc. severely curtailed. Nevertheless, the ideas that R. Feldman suggests are definitely worth exploring. We may not live in the ideal world in which such proposals would be easy to implement. But the idea that homosexuals – including those who have not exhibited the spiritual strength to remain totally celibate and lonely – should be encouraged to participate in communal life and thus be able to maximise their contribution to the Jewish people, in a healthy and halachically acceptable manner, is most definitely commendable.

To put it succinctly: Divine Providence guides every individual and helps him discover his mission in life and how he is to accomplish it. One who is equipped with the characteristics necessary for married life has an explicit commandment dictating his direction in life: get married and raise a family. Those who, for one reason or another, do not have the capacity to commit themselves to a long-term heterosexual relationship are exempt from doing so (in accordance with the principle *onnes rachamana patreih* – 'the All Merciful will exempt one who is unable'[34]) and, undoubtedly, they have a different – but, possibly, equally important – mission in life.

Understanding and empathy are of primary importance here. Awareness of one's purpose in life is one thing; to come to terms with it and make peace with it is another. When advising homosexuals, it is essential that one is sensitive to the trauma and complexes they may be suffering as a result of their realisation that they will probably not be able to get married and have children. When a person senses that his situation is understood and appreciated, he or she will then be more open to adopt a positive and optimistic attitude towards life. In this way, the approach that Rabbi Feldman advocates opens new avenues and opportunities for the homosexual to find his or her rightful place within the Torah community.

8
Questions and Responses

My article 'Homosexuality and Judaism', which was published in the *Jewish Chronicle* in February 2000, occasioned much correspondence, both written and oral. Parents of homosexual children, rabbis of communities, and many gay and lesbian people contacted me for clarification, discussion and – in some cases – advice. Whilst many of the ideas elaborated upon in my written correspondence have been included in this book, others have not. I therefore deem it appropriate to reproduce that article in this book (with the permission of the *Jewish Chronicle*) together with extracts from some of the questions I received in the wake of its initial publication and parts of my replies.

JUDAISM AND HOMOSEXUALITY
By Rabbi Chaim Rapoport

In his summary of the Orthodox position on homosexuality, Rabbi Dr Alan Unterman writes: '... it is not demanded that one should be sexually attracted to members of the opposite sex, but it is demanded that, attracted or not, one should still get married and have children'.

I disagree. To be sure, marriage and procreation are supreme values in Judaism. It is antithetical to the spirit of Judaism to initiate a procedure whereby children will be conceived, born and bred outside the normative family nucleus. Where the potential for a healthy and stable marriage exists, one ought to respond positively to the Divine calling 'Be fruitful and multiply'. Yet those unable to find a suitable spouse or are constrained by mental or physical incapacity are exempt from fulfilling this Commandment. Emotional incapacity for a heterosexual relationship may, likewise, exonerate the individual from embarking upon a marriage that is likely to bring untold suffering to both partners.

Hence, notwithstanding our high regard for marriage, a confirmed homosexual would be best advised to invest his or her energies and talents in other areas. Rabbi Aharon Feldman is closer to the mark when he writes that: 'a homosexual who does not have a family can make serious contributions to Judaism which others cannot'. Not being restricted to the rigours of family life, the homosexual can undertake many projects to which a married person could not commit himself. Rabbi Feldman speaks of individuals, highly respected for their communal achievements, 'even though it was well known that they had no interest in marriage'.

One should not jump to conclusions. Many people who have experienced manifestations of homosexuality may still be enabled, with therapeutic assistance, to engage in a mutually satisfying heterosexual relationship. Transitional homosexuality amongst teenagers, bisexuality, ambiguous sexuality or even confirmed sexuality amongst people who have been constrained in close-knit same gender settings, are all scientifically recognised phenomena. Even some 'confirmed' homosexuals have been able to get married and have children after intensive, albeit somewhat gruelling, therapy. But where therapy is either unattainable or ineffective, it would be inadvisable to draw a member of the opposite gender into a relationship where the basic ingredients for harmony and emotional security are lacking *ab initio*.

Jewish Law forbids premarital, extra marital, promiscuous and homosexual relations. Consequently the bachelor, the spinster, the homosexual or a person trapped in a sexless marriage, all face a formidable challenge: they have to remain celibate. It is, admittedly, theologically challenging to accept that Divine Providence has deprived the blessings of marriage and the bliss of intimacy from so many people. Yet the believing Jew accepts that ultimately the Torah's teachings are for the benefit of mankind, both the individual and society. Some temptations may require a Herculean effort to be overcome and as Rabbi Feldman asserts, cessation of homosexual activity will often 'be difficult and will have to be accomplished over a period of time'. Accordingly 'a Jewish homosexual has to make a commitment to embark on a course through which he will ultimately rid himself of homosexual activity'.

However, people cannot ordinarily be blamed or penalised for experiencing homosexual feelings. Rather, understanding and empathy for those facing such challenges are called for. The ethos of *imitatio Dei* – emulating God's kindness – particularly for the oppressed, surely dictates that we do not ostracise or alienate people who may well face untold loneliness, misery and sexual frustration. Sadly, some otherwise 'progressive' thinkers don the mantle of zealousness when dismissing the plight of homosexuals. In reality, they are merely projecting their own personal prejudices under the guise of religious teaching. Yet whilst we may not judge a person 'until we stand in his place', we are likewise forbidden to abandon all moral objectivity and allow chaos to reign in the hierarchy of Jewish and ethical values.

Furthermore, our advocacy of tolerance and patience for the homosexual refers to the individual. It does not apply to organisations that promote homosexuality as a *cause celebre* or even as an equally acceptable 'alternative lifestyle'. 'Gay Synagogues' are anathema to the religiously sensitive because their aim is not only to condone behaviour that the Torah proscribes but moreover to sanctify such practices. As to the retort sometimes advanced 'where should Gays *daven?*', the answer is: in the same Synagogue that Jews who eat shrimps, desecrate the Sabbath and behave promiscuously render service to their Father in Heaven. Would they be made welcome? Yes, provided they do not proselytise. Flamboyant displays of 'gay pride' demonstrate a lack of sensitivity for the teachings that the Synagogue represents.

Many Synagogues may sometimes offer an *aliyah* to someone who dined in MacDonalds the previous night, so long as he does not flaunt the bill for his cheeseburger in Shul. We would likewise welcome a Jew whose sexual life is not in accordance with the Torah unless there is reason to believe that he may parade his 'cause' or attempt to win over new 'converts'. Nothing is more objectionable in our Tradition than one who seeks to lead others astray.

Taking all the above into consideration, a number of conclusions emerge:

a) Homosexual intercourse is forbidden for Jews and Gentiles alike. Yet when counselling homosexuals it is unrealistic to expect that prohibited behaviour should cease immediately. In the interim, we must help the homosexual avoid the pitfalls of promiscuity, despair and the various ailments to which he may be more vulnerable. Depression and suicide attempts among homosexuals are not rare occurrences. Rabbis, teachers and counsellors must be alert to these issues and 'not stand idly by' in matters of *pikuach nefesh*. On a national level, we must endeavour to curb the worrying trend of personal attacks on homosexuals, which are reminiscent of Nazi policies.

b) Jewish Homosexuals should be encouraged to participate in every aspect of Jewish life that they feel able to. We are enjoined to promote the spiritual welfare of every Jew. Judaism does not advocate a 'take it or leave it' position. The journey to religious perfection is a long and indefinite one. Everyone should be supported to make progress on his or her own level.

c) God Almighty loves all His 'children' irrespective of their sexual orientations. He cares for the errant Jew even if his wrongdoing is inexcusable, *a fortori* when his or her behaviour has invariably been influenced by the predominantly secular and liberal nature of contemporary society and culture. We, too, should endeavour to emulate God's ways and befriend all our 'brothers and sisters'. In this way we can hope to create a society which will indeed reflect the Godly attributes of love and benevolence.

Dilemmas of Homosexual Women

Q. ... I am an orthodox lesbian woman. I am neither 'in the closet', or 'out' of it. Living as I do in Jerusalem where there are many single women, and the pressure to get married is less claustrophobic than in some other places, I do not feel the need to explain why I am single. If people know, that is fine with me, and if they don't, it is also. A friend of mine, likewise a lesbian, made the terrible mistake of getting married under parental and peer pressure. She married a wonderful young man, a Ben Torah (Torah Scholar), who really cared for her. She thought that she would be able to forge a close relationship with him, simply because she liked him as a person. Yet, in actuality, it was a disaster. She could not bear the thought of intimacy with a man, and he was very troubled by this. The couple went for counselling and therapy, but despite their perseverance, she was not able to come to terms with living intimately with him. The marriage came to a sad end. Although her husband was quite understanding, she suffered a lot of acrimony from members of his family who said that she was a 'moredet' (a woman who forfeits the rights of her marriage contract due to her 'rebellious' behavior). He faced further difficulties for as a Cohen (a member of the priestly tribe), he is not allowed to get married to a divorcee, and because of his previous marriage, he was not 'top of the market' for an untold number of eligible orthodox single ladies.

I would like to ask you for a clear answer on the following questions:

a) *Does a Jewish woman have an obligation to get married?*
b) *Does a Jewish woman have an obligation to submit herself to conjugal relationships with her husband when she would be extremely uncomfortable with this?*
c) *I understand that there is no biblical prohibition involved in Lesbian activity. This is in contrast to male homosexual activity, which is considered to be a very severe transgression. Is this true?*

A. Lesbian sexual activity is forbidden according to Jewish Law. It is true that there are different opinions regarding the status of this prohibition, namely whether it is of biblical origin, or a so-called rabbinical prohibition. It is also true that lesbianism does not carry the weight of severity that male homosexuality does, inasmuch as male homosexual intercourse can, at least in theory, be a capital crime, and is also subject to the strictures of *arayot* – they are forbidden even if human life is at risk. At any rate, lesbian sex remains forbidden and whatever the severity involved – as a negative commandment – must be avoided in all circumstances (unless life-saving considerations dictate otherwise).

Having said this, a woman who is of homosexual orientation ought not to get married, unless there is reason to believe that such a person will be able to become part of a successful marital union. A number of considerations are pertinent, of which I give you a brief outline.

Firstly, according to the strict letter of Jewish Law, a woman is not obliged to fulfil the commandment 'be fruitful and multiply'. This does not mean, however, that a woman has no religious duty to get married. She does. According to Rabbi Meir Simchah of Dvinsk (1843–1926), in his acclaimed *Meshech Chochmah* (in his commentary on *Parashat Noach* 9:1), one of the reasons that a woman is not commanded to get married is because she does not require the force of a commandment to do so. Based on the Talmud (TB *Bava Kamma* 110b) the *Meshech Chochmah* explains that the inherent desire that a woman has for the life-long companionship of marriage [and the natural yearning of a woman for motherhood], will work spontaneously. (A man, however, may, in certain circumstances, require the dogma of law to propel him to marry and have children; see *Meshech Chochmah* ibid. for the specifics.)

Whatever the reason is for the absence of a biblical mandate for the woman to marry, it is certainly considered the religious ideal. Wifehood and motherhood – the role of the so-called *akeret ha-bayit* (the main-stay of the home) – are of the greatest vocations that a Jewish woman can aspire to. There is more to religious duties than has been enshrined in the *halachah* as mandatory.

Nevertheless, in a situation where a person does not feel that she is able to enter into a marital relationship which includes marital intimacy, she ought not to get married, until she can be reasonably confident that she will be able to fulfil her responsibilities as a wife. If a person, man or woman, is aware that he or she could not painlessly tolerate sexual intercourse, he or she would be advised not to get married, unless his or her circumstances changed. In the case you

describe to me, where the woman was obviously aware of her homosexuality before she got married, it was wrong of her – or in all
probability, those who advised her – to assume that marriage would be
the answer to her problem. I am not suggesting that no lesbian can ever
get married. It is possible, however remotely so, that she may meet a
compatible spouse. In the event that a woman met such a person,
marriage may be an option, providing that she was honest with her
potential partner about her sexual orientation, and consulted a religious authority about the propriety of entering into marriage under
such circumstances. The same is true for a gay man. For a person to
draw a member of the opposite gender into such a relationship without
his knowledge, is, to say the least, unethical. As the case you described
demonstrated, it was the springboard for immense suffering for both
parties. Therefore, even a man, who is obliged to marry and sire
children under Jewish Law, may be advised not to fulfil this *mitzvah* at
the expense of such consequences.

There is no obligation for a woman to submit herself to intimate
relationships with her husband, if she is not emotionally or physically
fit to do so (see *Shulchan Aruch Even HaEzer* 77:2). What was wrong
in the scenario that you depicted was not that the woman wasn't
prepared to steel herself and endure intimacy at the cost of consistent
trauma. What was wrong was that she embarked upon a marriage
without the pre-requisite honesty with herself and with her spouse. I
am not suggesting that she is totally at fault. It is, as you indicated,
possibly a collective responsibility of all her family and friends, who
were not ready or able to confront the situation as it was, and as a
result, two innocent people had their lives shattered.

There are a number of institutions that offer psychological and
therapeutic assistance, which they claim is able to open the opportunity
for *some* gays and lesbians to be able to marry and have children. This
option *may* enable *some* homosexual people to enter a heterosexual
relationship and build a family, provided of course that they fulfil the
above-mentioned requirements of honesty and integrity. These psychologists and psychiatrists do not offer any simplistic solutions.

Also, there is considerable debate in the scientific and professional
arena about the effectiveness and desirability of such therapy. As a
rabbi, whose expertise lies ultimately not in the realm of modern
psychology, I cannot give you a *conclusive* opinion. I believe that the
answer to this question is very much subjective, as it varies from case
to case. My professional informants reflect a wide range of views,

ranging from those who believe that some sort of 'reparative' therapy is *sometimes* advisable, to those (including several observant Jews) who believe that such therapies are more often than not a waste of time, and moreover are extremely concerned about the negative effects of such therapy. Some say that therapy may be of assistance to support a determined homosexual in his or her pursuit of a celibate life, but cannot be relied upon for the type of results that would be necessary to make marriage possible and advisable.

I therefore advise you to consult a competent religious and understanding psychologist in your locale, and at the same time liase with your local rabbi, in order to determine whether or not you should try therapy. In the meantime, I believe that you have done right in not getting married. I also believe that you have no obligation to disclose the nature of your sexual orientation to anyone – even if they confronted you directly about it – simply because it is none of their business. [Jewish Law sometimes even permits 'being economical with the truth' in order to avoid the indignity of discussing matters of personal intimacy with another (see TB *Bava Metzia* 23b; Maimonides *Hilchot Gezeilah* 14:13; *Shulchan Aruch Choshen Mishpat* 262:21 and commentaries).] Yet whatever the categories of 'closeted' or 'out' may mean, you would probably gain from appointing for yourself a rabbi, rebbetzin, or another personal spiritual mentor in whom you could confide and who could provide guidance in the many complex situations and challenges that you may well encounter.

PS. ... The literature on conversion therapy and consultation with practising care professionals reveals a broad range of views with regard to the degree of effectiveness, if any, of the various techniques. Doctor Joseph Berger, in his article, 'The Psychotherapeutic Treatment of Male Homosexuality', in *American Journal of Psychotherapy* Vol. 48 (Spring 1994) pp. 251–61, argues that some *male* homosexuals can be successfully 'treated'. Berger believes that '*some* people who have had homosexual fantasies, behaviours or identified themselves as homosexual, can become *comfortably and fulfillingly heterosexual* with psychotherapeutic treatment' [emphasis added]. See also the article by Richard C. Friedman on 'Homosexuality', *New England Journal of Medicine*, Vol. 331 (6 Oct. 1994) pp. 923–30 *and references* who cites the findings that suggest that there is more variation in women with respect to the 'plasticity' of sexual attraction than with men. Nevertheless, Friedman writes, there are many women who have only experienced homosexual attraction since childhood and, in their case, change in sexual orientation is unlikely. For a more 'pessimistic' view on the effectiveness of conversion therapies see the article by D. C. Haldeman, 'The Practice and Ethics of Sexual Orientation Conversion Therapy', in the *Journal of Consulting and Clinical Psychology*, Vol. 62 (April 1994) pp. 221–27, where the literature in psychotherapeutic and religious conversion therapies is reviewed. The author seeks to demonstrate that there is no evidence indicating that such treatments are effective in their intended purpose. He also considers the potentially harmful effects of such treatments.

Gradualism in the Process of *Teshuvah*

Q. Your article regarding the attitude of Judaism to homosexuality and to homosexuals alerted me to some very important issues. However, I was somewhat disturbed by your quote from an article of Rabbi Aharon Feldman, that cessation of homosexual activity will often 'be difficult, and will have to be accomplished over a period of time … a Jewish homosexual has to make a commitment to embark on a course through which he will ultimately rid himself of homosexual activity'. If I understand you correctly, you seem to be of the opinion that a sexually active gay man, who wishes to abide by the Torah, does not have to cease engaging in prohibited behavior immediately. On what grounds would you, or Rabbi Feldman for that matter justify such an approach? Jewish Law seems to be unequivocal, homosexual practices are forbidden in all places, at all times, and for all people. Period.

A. I value your question greatly, for it provides an opportunity for me to elaborate upon a theme which is critical to the Torah's teachings regarding change, repentance, self-improvement and spiritual growth. Whilst this may be relevant to homosexuals it is by no means irrelevant to other people. We all struggle with temptations, religious setbacks, and the tensions involved in religious renewal and rededication.

It is, I believe, universally accepted that when offering guidance to potential returnees to Jewish faith and practice (*ba'alei teshuvah*) one ought to take a pedestrian and gradualistic approach. One contemporary halachic authority, Rabbi Moshe Sternbuch – senior member of the *Edah Chareidit* in Jerusalem – has dealt with this issue in his *Kuntres Dinei Ba'alei Teshuvah biZmaneinu*, which he published in his series of *Teshuvot veHanhagot* volume 1 no. 350 ff. Rabbi Sternbuch writes as follows:

I have been asked by people who are in the process of returning to the Jewish way of life what they should start observing first: the laws of Shabbos (the violation of which is a capital crime) or the laws of Kashrut (which are mandated by Biblical Negative Commandments that are not subject to capital punishment) ... The first principle is that in the guidance of a *Ba'al Teshuvah* one ought to start as with a young child, who at first only lies flat, then progressively learns to sit, crawl, stand, walk, and eventually to run. Similarly with a *Ba'al Teshuvah* one ought to train him according to his capabilities ... the rule (*din*) is that one teaches him according to what he is able to accept and commit himself to. Therefore in circumstances where it is easier for the *Ba'al Teshuvah* to start keeping the laws of Kashrut [than the laws of Shabbos] because Kosher food is readily available, the *Ba'al Teshuvah* should be guided to start with Kashrut notwithstanding the relative severity of the laws of Shabbos. In this manner the *Ba'al Teshuvah* is presented with a manageable challenge and will then progress, slowly but surely towards a full commitment.

Those who start off by imposing too heavy a burden upon the *Ba'al Teshuvah* and require that he commits himself in one go to observe all the commandments of the Torah – even those that are most difficult for him – have lost more than they have gained. Such an approach may cause the *Ba'al Teshuvah* to panic and, in fear of the overwhelming difficulties, he may retreat from his return [to the fold].

The main emphasis in the guidance of the *Ba'al Teshuvah* is to fortify his faith in the Holy One Blessed be He who controls the world and attributes reward and punishment [where due]. Once the 'spark of faith' has been kindled within the *Ba'al Teshuvah* he will then become more interested ... until eventually he will become completely committed.

In light of the above, it is clear that [no one system can be applied to all cases and] there is no need to start with Shabbos [which is one of the most severe laws of the Torah] but, as stated, one ought to start with what the *Ba'al Teshuvah* can manage. There are people who are able to undertake the laws of 'Family Purity' although they are not yet ready to keep Shabbos ...

I also refer you to the statement of Rabbi Sternbuch, *Teshuvot veHanhagot* vol. 1 no. 368 *s.v. Omnam da'ati noteh*, with regard to influencing the behaviour of people in what he considers to be the 'appurtenances of forbidden sexual relationships', and suggests that – in the given situation – it may be 'premature' to expect change: 'an endeavour [to effect change] at the wrong time has the potential to make things worse. Everything must be done at the correct point in time.' Similar advice and guidance has been given by many other rabbis (see, for example, the comments of Rabbi Chaim Pinchas Scheinberg published in *Sho'alim biTeshuvah*, a publication of the AJOP (Association for Jewish Outreach Professionals) Chapter 15, pp. 25–26). See also the discussion in *After the Return*, authored by Rabbis Mordechai Becher and Moshe Newman (both of Yeshivat Ohr Somayach in Jerusalem), Feldheim, 1994, Part One, Chapter 1 ('Evolution or Revolution?'). Cf. the view of Rabbi Menashe Klein, *Teshuvot Mishneh Halachot*, Vol. 9 no. 408.

However, all this begs the question, what is indeed the justification for taking a gradual approach? If a Jew is obliged to fulfil all the commandments of the Torah, how can we advocate counselling an approach which in effect means that the *ba'al teshuvah* will not fulfil his responsibilities to his Father in Heaven and will remain only partially committed to the requirements of the Torah until he 'slowly but surely' reaches the final stage of his return? I present the following ideas by way of answer to this question.

Essentially, every single Jew is obliged to perform all the commandments of the Torah. Namely, to observe all of the (practically relevant) 248 positive commandments, abstain from all the relevant negative commandments. In addition to our obligation to observe the biblical commandments, we are likewise obligated to observe all the rabbinical edicts and to refrain from violating any of their institutions. A Jew who wishes to 'return to the fold' and become 'observant' would therefore have to commit himself to the entire spectrum of Jewish Law. On the other hand, it is almost impossible, and in most cases quite literally impossible, for a person to change from one extreme to another instantaneously. Even if he were able to make a 'quantum leap' and effect a radical change 'overnight' it is not likely to be a long lasting change. We are therefore faced with a dilemma: On the one hand, if we advise the would-be 'returnee' that complete commitment – in the form of instant and radical change – is a prerequisite to his acceptability, we would be guilty of 'closing the doors of repentance'. If on the other hand, we would advise the beginner that he is 'allowed to commit certain sins', would we not be guilty of misrepresenting the Torah?

Take, for example, a married couple who do not observe *taharat ha-mishpachah* (the laws of family purity). Their rabbi or their friends have an obligation to encourage them to observe these laws, the violation of which is subject to the penalty of *karet* (Divine ex-communication) and must be avoided even at the cost of life (see *Chiddushei haRitva* on TB *Pesachim* 25a; *Bet Yosef, Yoreh De'ah* chapter 195 *s.v. ve'katav od biTerumat haDeshen; Siftei Cohen* on *Shulchan Aruch, Yoreh De'ah* ibid no. 20; *Levush* ibid. no. 17; *Chochmat Shlomoh* on *Yoreh De'ah* chapter 157. See also the exhortation of the *Chafetz Chayim* of blessed memory, in his *Sefer HaMitzvot HeKatzer*, Feldheim, Jerusalem, 1990, Negative Commandment no. 123, where he emphasises that the prohibition of *niddah* carries all the weight of severity that other forbidden sexual relationships entail; and in the commentary entitled *Chafetz Chayim al haTorah* (ed. Rabbi S. Greiniman) pp. 156–7, where the analogy between the severity of *taharat ha-mishpachah* and incest is made. Cf. *Teshuvot P'nei Yehoshua* vol. 2 no. 44; *Teshuvot Avnei Nezer, Yoreh De'ah* no. 461, section 10; *Teshuvot Chelkat Yo'av, Yoreh De'ah* no. 29; *Atvan De'Oraita*, section 21. The couple shows an interest in changing their ways and embracing the Jewish way of life. They may, however, not be ready to cease all forbidden activity simultaneously. How do we advise them? Do we tell them that they must immediately implement every aspect of the Law 'lock, stock, and barrel', or do we encourage a pedestrian approach? If we take a non-compromising attitude, we will almost inevitably not accomplish that which we seek to accomplish. If we take a realistic attitude, and recommend half measures – albeit with the ultimate goal of reaching 'perfection' – are we not 'intruding into God's domain'?

The answer, I believe, is well illustrated in an anecdote about Rabbi Menachem Mendel Schneerson, the Lubavitcher Rebbe of blessed memory. A Jew in distress once turned to him for advice and help with regard to a number of problems he was experiencing. The Rebbe, who sometimes gave his responses in the form of a small, somewhat terse hand-written message, replied to his letter with a brief note: 'You should conduct your daily life in accordance with the *Shulchan Aruch* (The Jewish Code of Law)'. The Jew who had turned to the Rebbe was baffled. He was not religious in any way, and here the great Rabbi, whose understanding he so desperately needed, seemed to be totally oblivious to the reality of his life. How could he expect a so-called 'secular' Jew to transform himself overnight to a person who would abide by a code whose detailed minutiae govern every aspect of a person's life from the moment one wakes up in the morning to the moment one wakes up the next morning? The distressed man asked his contact to convey his disappointment with this advice. In due course, he received a clarification from the Rebbe. Firstly, he was told to start with the observance of certain specified commandments. Secondly, he was told that commitment to the *Shulchan Aruch* includes not only the laws, but also the principles inherent in the Jewish Code of Law. Amongst the many maxims which govern Jewish thought and law is the pragmatic principle that *tafasta merubah, lo tafasta, tafasta muat, tafasta* (if you try to grasp a lot in one go, you'll lose your grip; if, on the other hand, you attempt to grasp a little at a time, you will be able to hold on to it). In other words, whilst the Rebbe had certainly intended to advise the Jew to make a general commitment to the entire scope of Jewish Law, he certainly did not expect him to be able to translate this into complete practice immediately. In a sense, such an expectation would also be in 'violation' of Jewish Law, which knows to differentiate between the ideal goal, for the future, and the pragmatics of the present. To put it succinctly, Judaism demands that everyone be committed to strive towards the fulfilment of every aspect of the Law. In principle, every *mitzvah* is within the reach of every person. Yet, Judaism likewise teaches that God does not demand the impossible from his creatures. To paraphrase an old Yiddish aphorism, 'Self sacrifice and martyrdom may enable a person to jump off a roof, and onto the ground. No amount of selflessness will enable the person to jump from the ground, onto the roof.' Provided that the essential commitment to the totality of Judaism is present, it is acceptable to encourage a measured, relatively slow, but ultimately more assured approach to spiritual growth.

To return to our case of a couple who are violating biblical Law in their intimate lives by not observing the dictates of *taharat ha-mishpachah*. The couple must be informed, in no uncertain terms, what the requirements of Jewish Law are in this area. To convey a false message would be tantamount to falsifying the Torah. Yet, they must also be given to understand that the commandments do not come to us in a vacuum. There is the factual, personal and cultural background that every would-be observer of the commandments has. This may affect the immediacy of a person's practical implementation of every aspect of the Law. Therefore, the couple must be advised as to the relative severity of the various component laws of *taharat ha-mishpachah*. In this way, they will be able to, slowly but surely, reach the level of observance mandated by the Law. At the outset, the interested couple may enquire into the details of the Law, and also develop an appreciation of the underlying philosophy. They may then move on to keep the basic aspects of the biblical law. They may then follow on to embrace all the requirements of biblical law. Finally, they may reach a stage where they apply even the strictures of rabbinical ordinances. They may even adhere to some rabbinical laws (which are easier for them to fulfil) before they commit themselves to certain biblical laws. To give the impression to the young couple that they confront an 'all-or-nothing' decision from the outset would be severely irresponsible.

To be sure, this is an extremely sensitive area of Jewish Law and thought, but it cannot be avoided. No blanket rulings and standardised procedures can be applied. This is an area in which subjective considerations feature prominently. The couple ought to be advised to seek personal guidance. That guidance, however, ought to reflect a sensitive and delicate balance – one which does not adulterate the teachings of the Torah, but at the same time, provides an opening for those who wish to hold steadfast to the 'Tree of Life'.

Furthermore, I do not believe that a rabbi or mentor necessarily has the right to advise the potential *ba'al teshuvah* that in his or her circumstances it is permitted to commit certain *specific* transgressions or abstain from fulfilling certain *specific* positive commandments. For even if it is presently impossible for the *ba'al teshuvah* to keep certain aspects of the Torah, how could his or her guide know – with any degree of certainty – what *is* and what *is not* possible for any given individual? What I maintain is that the teacher and mentor must not endeavor to propel the *ba'al teshuvah* towards complete commitment, at a speed that is, ultimately, likely to be counterproductive. As I said, the rabbi ought to inform his student of the laws and their respective severity and encourage the student to undertake what ever he is able to without insisting on the *ba'al teshuvah* taking a quantum leap. In this way the *ba'al teshuvah* will understand that God does not demand the impossible and expects of him to do that which he is able to in his present stage of spiritual development.

By the same token, when a gay or lesbian person approaches his or her 'Spiritual Mentor' and counsellor, the latter is required to state clearly the rules of the Torah ('The Written Law') and the rabbis ('The Oral Tradition') in this regard. It is forbidden to misrepresent the teachings of Judaism. However, at the same time, the 'Spiritual Guide' must be aware of and take into consideration the reality of the situation. Once again, no absolute or even standard procedure can be clearly stated. The art of education involves the delicacies of many details which cannot be subjected to uniform standards. It is conceivable that a given person would be best advised to refrain at the outset from practices that incur the penalty for the biblically proscribed act. He may then move on to refrain from all biblically prohibited activities. Ultimately, the individual would be faced with what we have described as 'the formidable challenge' of total celibacy including abstention from masturbation and any form of auto-eroticism including wilful indulgence and homosexual fantasy. This of course is what Jewish Law requires. But to demand immediate compliance with such a standard on behalf of all would be irresponsible and, quite frankly, wrong.

Whether or not this is what Rabbi Feldman had in mind in his article, I cannot say. Yet the approach outlined above and contained in 'short-hand' in my above-mentioned article, is based on the firm bedrock of Jewish Law and Philosophy. I hope that this somewhat lengthy expla-nation will suffice to answer your questions.

Homosexual Disposition – Secret or Public Knowledge?

Q. Your article came as a breath of fresh air to me, although it did by no means solve all my problems. I was always led to believe that being attracted to other men was a terrible sin. As a gay man, who has remained celibate, but experiences sexual longings for physical intimacy with a man, I have forever been guilt-ridden to the extreme. Sometimes I have felt close to despair. Your statement that people ought not to 'be blamed or penalised for experiencing homosexual feelings' gave me some hope. I feel that now I may be able to discuss my problems with close friends. However, I am concerned that as a result, I will eventually be exposed, as I know few people can really keep another's secrets. I would like to ask you whether according to Jewish Law it is permissible for a gay person to be 'out of the closet'? Also, I am worried about the reaction of some members of my congregation. In the synagogue where I pray, the Rabbi has often spoken harshly about homosexuals, and I am scared of the consequences, should I be 'out', or be 'outed'.

A. At the outset, I would like to applaud you for your courage and perseverance. Life must be very difficult for you given your sexual orientation and commitment to Torah. According to the Mishnah (*Avot* 5:23), the reward is 'according to the painstaking effort'. Our sages teach us (TB *Kiddushin* 39b) that: 'he who passively abstains from committing a sin receives a reward as though he had done a *mitzvah*.' Also the mystical teachings of Judaism (see *Zohar* vol. 2 128b; *Likkutei Amarim – Tanya* chapter 27) explain the great positive effect that is accomplished – for the entire cosmos – when a person subjugates his inclinations in accordance with the will of God. I realise that this may provide little solace for someone who has to confront the daily struggles that you obviously endure. I hope it will not come across as patronising, but I do empathise with your plight. It makes some of my own challenges appear insignificant and petty.

How can a person possibly be considered guilty for having desires? Surely we all, heterosexual and homosexual, are visited with many desires to do things that are contrary to our Creator's Laws. Throughout the generations there have been very few saints who have managed to completely eradicate their 'evil inclination'. In fact, it is usually counter-productive to try and 'kill' one's instinctive inclinations. The duty of man is to master his inclinations, not annihilate them. A heterosexual person is not considered guilty if he is seized by a desire for an illicit relationship. It is only if he welcomes the sinful thought and allows it to linger in his mind or if he translates it into action, that he is guilty of transgression. The same is true for a homosexual. You are not committing any wrongdoing towards God or towards your fellow man by virtue of your homosexual wants. It would be unfair and destructive for you or anyone else to hold that against you. What your Father in Heaven asks of you is that you exert every possible effort to avoid transgression.

If you exhibit all the strength you have to succeed in your attempt to live in accordance with God's will, who could ask more from you? Do you really think that the married heterosexual, who has a 'kosher' outlet for his sexual drive, is superior to you, who are confronted with the challenge of perpetual celibacy? True, he may not be 'plagued' with the same amount of 'sinful thoughts'. You too may not have had to contend with such struggles, had you been given the opportunity to express your sexuality in a permissible manner. Do not consider yourself to be inferior to your heterosexual acquaintances in this regard.

I would like to think that any Jew who has a basic understanding of his or her religion would respond to your situation with similar ideas and sentiments. However, I am only too aware that unjustified, even cruel prejudices prevail in relation to people of a homosexual orientation. Unfortunately, the Jewish Community is not immune to such prejudices. I do not know how and when this situation will change. However, I do hope that the article you refer to, and others like it, will contribute in a very small way to the refinement of society, so that slowly but surely we will cultivate a humane and sensitive ethos. In your particular case, however, I have reason to believe that you will be pleasantly surprised. The friends who you wish to confide in hold you, as you say, in esteem, and so does your rabbi. After all, you have contributed greatly to the community. Whilst they may still talk in harsh and even ridiculing terms about people with a homosexual orientation, it is unlikely that they will do so once you have shared your secret with them. Halachically, there would be no justification for any enmity or discrimination against you, *particularly* as you say that you are living a celibate life. As for the prejudices that are grounded in bigotry, I believe that since your friends have a highly positive appreciation of who you are as a person, they are unlikely to turn against you because of your idiosyncratic orientation. It is easy to condemn the far removed homosexual who can easily be stereotyped in a negative manner. It is, however, very difficult for a humane person to vilify a friend whom he knows to be a good person, even if he may find it difficult to accept that you are a homosexual.

With regard to your question about sharing your problem with others and whether or not Jewish Law permits a gay man to 'come out of the closet', I would like to offer the following guidelines. [Sometimes, the term 'coming out' refers to a gay person declaring or acknowledging to others that he has adopted a 'gay lifestyle', namely that he transgresses the prohibitions associated with homosexual practises. Needless to say, Jewish teachings frown upon such 'declarations'. (We are taught (TB *Moed Katan* 17a) that in the event that a person engages in forbidden sexual practises he should avoid publicising his sin. See, however, some relevant details and qualifications in *Iggerot Moshe, Orach Chayim* vol. 2, no. 95 (end); *Yoreh De'ah* vol. 2, no. 33.) However, in your case it is obvious that you refer to the question of being 'open' with others about your sexual orientation, since, as you write, you have remained celibate.] There is no intrinsic reason to prohibit disclosure of such information. Nor is there any intrinsic reason to obligate the disclosure to others of one's sexual orientation. Of course, there may be good reasons to adopt one or the other course of action. Your concern about the heightened degree of prejudice against homosexuals may justifiably suggest the advisability of prudence. Pragmatic considerations must always be taken into account.

Yet I can also think of many reasons why you may want to be more open with close friends about your private situation. Firstly, a person with any difficulty is advised by our sages (TB *Yoma* 75a) to 'pour out his heart' to another. The negative effects of having to carry such a burden alone can be considerable. If you manage to find an appropriate confidant with whom to share your daily concerns and trials, you may consider it a blessing. Secondly, the pressures of having to conceal the very real experiences of your daily life from all other people must be unbearable. It is therefore most advisable that you seek out someone who will be able to share your burden with you and empathise with your challenges. This will, hopefully, also help you overcome the unhealthy sense of guilt that you have for having desires that the Almighty does not allow you to fulfil. The feeling of desperation that you describe is extremely spiritually destructive. As one Chasidic master said: 'Depression is not a sin. [Nowhere in the Torah does it say 'Thou shalt not be depressed', nor is it always possible to avoid depression.] But no sin can lead to the spiritual abyss that depression can lead to.' I am concerned that the fact that you are carrying this secret and the unhealthy guilt it has engendered, alone, may lead you deeper into despair, God forbid. Indeed, other homosexuals have suffered greatly, both emotionally and spiritually as a result of their having to constantly hide the truth about themselves and tell white or black lies day in and day out. If it is in the interest of your peace of mind to share your predicament with your nearest and dearest, then the Torah would most definitely advise you to do so.

Ultimately, however, I do not know if it is really feasible to keep it a complete secret. As you yourself wrote, word has a way of getting around. You mentioned that *shadchanim* (matchmakers) have been persistently nagging you to meet an eligible young lady, as indeed are your family and friends. This sort of pressure is only likely to accelerate in the course of time, for obvious reasons. I reckon that the pressure of having to put on some façade every time the issue of marriage is brought up must be emotionally draining. You may find, therefore, that you have no choice but to be more frank with others if you want to avoid such trauma.

Also, given your powerful sex drive you ought to take certain precautions in order to avoid temptation. In practical terms this means that you may have to avoid certain contact with other men that would be completely innocuous for heterosexual people. The particular constraints you put upon yourself in order to avoid sexual provocation will inevitably attract curiosity. This may necessitate you to disclose your particular challenges to those in your immediate social circle. Once it becomes known to a number of people that you are a homosexual, you may feel compelled to share it with others. Otherwise people may accuse you, rightly or wrongly, of concealing information that they feel they ought to be privy to. For example, if, as you say, you are sharing accommodation with someone, they may feel that there are certain issues of their behaviour towards you that they would modify had they known of your orientation. Similarly, should you choose to go to yeshivah and immerse yourself in intense learning, there may be good reason to share with the rabbis of the yeshivah your particular issue. Once again, it may be inevitable that others will find things out in the course of time. Depending on how the information is 'leaked' and circulated, it could be quite damaging.

As a person with a homosexual orientation, you may be best advised to seek employment in a predominantly female environment. In this way, you will be able to avoid, more easily, the temptations and provocative thoughts that you are prone to. As an unmarried man, you may have some difficulty finding such employment in a religious environment. Once again, honesty and integrity are crucial. In such a situation you may benefit from a candid exchange rather than camouflaging the issue with a maze of deceit. Taking all the above into consideration, I contend that it might be in your best interest, and that of others around you, to 'come out' in certain contexts.

You mention the view of Rabbi Reuven Bulka (in his book *One Man, One Woman, One Lifetime*) that 'The dictates of modesty and the imperative to walk humbly with God make the labelling of anyone as homosexual, or heterosexual for that matter, totally inappropriate.' You are therefore concerned that disclosure of your sexual orientation may violate the norms of modesty (*tzniut*).

I am not sure what the meaning of Rabbi Bulka's statement is. To be sure, the dictates of modesty require that all matters of sexuality are discussed discreetly and in an appropriate setting. The trend in some Western circles for people to display their sexual orientation through badges, slogans or sexually suggestive behaviour is clearly antithetical to the values of Judaism. Nor do I believe that people should ultimately be categorised according to their sexual desires. But acknowledgement to oneself and to others, *in a relevant context*, of one's sexual orientation (a matter that from a halachic perspective constantly effects many aspects of a person's life) – call it 'labelling' if you like – is certainly not a breach of the dictates of *tzniut*. This is true both for the homosexual and the heterosexual.

I therefore advise you to think carefully about these issues. Do not make rash decisions. If you do choose to disclose the matter of your sexuality to others, remember that you may get an initially adverse reaction from some people. Whatever decision you make should be 'for the sake of Heaven'. May the Almighty grant you success and happiness always.

Is there Room for Empathy?
Q. I was quite horrified by your article in the Jewish Chronicle. I thought that as an Orthodox Rabbi, you would know better than to single out homosexuals, who violate prohibitions for which one must sacrifice one's life (rather than violate) for special 'understanding' and 'empathy'. It appears to me that you have been brainwashed by the forces of political correctness into distorting, even if slightly, the Torah view. Sodomy is not just another sin like eating a cheeseburger in McDonalds. Sodomy is non-negotiable.

A. It is precisely because I am an Orthodox Rabbi that I take the view expressed in my article in the *Jewish Chronicle*. Or perhaps, I should say that it is because I espouse the compassionate attitude delineated in my article, that I am able, with God's help, to serve as an Orthodox Rabbi to a community that consists of members across the spectrum of religious observance, or the lack of it. The Jewish people to whom I minister vary in their backgrounds, social position, faith, and observance of Jewish Law. I have had occasion to attend to the needs of Jewish prisoners, guilty of minor or major offences; people brought up in orthodox homes and in irreligious homes; healthy family environments, and unhealthy ones. Naturally, it is part of the awesome responsibility of a rabbi to reprove people for their shortcomings and inspire sinners to repent. Yet surely a pre-requisite to all the above is the ability to be compassionate and understanding. If a rabbi cannot adopt such an attitude, he would be better off avoiding the pastoral ministry. Any counsel, or rebuke for that matter, can usually only have a positive effect if it is administered in a compassionate and understanding manner.

I take it that as an Orthodox Rabbi, you have probably had occasion to counsel young couples about the observance of *taharat ha-mishpachah*. You are surely aware that sexual intercourse with a *niddah* is a most severe infraction. It is likewise a sin for which one is obliged to forfeit one's life, rather than violate. It is also 'not just another sin like eating a cheeseburger in McDonalds'. Intercourse with a *niddah* (whether within or without the bonds of marriage) is 'non-negotiable'.

When you seek to inspire observance of *taharat ha-mishpachah* of those of your members who totally disregard these laws, do you succeed with fire and brimstone alone? Or do you try and appreciate their backgrounds, circumstances, and trials? I, for one, have found that the only way to communicate Torah ideals to the uninitiated is by adopting an extremely sensitive and sympathetic approach.

The reason that I singled out homosexuals for 'special' understanding is stated explicitly in my article. As I wrote, 'the bachelor, the spinster, the homosexual or a person trapped in a sexless marriage' may face untold loneliness, misery and sexual frustration. Is that not a good enough reason to advocate 'special' consideration for people who may face such a predicament through no fault of their own? Do you not think that a homosexual who does not have any legitimate sexually emotional outlet, and who may be compelled constantly to face temptation, is a subject worthy of compassion? At any rate, the challenges of a homosexual must be inconceivably greater than those of a married couple who have to abstain from relationships during the days of the wife's ritual impurity. It is for this reason that I maintain that, if we can be kind and understanding to all other people, irrespective of their religious or moral shortcomings, then *a fortiori*, we must adopt the same attitude towards those who face the challenges, say, of an exclusive homosexual orientation.

If I were not an Orthodox Rabbi, but, say, a Reform of Liberal thinker, I may be 'justified' in taking a more harsh attitude towards homosexuals. For those who are not bound by the Laws of the Torah, and who mould their Judaism in accordance with their personal conscience – which is naturally affected by personal and social prejudices and biases – may indeed take the liberty of projecting their personal bigotry onto the Torah. It is, as I said, precisely because I am an Orthodox Rabbi that I cannot allow my personal aversion for homosexual intercourse and discomfort with the whole concept to corrupt the correct attitude to brothers and sisters of homosexual orientation. As you wrote, 'Sodomy is non-negotiable' – but for that matter, neither is *ahavat Yisrael* ('Love Thy Neighbour'), at least in the school I come from.

Condemnation and Compassion – Are They Compatible?

Q. I read your sensitive and nuanced article in the Jewish Chronicle. *Whilst I agree with many of the points that you made, I have my reservations about others. You state that 'we must endeavour to curb the worrying trend of personal attacks on homosexuals, which are reminiscent of Nazi policies'* [some 25,000 homosexuals were killed during the Holocaust because of their sexual orientation. See the study of W. Roll, *Homosexual Inmates in the Buchenwald Concentration Camp*, published in the *Journal of Homosexuality*, Vol. 31 (1996) pp. 1–28 for an example of the type of conditions homosexuals were exposed to in the concentration camps]. *But surely, this may give the false impression that Judaism condones homosexual behaviour? I understand that you do not condone it, but any compromise in the rigid stance we have taken towards homosexuals is likely to be mis-construed as a quasi-approval of the homosexual lifestyle. I am also concerned about the invitation you have extended for Jewish homo-sexuals 'to participate in every aspect of Jewish life that they feel able to'. How can we possibly allow such deviants to infiltrate the Jewish Community?*

A. Two wrongs do not make a right. There is a dangerous tendency to avoid complexity when it comes to paramount moral issues. Yet to take an uncompromising and inconsiderate view is not – as some people think – an issue of 'being *machmir* (stringent)'; it can often lead to leniency. If a leader, in his eagerness to condemn homosexual practices, does not emphasise the importance of understanding and inclusivism, his 'stringency' may lead to fatal 'leniency'. I trust you are aware of the anecdote attributed to Rabbi Chaim Soloveitchik of Brisk, who was asked why he was so lenient with regard to the obligation of fasting – apparently he often ruled that people do not need to fast, even if the danger seemed remote. 'I am not', said Rav Chaim, 'lenient with regard to fast-days. I am stringent with regard to the imperative to protect life (*pikuach nefesh*)'. A more dogmatic stance with regard to the *mitzvah* of fasting on the proscribed days may possibly have sown less confusion, but ultimately it would have endangered more lives.

The fact is that the moral issues related to homosexuals and homosexuality are multi-faceted. To be sure, promoting Jewish sexual ethics and combating the ever-increasing permissiveness of society is of paramount importance. That does not mean that there are no other issues of equal importance. Nor does it mean that one matter of importance should, by necessity, over-ride the other. In our context, protecting our brothers and sisters who are gay and lesbian from harassment, attack, and even death – through homicide or suicide – is also of paramount importance. We cannot condone a system of religious exhortation that seeks to address the first issue at the expense of the second. I realise that the need for such sensitivity does not make things simple. But whoever said that moral dilemmas are easy to cope with? Where does the Torah say that it is acceptable to encourage unjustifiable prejudice in order to promote compliance? The end does *not* justify the means. Some people may not be equipped to deal with issues so delicate, where the over-emphasis on one or the other aspect could yield disastrous results. But, once again, such people should not try to deal with issues that are beyond their capacity.

You are undoubtedly aware of the distinctions that have been drawn between various types of transgressors of the prohibitions associated with homosexuality. One can easily appreciate the difference between the homosexual act committed by a heterosexual or bisexual person, and that same act committed by the exclusive homosexual; between the homosexual who disregards the word of God, and the one who struggles but ultimately succumbs to natural temptation; between the practising homosexual who had a religious education, and the one who may be seen, to one extent or another, as a product of his or her secular environment – a *tinok shenishbah*.

These differences all have halachic bearing. Yet, when it comes to helping the sinner – homosexual or heterosexual – whose life is in danger, we are enjoined to do whatever is within our ability to help him or her. Judaism does not seek the death of the sinner, even in circumstances where he may be responsible for the danger in which he has become entangled. How much more so when he or she is an innocent victim of extraneous circumstances. In this context, the words of Rabbi J. David Bleich, in his *Bioethical Dilemmas* (p. 139), are most appropriate:

> Accordingly, the question of punishment is one that should not arise with regard to our relationship vis-à-vis individuals who engage in deviant sexual behavior or, for that manner (sic), with regard to our relationship vis-à-vis any person who violates any of the commandments of the Torah. Insofar as our attitude is concerned, the act must be deplored, but the person who commits such acts remains a Jew to who our hearts and arms are open. Such a person remains a brother and our relationship to him must be the fraternal relationship one has with a brother who has strayed from the values and mores of the family, i.e., a brother to who one's arms are always open and who will be warmly and affectionately welcomed at all times.

You are also surely aware of the many dangers that seek to threaten the lives of homosexuals. The causes of such danger are various. There exists a consensus of opinion that homosexuals form one of the largest groups of people who are liable to commit suicide. (See Richard C. Friedman, 'Homosexuality', in *The New England Journal of Medicine*, Vol. 331, pp. 923–30 in the section on 'Suicide and Gay Youth' and the references thereon.) Self-hatred, leading to depression, often ends in suicide attempts. Isolation and loneliness and the devastating feeling of helplessness are likewise perilous for the homosexual. Teenage and adult depression; bullying and physical persecution; perceived and, unfortunately, often very real rejection by family and friends – for the mere 'sin' of having a different sexual orientation – are among the causes of depression that lead to life-threatening situations. Feelings of inadequacy and inability to build a family, especially in a community that revolves around the family nucleus, may likewise contribute to the dangerously traumatising emotions experienced by homosexuals. The feeling of being ridiculed, hated, and even threatened by other people is an additional factor that we must take into consideration when assessing the plight of contemporary homosexuals.

With all the above in mind, I wrote and maintain that it is the sacred duty of religious leaders and communities to convey the word of God as expressed through the *halachah, without* compromise. This applies equally to the *halachah* with regard to love for one's neighbour, as it does for the *halachah* with regard to the prohibitions associated with homosexuality.

I believe that we also have an obligation to do whatever we can to protect sexually active homosexuals from the various diseases that they may contract. Unless you maintain that we have no duty to save the homosexual sinner (and I would want to know why you isolate him from amongst all other sinners of today's day and age), I presume that you would agree with me. I therefore wrote in my article that we must help the homosexual 'avoid the pitfalls of promiscuity, despair and the various ailments to which he may be more vulnerable'. It is my considered opinion that such 'help' cannot be restricted to referrals for reparative therapy. To do so would be naïve at best, and wicked at worst. It is *possible* that some homosexuals *may* find hope and even the amelioration of their problems through such therapeutic endeavours. But we cannot deny solicitude and advice from those who either cannot or, for one reason or another, will not pursue the avenue of therapy. Even if they do opt for therapy, it would be a simplification to assume that they will cease all forbidden activity immediately. In some cases, therapy may actually promote increased sexual activity, at least initially. Therefore, we have no other route but to advise those homosexuals who seek our counsel, according to the context of their behaviour, whether or not it is 'ideal'.

The same principles must govern our behaviour when confronted with homosexuals or promiscuous heterosexuals that have contracted AIDS as a result of their activity. The variety of convoluted debates that emerged in the late 1980s as to whether AIDS, for example, could possibly be a manifestation of Divine retribution, are irrelevant to this position. Even if it could be demonstrated that a person is suffering illness as a punishment or a consequence of his own sin, we are still duty bound to do whatever we can to save his life. The same God who brought illness to the individual has commanded us to endeavour to ameliorate his suffering. The same God who has brought the patient to the threshold of death, has invited us 'into his domain' and asked us to do our utmost to keep the flame of life burning. Failure to act in a situation of *pikuach nefesh* is sometimes compared with the horrific crime of 'shedding blood'. When a life is in peril, discussions about the theology of suffering must be put on the back burner and immediate action is called for.

With regard to the second issue you raise, namely the 'infiltration' of homosexuals into the Jewish Community, I am not sure I understand your difficulty. I take it that you have no problem welcoming known celibate homosexuals and according them equal rights to all other members of the community. You would not like to see such innocent – if not heroic – members of the Jewish people humiliated, never mind alienated. Your reference must obviously be to sexually active homosexuals. Once again, I cannot agree. Communities that only welcome Jews that are completely observant, would invariably shut their doors on such homosexuals, as they would indeed on those who violate any aspect of the sexual code in Leviticus, the laws of *Shabbat*, *kashrut*, and the like. But why should communities who open their doors welcomingly to all Jews, regardless of level of observance, single out homosexuals for unparalleled censure? Furthermore, such ostracism is likely to drive all such people to join non-Orthodox denominations, or to create separate congregations for themselves. The notion that such homosexuals should be treated like lepers, just because of their religious failing in this area, goes against the grain of my religious conscience.

Finally, the implication of your comment is that the Jewish Community is composed of heterosexual people exclusively. The question for you is: do we open our doors and provide religious asylum for practising homosexuals? This is, however, far from the truth. The fact is that there are many practising homosexuals amongst Jewish families that are very much part of the Jewish Community. Many of them want to fulfil all the *mitzvot* that they feel able to, and to contribute harmoniously to the greater good of the community. The question therefore is, do we declare that the practising homosexual is *persona non grata* in the Orthodox synagogue? Do we conduct an 'inquisition' to expose and expel all closeted homosexuals? Or conversely, do we insist that all homosexuals – practising or otherwise – that wish to remain in our midst remain closeted forever?

Communicating with Parents and Family

Q. I am a modern orthodox homosexual who has recently 'come out' to my parents and family. For years I kept my homosexuality a secret, but there came a point in time where I was no longer able to do so. My brothers and sisters took it quite well, but my parents were devastated. They exclaimed hysterically: 'How could you do this to us? Is this what we deserve? If you have a problem, go and see a shrink and sort yourself out. Whatever you do, do not embarrass us.' I had actually been in long term therapy to try to get rid of my homosexuality. I had a gay friend who did go through therapy and, whilst he still considers himself a homosexual, has been able to find a wife with whom he says he can maintain an emotionally fulfilling relationship. I was hoping that I would be able to be like him. It still grieves me very much that I will not be able to get married and have children. Unfortunately, however, therapy did not help matters and after a long period of perseverance my therapist, who by the way is ultra-orthodox, advised me to quit therapy, as it was becoming counter-productive. I am aware of the prohibitions in the Torah regarding homosexual behaviour. Fortunately, I have managed to abstain from anal intercourse, although I have sometimes after long periods of celibacy, allowed myself to engage in other physical intimacies with a close gay friend, who has been very supportive to me throughout my ordeal. I have never been promiscuous, and I make sure to avoid bad company and risky conduct. My parents do not know that I have ever engaged in homosexual intimacy, but they simply cannot come to terms with my homosexuality. I love them dearly, and would literally do anything to make them happy. What should I do?

A. It is with certain trepidation that I venture to respond to your heartbreaking letter. I wish I could refer you to someone who has the solution to a problem like yours. Unfortunately, I cannot. It is in the spirit of *ahavat Yisrael* (love thy neighbour) that I feel obliged to offer a few words of advice, however lacking and unsatisfactory it may seem to you. I am guided by the words of our sages (*Avot* 2:16): 'It is not your duty to complete the task, but neither are you free from to desist from it'. I do hope that you will gain something from the ideas I am about to share with you.

Your ability to communicate and effect a reconciliation with your parents depends, to a certain degree, upon your understanding of 'where they are coming from' and their understanding of 'where you are coming from'. Therefore, whilst it will undoubtedly be painful for you to read the following sentences I feel duty bound to explain what I feel you need to understand about their experience.

There are two emotional reactions which are closely linked and are often confused with each other: they are (a) pain and (b) anger. By pain I refer to the emotional trauma and suffering that a person endures as a result of experiences that hurt. The expression of pain and the process of grief may have many nuances including, feelings of guilt, frustration, desperation, intolerant behaviour and depression. By anger I refer to the emotional response of passionate 'animosity' towards one who is to be blamed or whom one would like to blame for causing such hurtful experiences.

A simplistic analogy may help. Imagine the following scenario: a woman received an expensive diamond ring from her husband. Some twenty-five years into her happy marriage, her young child took the ring and misplaced it. Several weeks later the ring, valuable financially and invaluable sentimentally, was still not found. To add salt to the wounds, the ring was not insured. This woman is likely to experience pain (as a result of her loss), guilt (for having been careless), frustration (for not being able to find the ring), etc. This would all be understandable. Yet for the woman to harbour feelings of anger towards her infant child would be an illogical reaction. After all, how can one blame a child of a young age and hold him or her responsible for the loss of a precious item? Surely the child cannot be held accountable for incurring the loss and pain of the mother. Nevertheless, some mothers may, at least temporarily, allow their pain to be translated into anger with the child. It is illogical but a fact of life that sometimes people channel their emotions of pain through the conduit of anger. Sometimes finding a scapegoat on whom one can vent one's anger is quite 'therapeutic' in terms of alleviating or ameliorating one's pain.

This rather simplistic analogy may be 'useful' in your situation. For in more 'complex' situations than the above, it is easier for people to erroneously apportion blame where it does not belong and thus confuse pain with anger, which they then vent on an innocent 'scapegoat'. Your parents quite naturally and understandably are experiencing much pain as a result of their new 'discovery'. Whilst they may be expressing anger towards you and seem to be harbouring ill feelings towards you, it is essentially a feeling of intense pain that is being expressed, albeit in a way that is most unfair to you. Your parents are confusing pain with anger and as a result are expressing the type of knee-jerk condemnations and fury that you describe.

The harsh reaction of your parents towards you, whilst illogical, may even be symptomatic of their special feelings of affection for you. Naturally, most parents hope that their children will grow up, find a spouse, get married, and have children. You can surely relate to this feeling, for as you said yourself, it is difficult for you to come to terms with remaining single and childless. Even if your parents were irreligious and had no qualms about homosexuality per se, they would invariably be upset to learn that their son will not in all probability be able to settle down to a stable married life and produce – their reward for surviving parenthood! – grandchildren. How much more so that your parents are religious and having children is a sacred duty and privilege for which a Jew ought to be prepared to suffer much inconvenience in order to fulfil. Given the social norms and the prevalent prejudices in society, the almost irrational preoccupation with 'embarrassment' may also be understood. For it is unfortunately not unheard of, even in today's day and age, for parents and siblings to be penalised and ostracised if a member of the family does not conform to society's expectations. If there is someone 'different' in the family, the whole family is often stigmatised. Unfortunate, unjustifiable, but very often true.

Furthermore, your parents probably realise that the loneliness and celibacy that are almost inevitably the fate of a religious homosexual, will present you with an awesome challenge. Even though they do not know that you have engaged in homosexual activity, they must be aware of the almost impossible situation in which you find yourself. Naturally, therefore, they are no doubt concerned about the spiritual and physical malaise associated with physical intimacy outside of marriage, and particularly those related to homosexual intercourse. These and other considerations all cause severe pain for your parents even if you cannot be blamed and you bear no responsibility whatsoever. In truth, you both need and deserve understanding and support, but at this stage your parents are too preoccupied with their own feelings to be able to respond, correctly and responsibly, to their parental duties. However, the knowledge that at the depth of their pain lies a strong feeling of love towards you should encourage you to take the right steps towards reconciliation with them.

I hope that the above will help you put your parents' anxiety into context. As far as your own conscience is concerned, I do not think that you have to feel responsible for your homosexual orientation and the awkward consequences it has given rise to. As you wrote, you have never had any attraction to girls and you have always been sexually attracted to men. In the interest of avoiding pain, for yourself and your family, you kept it a secret for many years. Your religious convictions led you to seek help in therapy with the hope that you would be able to get married and fulfil the biblical commandment of procreation. The same religious convictions led you to quit therapy on the advice of a God-fearing professional, and with the awareness that your physical and spiritual health was suffering as a consequence. Your friend was able to benefit from therapy. You were not. Finally, you felt unable to hide your problem, and in desperate need for support and love, confided in your nearest and dearest. The pain you must have experienced and continue to experience as a result of your parents' reaction must be horrifically tortuous. I can only cry with you and for you, realising as I do the intensity of your suffering. The tensions, the guilt, the regrets, the anger, the feelings of inadequacy and impotence must be unbearable. But the fact that you have experienced all this may not be attributed to your fault. I know this will provide meagre, if any, comfort. But it is important that you should know it. Do not take on board greater measures of responsibility than can be reasonably apportioned.

I do hope that you will be able to help your parents, whom you so dearly love. However, you must realise that their reconciliation with you will invariably not happen overnight. Your disclosure of information to them, which was done in good faith, gave them a shock that they are apparently not equipped to cope with. You yourself struggled for many years to avoid confronting what you have now accepted, as – in all probability – an unalterable homosexual disposition. Your parents, to whom the whole issue is alien, will need time and patience to acclimatise themselves to your predicament, just as you did yourself.

I suggest that you identify someone for whom your parents have great respect, and confide in him. Find a rabbi who is knowledgeable, sensitive, and will command the respect of your parents. As someone who is not immediately affected by your homosexuality, he will be able to retain his objectivity. Hopefully, in the course of time, he may be able to help your parents come to terms with the disillusionment of their expectations and the shattering of their hopes. In your own way, you may also be able, in the course of time, to provide your parents with some solace, if not compensating *nachas*. You may achieve great accomplishments in your work for the community, in your personal occupation, and your efforts in Torah study, or deeds of benevolence and kindness. Like other great people who never married or had children, your contribution to the Jewish people may be equally as great, if not as fulfilling. You may teach, inspire, and support others. Your personal behaviour towards your parents will slowly but surely help communicate to them the message that there is no malice intended on your behalf.

As far as you yourself are concerned, it is important that you seek to identify your unique mission in life. You would be best advised to find an area of study or communal or worthy universal campaign in which you will be able to invest your energy. Try and avoid the temptation to become obsessed with your sexual struggles. Such exclusive preoccupation can only be detrimental. Rather, remember that our sexuality and the challenges it entails are not the be all and end all in life. There are so many areas of religious endeavour that require great attention and may promise magnificent reward. Even if you have reason to believe that some day you may be able to get married – wonders never cease – it would be a dangerous mistake to put your life in suspense, even if this hope will be fulfilled. The Almighty granted you days and years to utilise in the best possible way. No one knows for sure what the future may tell, but in the interim you most definitely have a mission. Try and identify it and throw your whole heart and soul into it.

Regarding your sexual behaviour, it is most admirable that you have abstained from the more serious offences and that you have avoided the pitfalls of a promiscuous lifestyle. I understand that this has not been easy and I stand in awe of your stamina and perseverance. 'Rome was not built in a day', neither was Jerusalem. The Almighty expects you to try your best. More than that, you cannot do, and less than that you may not do. Ultimately, it is only the Almighty who can measure your abilities, trials, and efforts (Maimonides, *Hilchot Teshuvah* 3:2), and it is to Him alone that you are accountable. All of us struggle constantly with our particular challenges, and very few of us reach perfection. It is a mistake to think that success in life means reaching a point of no struggle. Whether we like it or not, struggles are an integral part of the human condition. We pray daily to be spared from spiritual tests (*al tevi'einu li'yedei nisayon*) but almost no day goes by without challenge. Our efforts to perfect ourselves are not just a means to an end. They are an end in themselves. The intensity of our endeavour to sanctify our lives is the true measure of our relationship with our Father in Heaven, which ultimately is the *raison d'être* for our existence. I hope and pray that you will be granted special Divine assistance to overcome the many obstacles that appear to be in your way. I hope and pray that the Almighty will grant you success in your personal endeavours, and in your work on behalf of our people. I hope that you will be granted good health, happiness, prosperity and all the material and spiritual blessings that we constantly pray for.

Is Orthodoxy Equipped to Face the Challenges of Homosexuality?

Q. I am an observant Jew, single and aged 36, who has ever since puberty always been attracted to men exclusively. Due to the taboo on the subject in my community, I have carried my burden quietly and it is only recently that I have begun to discuss my situation with friends, and to explore different avenues of progress. One rabbi told me 'to get married and it will be O.K.'; another one said, 'Your Judaism and homosexuality are irreconcilable – go to Reform' and I do not know who to listen to. I have been praying incessantly for God's salvation, but alas, to no avail. I would love to get married and have children, and I know that only in this way will I be respected in my congregation as a valued member of the community. I really do not know which way to turn. Please can you help me.

A. You write about your struggles as a person who wants to be completely observant, and the difficulties you have because of your homosexual disposition. I offer some guidance in the order of your questions. It is impossible for me to provide an adequate response to your searching letter, rather consider what I write as a sort of short-hand from which you may glean certain ideas, and extrapolate upon them.

It is important that you identify a learned, kind and pious Rav in your city with whom you will have the opportunity to discuss your personal circumstances, and the practicality – or lack of it – in assuming some of the ideas mentioned in my letter.

With regard to the exact nature of your homosexual leanings, it is necessary for you to identify a professional expert in the field who is sensitive to the Jewish teachings in this regard. He will be able to help you clarify what your situation is, and whether or not therapy would have anything to offer. It is, however, clear that at this moment in time, your homosexual longings are dominant and – whatever the future will bring – you cannot put your life on hold. You must therefore find solutions that you can apply with immediacy to enable you to live healthily, both materially and spiritually.

You seem to be under the impression that your homosexuality and your Jewishness are irreconcilable. I hope that the following quote from Rabbi J. David Bleich will help put matters into perspective. In his book, *Judaism and Healing* (page 70), Rabbi Bleich writes: 'One should be aware of the distinction between homosexuality, and homosexual conduct. Some individuals are sexually attracted to members of their own sex, but feel no similar attraction to members of the opposite sex. This deeply felt attraction may or may not find expression in overt sexual activity.' Such people '*are homosexuals, even if they remain celibate or engage in heterosexual activity exclusively*'.

The fact that you have the feelings that you do definitely creates new challenges insofar as your Judaism is concerned, but it is not irreconcilable with your Judaism.

Judaism demands of you not to engage in homosexual activities and for this you will require tremendous strength. It may be *almost* impossible for you to discipline your desires completely, but our sages tell us that ultimately a person has the ability to harness his sexual desires, even when a Herculean effort is necessary.

Yet, Judaism has never preached an 'all-or-nothing' policy. *The fact that any given person has difficulty with regard the observance of any commandment, is not a reason to abandon his or her Judaism.* It is totally antithetical to Jewish teachings to suggest that failure in one area is grounds to desert what is rightfully yours, namely the Torah, which is 'an inheritance for the entire Congregation of Jacob'. The rabbi who told you to 'go to Reform', where homosexual conduct is condoned, is totally irresponsible. Every Jew, man and woman, whatever their circumstances are, must be able to find a home in the

Community of the Torah. To suggest that you may as well look elsewhere, because the Almighty has imposed upon you additional challenges, is scandalous. Even with regard to a sinner who deserves the title *rasha*, Maimonides (*Hilchot Nesiyat Kappayim* 15:9) states categorically: 'we do not say to the *rasha*: "indulge in sin and refrain from performing *mitzvot*"'. How much more so with regard to someone who is truly desirous of being loyal to the Torah and is in the process of an upward struggle towards total observance. Such a person must not be in any way disenfranchised or discouraged, God forbid, even if he succumbs to the all too human desire for physical intimacy.

You write about your desire to marry and raise a family. You feel a strong yearning to create a family home. In addition to the *mitzvot* involved, you know that in your community, you will be considered defective, a '*halber mensch* (half-man)' unless you get married. In your present situation, you do not feel able – and rightfully so – to marry. You say that you have prayed for many years that you should be able to find some way of getting married, and having children. You feel, however, that your prayers have gone unanswered.

Prayer is not without its complexities. On the one hand, a person who prays for the opportunity of marriage and children really wants his prayers to come true. Insincere prayer is severely condemned. Furthermore, the believing Jew accepts that sometimes prayers are fulfilled only after a long time, and that the fact that prayers have not changed his circumstances up until now does not mean that they will never do so. On the other hand, the believing Jew is also aware that whilst God answers prayers, sometimes His answer is 'No'. It is possible that God Almighty has a designed a different destiny for the petitioner, in which his requests cannot be fulfilled. Therefore, whilst we persevere with our prayers, we cannot postpone the fulfilment of our life's mission until such time as our prayers are answered in the way we would like them to be. (I say 'in the way we would like them to be', for as Rabbi Yisrael *Baal Shem Tov* taught, no prayer is wasted, for every prayer has an effect somewhere and somehow, even if not in the particular area of the petitioner's request.)

In your circumstances, therefore, it is necessary for you to invest your time and energy in an area of Judaism in which you can be successful at the moment. The commandments of God Almighty that you will fulfil, the lives of people that you will change for the better, the disciples that you will raise, will be your 'offspring', providing you with the merit and fortitude of posterity and eternity. If God does respond favourably to your prayers – in their literal sense – and you find yourself able to embark upon the *mitzvah* of marriage and pro-creation, you will be doubly rewarded.

I pray to God Almighty that He should help you and guide you in what is obviously something of a maze for you. He should give you the stamina to persevere, and the courage to meet your particular destiny. I pray that you should realise your full potential.

PS. With regard to the question of teaching Torah to someone who does not abide by its laws, see the discussion and references in Rabbi Moshe Weinberger, *Jewish Outreach: Halakhic Perspectives*, KTAV, New Jersey, 1990, Chapter 4, pp. 32–40, 136–8. See also *Likkutei Sichot*, Vol. 1, pp. 86–7. Incidentally, there is a specific reference to teaching Torah to practising homosexuals in the work *Lekket Yosher*, written by a disciple of the author of *Terumat haDeshen*, Part 2, p. 39. The author reports that he consulted his teacher about the propriety of teaching Torah to a 'child' who 'is going in a bad way, for example: he practises *mishkav zachar* and transgresses the negative command-ment against theft (*lo tignov*)'. The answer he was given was in the affirmative: it was correct to teach such a 'backsliding' student.

9

Summary and Conclusion

I am sorry if I have disappointed the keen reader. One may have set out to read this book with the intention of solving all the problems and yet, having read it, will realise that none of them have been completely solved. Indeed, it was not my aim in writing this book to provide an answer for all the questions. Rather, in a sense, it was my aim to provide many thought-provoking questions for those who assumed that they had all the answers or, worse still, thought that there are no questions at all.

Is this not a futile exercise? Definitely not. 'The awareness of the problem is half the solution', goes the old adage. In the sensitive subject we have undertaken to explore in this book, this is most pertinent. The degree of ignorance and insensitivity that often leads to tragic consequences is far too great. It is sincerely hoped that the chapters of this book will have helped dispel much of the confusion and erroneous assumption about Judaism's attitude to the issue of homosexuality.

I hope to have provided the outline of a framework for those of homosexual orientation to be able to reach a *modus vivendi* with themselves, their parents, their communities and, above all, their Father in Heaven. I also hope to have provided a resource for heterosexual people to be more familiar with the problems and challenges that gays and lesbians, their families, friends and communities face.

Amongst the multitude of issues that have been clarified, brief mention can be made of the following:

i. That in contrast to certain revisionist trends, Jewish Law clearly proscribes homosexual activity for both males and females;

ii. That this prohibition does not necessarily defy, but is likewise not contingent upon, reason;

iii. That it is in no way contradictory to the Jewish faith to accept the possibility that a person may be of exclusive homosexual disposition, without any choice in the matter;

iv. That it is badly wrong to condemn people for their natural sexual orientation;

v. That, however strong temptation may be, a person does, ordinarily speaking, have the ability to control and discipline his desires. People of whatever sexual orientation must abstain from all sexual expression outside of marriage;

vi. That homosexual people are more often than not confronted with a formidable challenge, the likeness of which is rare in other spheres;

vii. That appreciation by heterosexuals of the difficulties endured by gays and lesbians is of paramount importance;

viii. That most practising gays and lesbians do not fall into the category of 'defiant rebels' and, therefore, should not be disenfranchised by co-religionists;

ix. That in contemporary times, most practising homosexuals fall under the halachic category of *tinok shenishbah* and are therefore not 'hedonistic renegades'. Rather, their attitude towards religion must be attributed to the secular climate of Western society. Such homosexuals should be encouraged to study Torah, observe the *mitzvot* and, ultimately, adhere to all the laws of the Torah, including those which pertain to their intimate lives;

x. That homosexuals are essentially no different to any other Jew. The commandments to love and be compassionate, benevolent and kind apply to all Jews;

xi. That homosexuals should be encouraged to participate in every area of Jewish life that they feel able to;

xii. That moral judgmentalism should be tempered with subjective consideration in accordance with the rabbinic teaching 'Do not judge a person until you stand in his place';

xiii. That homosexuals should, ordinarily speaking, not be encouraged to embark upon a marriage. Rather, they should invest their talents and energies in other important areas of endeavour and accomplishment.

To the best of my knowledge, this is one of the first books to be written by an Orthodox rabbi on the subject of homosexuality. As such, I am aware that many areas will require further development and discussion, in a manner beyond the scope of this introduction. I hope and pray that this book will serve as a springboard for further treatment of this subject from an informed perspective.

Notes

1 THE PROHIBITION OF HOMOSEXUAL PRACTICES

1 Chapter 18 (*Parashat Acharei Mot*) and Chapter 20 (*Parashat Kedoshim*) verse 10 ff.
2 See *Torat Cohanim* on Leviticus 14:4; TB *Mo'ed Katan* 28a; TJ *Bikkurim* 2:1. See also Tosafot *Mo'ed Katan*, ibid. *s.v. met* and *s.v. umitah*; *Shabbat* 25a *s.v. karet*; Tosafot *Yevamot* 2a *s.v. eishet*. Cf. Rabbeinu Asher (c.1250–1327), *Tosafot HaRosh Yevamot*, ibid. *s.v. eishet*. See also R. Boronstein (1839–1910), *Teshuvot Avnei Nezer*, *Even HaEzer*, no. 45.
3 See Maimonides, *Mishneh Torah*, *Hilchot Teshuvah* 8:1; *Perush HaMishnah*, *Sanhedrin* ch. 9. According to Rabbi David ibn Zimra (1479–1573) in *Teshuvot HaRadvaz* vol. 8, no. 70, Maimonides does not dispute the talmudic interpretation of *karet* as premature death, but merely adds an alternative possibility, namely that of a 'spiritual excision' in the World to Come. See also the commentary of Nachmanides (1194–1270) on Leviticus 18:29 and his *Sha'ar HaGemul* in *Kitvei HaRamban*, vol. 2, p. 291; Rabbeinu Yonah of Gerona (c.1200–1263), *Sha'arei Teshuvah*, *Sha'ar Shlishi*.
4 The theoretical nature of these punishments, in the majority of cases, is based on the fact that capital punishment, as well as the punishment of *karet*, is only administered in circumstances where the violator of the law did so *b'meizid*, a halachic definition which denotes not only deliberate intention to commit the forbidden act, but also a proper awareness and appreciation of its severity (see Maimonides, *Hilchot Shegagot* 2:2; See also R. Karelitz (1878–1953), *Chazon Ish*, *Yoreh De'ah* 2:15 *s.v. ve'nireh*. See also – with regard to homosexual intercourse – R. Yossef Chaim of Baghdad (1834–1909), *Teshuvot Torah Lishmah*, *Teshuvot b'Inyanim Shonim*, no. 379). Furthermore – with regard to capital punishment – nowadays, for a variety of reasons, Jewish courts are no longer empowered to execute capital punishment. Even during the period of the Second Temple when the Sanhedrin had the authority to execute such punishment it seems evident that such execution rarely took place. The Mishnah (TB *Makkot* 7a) states that a Jewish court that imposes the death penalty even

once in seven years is considered a 'destructive' court. According to one view in the Mishnah, this title applies to a court that imposes the death penalty but once in seventy years. The laws of evidence and the mode of examination to which witnesses were subjected made it difficult – almost impossible – to secure a conviction in the vast majority of cases. Even if the witnesses would withstand the cross-examination and interrogation, capital punishment would generally only be incurred by a person who committed the capital crime in the presence of the witnesses immediately after having received a formal warning, *hatra'ah*, from the witnesses (see Maimonides, *Hilchot Sanhedrin* 12:2; 18:5). The likelihood of violating a prohibition of a sexual nature under such circumstances is remote (see also R. Bulka, *One Man*, p. 39).

In connection with the penalty of *karet* which is 'in the hands of Heaven' different considerations apply. R. Schneur Zalman of Liady (1745–1812) writes in his *Iggeret HaTeshuvah*, ch. 4 (p. 186): 'In every generation there are so many guilty of excision and death who enjoy extended and pleasant days and years!' He explains that the mystical reason for this phenomenon is due to the fact that the 'mechanism' for *karet* only operated 'when Israel was on a higher plane, when the Divine Presence dwelt among Israel in the *Beit HaMikdash*. Then the vitality of the body came only through the Divine soul ... but after they had fallen from their estate, and through their actions caused the mystery of the exile of the Divine Presence ... the benevolence and vitality proceed through the hosts of Heaven and those charged over them to every living physical being in this world, even to vegetation ... Thus even the sinful and deliberate transgressors of Israel may receive vitality for their bodies and animal souls exactly as other living beings do ...' (for an elucidation of several ideas mentioned by R. Schneur Zalman see R. M. Schneerson (1902–1994), *Likkutei Sichot*, vol. 5, p. 104 ff. and the footnotes thereon). Consequently, premature death does not necessarily take place in the literal sense of the word in the post-Temple era. Given that repentance has the effect of annulling the *karet* punishment (see TB *Makkot* 13b) – in contrast to capital punishment, which is executed by the Court, who are not in a position to take repentance into consideration (see R. Landau (1713–1793), *Responsa Noda BiYehudah, Orach Chaim, Mahadura Kamma* no. 35 *s.v. ella she'omer ani*. See also R. Chayim Yosef David Azulai (1724–1806), *Eyn Zocher, Erech Malkut, Ot Chaf*; *Teshuvot Chayim Sha'al*, vol. 2, no. 3, s.v. *u-mei-eyn dugma*; *Tov Ayin*, no. 6 (8a–b); R. Loew (the Maharal) of Prague (c.1512–1609), *Netivot Olam, Netiv HaTeshuvah* ch. 2 and the discussion in R. Engel (1859–1919), *Gilyonei HaShas* on TB *Makkot* 13b and R. M. Schneerson, *Likkutei Sichot*, vol. 9, pp. 111–12 and the footnotes thereon) – the fact that we no longer witness *karet* as they did when the Jewish people were on a 'higher plane' has, somewhat ironically, its advantages. This phenomenon, which is associated with the 'exile' of the Divine Presence, affords additional opportunity for one who is deserving of *karet* to repent and make amends for his sins. See the discussion of R. M. Schneerson, *Torat Menachem – Hitva'aduyot*, 5745, vol. 4, p. 2581. For another explanation of the phenomenon that many people who are deserving of *karet* live to a ripe old age, see R. Chayim ben Attar (1696–1743), *Ohr HaChayim* Leviticus 18:24. See also R. M. Schneerson, *Likkutei Sichot*, vol. 9, p. 117 footnote 20; vol. 22, p. 308. Cf. R. Poczanowski (early twentieth century) *Pardes Yossef* on Exodus 31:14, no. 13; R. Henkin, *Teshuvot B'nei Banim*, vol. 2, *Ma'amar 5*: 'Ha'im tzibbur nichrat'.

None of the above is intended to suggest that man can 'escape' Divine justice. It is a cardinal principle of Judaism that the Almighty rewards and punishes each person according to his deeds. This is the eleventh principle in Maimonides' *Thirteen Principles of Faith*, and there are no rabbinic authorities who do not endorse this principle (although there are differences with regard to the exact nature of reward and punishment). However, such reward or punishment is meted out by the Almighty Himself, Who knows the circumstances, intensity of temptation and challenge that a person encountered before succumbing to sin (see Maimonides *Hilchot Teshuvah* 3:2). As R. Goldberg (*Homosexuality: A Religious and Political Analysis*, p. 28) writes in connection with people who are confronted with the challenges of a homosexual predisposition: '... God measures each violation of the ritual, ethical character, and attitudinal norm not only, and not even primarily, against its objective magnitude, but against the magnitude of the subjective struggle necessary to prevent it. The stronger the inherent drive toward the violation, the greater the Divine mercy toward the violator.'

With regard to the above-mentioned penalty of *karet*, it is also worthy of note that according to several talmudic and midrashic teachings, the punishment of *karet*, as indeed any form of penalty left to the jurisdiction of 'Heaven', is only meted out to those over the age of 20. See TB *Shabbat* 89b; TJ *Bikkurim* 2:1; *Midrash Bemidbar Rabbah* 18:4; the commentary of Rashi on Numbers 16:27; Maimonides, *Perush HaMishnah Sanhedrin*, 7:4; R. Ovadiah of Bertinoro (c.1440– c.1516), commentary on *Pirkei Avot* 5:21.

However, see R. Ashkenazi (1660–1718), *Teshuvot Chacham Tzvi*, no. 49 and R. Moshe Sofer (1762–1839), *Teshuvot Chatam Sofer Yoreh De'ah* no. 155, who argue that this teaching is by no means conclusive and may refer only to specific circumstances or forms of *karet*. In their opinion, punishments by 'Heaven' are indeed, generally speaking, executed, even for those under the age of 20. There is no blanket exemption for teenagers. See the discussion in the various works cited in *Likkutei He'arot* on *Teshuvot Chacham Tzvi*, pp. 54–56; R. Goldstein, *Likkutei He'arot* on *Teshuvot Chatam Sofer Yoreh De'ah*, vol. 2, pp. 393–4.

For a list of sins that incur capital punishment, see Maimonides, *Hilchot Sanhedrin* 15:10–13. For a list of sins that incur the penalty of *karet* see Mishnah *Keritot* 1:1.

5 The common translations of *giluy arayot* as 'adultery' or 'incest' are inadequate as they do not include all the prohibitions that are enumerated in the above-mentioned chapters in Leviticus and which are subject to the halachic strictures regarding *giluy arayot*.

6 See TB *Sanhedrin* 74a; TJ *Shevi'it* 4:2; Maimonides, *Hilchot Yesodei HaTorah* 5:1–2; *Shulchan Aruch Yoreh De'ah* 157:1. R. Krauser, in *Devar HaMelech* on Maimonides' *Hilchot Issurei Bi'ah* 1:9, infers from Maimonides' phraseology that *yehareg ve-al ya'avor* applies to the prohibition against male homosexual intercourse, as it does to other forbidden sexual relationships. R. Krauser then proceeds to argue that other authorities (particularly Tosafot on TB *Yevamot* 54b *s.v. be-zachur mahu*; and TB *Sanhedrin* 73a *s.v. chayavei keritot*) may disagree with Maimonides on this matter. However, an explicit reference to the obligation to forfeit one's life rather than perform the act of in *mishkav zachar* can be found in R. Yom Tov ibn Asevilli (early fourteenth century), *Chiddushei HaRitva* on TB *Pesachim* 25a. See also R. Shlomoh ben Aderet (1235–1310), *Teshuvot HaRashba*, vol. 1, no. 1237. There is some debate whether this stricture applies to one who is under threat of being sodomised. According to some views, a person is not obliged to choose death rather than submit himself – passively – to the homosexual act; see R. Emden (1697–1776), *Birat Migdal Oz, pinah aleph, Even Bochen*, section 60. R. Emden refers to the views that a woman is not obliged to forfeit her life rather than submit herself to rape (see R. Moshe Isserles, the Rama (c.1530– 1572), *Yoreh De'ah* ibid) because she is merely *karka olam* – a technical halachic term employed to describe passive rather than active accommodation for sexual assault. By the same token, R. Emden argues that the victim of sodomite rape is not required to give up his life rather than 'accommodate' the assailants.

Whether the principle of *yehareig v'al ya'avor* applies when subjected to coercion to commit an act of bestiality, see *Chiddushei HaRitva*, ibid.; R. Nissim of Gerona (c.1290– c.1375), *Chiddushei HaRan* on TB *Sanhedrin* 74a. See also *Teshuvot Penei Yehoshua* cited below, note 11; R. Perlman (1835–1896), *Ohr Gadol*, no. 1 (8a); and R. Feinstein (1895– 1986), *Teshuvot Iggerot Moshe, Yoreh De'ah*, vol. 2, no. 127, section 6. Regarding forfeiting one's life rather than cohabiting with a *niddah* (a woman who is ritually impure after menstruation), see the references cited below in Chapter 4, note 13.

With regard to the difference between *giluy arayot* and other crimes, it should be mentioned that there are exceptions to the rule. In circumstances where a person is being forced to violate *any* commandment publicly (in the presence of ten Jews) where the agenda is, not the personal gain of the assailant, but simply an attack on the religious beliefs of the victim (*le-ha'aviro al dato*), one is obliged to forfeit one's life rather than succumb to pressure and violate the commandment. Similarly, in circumstances where the Jewish people are being forced en masse to desert Judaism by tyrants such as Nebuchadnezzar (*sha'at ha-shmad*), one is also obliged to forfeit one's life rather than violate any commandment of the Torah, even if the attempted coercion takes place in total privacy. The obligation to do so comes under the commandment 'to sanctify God's Name' (*kiddush ha-Shem*); see Maimonides' *Hilchot Yesodei HaTorah* 5:1–2; *Shulchan Aruch Yoreh De'ah* 157:1.

In circumstances where a particular *mitzvah* is being severely undermined, as a result of widespread laxity and neglect, it is appropriate and praiseworthy for the pious person to persevere in the fulfilment of the particular *mitzvah* even in the face of life-threatening situations (in order to impress upon society the severity of the *mitzvah* at hand); see R. Caro (1488–1575) *Kesef Mishneh* on Maimonides, ibid., paragraph 4; *Bet Yosef* on Tur *Yoreh De'ah* ibid.; R. Shabbtai HaCohen, the *Shach* (1622–1663) *Siftei Cohen* ibid., no. 2.

Whether or not it is permissible for a person to give up their life 'voluntarily', rather than perform a sin of commission or omission (in circumstances where the above-mentioned considerations do not apply) is a subject of much dispute and debate. See Maimonides, ibid., paragraph 4; Tosafot *Avodah Zarah* 27b *s.v. Yachol*; Tur and *Shulchan Aruch* ibid.

7 Maimonides, *Hilchot Issurei Bi'ah* 1:14, based on Mishnah and Talmud *Sanhedrin* 54a–b. See also *Tur, Shulchan Aruch* and commentaries, *Even HaEzer*, chapter 24.

In addition to the above-mentioned verses in Leviticus, the Talmud, ibid., explains the verse in Deuteronomy 23:18 '... and there shall be no *kadesh* amongst the Children of Israel' as a reference to a male who is 'designated for homosexual congress'. Cf. Targum *Onkelos*, Rashi and Nachmanides on Deuteronomy, ibid. Nachmanides explains the verse, in light of the halachic midrash *Sifrei*, to mean: '... and so the verse issues a warning to the Courts regarding one who is designated to be sodomised by males [the male prostitute]. The "*kadesh*" in this verse must be understood in the same vein as that which is written (Kings I 14:24): "The male prostitute was also in the land; [they did all the abominations of the nations]". In addition to the forewarning directed at the transgressors themselves, the Torah here warns the Beth Din that they should not allow the male prostitute to stand [available for passers by] at the crossroads by the road, in a manner that is known to occur in Egypt, whereby such prostitutes stand on the road, veil their faces like women, ready to perform this abominable act.'

In addition to the negative commandment forbidding all male homosexual intercourse, there is an additional commandment forbidding (and imposing additional severity on) male homosexual intercourse between father and son and between a man and his father's brother. Such incestuous homosexuality is referred to in Leviticus 18:7; 14 ('The nakedness of your father ... you shall not uncover ... The nakedness of your father's brother ... you shall not uncover') as interpreted in *Sanhedrin* 54b. See Maimonides, *Sefer HaMitzvot* Negative Commandments nos. 342 and 351; *Hilchot Shegagot* 4:1 (end); *Sefer HaChinuch* Commandment nos. 189 and 199.

8 Leviticus 18:6. See Maimonides (note 7) 21:1; *Shulchan Aruch Even HaEzer* 20:1. See, however, Nachmanides in his 'Critique' to *Sefer HaMitzvot* Negative Commandment no. 353 (cited in R. Shmuel ben Uri Shraga Feivush (c.1640– c.1700), *Bet Shmuel, Even HaEzer* 20:1). See also R. Eliyahu of Vilna (1720–1797), *Biurei HaGra* to *Even HaEzer* 20:1 and *Otzar HaPoskim Even HaEzer* 20:5.

9 See Rama, *Yoreh De'ah* 157:1 and *Siftei Cohen*, ibid. no. 10. See also R. Feinstein, *Teshuvot Iggerot Moshe, Even HaEzer*, vol. 1, no. 56 with regard to a person who is subjected to force, compelling him to gaze at a naked woman with the intention of fornicating with her, that he would have to forfeit his life rather than submit to the coercion and violate the prohibition of *histaklut* (gazing) *per se*.

10 See Numbers 15:29; TB *Berachot* 12b; Maimonides, *Sefer HaMitzvot*, negative commandment No.47; see also Deuteronomy 23:10; TB *Ketubot* 46a; Tosafot on TB *Avodah Zarah* 20b s.v. *shelo* (Cf R. Te'omim (c.1727–1792), *Peri Megadim, Petichah Kollelet*, part 5, subsection 34; R. Grodzinski (1863–1940), *Teshuvot Achiezer*, vol. 3, no. 24, sub section 5 s.v. *v'od nireh*); Maimonides, *Hilchot Issurei Bi'ah* 21:23 – *Shulchan Aruch Even HaEzer* 21:1–7. (See also R. Feinstein, *Teshuvot Iggerot Moshe, Even HaEzer*, vol. 1, no. 69.)

[The prohibition against indulging in sexual fantasy (outside of marriage) also applies to women: See *Sefer HaChinuch* commandment no. 188 (end); R. Halberastam (1904–1994), *Teshuvot Divrei Yatziv, Even HaEzer*, no. 35.]

11 However, not all these prohibitions are subject to the rule of *yehareg v'al ya'avor* (forbidden even in life-threatening situations). See R. Yehoshua ben Yosef of Cracow (d. 1648), *Teshuvot P'nei Yehoshua*, vol. 2, no. 44 and R. Karelitz, *Chazon Ish, Yoreh De'ah* 104:3, that masturbation is not governed by this stricture as it does not come under the category of *giluy arayot*.

Notwithstanding the severity of the prohibition of masturbation (see Maimonides (note 7) 21:18 and *Shulchan Aruch Even HaEzer* 23:1–7 and commentaries) there is, according to some 'weighty' authorities, a 'caveat' to the law. Based on R. Yehudah HeChasid (c.1150–1217), *Sefer Chasidim* (no. 176), some authorities rule that if a person is on the verge of committing a more serious prohibition – for example, adultery or co-habitation with his wife whilst she is in a state of ritual impurity after having experienced her menstrual flow – 'it is better for him to spill the seed' by masturbation rather than risk succumbing to the more severe sin. Afterwards, the person is obliged to take upon himself the appropriate penitential measures. See R. Moshe b. Yitzchak Yehudah Lema (c.1605–1658), *Chelkat Mechokek* and R. Shmuel b. Shraga Feivush (c.1640– c.1700), *Bet Shmuel Even HaEzer* 23:1, who cite the words of the *Sefer Chasidim* in this context. See, however, R. Azulai, *Petach Eynayim* on TB *Niddah* 13a, who interprets the *Sefer Chasidim* in such a manner that it does not serve as a precedent for the ruling as articulated by *Chelkat Mechokek* and *Bet Shmuel*.

The reason for this rather 'curious' ruling (we do not usually find halachic authorities sanctioning the commitment of transgressions in order to curb temptation for more severe transgressions) may be debated. R. Berlin (1817–1893), the Netziv, and his correspondent, R. Moshe Tarashchanskij (1858–1942), *Teshuvot Meishiv Davar*, part 2, nos. 43–44, actually understand this ruling as a general principle in *halachah*: if a person is bent on committing an infraction of *halachah*, he ought to be advised to violate a lighter transgression in order to avoid violating a more severe transgression. The Netziv suggests that this principle is the subject of a dispute between the commentaries on the Talmud. TB *Chagigah* 16a, *Moed Katan* 17a and *Kiddushin* 40a state: 'If a person sees that his evil inclination is overwhelming him, he should go to a place where he is not known, clothe himself in black and wrap himself in black, and he should do what his heart desires, but he should not desecrate God's Name in public'. Rashi (s.v. *heicha*) and Tosafot (s.v. *v'ya'aseh*), on *Chagigah*, explain that the Gemara counsels a person who has succumbed to his inclination to sin to do so in a manner that does not entail the additional burden of sin, namely that of *chillul HaShem* (the desecration of God's Name). Rav Hai Gaon (939–1038), cited by Rashi (*Moed Katan*, ibid., s.v. *mah she-libo chafetz*) and Rabbeinu Chananel (d. c.1055), cited by Tosafot (*Chagigah* and *Moed Katan* ibid., s.v. *im ro'eh*; *Kiddushin* ibid., s.v. *v'ya'aseh*; see also Rashi, *Kiddushin*, ibid., s.v. *yilbash*), however, explain that the Gemara never intended to prescribe a formula for sinning. Rather, the Gemara means that travelling to a place where one is unknown, and hence not respected, wearing humbling attire etc., will help the potential sinner subdue his passions and he will thereby refrain from sinning. Consequently, the Netziv states that the ruling of the *Sefer Chasidim* and the subsequent authorities who counsel one who is on the verge of engaging in forbidden intercourse to 'spill his seed' reflects the view of Rashi and Tosafot, in contra-distinction to the view of Rabbeinu Chananel and Rav Hai Gaon. On this analysis of *Sefer Chasidim* and the Codes who cite his ruling, the *halachah* does not actually provide a sanction for anyone to commit a minor transgression. It is merely providing sound advice and counselling 'spiritual economising' to the determined sinner: if you are going to sin, do so minimally rather than maximally. (See also Rabbeinu Asher, *Tosafot HaRosh* on *Kiddushin* ibid., s.v. *v'ya'aseh*.)

A completely different, albeit most novel, understanding of the ruling of the *Sefer Chasidim* is advanced by R. Kluger (1785–1869) in his *Chochmat Shlomo (Even HaEzer*, ibid., no. 1) and in a similar vein by R. Gruenfeld (1881–1930) in his *Teshuvot Maharshag*, vol. 2, no. 243, *s.v. v'hinei lo*. The gist of their explanation is that the prohibition of *hashchatat zera* ('producing seed in vain') only prohibits masturbation when it is performed for no *positive* purpose; that is, a purpose that Torah teachings inform us is positive. Consequently, if a person feels that he is on the verge of committing a serious prohibition which he could avoid by 'spilling his seed' in masturbation, he would not – by definition – be producing his seed 'in vain'. In such a case, his masturbation is regarded as a preventative measure, performed in order to *avoid transgression*. This means that, according to the intrinsic meaning of the term 'spilling seed in vain', he *has not really committed this sin*. (This may be analogous to the injunction of *bal tashchit* (Maimonides, *Hilchot Melachim* 6:8–10), destroying useful human resources. If the destruction of an item is performed for a constructive purpose, it does not fall under the rubric of this transgression, so that, for example, when one is unable to access earth for the purposes of fulfilling the *mitzvah* of *kisuy ha-dam* – covering the blood of an undomesticated animal or bird after ritual slaughter (Leviticus 17:13; Maimonides, *Hilchot Shechitah*, ch. 14; *Shulchan Aruch Yoreh De'ah* ch. 28) – a garment may be burned to provide ashes for this purpose, even though burning a garment would ordinarily be forbidden under the rubric of *bal tashchit* (see TB *Chullin* 88b; R. Schneur Zalman of Liady, *Shulchan Aruch HaRav, Hilchot Shemirat Guf VaNefesh*, no. 14). The injunction of *bal tashchit*, by its very definition, does not include 'constructive destruction'. In a similar vein, R. Gruenfeld suggests that the injunction against *hashchatat zera*, by its very definition, does not include 'constructive destruction' or waste of seed.) R. Gruenfeld also states his view that, in light of the above, it would be correct to 'spill seed' even in order to save oneself from the violation of a rabbinical sexual prohibition. Once it has been established that such 'spilling of seed' is not considered to be completely 'in vain', it follows that such a practice must be preferable even to the transgression of a rabbinical edict.

It ought to be mentioned that the logic of *Chochmat Shlomo* and *Teshuvot Maharshag* is evidently rejected by a number of prominent halachic authorities. The responsa literature features many a responsum written about the propriety of a man procuring semen for the purpose of fertility testing or AIH (artificial insemination using the husband's sperm). The controversy with regard to this procedure also revolves around the issue of *hashchatat zera*. Whilst it is currently, almost universally, accepted that a man may, in certain circumstances, provide sperm for such testing – preferably by the retrieval of the sperm from his wife following cohabitation – the responsa literature on this issue is fraught with debate. Even those authorities who allow it do so on the basis that the purpose of the procurement of seed *is for procreation*. Since the prohibition of *hashchatat zera* is seen as the very antithesis of procreation, this yields the conclusion of some halachic authorities that where the spilling of the seed is done in order to facilitate procreation, there is no prohibition; see R. Grodzinski, *Teshuvot Achiezer*, vol. 3, 24:4; R. Schwadron (1835–1911), *Teshuvot Maharsham*, vol. 3, no. 268; R. Yossef, *Teshuvot Yabia Omer*, vol. 2, *Even HaEzer*, no. 1. However, none of these authorities indicates that the procurement of seed is permitted for any other purpose than procreation, however positive and 'constructive' it is. This suggests that the argumentation of Rabbis Kluger and Gruenfeld is by no means representative of mainstream *halachah*. (See, however, the presentation of *Chochmat Shlomo*, who, in a rather homiletical style – not frequently attributed such weight in the resolution of a halachic problem – suggests that 'spilling seed' in order to avoid transgression is also a form of procreation! The Hebrew word *toldot*, which usually refers to progeny, is also interpreted to refer to the 'spiritual offspring' of the righteous man, namely his *mitzvot*; see *Bereishit Rabbah* 30:6, cited in Rashi on Genesis 6:9. Consequently, the '*mitzvah*' of abstaining from violating a severe prohibition is in itself a form of procreation – sufficient to justify the act of *hashchatat zera*.)

However, notwithstanding any qualms that may be raised with regard to the above-mentioned thesis, the ruling of the *Chelkat Mechokek* and the *Bet Shmuel* – whatever its rationale may be – may provide rabbis and counsellors with useful guidelines when instructing homosexuals. In what almost inevitably amounts to commitment to lifelong celibacy, there are bound to be situations in which some homosexuals will find themselves on the verge of violating the biblical prohibition of male-to-male intercourse or the rabbinic extensions of that prohibition. Also, in the event of practising homosexuals attempting to return to the ways of the Torah and abstain from all forbidden acts, it may be nearly impossible for them to change their *modus vivendi* from one extreme to another. In all such situations, it is possible that the mentor may be justified in taking recourse to the views expounded by the above-mentioned authorities when forming their advice to their charges.

12 Leviticus 18:3.

13 *Torat Cohanim* on Leviticus (previous note) cited in Maimonides, *Sefer HaMitzvot*, Negative Commandment no. 353 and Tur, *Even HaEzer*, ch. 20. Cf. R. Sa'adiah Gaon (882–942), commentary on Leviticus 18:23 (cited also in *Perush Rasag* on Genesis pp. 388–9, note 183).

14 The Gemara, TB *Yevamot* 76a, cites the opinion of Rav Huna that women who are '*mesolelot*' [generally understood as a reference to their engagement in lesbian activities] with each other are disqualified from marrying *cohanim*. Rav Huna considers this practice to be a form of licentiousness that comes under the category of *zenut* and therefore maintains that, in light of the injunction in Leviticus 21:7 which prohibits a *cohen* from marrying a *zonah* (a 'harlot'), women who have indulged in such activities cannot subsequently marry and have relations with a *cohen*. See R. Feinstein, *Dibrot Moshe* on *Shabbat*, vol. 2, ch. 59, section 34 and R. Greinemann, *Chiddushim U'bi'urim* on *Shabbat*, ch. 13 (42d) *s.v. leima*, who explain that,

on a biblical level (*mid'Oraita*), the lesbian activity does not render her a *zonah*. This is merely a rabbinic stringency (*chumrah deRabbanan*).

[Rashi, in his commentary on TB *Shabbat* (note 17), explains that Rav Huna would consider such a woman ineligible for marriage with a *cohen gadol* (High Priest) only. This is because, whilst a woman who has been *mesolelet* is not considered to be a *zonah*, she is nevertheless not considered a proper 'virgin' (*betulah*). The *cohen gadol* must marry a girl whose hymen and virginity is still intact. See R. Feinstein, *Dibrot Moshe* on *Shabbat*, vol. 2, ch. 59, section 34 for a suggestion as to why Rashi maintains that even R. Huna does not forbid such a woman to marry an ordinary *cohen*. R. Feinstein argues that, since lesbian relationships involve no intercourse (*bi'ah*) in the halachic sense of the word, Rashi is of the opinion that it is inconceivable for a woman who had engaged in lesbian activity to be categorised as a *zonah*, a term which by its very definition is reserved for a woman who had engaged in some forbidden form of *intercourse*.]

However, Rava disagrees with him and says that, even according to the stringent opinion of Rabbi Elazar (which, incidentally, is not accepted as normative *halachah* – see Maimonides, *Hilchot Issurei Bi'ah* 18:2; *Shulchan Aruch Even HaEzer* 6:8) – who says that if a woman has engaged in 'casual' premarital sex even with a man of 'untainted' lineage (whom she would be allowed to marry according to Jewish Law), she is forbidden to marry a *cohen* – a woman who has engaged in sexual activities with another woman may marry a *cohen* because her activities cannot be described as *zenut*; such interaction between one woman and another is *peritzuta be'alma* (mere lewdness). See TJ *Gittin* 8:8 where the dispute between the Amoraic sages, Rabbi Elazar and Rava, seems to be attributed to the schools of Shammai and Hillel respectively (instead of the term *mesolelot* employed by the Babylonian Talmud, the Jerusalem Talmud uses the term *mesaldot*). However, based on the teaching of the *Torat Cohanim*, cited in note 13, it is understood by the commentaries on the Talmud as well as the authors of the halachic codes that this entire debate is only with regard to the status of the woman who has engaged in such activities: whether or not she comes under the category of a *zonah* and is forbidden to marry a *cohen*. All opinions, however, would agree that such activities are forbidden. Therefore, whilst the halachic ruling is in accordance with the opinion of Rava that such activities do not render the woman disqualified in terms of marrying a *cohen*, it equally endorses the 'unanimous' injunction against the lesbian activities *per se*.

For the exact definition of which activities come under the category of '*mesolelot*' see note 17.

15 *Mishneh Torah, Hilchot Issurei Bi'ah* 21:8. See also R. Moshe of Coucy (thirteenth century), *Sefer Mitzvot Gadol*, no. 126.
16 See *Shulchan Aruch Even HaEzer* 20:2.
17 The exact definition of the Hebrew term *mesolelot* is subject to dispute. Rashi *Yevamot* (note 14) *s.v. ha-mesolelot* (cited in *Bet Yosef, Perishah* and *Levush Even HaEzer*, previous note) explains that this term refers to women who engage each other in a 'manner similar to male-to-female intercourse, [they do so by] rubbing their genitalia against each other'. Rashi cites the Gemara (TB *Sanhedrin* 69b) which discusses the case of a woman who is *mesolelet* with her son who is yet a minor and the son initiates intimate contact with her. (There it is clear that the term denotes, at the very least, contact between the male and female sexual organs.) Cf. Maimonides, *Perush HaMishnah, Sanhedrim* 7:4 and R. Menachem HaMe'iri (c.1249– c.1306), *Bet HaBechirah* on *Yevamot* (p. 275), who explain that the term *mesolelot* is related to the term *mesilah* (a path on which one walks). HaMe'iri explains that women who perform this practice simply 'trample' on each other as some does on a flat surface without making any penetration. Tosafot *Yevamot* (note 14) *s.v. Ha-mesolelot*, however, cite the opinion of the disciple and son-in-law of Rashi, R. Yehudah ben Nathan (early twelfth century), the Rivan, who explains that the term *mesolelot* refers to (married) women who, *post coitus*, 'transfer the semen that with which their husbands had impregnated them into each other's vaginal canal'. This interpretation is also cited, alongside Rashi's interpretation, in the *Bet Yosef Even HaEzer* (previous note). *Maggid Mishnah* on Maimonides (note 15) only cites the interpretation of the Rivan. As explained by R. Navon (eighteenth century), *Kiryat Melech Rav*, no. 26 (89b) and R. Kallir (1728–1801) – a disciple of R. Yechezkel Landau, author of the *Noda BiYehudah* – in his work *Cheker Halachah, chakirah* no. 14, according to the interpretation of the Rivan, the issue of *mesolelot* has no bearing on lesbian activity in the 'conventional' sense of the term. Nevertheless, since the interpretation of Rashi is cited by numerous later

codifiers as the definitive one and is implied by Maimonides (note 15) and the *Shulchan Aruch* (note 16), as has been argued by R. Yoel Teitelbaum, the late Rebbe of Satmar (1888–1979), *Teshuvot Divrei Yo'el*, vol. 2, *Even HaEzer*, no. 107, p. 411, and since, according to Rashi, it would appear that the prohibition of *mesolelot* applies to all forms of lesbian activity, normative *halachah* would proscribe lesbian activity. (My contention that according to Rashi the contact of the genitalia is not essential to the prohibition against lesbian practices is based on the fact that such relationships are defined as *peritzuta b'alma* (mere lewdness), a category of behaviour which denotes – in this context – engagement in erotic interplay between two people and is therefore not dependent upon genital contact, since even such contact does not constitute intercourse when performed by two women. See Rashi on TB *Sotah* 26b *s.v. derech eivarim peritzuta b'alma* who defines such 'lewdness' as two people (in his case a man and a woman) lying together in the nude (see also Rashi on TB *Gittin* 89a, s.v. *peritzuta b'alma*). See also *Dibrot Moshe* on Tractate *Shabbat*, vol. 2, ch. 6, section 35, who refers to touching the genitals 'with the hand' (i.e. mutual masturbation) in his description of '*nashim ha-mesolelot*'). See also the cryptic remarks of R. Schneur Zalman of Lublin (d. 1902), *Teshuvot Torat Chesed*, *Even HaEzer*, no. 43 in a footnote to subsection 2 (109d) where, apparently, female masturbation is associated with *mesolelot* and forbidden under the same principle. See also R. Yosef Chayim of Baghdad, *Teshuvot Torah Lishmah* (section entitled '*Sod Yesharim*'), no. 504, who also suggests that the prohibition against female masturbation is rooted in the prohibition against lesbian practices. All this supports my contention that contact of the genitalia of the two women is not essential to the prohibition against lesbian practices: if it were, the extrapolations of these two authorities would be unfounded.

The prohibition of *mesolelot* as derived from the *Torat Cohanim* has raised a problem with regard to another relevant discussion in the Gemara, TB *Shabbat* 65a–b. There, the Gemara discusses various strictures that an Amoraic sage imposed upon his daughters. Amongst other things, 'the father of Shmuel ... did not allow his [virgin] daughters to sleep together with each other [in the same bed]'. The Gemara then discusses the reason for the father of Shmuel's objection to such a practice. The Gemara suggests: 'does this support the teaching of Rav Huna, for Rav Huna said that women who are *mesolelot* with each other are disqualified from marrying a *cohen*?'. Accordingly, it is possible that Shmuel's father was in agreement with Rav Huna and therefore did not want his daughters to sleep in such close proximity to each other which could possibly lead to the type of behaviour that would render them disqualified for marriage with a *cohen*. The Gemara then rejects this suggestion and says that there is no reason to assume that the father of Shmuel shared Rav Huna's view (i.e. the father of Shmuel would not agree with the strict stance of Rav Huna, rather he would take the view of the latter's disputant (note 14), who holds that the practice of *mesolelot* does not render the woman unsuitable for a *cohen*). The reason that the father of Shmuel was particular that his daughters should not sleep huddled up together was 'so that they should not become accustomed to [sleeping in physical contact] with another body'. Rashi explains that he was concerned that this habit may make them desire to sleep with a man [before they were married], and it was from this that Shmuel's father sought to protect his daughters. Consequently, there is no evidence from the Sage's fatherly instructions that he supported the view of Rav Huna.

Some commentaries (R. M. Sofer, *Hagahot Chatam Sofer al HaShas*, R. Navon, *Kiryat Melech Rav*, ibid. and R. Feinstein *Dibrot Moshe* ibid.) are puzzled by the fact that the Gemara initially suggests that what motivated the father of Shmuel to instruct his daughters against sleeping with each other was the 'controversial' teaching of Rav Huna. Surely, even if the father of Shmuel did not agree with Rav Huna about the consequences of *mesolelot* in terms of marrying a *cohen*, he would not have wanted them to engage in this practice, which is forbidden according to all opinions under the category of 'the practices of the Egyptians', as taught in *Torat Cohanim* (and cited in the halachic codes). *Chatam Sofer* adds that, even if his daughters were minors at the time that he issued his prohibition, Shmuel's father would have been obliged to prevent them from transgressing such a prohibition on the grounds of the rabbinically mandated law of *chinnuch*, whereby every father has to make sure that his young children abstain from such sins. (This question is also cited in the name of the *Chatam Sofer* by R. Haas (d. 1847) on *Shulchan Aruch Even HaEzer* 20:2.)

R. Greinemann (note 14) suggests that Shmuel's father never really suspected that his daughters would indulge in lesbian activity and the mere fact that such activity is forbidden would have been insufficient grounds to impose the strictures of separation upon his daughters. However, if Shmuel's father followed the view of R. Huna, who holds that lesbian activity would effect a disqualification (*pesula*) in the woman that would render her ineligible to marry a *cohen*, the Gemara suggested that it may have been reasonable for him to impose an additional precautionary measure to avoid the possibility – however remote – of such a stigma. In a similar vein, R. Feinstein (note 14) suggests that the Gemara maintained that, according to Rav Huna, who holds that *mesolelot* are ineligible to marry a *cohen*, it may be reasonable to enforce a rather extreme precautionary measure, as the father of Shmuel did when he forbade his daughters from sleeping huddled together, because in the unlikely event that this would lead to lesbian activity, it would not only entail the violation of a prohibition, but it would bring about a 'stumbling block (*michshol*)' for the *cohen*, who may end up marrying the *mesolelet*.

R. Feinstein also suggests that it is possible that the Gemara never meant to suggest that Shmuel's father shared Rav Huna's view with regard to the ineligibility of women who have indulged in the practice of *mesolelot* for becoming the wives of *cohanim*. The Gemara's initial suggestion was merely that Shmuel's father's objection to his daughters' sleeping together may support the prohibition *implied* by Rav Huna's teaching – to which even Rav Huna's disputants would agree – namely that it is forbidden for women to be *mesolelot* with each other. (Were this not the case, such a practice could not render them ineligible for *cohanim*.)

Yet, why did the Gemara not cite the teaching in *Torat Cohanim*, in which the prohibition of *mesolelot* is *explicit*? According to R. Feinstein, the Gemara did not cite the teaching of *Torat Cohanim* as the source for such a prohibition because, although the teaching is *explicit* in that source, it could leave room for doubt. The text of the *Torat Cohanim* mentions four practices which are labelled as 'Egyptian practices'. These are (a) a man marrying a man; (b) a woman marrying a woman; (c) a woman marrying two men; and (d) a man marrying a woman and her daughter. This conglomeration is somewhat odd, says R. Feinstein. For practices (a) and (c) are severe prohibitions which are forbidden under the Noachide code for all of mankind. In contrast, practice (d) is not forbidden under the Noachide code (and is a less severe prohibition even for Jewish people) whilst practice (b) is not forbidden at all under the Noachide code, and even in Jewish law it is probably a rabbinical prohibition. This could lead one to the erroneous conclusion that this teaching of the *Torat Cohanim* is not a 'halachic' one, on which the legal status of any of the activities described can be based. One may have maintained that the *Torat Cohanim* merely mentions an array of practices which are symptomatic of a hedonistic society which indulges in the pursuit of pleasure for pleasure's sake. Whilst not all the practices may be 'forbidden' in the strict sense of the word, this would not stop the *Torat Cohanim* from mentioning them in tandem because of the common factor that they all share. Therefore the Gemara cited the teaching of Rav Huna in which it is evident that the practice of *mesolelot* is not just 'frowned upon' but is actually forbidden (as is evident from the fact that Rav Huna holds that a woman who has engaged in such a practice is not allowed to marry a *cohen*).

18 R. Falk (1680–1756), *Perishah* on *Even ha-Ezer* 20:2; R. Y. Teitelbaum (note 17), p. 110 *s.v.* *ve'ha'emet* (end). See also R. Feinstein (note 14), p. 401, who is inclined to say that, according to Maimonides (note 15), lesbian activity is only forbidden under rabbinical injunction. R. Feinstein argues that whilst the first reason that Maimonides presents for the absence of biblically-mandated corporal punishment (*malkut*) for lesbian activity ('since there is no *specific* prohibition against it') would imply that the prohibition itself is of biblical origin, the second reason that Maimonides offers ('no sexual intercourse takes place') implies that there is no infraction of a biblical commandment in lesbian activity. R. Feinstein suggests that Maimonides sees lesbian activity as analogous to non-penetrative sexual activity between men and women who are forbidden to each other. Maimonides considers the latter to be forbidden on biblical grounds (see note 8), because such activity could lead to proper penetrative intercourse. By the same token, lesbian activity – which, in contrast to heterosexual unions, does not have the potential for penetrative intercourse in the halachic sense of the word – is certainly not forbidden on biblical grounds. According to R. Feinstein, Maimonides cannot conceive of a biblical infraction for lesbianism, where – by definition – no 'intercourse' can really take place.

However, this argument is by no means convincing, for it is possible that whilst non-penetrative intercourse does not constitute a violation of a biblical commandment under the rubric of *giluy arayot* (unless it has the potential to lead to proper intercourse), it is nevertheless forbidden under the category of 'Egyptian practices', which includes a broader range of actions beyond those that may reasonably be included under the parameters of *giluy arayot*. According to this interpretation, the two reasons Maimonides provides would be understood as follows: the fact that 'there is no specific prohibition against' lesbian activity explains why there is no biblical corporal punishment for such transgression even though it is biblically forbidden under the commandment 'According to the deeds of the Land of Egypt …'. The fact that 'no sexual intercourse takes place at all' explains why there is no biblical corporal punishment for such transgression, under the injunction '*lo tikrevu* – do not approach'. For as R. Feinstein explains, since 'no sexual intercourse takes place' any lesbian activity could not possibly lead to sexual intercourse. According to this interpretation of Maimonides, the views of those authorities (cited below, in notes 19 and 20) – who are of the opinion that Maimonides considers female homosexual practices to be biblically pro-scribed – are not contradicted by the reasons Maimonides provides for the absence of biblical *malkut*.

Alternatively, one could argue that there are no two reasons given by Maimonides as R. Feinstein suggests. Rather the two factors that Maimonides mentions are components of one essential reason. If there were to be a specific, and categorically defined lesbian act that would be forbidden by the Torah, this transgression may indeed have been punishable by biblical *malkut* (even though other acts may have been forbidden under the same title – commandment). However, since there is no categorically defined lesbian act that is forbidden under the commandment 'according to the deeds of the Land of Egypt …' – as 'no sexual intercourse takes place' and the prohibition encompasses any activity which falls under the category of *peritzuta* (as explained above in note 17) – the commandment falls under the classification of *lav shebichlalut*, the violation of which does not incur biblical *malkut*. For an understanding of this interpretation of Maimonides, see the thesis of R. Joseph B. Soloveitchik (1903–1993), *Reshimot Shiurim*, p. 192 ff.

19 R. Moshe di Trani in his *Kiryat Sefer* on Maimonides (note 15) and R. Jaffe, *Levush Malchut* on *Even ha-Ezer* 20:2. For an understanding of the concept '*lav shbichlalut*' see Maimonides, *Sefer HaMitzvot*, '*Sharashim*', no. 9; *Hilchot Sanhedrin* 18:3 and the commentaries thereon.
20 R. Rozin, *Teshuvot Tzofnat Pa'aneach*, Dvinsk, vol. 1, no. 90 and no. 113; Warsaw, no. 164 and Jerusalem, no. 6, who suggests that whether or not the prohibition of *mesolelot* is biblical or rabbinical is the subject of a dispute between Maimonides (who, he maintains, opines that it is a biblical prohibition) and Tosafot (*Yevamot* 82b *s.v. Tenan*) who indicate that it is a rabbinical prohibition.

A 'middle way' is suggested, albeit tentatively, in *Kiryat Melech Rav* (note 17) who suggests that it is possible that lesbian activity *per se* is only a rabbinic prohibition, whereas 'lesbian marriages' – namely institutionalised relationships between two women – are biblically forbidden. (See also *Teshuvot Torah Lishmah,* cited in note 17, where it is suggested that lesbian practices – like female masturbation – are only forbidden when performed on a regular basis, because only then does such behaviour fall under the category of Egyptian 'statutes'.) This would add an extra severity to the recent campaign in certain circles for the recognition of lesbian 'marriages'.
21 It is as a result of this dispute that contemporary writers are somewhat vague in their discussions of lesbianism. For example, R. Bleich, *Judaism and Healing*, p. 69, writes: 'Lesbianism *is included in the Biblical admonition* against participation in the deviant sexual practices associated with the Egyptians and Canaanites of antiquity, but it is not a capital offence'. This statement gives the impression that lesbian activity is biblically forbidden, but the cautious phraseology allows for some flexibility in its interpretation.
22 See also R. Rozin (note 20). R. Lamm, *Judaism and the Modern Attitude to Homosexuality*, p. 197 writes, 'Jewish Law treated the female homosexual more leniently than the male. It considered lesbianism an *issur*, an ordinary religious violation, rather than *arayot*, a specifically sexual infraction regarded much more severely than *issur* ….' Spero, *Further Examination of the Halakhic Status of Homosexuality* (p. 6 and note 37 thereon) argues somewhat tentatively that the designation of female homosexual practices as 'non-*giluy*

arayot' infractions, means that certain problems regarding psychological 'treatment' of female homosexuality 'are lessened'; for an understanding of this see Chapter 2, note 9.

Paul, in his 'Troubled Times for Orthodox Homosexuals', writes: 'Female homosexuality suffers no similar biblical damnation but is widely discussed in the teachings of the rabbis. There it is denounced as an obscenity, tantamount to harlotry and warranting, according to the strictest, the punishment of "lashes".'

Paul's statements are inaccurate. As has been demonstrated, the penalty of disciplinary lashes (*makat mardut*) is advocated by Maimonides for those who engage in lesbian activity and no authority seems to dispute him on this matter. Indeed, *makat mardut* is a statutory punishment – administered at the discretion of the Bet Din – for the violation of rabbinic law (or even biblical transgressions that do not incur a biblically prescribed penalty) and does not necessarily indicate any special severity. *Makat mardut* are administered by Jewish courts to people who violate the rabbinical prohibitions related to Shabbat (Maimonides, *Hilchot Shabbat* 1:3; 6:8; 27:2); eat *matzah* on the eve of Pesach (Maimonides, *Hilchot Chametz u-Matzah* 6:2); drink unsupervised milk (Maimonides, *Hilchot Ma'achalot Asurot* 3:15) or wine handled by gentiles (ibid. 11:3); and eat in unhygienic conditions (ibid. 17:30). Likewise, members of the Jewish community who refuse to contribute to the local charity collections, violate the injunction of *bal tashchit* by destroying useful human resources (other than trees), and members of the priestly tribe (*cohanim*) who walk within four cubits of a grave are amongst the candidates for *makat mardut* (see Maimonides, *Hilchot Mattenot Aniyim* 7:10; *Hilchot Melachim* 6:10; *Hilchot Evel* 3:13).

Another inaccuracy, regarding the penalty of *makat mardut* for women who engage in homosexual activity, occurs in R. Bulka (note 4), p. 61: 'The penalty for such activity is not of a capital nature; it is limited to flagellation and also subject to the requirement of prior forewarning and its taking place in the presence of two eyewitnesses'. See R. Shlomoh Duran (1400–1467), *Teshuvot HaRashbash*, no. 210 (p. 511), who states explicitly on the basis that no forewarning is necessary before administering lashes for lesbian activity.

23 TB *Makkot* 23b; Maimonides, Introduction to *Mishneh Torah*.

24 See Maimonides, *Hilchot Melachim*, 8:10–11; 9:1–14.

25 See TB *Sanhedrin* 58a; Maimonides (previous note) 9:5. The Gemara, ibid. derives the ban on *mishkav zachar* for gentiles from Genesis 2:24: 'therefore a man shall leave his father and his mother and he shall *cling* to his wife'. The Talmud says that the word *ve'davak* – 'and he shall cling' – excludes relationships with males. Rashi, ibid., *s.v. ve'davak* explains that homosexual unions do not have the capacity for long-term 'clinging' since, in contrast to a woman who receives pleasure from intercourse, the male does not receive pleasure from being sodomised. Consequently, the passive homosexual partner will not be inclined to remain steadfast in his relationship with the active partner (cf. Maimonides, ibid., and R. Shor (d. 1632), *Torat Chayim* on TB *Sanhedrin*, ibid.). See also the comments of the famous nineteenth century biblical commentator, R. Meir Leibush Malbim, *HaTorah ve-HaMitzvah* on Leviticus 20:13, who referes to this idea when explaining the reason that the Torah uses the expression '*v'et zachar*' (*v'et* indicates the object of the verb) rather than the seemingly more appropriate wording '*v'im zachar*' (with a male) when introducing the prohibition against *mishkav zachar*: '... that which is written here is *v'et zachar*, for in this case the passive partner does not enjoy this mode of intercourse'. See, however, Tosafot on TB *Sanhedrin* 9b, *s.v.* li'retzono (discussed in some detail in chapter 6, note 26), where it is evident that the Tosafists were of the opinion that the passive participant in the act of sodomy could derive much pleasure from this act. (The fact that an untold number of present-day homosexuals do, evidently, experience significant pleasure from being penetrated may be explained, according to Rashi, by recourse to the general halachic principle *nishtanu ha-tivim*, namely that certain aspects of empirical scientific phenomena, including human biology and psychology, may have changed since the era of the Talmud and the early Codes of *halachah*. See R. Guttel, *Hishtanut Ha-tivim ba-Halachah*, for a comprehensive study of this principle and its far-reaching ramifications.)

The degree of the universality of the prohibition of male homosexual conduct is further emphasised by the fact that even a 'Canaanite slave' (who is not subject to many prohibitions in the realm of sexual intercourse) is subject to the prohibition against male-to-male intercourse: See Maimonides, *Hilchot Issurei Bi'ah*, 14:18 and commentaries; *Sefer HaChinnuch*, Commandment no. 209.

In the first section of this chapter, it was explained that in Jewish Law any form of homosexual intimacy – even if not penetrative – is forbidden. According to R. Steif (1877–1959), *Limmudei HaShem on Genesis*, p. 274, this is true for gentiles as well and comes under the title of *arayot*, which is part of the Noachide Code.

The rational approaches to the prohibition against male homosexual practices – to be outlined later in this chapter – would serve to explain why the prohibition is included in the Noachide code, which is essentially a code of universal ethics and therefore applies to gentiles as well as Jews (see Maimonides, *Hilchot Melachim* 8:11; 9:1). See also R. Epstein (1829–1908), *Aruch HaShulchan HeAtid, Hilchot Milachim* 78:2 and R. Meir Simchah HaCohen of Dvinsk (1843–1926), *Meshech Chochma* on Deutoronomy 30:2 (end), amongst many other authorities, who explain that the seven Noachide commandments were designed for the benefit of a humane and dignified society.

There has been little if any discussion about the source of the prohibition for gentiles to engage in lesbian practices. R. Feinstein, *Dibrot Moshe* (note 16) asserts that gentiles are certainly not subject to this prohibition. However, considering the fact that the Torah describes female homosexual activity as corrupt 'Egyptian practices' which are to be scorned and repudiated, it appears to this writer that whilst there may be no formal halachic ruling, biblical or rabbinical, preventing gentile women from such practices, it is certainly against the spirit of the Torah's teaching for all humanity that any women – Jews and gentiles alike – should indulge in lesbian practices. It must be emphasised that the very same *Torat Cohanim* (cited above) also comments, on the very same verse in Leviticus, that the deeds of the Egyptians and Canaanites (referred to in the verse) were 'more corrupt' than those of any other nation. As R. Feinstein writes (*Dibrot Moshe*, ibid.): 'such practices [including lesbian practices] that are performed for mere lustful indulgence generally lead to even greater and more abominable deeds'. In other words, whatever their legal status may be, lesbian practices are deemed by the Torah as part of the morally degenerative lifestyle adopted by hedonists. Consequently, one can definitely state that the Torah opposes lesbian practices for all humanity. See also Clorfene and Rogalsky, *The Path of the Righteous Gentile*, 8:16 (p. 88): 'Though it violates the spirit of the Seven Universal Commandments, lesbianism is not explicitly stated [in the Noachide Code] as one of the forbidden relationships. Lesbianism is, however, deemed an immoral and unnatural relationship that destroys the order of the world' (no sources are cited).

After having written the above, my esteemed friend and colleague R. N. D. Dubov drew my attention to the manuscript (prepared for publication) by R. Steif, *Sefer Mitzvot HaShem – Kuntres Dinei B'nei Noach*, ch. 76, section 8 (p. 81), in which he states: 'it is certain that gentiles are also forbidden to engage in this [lesbian activities], since they are proscribed under the "abominations of Egypt", which God despises. Consequently, gentiles also have to abstain from such practices.'

26 The general principle behind this obligation is that of guarantorship (*arvut*). The Talmud, TB *Shavuot* 39a; *Sanhedrin* 27b (see also TB *Sotah* 37b and commentaries) declares that all Jewish people are 'guarantors' for each other and thus assume responsibility for the negative behaviour of a fellow Jew, in circumstances where they could have prevented such. Other commandments that provide a mandate for 'interference' and 'intervention' in the behaviour of a fellow Jew include the commandment to 'admonish one's neighbour' and the commandment to 'love one's fellow Jew' (manifest also in one's concern for the spiritual welfare of one's fellow) and – in certain circumstances – the commandment to save the life of one's fellow, which also includes the 'soul' of one's fellow, namely his spiritual life.

27 See Maimonides (note 24) 8:10.

28 R. Yom Tov Lipman Heller (1579–1654), *Tosafot Yom Tov*, on the *Ethics of our Fathers*, 3:14.

29 For an elaborate discussion of this obligation as it applies in contemporary society, see R. Menachem Schneerson, *Likkutei Sichot*, vol. 26, pp. 132–44.

30 One of the Thirteen Principles of Faith is that the commandments of the Torah are eternal: the Divine Dictates that it contains are never to be revoked or superseded by other commandments. The principle that the laws of the Torah will never be abrogated is expanded upon by Maimonides in his Ninth Principle of the Thirteen Principles. See also his *Mishneh Torah, Hilchot Yessodei HaTorah* 9:1. The eternity of the Torah is a concomitant of the Divine source of the Torah. If the commandments are the will of God, then just as God Himself is not

subject to change, due to His absolute eternity, neither is His will (a manifestation of His essence) subject to alteration; see the discussion in Abarbanel (1437–1508), *Rosh Amanah*, ch. 13; R. Moshe di Trani, *Bet Elokim, Sha'ar haYesodot*, ch. 34 ff. Cf. R. Albo (c.1380–c.1444) *Sefer halkkarim* 3:19–20.

31 Often, only the two 'extreme' categories, *chukkim* and *mishpatim*, are mentioned. See, for example, Maimonides, *Hilchot Temurah* 4:13 and *Hilchot Me'ilah* 8:8 (see also his *Shemonah Perakim* chapter 6), where *chukkim* are described as *mitzvot* for which there is no *known* reason and the term *mishpatim* is used to describe all the commandments that have a *known* reason and the benefit of whose performance is manifestly clear in this world. See also *Torat Cohanim* on Leviticus 18:4 and TB *Yoma* 67b (cited in *Shemonah Perakim*, ibid.).

In other places, however, a distinction is drawn between two types of 'understandable' commandments: those that are logical imperatives, and those that are logically conceivable. The former alone are termed *mishpatim*, whilst the latter are termed *eidot*. See, for example, the commentary of Nachmanides on Deuteronomy 6:20. See also R. M. Schneerson, *Gidran shel Mitzvot*, page 7 ff.

32 A survey of the reasons for the commandments of the Torah, forwarded by the mediaeval philosophers (see, for example, R. Sa'adiah Gaon (882–942), *Emunot veDeot*, Third Discourse; Maimonides, *Guide for the Perplexed*, part 3; R. Yehudah HaLevi (c.1080–c.1145), *Sefer HaKuzari*, Second Discourse; *Sefer HaChinnuch* – particularly commandments nos 95, 159, 545) and other works, suggests a broad range of ethical dynamics which, I believe, cannot be 'strait-jacketed' into one particular system or school of moral philosophy.

33 Even the observance of the *chukkim* may not be totally devoid of logic. It is possible for a 'rationalist' to justify the observance of what appear to be irrational commandments, on the grounds that whilst from the perspective of the puny mortal they cannot be comprehended, it is reasonable to assume that the Supreme Commander has 'solid' reasons for instructing us to fulfil these commandments. (See, for example, *Midrash Bemidbar Rabbah* 19:6, where God reveals to Moses the *reason* of the most difficult *chok*, namely the law of the *Parah Adumah* detailed in Numbers, chapter 19. The midrash (ibid. 19:3) tells us that King Solomon understood the reason for all other *chukkim*.) Some Jewish thinkers seem to advocate this sort of 'rationalistic' approach to *chukkim*. (See, for example, Nachmanides' commentary on Deuteronomy 22:6; R. Shlomoh ben Aderet, *Teshuvot HaRashba*, vol. 1, no. 94.)

However, notwithstanding the authenticity of this idea, it should be emphasised that the ultimate *raison d'être* for the observance of the *chukkim* – or for that matter, even the rationally comprehensible *eidot* and *mishpatim* – is not any underlying rationale that these commandments may contain. The reason we, the Jewish people, fulfil these commandments, is ultimately because they are the will of God. See R. Y. D. Soloveitchik, *Bet HaLevi* (1820–1892) on Genesis 17:1. For an overview of a Chabad-Chassidic approach to this issue, see the discussion in R. Schneerson *Gidran shel Mitzvot* (note 31), pp. 9–14.

34 See Maimonides, *Guide for the Perplexed*, 3:26.

35 See R. M. Schneerson, *Likkutei Sichot*, vol. 32, p. 179; *Gidran shel Mitzvot* (note 33).

36 For example, several mediaeval Jewish philosophers (R. Sa'adiah Gaon, *Emunot VeDeot*, 3:2; Maimonides, *Guide for the Perplexed*, 3:49 – cited in *Sefer HaChinnuch* Commandement no. 190; R. Abraham ibn Ezra (1089– c.1164), *Yesod Mora*, no. 7) all offer an explanation for the Torah's prohibition against incestuous cohabitation. The gist of their explanation is that the function of these prohibitions is to curb man's sexual indulgence. Immediate relatives, such as parents, siblings and children, are most readily 'available' to a person, due to the fact that they live in close proximity to each other, share the same home and are most familiar with each other. Were it to have been permitted to cohabit with one's (unmarried) sister, for example, people would be provided with an opportunity for over-indulgence in libidinal pleasure. This rationale may ring 'peculiar' to us. (See Nachmanides on Leviticus 18:6 who points out the weakness of this rationale. R. M. Sofer in the addendum to his commentary on TB *Ketubot* 7b (*Mahadura Batra*), describes this philosophical reason as '*hevel*' – nonsense – and explains that the prohibition against incest is based on the 'mysteries of the Torah'. They are rooted in a special 'sanctity' conferred upon us by God.) R. Sa'adiah, ibid., also suggests another 'reason' for the prohibition on marrying one's sister. If a man could marry his own sister, he says, homely girls would end up as old maids because their own relatives

would not be interested in them and every potential suiter would say that these girls are so ugly that not even their own brothers would marry them. Once again, a notion that is hardly palatable to the modern ear. Yet these types of rationalisations are quite typical of Jewish mediaeval thought. Such reasons must be appreciated as an attempt to explain the function of the commandments through the prism of mediaeval philosophical ideas.

One is reminded of the explanation that Maimonides gives for the concept of animal sacrifices. In the *Guide for the Perplexed* 3:32; 46, Maimonides asserts the notion that sacrifices were instituted only as an expedient to wean the Jewish people of the idolatrous practices to which their environment, particularly in pagan Egypt, had accustomed them. Sacrifices were a concession to human nature, which required the gradual adjustment in stages from one form of worship to another. Once again, Nachmanides on Leviticus 1:9 challenges Maimonides on this issue describing his rationale as 'words of vanity'. Nachmanides argues that if the sacrifices were merely meant as an antidote for a people who were submerged in a pagan society, why does Scripture state – time and again – that the sacrifices provide for a 'pleasant fragrance' for the Almighty? Why did God respond favourably to the sacrifices of Abel and Noah, which were offered at a time when pagan sacrifices were unheard of and there was no need for any 'concession' or 'compromise'? However, it is seems evident that even according to Maimonides sacrifices are much more than a response to paganism. As R. Yom Tov ibn Asevilli, the *Ritva*, writes in his *Sefer HaZikaron*, chapter 2, Maimonides in his *Guide* was explaining the function of the sacrifices in a manner that could be appreciated by the mediaeval rationalists. He obviously did not intend to suggest that the rationale he offered for the phenomenon of sacrifices in the Jewish religion was the 'be all and end all' of the concept of *korbanot*. Indeed, the same Maimonides emphasises in his code the primacy and permanence of sacrifices in the Divine order. In *Hilchot Me'ilah*, 8:8, Maimonides underscores the supremacy of sacrifices when he codifies the rabbinic teaching that 'the world stands on the practice of sacrifices'. According to Maimonides, *Hilchot Melachim*, 11:1 one of the functions of the Messiah and the utopian era he will introduce to the world is the restoration of the sacrificial order in the Third Temple. All this suggests that Maimonides recognised in the sacrificial rite much more than a (temporary) pedagogic function, in helping a people who had only recently emerged from an idolatrous society to serve God. Indeed, I believe that this understanding of Maimonides is implied by his teaching in *Hilchot Me'ilah*, ibid., where he says that 'all the sacrifices come under the category of *chukkim*' which transcend human intellect and his subsequent teaching in *Hilchot Temurah*, 4:13 that '*notwithstanding* the fact that all *chukkim* are Divine decrees as we have explained in *Hilchot Me'ilah*, it is appropriate to contemplate on their meaning and attempt to provide reasons for them'. (See also *Midrash Rabbeinu Bachya* on Deuteronomy 29:28 in the name of Maimonides. Cf. R. Cardozo, *On Silence, Sacrifices, and the Golden Calf* for a somewhat different approach to this issue.)

With regard to incest and other illicit sexual unions as with regard to sacrifices and numerous other issues one must not make the error of assuming that the rationalisations of Maimonides and other authorities are by any means *primary*. Sometimes they create more problems than they solve. See, for example, R. Shlomoh ben Aderet, *Teshuvot HaRashba*, vol. 4, no. 253, who urges his interlocutor not to pay too much attention to the reasons that Maimonides gives for the various commandments, for the majority of these reasons 'are most problematic'. See R. Eidels (c.1555–1632), *Chiddushei Aggadot* on TB *Chagigah* 11b *s.v.* *ba'arayot* who addresses the problems inherent in rationalising the prohibition against incest.

37   In recent years, this attribution has been strongly disputed on weighty, scholarly grounds; see introduction of D. Metzger to *Sefer HaChinnuch* published by Machon Yerushalayim (1988), pp. 16–19.

38   Mark Solomon, *Jewish Explorations of Sexuality*, p. 75 ff.

39   See Solomon (previous note) pp. 81–2: 'It is my deeply-held belief, shared by many lesbians and gay men, that this homosexual nature was implanted in me by my Creator. The purpose and precise means of this are open to endless speculation, but the fundamental conviction remains that God created me, and wills me to be, gay. What, then, of the divine will as expressed in Leviticus 18:22? A variety of responses is possible ... sustained reflection on my situation led me, for the sake of religious and sexual survival with integrity, to reject the commandment altogether ... the logic of this position led me to revise my whole conception

of the Torah, which I have come to regard not as the unmediated revelation of God's immutable will, but as an earthly record of the sustained encounter of our people with God, at times expressing the highest wisdom, beauty and goodness of which inspired humanity is capable, at others *reflecting the prejudices and fallacies of a primitive and patriarchal society*' (emphasis added). See also Matt, *Homosexual Rabbis?*, pp. 31–32: 'As for the Torah's condemnation of homosexuality, we follow those teachers who have taught us that though The Torah *contains* God's word, it is not *identical* with God's word; it is both divine and human ....'

40 As has often been pointed out, this type of attitude – in addition to its intrinsic heresy – renders the Torah a completely impotent text in terms of moral and religious authority. One who – like Solomon, or for that matter more 'traditional' progressives – maintains that the Torah's commandments contain 'harmful' ones (see Rabbi Dr L. Jacobs, *A Jewish Theology*, pp. 226, 228–9) and that some of the commandments were the products of primitive man, there is indeed no binding reason to keep any of the Torah's commandments. For, if the commandments under discussion are considered to be morally unacceptable, according to the subjective perspective of the individual or the collective *zeitgeist* of society, they would have to be disregarded, if not repudiated. (Given the possibility of an extreme 'vegetarian' society, even the relatively 'innocuous' commandments of *Sefer Torah*, *tefillin* and *mezuzah* may become regarded as the immoral products of a barbaric and inhumane 'tribe'. Cf. R. Schneerson, *Likkutei Sichot*, vol. 39, p. 245.) In the event that the commandments are regarded as morally 'harmless', they would nevertheless – as any other human innovation – ultimately be optional. Given the extremely relativistic and subjective appeal of any of the Torah's commandments, the consistent progressive would have to acknowledge that, as a whole, the Torah's commandments – for him – are no more than ancient fossils whose influence and meaning for contemporary Judaism are minimal.

41 See R. Cardozo, *Thoughts to Ponder*, no. 42. It is worthwhile quoting R. Cardozo's eloquent presentation:

> We have been witness to a great amount of debate about such topics as homosexuality, a marriage between people of the same sex, and abortion. Both sides try to prove their point of view with learned dissertations and heavy arguments. But those who survey this literature have long since been convinced that such debates will lead nowhere. There is no reconciliation or any *modus vivendi* that will bring these camps any closer. The reason is obvious: there is no common ground which could be used to allow for any kind of useful debate ... All discussions of why certain marriages or sexual relationships are forbidden are doomed to fail! No human reasoning is able to explain them in any consistent way. It is for this reason that religious thinkers should distance themselves from giving primary reasons for these prohibitions. It would be counter-productive and dangerous.
> This is true when discussing homosexuality or even abortion. Although these relationships are forbidden since the days of the creation of Man, they are beyond human comprehension and should be accepted as such. It is here, we believe, that a difficulty arises for secular philosophy and ethics. On the basis of which rational principle should a homosexual relationship be permitted, but incest forbidden? However ghastly our argument may sound, we are forced to ask what could there be wrong with incest, pederasty, fetishism, or bestiality from a secular perspective? As long as such a relationship takes place by mutual consent and nobody gets physically hurt, there should be no reason why these relationships should be forbidden. While several philosophers have attempted to give secular reasons why such acts should even be forbidden by secular law, we have to conclude that no consistent and rational argument has yet been forwarded which is fundamentally sound. Arguments such as the 'need for human dignity' or 'social conduct' are of little meaning, because it is completely unclear why human dignity or social conduct should in fact be unchallenged norms in our society. Philosophers are not even in agreement what the definitions of these phrases should be. We are therefore forced to conclude that when secular law forbids certain sexual acts, it borrows from a system alien to its own philosophy.
> The secular understanding of sexual morality does not make any sense unless one admits that it is founded on religious premises. Religious thinkers, however, should not forget ...

that neither can religious philosophy explain the subject for them. These prohibitions cannot be the result of rational deduction or ethical contemplation, but must be rooted in a 'will' which is external to man. Either one accepts this external will, or one rejects it. Once one rejects such an external will, there can be no distinction made between matters such as homosexuality and incest, and as such, both relationships should be permitted.

42 Leviticus 18:22; 20:13. See also Deuteronomy 32:16 and the commentary of Rashi thereon (Cf. Nachmanides there). See also the mediaeval compilation of *Midrash Yalkut Shimoni* on Deuteronomy no. 945. See also TB *Sanhedrin* 82a which interprets the phrase 'and abomination has been committed in Israel' (Malachi 2:11) as a reference to male homosexual conduct.

It is true that Leviticus 18:29–30 states (in reference to all the forbidden sexual unions enumerated in that chapter): 'For if anyone commits any of these *abominations*, the people doing so will be cut off from among their people. You shall safeguard my Commandment not to do any of these *abominable* practices that were done to you …'. However, as R. Yosef Chayim of Baghdad explains in his commentary to *Sanhedrin* ibid., the Torah refers to all the *arayot collectively* as 'abominations'. In contrast, *mishkav zachar* is singularly given the appellation '*to'evah*'. The same explanation is offered by *Chiddushei Aggadot* (next note). See also *Rabbeinu Meyuchas* (twelfth century) in his Commentary on Leviticus 18:22, (p. 231): '*It is an abomination:* from this we learn that this [homosexual practice] is *more than all other forbidden sexual relationships,* for whilst they are all described as abominations, this practice is more abominable than all of them'.

Alternatively, it has been argued that – according to a recorded midrashic hermeneutic – the term 'abomination' in these two verses also refers specifically to homosexuality and bestiality. R. Gombiner, the Magen Avraham (c.1634–1682), in his commentary *Zayit Ra'anan* on *Yalkut Shimoni* ibid., suggests that this *novel* interpretation is indicated by the order in which the prohibitions are arranged in Leviticus Chapter 18. First the Torah lists all the forbidden sexual relationships (in verses 6 to 20), then interjects with the prohibition against offering one's children to the idol *Molech* (verse 21), and only then returns (in verses 22 and 23) to the prohibition against homosexuality and bestiality. After all the above, the Torah presents its exhortation (verses 24 to 30): 'Do not become defiled through any of these; for through all of these, the nations that I drive away before you became defiled … and the land expelled (literally: vomited out) its inhabitants … Let not the land expel you for having defiled it as it expelled the nation that was before you …'

Zaayit Ra'anan explains that by interrupting between all the other forbidden sexual relationships and homosexuality and bestiality, the Torah makes it clear that the subsequent exhortation which contains a reference to abominations – *to'evah* – refers specifically to these two offences. In this way, he explains the meaning of the *Yalkut Shimoni* on Leviticus 20:13, no. 622, which states as follows: '*Mishkav zachar* and intercourse with an animal were included with all the *arayot* (illicit sexual unions), yet the Torah singles them out and calls them *to'evah*. This comes to teach that, just as these forms of *arayot* – which are subject to the penalty of *karet* when performed deliberately, and necessitate the bringing of a sin-offering when performed inadvertently – caused the exile of the [ancient] Canaanites [from their land], so too all other *arayot* – which are subject to the penalty of *karet* when performed deliberately, and necessitate the bringing of a sin-offering when performed inadvertently – were the cause of the exile of the Canaanites'. At face value, two problems are raised by this teaching. Firstly, where does the Torah use the term *to'evah* in connection with bestiality? Secondly, where does the Torah indicate that homosexuality and bestiality were *the* sins that caused the expulsion of the ancient Canaanites from the Land of Israel? According to *Zayit Ra'anan* these problems are solved. For the exhortation (verses 24 to 30) in which repeated reference to *to'evah* is made, and which clearly attributes the expulsion of the Canaanites to these abominations, refers specifically to the two crimes of sexual intercourse between males and between humans and animals.

43 TB *Nedarim* 51a. (The commentary attributed to Rashi on *Nedarim*, ibid. implies that the Gemara is commenting on the word '*to'evah*' as it occurs with reference to all sexual transgressions, particularly adultery. Rashi states: '[you go astray because of her] that is to say, he abandons his wife who is permissible to him, in favour of one [*ve-tafas et zo*] with whom relationships are in the category of *zenut*.' However, all other commentaries

apparently understand the Gemara to be commenting on the word '*to'evah*' as it is found in the context of the proscription against homosexual intercourse.) See R. Eidels, Maharsha (c.1555–1632), *Chiddushei Aggadot* on *Nedarim* ibid., who explains that the Talmud is dwelling on the fact that the word *to'evah* is mentioned *specifically* only in connection with male homosexuality, and this term is employed *twice*: when the Torah introduces the prohibition (in *Parshat Acharei*) and when the Torah reiterates the prohibition and its penalty (in *Parshat Kedoshim*).

See also *Rabbeinu Meyuchas* in his Commentary on Leviticus 18:22 (p. 231): '*It is an abomination*: from this we learn that this [homosexual practice] is *more abominable than all other forbidden sexual relationships*, for whilst they are all described as abominations, this practice is more abominable than all of them'.

R. Boteach, in his essay 'Does Homosexuality differ from Heterosexuality', pp. 39–40, has rejected the idea that the use of the word *to'evah* with regard to homosexuality is indicative of a particularly emphatic stance regarding male-to-male intercourse. He writes:

> Many observant Jews reject this 'soft' view of homosexuality by pointing out that the Torah uses the word *to'evah* 'abomination', in describing homosexuality. What these individuals, however meritorious, seem to ignore easily is the Torah's use of the same word in describing the prohibition in eating a *sheretz* (invertebrate) and other non-kosher foodstuffs: 'Thou shalt not eat any abominable thing' (Deuteronomy 14:3). The same word *to'evah* is used to describe the prohibition of a woman returning to her first husband, from whom she has been divorced, after she has already been married to someone else (Deuteronomy 24:4). Again, the word *to'evah* is used in Deuteronomy 17:1. 'Thou shalt not sacrifice unto the Lord thy God any bullock, or sheep wherein is blemish, or any evilfavouredness, for that is an abomination unto the Lord thy God.' Similarly, there are many other uses of the word *to'evah* in the Torah which would not depict a social loathing or repulsion of a particular mode of human behaviour.'

This argument bespeaks an ignorance of the rabbinic interpretation and elaboration of the term *to'evah* as a peculiarity of male-to-male intercourse. The fact that the term *to'evah* is used in connection with other sins, both of a sexual nature and otherwise, does not undermine the notion that homosexuality is unique in its perversity. For as mentioned, it is not merely the description of the homosexual act as a *to'evah* that served as a basis for the rabbinic elaboration. Rather it is the fact that homosexuality was singled out as an 'abomination' amongst abominations that served as a springboard for the above-mentioned interpretations.

44 *Pesikta Zutrata* Leviticus 18:22 (p. 52). (R. Riskin, 'Homosexuality as a Tragic Mistake', suggests that this is alluded to in the biblical context wherein the prohibition against male homosexual intercourse appears: 'it is not by accident that the verse preceding the prohibition against homosexuality reads "And thou shalt not give any of they seed to Moloch" (Leviticus 18:21). One sacrifices potential future generations through homosexuality.' Feldman, 'Homosexuality in Jewish Law', p. 428, surprisingly, does not recognise any inference from Leviticus for this idea. He writes: '… certainly, the context of the Bible gives no support to that explanation. Homosexuality is declared an abomination in the context of other prohibitions – adultery, incest, and bestiality – all of which are quite removed from the question of procreation'.)

45 *Sefer HaChinnuch*, commandment no. 209.

46 Nachmanides on Leviticus 18:12. R. Bachya (d. c.1340), *Midrash Rabbeinu Bachya* on Leviticus 18:6 cites the view of Nachmanides that the reason that the Torah forbade many of the sexual unions detailed in that chapter of Leviticus is because those unions do not facilitate the 'perpetuation of the species' (at least), in a healthy manner. R. Bachya challenges Nachmanides: 'What would the Rabbi say about a person with crushed testicles who may marry a convert to Judaism, and the like. Surely this is conclusive proof that the Torah does not forbid sexual intercourse where it does not contribute to the "perpetuation of the species".' R. Bachya quotes the famous formula of R. Abraham ben David of Posquières (c.1120–1197) in which that latter explains that there are five reasons that people may engage in sexual intercourse. The first is for the purpose of the 'perpetuation of the species'. The second is for the fulfilment of one's conjugal duties towards one's wife. The third is for

therapeutic reasons – intercourse is necessary as part of one's physical regimen for good health. The fourth is in order for a person to retain his mental sanctity. (By engaging in intercourse, in a permissible way, he will not be plagued with carnal thoughts.) The fifth is simply for delight and animalistic pleasure. Whilst the fifth reason is to be scorned upon, the first four reasons for engaging in physical intimacy are all honourable motivations although the fourth reason is not as praiseworthy as the first three. R. Bachya therefore dismisses the idea of Nachmanides and argues that there must be a reason grounded in mystical phenomena for the biblical prohibitions against the sexual unions outlined in Leviticus.

47 R. Sacks, *Tradition in an Untraditional Age*, pp. 169–70, writes: '… the underlying logic is apparent in the first chapter of Genesis. All of nature shares with God the property of being creative, of bringing new life into being, but only humanity shares with God the *moral choice* of bringing new life into the world. Only for Adam and Eve is the phrase "Be fruitful and multiply" experienced not just as a blessing but as a command. Bringing children into the world thus presupposes moral responsibility, for one might have chosen otherwise …'.

48 Commentary of Tosafot and Rosh on TB *Nedarim* (cited in note 43), *s.v. To'eh atah bah.*

49 See, for example, R. Lamm (note 22), p. 197: 'Another interpretation is that of the *Tosafot* and R. Asher Ben Jehiel … which applies the "going astray" or wandering to the homosexual's abandoning his wife. In other words, the abomination consists of the danger that a married man with homosexual tendencies may disrupt his family life in order to indulge his perversions.'

50 R. Bleich, *Judaism and Healing*, p. 70. Bleich concludes: 'The homosexual cannot lead a normal family life'. See also the commentary of *Ba'alei HaTosafot al HaTorah* (on Leviticus 18:22): 'You go astray … because you did not pay heed to that which is written in Proverbs 5:15 "drink water from your own cistern, and flowing water from your own well".' (It is, however, possible that this commentary understood the talmudic phrase 'to'eh atah bah' with reference to adultery rather than homosexual intercourse, see above beginning of note 43.)

It should be noted, however, that R. Feinstein (note 51) argues that Tosafot and the Rosh did not intend to explain the term *to'evah* (and its talmudic rendition 'you go astray in it') as a reference to the capacity of homosexual relationships to destroy family units. He writes that they really refer to the very fact that homosexual indulgences are intrinsically repulsive in as much as there cannot be any natural desire for homosexual activity. The word *neshoteihen* in Tosafot and the Rosh must be seen as a 'synonym' for the term *mishkevei ishah* employed by R. Nissim. The intent of all these authorities, R. Feinstein says, is that homosexual relationships are unnatural and inexcusable, as will be elaborated in our forthcoming citation from R. Feinstein.

51 R. Feinstein, *Iggerot Moshe Orach Chayim*, vol. 4, no. 115.

52 R. Feinstein's comments on this matter came against an interesting background. In 1975, Dr I. Lange, who resided at the time in Switzerland, collated a number of mediaeval manuscripts and published them under the title of *Perushei HaTorah le-Rabbi Yehudah HeChasid* (Jerusalem, 1975). Rabbi Daniel Levy, the spiritual leader of Lange's congregation, detected what he thought was heresy in this work. A number of comments attributed to R. Yehudah HeChasid (late twelfth century) were thought to be of a heretical nature and whilst no-one accused Lange himself of forgery, the suggestion was made that the attribution of a book containing such heresy to R. Yehudah HeChasid was unthinkable.

R. Levy consulted, amongst others, R. Moshe Feinstein, who dealt with the issue in two letters which were subsequently published in his above-mentioned responsa. R. Feinstein argued that the work was a forgery – a mediaeval heretic was responsible for the sham – and voiced his opinion that the book should be banned. R. Levy personally informed this writer that when he visited the contemporary halachist R. Yosef Shalom Elyashiv, the latter did not even want to allow the book – 'an abomination' – to be brought into his home. (Subsequently, a 'censored' edition of the book was published under the same title and in the same format containing a brief note from Dr Lange in which he writes: 'I consider it appropriate to make it known that after consultation with Torah Authorities – and based on their opinion – I have omitted a few passages [from the book] regarding which it is forbidden to entertain the idea that they were expressed by the holy mouth of Rabbi Yehudah HeChasid and regarding which one must assume that "strangers" got hold of the manuscripts and tampered with them.')

Three passages in the book were cause for concern. The 'worst' of them was a comment on Numbers 21:17, where Scripture states: 'Then Israel sang this song'. According to the manuscript, R. Yehudah HeChasid said that the song that they sang was the one recorded in Psalm 136, known in rabbinic literature as *Hallel HaGadol* ('the Great Hallel'). Originally this was recorded in the Pentateuch. However, King David removed all the unattributed Psalms of Moses that were found in the Pentateuch, and placed them in his book of Psalms.

In R. Feinstein's first correspondence with Rabbi Levy, he quotes the teaching of the Mishnah in Sanhedrin which states that one who said that even a single verse of the Torah was not from Heaven despises the word of God, and the ruling of Maimonides that the same is true of one who says that even a single word of the Torah was not from Heaven. To say, as R. Yehudah HeChasid is reported as saying (in two passages in the book), that Joshua or the Men of the Great Assembly added words or verses to the Torah is tantamount to a denial that the entire Torah – as we have it – was written by Moses at the command of God. To say that anyone, however great a prophet he may have been, deleted words from the Torah is likewise unthinkable. The idea that King David extracted Psalm 136 from the Pentateuch is, says R. Feinstein, sheer nonsense. Moreover, it is worse than the other comments in that there is no reason at all for saying this, unless it is simply to be provocative for provocation's sake. For David to have taken away a portion of the Torah would have meant that he tampered with the words given by God to Moses, and that would have been a worse offence than that of the person who says that a particular verse was not given by God to Moses. (At the end of the responsum, R. Feinstein records that his attention was drawn to the fact that the above-mentioned idea attributed to R. Yehudah HeChasid was also recorded in his name by a fifteenth century kabbalist, R. Menachem Tziyoni, in his *Perush al haTorah* 64d. R. Feinstein was not impressed. He writes that 'we do not know exactly who R. Menachem Tziyoni was' and, at any rate, he must have just copied, somewhat absent-mindedly, the above-mentioned idea from an earlier manuscript, without paying attention to its heretical nature.)

In the second responsum, addressed to the world-renowned halachist R. Shlomo Zalman Auerbach, R. Feinstein says that he has discussed the matter with R. Levy in Switzerland over the telephone and that he suggested that the latter should try to persuade Dr Lange not to publish the work, but that it should all be done privately lest contemporary heretics, hearing of the existence of such a work in manuscript, should try to have it published and lead the masses astray. Dr Lange, however, had insisted that the book be published and many copies had already been sold. R. Levy had also told R. Feinstein that R. Auerbach and R. Elyashiv had made Dr Lange promise to produce a new edition of the work, from which the offending passages would be omitted. Rabbis Auerbach and Elyashiv maintained that there would be no objection to such a publication provided that it was made clear in the introduction to the new edition that the earlier edition contained the three above-mentioned forgeries.

R. Feinstein, however, argued that the detection of these three heretical ideas placed the whole book under suspicion. Who knew what other heresies and obscenities would be found when the work was closely scrutinised? R. Feinstein goes on to demonstrate the likelihood of the discovery of further heresies by referring to a comment in this book (pp. 147–8) on the subject of homosexuality. The comment states as follows:

The reason that the Torah forbade for a man to lie with a man or with an animal is all in order that men should marry women and fulfil the commandment to procreate. Notwithstanding the fact that these sins [homosexual intercourse and bestiality] are punishable by stoning, whereas this commandment [to be fruitful and multiply] is merely a positive commandment, [why therefore should activities that would distract from procreation be punished with such a severe penalty? The answer is that] the Torah found it necessary to make a great barrier [against activities likely to detract from procreative endeavours].

R. Feinstein argues that this is yet another example of how the wicked sinners intended to undermine the prohibition of homosexual intercourse. Firstly, by implying that there is a [legitimate] 'question' as to why the Torah forbade this. This in itself is an enormous evil and undermines the severity of the prohibition for the evildoers who are engaged in this grotesque form of lust – one of the greatest abominations – which even the Nations of the World acknowledge as the most depraved of abominations. There is no need for a reason for this prohibition ... and by articulating the very question 'why did the Torah forbid this?' [the evildoers have] removed the disgust and associated embarrassment and disgrace associated with homosexuality. Secondly, the answer that the author gives to his question, namely that the prohibition was designed to encourage marriage and promote procreation, is a gross minimisation of the prohibition, inasmuch as it suggests that the prohibition of homosexual intercourse is not intrinsically *ervah* (sexual immorality), it merely underscores the performance of a positive commandment which people do not consider to be as important. Such ideas are tantamount to heresy and are forbidden to be printed.

In light of all the above, R. Feinstein concluded that the so-called commentary of R. Yehudah HeChasid should be banned and destroyed.

However, it should be noted that, in addition to the above-mentioned source for R. Yehudah HeChasid's rationalisation of the prohibition against homosexual practices, the idea is also attributed to him in another mediaeval commentary, *Moshav Zekeinim al Ha-Torah*, p. 339. The text reads as follows:

> Nachmanides wrote that the reason for the prohibition against male-to-male and human-to-animal intercourse is well known, for it is an abominable practice and does not facilitate the perpetuation of the species, for [the cohabitation of] man and animal does not lead to reproduction ... and Rabbi Yehudah HeChasid explained that the reason that the Torah forbade male-to-male intercourse is so that people should marry women and thus fulfil the commandment *p'ru u-r'vu*.

At any rate, the rationalisation of the prohibition of *mishkav zachar* – on the grounds that it undermines marriage and procreation – is certainly not unique to R. Yehudah HeChasid. It is referred to, amongst others, by Nachmanides, *Sefer HaChinnuch* and *Radvaz*. I am, therefore, not able to explain why R. Feinstein considers the notion as advanced in the name of R. Yehudah HeChasid 'tantamount to heresy'. Moreover, in light of the general trend in mediaeval rationalisation of the commandments (see above note 36), it is difficult to appreciate R. Feinstein's problem with the above-mentioned teaching of R. Yehudah HeChasid.

53 See R. Feinstein (note 51), *s.v. u'shlishit*.
54 See R. Feinstein (note 51), and *Iggerot Moshe Even HaEzer*, vol. 4, no. 113, p. 176, *s.v aval*.
55 Gersonides, Commentary on Leviticus 18:22. See also R. David Hoffman, *Leviticus with a Commentary*, p. 23. See also R. Avraham ibn Ezra, commentary on Leviticus 18:22, where he states that *to'evah* means 'something which is naturally abhorred by a refined spirit (*nefesh kedoshah*)'.
56 R. Lamm (note 22), p. 198.
57 *Sefer HaChinnuch* (note 45). See also *Sefer HaChinnuch*, commandment 189, which discusses the prohibition against homosexual congress with one's father (which is added to the general prohibition against homosexual relationships, 'in order to impose punishment for violating two commandments' in the event of a man who copulates in his father). The *Sefer HaChinnuch* says: 'The significance of this injunction is obvious. There is no need to write at length about its root reason: for it is fitting to remove this great ugliness from human beings and to punish a transgressor for it with a great penalty. He is therefore sentenced to death by stoning.'
R. David ibn Zimra, *Metzudat David (Ta'amei Mitzvot leRadvaz)* Commandment no. 157 also offers two reasons for the prohibition of *mishkav zachar*: (a) *Mishkav zachar* detracts from pro-creation; (b) *Mishkav zachar* is intrinsically repugnant. He writes: 'The reason for this commandment according to the simple meaning [of the Torah] is because it is a shameful, repugnant and ugly act, in addition to the fact that it wastes the seed which has the potential to perpetuate the human species. Through this disgraceful act the person overturns the intent of creation concerning which it says that He created them male and female. Know that even animals and birds only copulate with members of the opposite sex for this is the method through which the species will remain viable.'
Radvaz then goes on to give a mystical reason for the prohibition of male-to-male intercourse. He concludes his words with the following: 'because these two abominations [sodomy and bestiality] are far from the intellect our sages have said that the Jewish people are not suspect to engage in sodomy or buggery even though they are suspect to engage in other illicit sexual unions ...'

58 R. Epstein, *Torah Temimah*, Leviticus 18:22, writes as follows: 'You are going astray from the foundations of creation'. R. Lamm (note 22) understands R. Epstein to mean that homosexuality 'defies the very structure of the anatomy of the sexes, which quite obviously was designed for heterosexual relationships'.

59 See also *Midrash Vayikra Rabbah*, 18:13.

The idea of the 'unnaturalness' of *mishkav zachar* is elaborated upon in a rather novel way by R. Ettlinger (1798–1871), in his *Aruch LaNer* on TB *Sukkah* 29a, where the Gemara mentions four sins which cause the sun not to function properly as a luminary. *Aruch LaNer* explains that the male is supposed to be the *mashpia* ('giver') and the female the *mushpa* ('receiver'). One who [actively] copulates with a male subverts the natural order (*seder ha-olam*) by turning the *mashpia* into a *mushpa*. It is for this reason that *mishkav zachar* causes (*middah k'neged middah* – measure for measure) the dysfunction of the sun, whereby the sun, which is supposed to serve as a *mashpia* to the earth (which is supposed to be the *mushpa*), no longer does so efficiently. In this vein, *Aruch LaNer* explains why the heavenly constellations did not function as luminaries during the period of the Flood (*Midrash Bereshit Rabbah* 25:2; 34:11; Rashi to Genesis 8:22). Since that generation had sinned by violating, amongst other transgressions, the prohibition against *mishkav zachar* (*Midrash Bereshit Rabbah* 26:9; *Vayikra Rabbah* 23:9), it caused the dysfunction of the luminaries, whereby the '*mashpia*' was not effective in this capacity.

60 See Maimonides, *Perush HaMishnah*, *Sanhedrin* 7:4, who explains the talmudic teaching (TB *Kiddushin* 82a) that Jewish people are not suspect to engage in sodomy or bestiality is because 'the Jewish people do not desire such *unnatural* acts'.

61 R. Bulka, *One Man*, p. 48, for example, writes as follows:

> The precise act of homosex which the Torah (Bible) brands as a capital breach is penetration of the male generative organ into the anus of another male ... It should be noted that anal intercourse and sodomy have been described by homosexual writers as *the* sex act that epitomises homosexuality. The anus, whether it be of the male or female, was not designed for the purpose of sex. The fact that some may be sexually aroused and satisfied by anal sex is no more to the point than if someone is sexually aroused and satisfied by a cow, a vacuum cleaner, a vibrator, or a pet rock. The anus is designed to be the evacuatory channel for human faeces. It is not for sex, and it is unsafe for sex, precautions and all – unsafe for homosexuals and for heterosexuals.

Notwithstanding the rather unsavoury comparison between anal sex practised between two human beings (which in the case of married couples Jewish Law does allow, albeit with 'reluctance') and auto-eroticism with the aid of a beast or inanimate object, the point is well taken that nature – created by God – clearly indicates that the sexual organs are specifically designed, and were obviously created, to accommodate heterosexual intercourse. Without recourse to exaggerated analogies, we may simply say that the most superficial study of human biology and the details of the male and female sexual organs demonstrate that they were created to interact with one another. Consequently, any other sexual use of these organs may be described as 'unnatural'. The fact that some individuals may only find sexual fulfilment through the 'unnatural' use of these organs does not undermine the undeniable fact that such activities go against the prescription of nature.

Parenthetically, Bulka, ibid., argues that nowadays all anal sex should be forbidden, even in a heterosexual marriage: 'Given what we now know of the potential hazard posed by anal intercourse, both to the person whose anus is breached and to the perpetrator, it is appropriate to suggest that we remove anal intercourse from human sexual interaction between husband and wife. This ban would be somewhat like the matter of cigarette smoking, which was sanctioned in previous generations because its ill effects were not known. Now that we know, cigarette smoking is in the category of ingesting poison and is forbidden. Knowing what we now do about anal intercourse, it should follow cigarette smoking into the sphere of forbidden activity. The best defence against the pain, the hurt, and the potential long range health implications of anal intercourse is to cease and desist.' Whatever the virtues of R. Bulka's argument are, I am surprised that he states categorically, that nowadays cigarette smoking 'is forbidden'. Whilst some contemporary authorities have indeed asserted that it is forbidden to smoke (see R. Waldenberg, *Teshuvot Tzitz Eliezer*, vol. 15, no. 39; vol. 17, nos. 21–22; vol. 21, no. 14), at least two pre-eminent halachic authorities are of the opinion that the dangers inherent in cigarettes are insufficient to impose a prohibition on smoking. R. Feinstein (*Teshuvot Iggerot Moshe, Yoreh De'ah*, vol. 2, no. 49; *Choshen Mishpat*, vol. 2, no. 76), and R. Elyashiv (*Kovetz Teshuvot, Choshen Mishpat* no. 219) asserted that it is permitted to smoke cigarettes, despite considerable medical evidence regarding the dangers of smoking. The basis for their ruling is the talmudic principle '*shomer pe'ta'im Hashem*' – 'God preserves the simple'. This concept is applied to low incidence natural dangers in situations whereby *dashu bo rabbim* – the multitude are accustomed to doing so (TB *Shabbat* 129b). Rabbis Feinstein and Elyashiv maintain that although many people refrain from smoking because of the inherent dangers, it cannot be categorised as involving definite danger; it may be compared to overeating or failure to exercise properly – neither of which are strictly forbidden by the *halachah*. It is noteworthy that R. Elyashiv, in his above-mentioned responsum, takes into consideration the fact that 'those people who are regular smokers perceive smoking as an absolute necessity, without which they could hardly exist'. Moreover, R. Elyashiv – in contradistinction to R. Feinstein, see *Teshuvot Iggerot Moshe, Yoreh De'ah*, vol. 3, no. 35 – maintains that, strictly speaking, a person is entitled to smoke in the public domain where others will be compelled to suffer the consequences of passive smoking.

It is possible that the above-mentioned reasoning may apply to the practice of anal intercourse in marriage, which is arguably no more dangerous than smoking cigarettes.

62 See Maimonides, *Hilchot Issurei Bi'ah*, 21:9; *Shulchan Aruch Even HaEzer*, 25:2 and commentaries thereon.
63 See Steinberg, *Encyclopaedia*, p. 636, footnote 81. See also Jakobovits, *Pioneers*, p. 127 ff.
64 Jakobovits, *Halachic Perspectives on Aids*, p. 14 (all emphasis added).
65 Jakobovits (previous note), p. 15.
66 R. Bulka, *One Man*, pp. 45–46 elaborates on this point:

> … There is perhaps another facet to the notion of homosexuality as *to'ayvah*. A study by Bell and Weinberg, published by the Kinsey Institute in 1978, showed that 28 percent of male homosexuals had sexual encounters with one thousand or more partners. Furthermore, 79 percent said more than half of their sex partners were strangers. In that survey, only 1 percent of sexually active men had fewer than five lifetime partners … This is not to suggest that there is no promiscuity among heterosexuals. But, it does suggest that some inherent deficit in the homosexual condition that makes promiscuity, which is a *to'ayvah* (abomination) in itself, more likely.

> (Some support from Jewish sources for this rationale may be derived from TB *Sanhedrin* 58a, where the Talmud states that *mishkav zachar* is forbidden under the Noachide Code. The Gemara derives this from the verse in Genesis 2:24, '… a man shall leave his father and his mother and he shall cleave to his wife and they shall become one flesh'. The Gemara comments: '*ve-davak* (and he shall cleave)" – not to a male'. Rashi explains this to mean that the Talmud sees 'cleaving' and male homosexual relationships as mutually exclusive. However, as mentioned above, note 25, Rashi explains that this is so because the passive partner in male homosexual intercourse does not derive any pleasure from the act and, therefore, he is unlikely to remain committed to the relationship. Although the Tosafists were clearly of the opinion that the 'passive' partner also derives pleasure from *mishkav zachar* (as explained in note 25), the idea that '*ve-davak* (long-term relationships)' excludes male homosexual relationships is clearly implied in the Gemara and may be seen as a Jewish basis for Bulka's theory.)

For all its value, this argument is based on a premise that the promiscuity amongst homosexuals is due to an inherent characteristic of homosexual orientation and desire, rather than an equally plausible hypothesis that this is due to the fact that society, quite rightly, does not provide a forum and 'support system' for the cultivation of stable, long-lasting homosexual relationships. As we shall yet argue, the opposition to homosexuality based on its presumed association or even synonymy with promiscuity does not contain adequate potency to negate homosexual relationships which are based on the firm bedrock of commitment, love, care and hence stability.

67 It must be remembered that, as Maimonides explains in his *Guide for the Perplexed*, part III, ch. 34, the commandments of the Torah (as indeed those of secular constitutions) – when viewed from the rationalistic vantage-point – are determined by the normative majority.
68 R. Bleich, *Bioethical Dilemmas*, p. 134. R. Bleich (p. 135) cites Maimonides, *Shemonah Perakim*, chapter 6, in his famous essay, where he elaborates upon the difference between what the philosophers describe as the superior 'pious man' and the inferior person who 'overcomes his desires'. The latter has to battle to discipline his desires and constantly struggles to do the opposite of his natural tendencies. The former, by contrast 'conducts himself according to the manner in which he is prompted by his desires and disposition. He performs worthy deeds because he wants to, and because this is his nature.'

Maimonides explains that the sages would agree with the philosophers with regard to those practices 'that all people will appreciate as evil – for example, murder, theft, robbery, cheating, damaging a person who has performed no harm, repaying good with evil, demeaning one's parents, and alike'. With regard to these the sages, like the philosophers, consider the person who finds such practices naturally abhorrent, and 'suffers no discomfort from refraining from these practices', the 'ideal' man. The person who does desire such evil suffers from 'depraved qualities'.

In contrast, those commandments which 'had the Torah not forbidden them, they would not be considered evil at all', our sages teach us that a person 'should continue to desire them, and should feel that the only thing preventing them is the Torah's [decree]'. Examples of commandments which should be observed only out of obedience (and are not supported by natural repulsion on behalf of the 'pious man') are '[the avoidance of forbidden combinations of] milk and meat; wool and linen garments; and *forbidden sexual relationships*'. Maimonides, it would seem, includes sexual relationships amongst those commandments which 'had the Torah not forbidden them, they would not be considered evil at all' because essentially violation of the Torah's sexual code is considered – by Maimonides at least – to be in the category of sins between man and God (*bein adam la-Makom*) and not in the class of sins between man and man (*bein adam la-chaveiro*); see Maimonides, *Hilchot Teshuvah*, 2:9: '*Teshuvah* and the Day of Atonement only afford atonement for *sins between man and God*; for example, a person who ate a forbidden food or *performed a forbidden sexual act*, and the like. However, sins between man and man; for example, someone who injures his fellow, curses him, steals from him, or the like, will never be forgiven until he gives his fellow man what he owes him and appeases him'. See also Maimonides, *Hilchot Rotz'each*, 4:9 and the sources cited below in Chapter 4, note 35.

In the Talmud (TB *Yoma* 67b), however, illicit sexual unions are reckoned amongst those commandments that 'had the Torah not forbidden them', they ought to have been forbidden anyway. It is possible that there are differences between different types of sexual prohibitions, some (e.g. cohabiting with someone else's wife, etc.) which ought to have been forbidden anyway, and others (such as those that do not involve infidelity and assault, etc.) which come under the category of *chukkim*.

R. Plotzki (1867–1928), *K'lei Chemdah al HaTorah*, vol. 1, p. 44 (on Genesis 19:8, subsection 3, s.v. *omnam*), suggests that a distinction should be drawn between those sexual relationships that are forbidden for gentiles and those which are forbidden for Jews. The former form part of the Noachide Code and as such 'can be rationalised to some degree', whilst the latter – which includes the prohibitions against marrying one's siblings' spouses *even after the death of one's siblings*, and the prohibition against marrying one's spouse's offspring from another marriage *even after the death of one's spouse* – 'are illogical'. According to R. Plotzki, Maimonides in his *Shemonah Perakim* refers to those sexual prohibitions that are unique to the Jewish people, whereas the Gemara in *Yoma* refers to those sexual prohibitions that are enshrined in the universal code and which human logic ought to dictate.

According to this thesis, we would have to conclude that the prohibition against male-to-male intercourse, which is included in the Noachide code, is actually a logical imperative. The reasons that have been set forth for this prohibition in this chapter demonstrate how this prohibition can also 'be rationalised to some degree'.

However, Maimonides' treatment of incest and adultery cited in note 36 indicates that, whilst he did offer 'reasons' for some of the sexual prohibitions of the Torah, he did not necessarily remove them from the category of *chukkim*. Rather, as we have explained (ibid.),

Maimonides attempts to offer tentative explanations even for the *chukkim* of the Torah. This is despite the fact that most of the laws of incest (with several exceptions, most notably one's daughter! – see TB *Sanhedrin* 58b; Maimonides, *Hilchot Issurei Bi'ah*, 14:10. Cf. Tosafot on TB *Nazir* 23a, *s.v. leLot*; and Tosafot on TB *Sanhedrin* 57b *s.v. la-na'arah*) are explicitly enshrined in the Noachide Code. All this makes it extremely difficult to support the notion that the commandments against *arayot* included in the Noachide Code *all* fall under the category of logical imperatives (notwithstanding the various reasons that have been offered for these prohibitions).

R. Goldberg, *Homosexuality: A Religious and Political Analysis*, pp. 31–32, in dismissing the argument of those who maintain that the Torah only forbade 'loveless, impermanent or coercive homosexuality' writes: 'Jewish sacred literature divides between the norm that is and is not understandable to human reason, respectively, the *mishpat* and the *hok*. The prohibition against homosexuality is a *hok*, a revelation of the Divine mind, a Divine decree independent of any cultural norm.'

R. Goldberg then struggles with the apparent paradox of designating the prohibition against homosexual conduct as a 'Divine decree', and the claim implied by the term *to'evah*, which implies that homosexual practices ought to inspire 'instinctive repugnance'. Somewhat inconsistently, R. Goldberg then suggests that the prohibition against homosexual conduct is only a *chok* for those who have indulged in homosexual behaviour (and the like). These people, he says, who 'cannot intuitively grasp homosexuality's repugnance' must have become spiritually desensitised: 'such spiritual atrophy spurs the rationalisation of homosexuality. For the rationaliser, the biblical prohibition will indeed seem to be beyond reason and in that sense a *hok*.'

I am not convinced that there is necessarily any contradiction between the idea that homosexuality evokes 'instinctive repugnance' and the designation of the prohibition against *mishkav zachar* as a *chok*. Eating creeping creatures and carrion are also described as evoking 'instinctive repugnance', but the prohibition against eating them could hardly be described as a logical imperative (indeed, gentiles are allowed to eat them). The idea that homosexual behaviour may provoke an innate and powerful response of revulsion on behalf of most people does not *necessarily* serve to designate the prohibition against *mishkav zachar* as a *mishpat* in the full sense of the word.

At any rate, R. Goldberg does clearly concede that in today's culture many people will only be able to relate to the prohibition of homosexuality as a Divine decree, one which will not necessarily withstand the critique of the moral philosopher. To this extent, I agree with him. However, as I have indicated, my personal understanding of why some people may not be able to grasp 'the impropriety of homosexuality intuitively' may have less to do with spiritual sensitivity and more to do with their personal orientation and psychological conditioning. (R. Levi, *Modern Liberation*, p. 38, for example, brings 'evidence' for 'the instinctive feeling of revulsion' – *to'evah* – that homosexual practices 'normally arouse' from 'French society', which confirms 'the naturalness of the feeling of disgust normally generated by homosexual practice. There, the homosexual still lives in shame and secrecy almost two centuries after all relevant legal restraints were abolished.' It would, however, be extremely far-fetched to argue that French society has preserved a level of spiritual sensitivity and intuitive sexual morality that the rest of the civilised world has lost.) A person who is of an exclusive homosexual orientation, even if he has never indulged in 'repeated sin, such as homosexual behaviour' and has not deadened his 'spiritual sensitivities', may nevertheless more easily relate to the Torah's prohibition coupled with his very tangible awareness of his own orientation, as a Divine mystery, one which the human mind cannot fathom.

69 It is noteworthy that, in rabbinic literature, there are several passages cautioning against over-emphasis on rationalisation of the commandments (*ta'amei ha-mitzvot*), due to the fact that this could lead to the rejection of certain commandments in circumstances where the rationale would not seem to apply. See, for example TB *Sanhedrin* 21b: 'why were the reasons for the commandments not revealed? [Rashi explains that the reasons for the *chukim*, the Gemara answers], because when the reasons for two commandments were revealed the great man [King Solomon] stumbled and transgressed them.' The Gemara explains that the Torah (Deuteronomy 17:16–17) provides the reason for the Negative Commandments restricting the number of wives and horses a king may have. Scripture states that these commandments

were designed to prevent the king from turning his heart away from God and causing the nation to return to Egypt. King Solomon argued that he would not be led astray by many wives, nor would he allow his interest in horses to encourage a return to Egypt. Consequently, he married many wives and acquired an enormous amount of horses, which ultimately brought about the very problems that the Torah sought to forestall by these prohibitions.

2 THE NATURE OF HOMOSEXUALITY – A JEWISH PERSPECTIVE

1 There exists a voluminous literature on this subject. The reader interested in broadening the horizons of his knowledge and exploring the variant views with regard to the issues discussed under this subtitle is referred to the following books and articles: Bancroft, 'Homosexual Orientation: The Search for a Biological Basis', pp. 437–40; Berger, 'Theories of Sexual Orientation', p. 432; Byne, 'Human Sexual Orientation: The Biologic Theories Reappraised', pp. 228–39; Byrne, 'Theories of Sexual Orientation', pp. 432–33; Eckert et al, 'Homosexuality in Monozygotic Twins Reared Apart', pp. 421–25; Friedman and Downey, 'Neurobiology and Sexual Orientation', pp. 131–53; Friedman, 'Homosexuality', pp. 923–30; Gordon, 'Sexual Orientation: Born or Bred?', pp. 313–321; Greenberg, *The Construction of Homosexuality*; Haynes, 'A Critique of the Possibility of Genetic Inheritance of Homosexual Orientation', pp. 91–113; Hershberger, 'A Twin Registry Study of Male and Female Sexual Orientation', pp. 212–222; Johnston and Bell, 'Romantic Emotional Attachment: Additional Factors in the Development of the Sexual Orientation of Men', pp. 621–625; LeVay, *The Sexual Brain*, pp. 105–130 (*and the many works cited, ibid., pp. 144–147*); Lidz, 'A Genetic Study of Male Sexual Orientation', p. 240; McConaghy, 'Biologic Theories of Sexual Orientation', pp. 431–432; McGuire, 'Is Homosexuality Genetic?', pp. 115–145; Pillard, 'Evidence of Familial Nature of Male Homosexuality', pp. 808–812; Rosenberg, 'Biology and Homosexuality', pp. 147–151; Ruse, *Homosexuality: A Philosophical Inquiry*; Ruse, 'Nature/Nurture: Reflections on Approaches to the Study of Homosexuality', pp. 141–151; Suppe, 'Explaining Homosexuality', pp. 223–268.

2 For examples of homosexual conduct recorded in the Holy Scriptures, see I Kings 14:22 ff, where Scripture describes the sinful behaviour of the Jewish people under the reign of Rehoboam. Verse 24 states: 'There was also *kadesh* in the land, and the people did as all the abominations of the nations that the Lord had driven out from before the children of Israel'. According to the Talmud (TB *Sanhedrin* 54b) and some commentaries on the Scriptures, the meaning of *kadesh* is male prostitution. In a later chapter (ibid. 15:12) Scripture describes how Asa King of Judah abolished the *kedeishim* [the homosexual prostitutes] from the land of Israel. See also II Kings 23:7.

   Commenting on the verse in Malachi 2:11, 'Judah has behaved treacherously, *and an abomination has been committed in Israel and Jerusalem*', the sages (TB *Sanhedrin* 82a) say that the reference is to male-to-male intercourse. Commenting on the corruption of the generation that was ultimately obliterated by the Flood (Genesis 6:2): '... and they took themselves wives from whomever they chose', the *Midrash Bereshit Rabbah* 26:9; *Vayikra Rabbah* 23:9 (cited in Rashi Genesis ibid.) explains that the generation of the Flood indulged in, amongst other perversions, homosexual relationships. The midrash says that 'the generation of the Flood was not blotted out from the world until [their corruption reached such low levels that] men arranged "ketubot" – "marriage contracts" – for relationships with other men and with animals'. (The implication of this teaching is that their endeavours to formalise such relationships and make them 'politically correct' constituted 'the last straw' before the verdict for their annihilation was sealed. See the commentaries *Matenot Kehunah* and *Etz Yosef* on the midrash. See also TB *Chullin* 92a–b, where the Gemara speaks about the minimal 'observance' of the nations of the world, who 'do not write marriage contracts for their homosexual relationships'. Rashi, ibid., *s.v. she'ein kotvin*, explains that whilst the nations are suspect of engaging in male-to-male intercourse, and people 'set aside a specific male for their service' in this capacity, 'they do not treat the commandment [against homosexual intercourse] so lightly that they would actually [formalise this procedure] by documenting it in a contract'.)

For an example of homosexual rape and sadistic torture, see Genesis 19:4–5: '... the town's people, the people of Sodom, converged upon the house, from young to old, ... and they called to Lot and said to him, "Where are the men who came to you tonight? Bring them out to us that we may know them"'. The *Midrash Bereshit Rabbah* 50:10 (cited by the commentary of Rashi, verse 5) explains: 'that we may know them – by homosexual relationships'. The midrash states that the Sodomites had a 'rule' that any visitor that would come to the town should be raped and have his money confiscated.

See also Genesis 9:22: 'And Ham, the father of Canaan, saw his father's nakedness ...'. According to some rabbinic authorities, the meaning of this 'euphemistic' phrase is that Ham performed sodomy upon his father, Noah, when the latter was lying in a drunken stupor (see TB *Sanhedrin* 70a cited in Rashi's commentary to Genesis ibid.).

Similarly, Genesis 39:1 records how Joseph was purchased as a slave by Potiphar, a courtier of Pharaoh in ancient Egypt. The Gemara (TB *Sotah* 13b) explains that Potiphar purchased Joseph for homosexual purposes, but God intervened and sent the angel Gabriel to castrate Potiphar.

The decimation of the tribe of Benjamin recorded in the book of Judges chapter 20 resulted from the notorious incident of a group of that tribe in Gibeah who sought, amongst other things, to commit homosexual rape (ibid., 19:22). See Nachmanides on Genesis 19:8, who explains in great detail why the crime of the Sodomite people was worse than the crime of the members of the tribe of Benjamin. Amongst various factors he notes that the latter were motivated by lust, whereas the former were motivated by wicked cruelty and the institutionalised persecution of strangers.

The Gemara (TB *Shabbat* 149a) discusses the homosexual indulgences of Nebuchadnezzar, who used to sodomise the kings who were subject to him. The Gemara relates that Nebuchadnezzar used to cast daily lots to decide which members of royalty he would sodomise on any given day. Commenting on the verse in Isaiah (14:18), the Gemara explains that when Nebuchadnezzar died, his victims were finally freed from the humiliation that Nebuchadnezzar had imposed upon them. The Gemara there relates that when Nebuchadnezzar attempted to sodomise Zedekiah the king of Judah, Divine retribution was immediately inflicted upon Nebuchadnezzar, who was publicly humiliated and disgraced by a miraculous occurrence: 'his foreskin extended 300 cubits and encircled the entire gathering' of kings seated before him. This, says the Gemara, is the homiletical meaning of the verse in Habakkuk (2:16): 'you have been sated with shame rather than honour'. The reference is to the great embarrassment Nebuchadnezzar endured in the above-mentioned scenario. The verse in Habakkuk continues: 'you too will drink *ve-he'arel*' (and be confounded). The Gemara, in a homily on the word *ve-he'arel*, explains that the reference is to the exposure of Nebuchadnezzar's prepuce. The word *arel*, which is the root of the word *ve-he'arel*, means 'uncircumcised'; hence it is a reference to the foreskin. Furthermore, the numerical equivalent of the word *arel* (as spelt in Hebrew: *ayin* – 70, *resh* – 200, *lamed* – 30) is 300; a reference to the 300 cubits which was the extended length of Nebuchadnezzar's foreskin (see R. Yosef Chayim of Baghdad, *Ben Yehoyada* on *Shabbat*, ibid., who suggests that the 300 cubits are significant because they constitute the numerical equivalent of the word *yetzer* (spelt *yud* – 10, *tzadi* – 90, *resh* – 200), 'inclination', referring to the impetus of the evil inclination for sin).

See also JT *Sanhedrin* 6:3 which recounts the story of R. Yehudah ben Pazi, who discovered two men having intercourse in the attic of the *Bet HaMidrash* (the house of study). They warned him to keep silent, since as a lone witness in court, his testimony would be outweighed by theirs.

For 'case studies' in which the sin of *mishkav zachar* features in the responsa literature, see R. Shlomoh ben Aderet, *Teshuvot HaRashba*, vol. 5, no. 177; R. Berdugo (1747–1822), *Teshuvot Mishpatim Yesharim*, vol. 1, no. 111; R. Pallaggi (1788–1869), *Teshuvot Chikekei Lev*, vol. 1, no. 47 (cited below in chapter 4, note 42); R. Yosef Chayim of Baghdad, *Teshuvot Torah Lishmah, Teshuvot b'Inyanim Shonim*, no. 413; R. Kook (1865–1935), *Teshuvot Da'at Cohen, Yoreh De'ah*, no. 3.

R. Eliyahu Mizrachi (d. 1526), was consulted about a case in which it had been testified by two perfectly valid witnesses that the beadle of a synagogue in Aragon had performed homosexual activities with a boy in the synagogue. The question was whether this act desecrated the synagogue to the extent that it would be forbidden thereafter to pray there.

R. Mizrachi replied that, since a rumour had been spread to the effect that it was forbidden to pray there, or even to keep a *Sefer Torah* there, he felt obliged to declare that such an opinion is wrong. Moreover, it is even wrong to express such a view. If such a view were correct, it would mean that it was forbidden to pray in any house that was once occupied by Christians, since they all have icons before which they burn incense. Even though idolatry – which is the most severe and most repugnant of all sins – has been practised in such houses, it is the universal Jewish practice to rent houses from Christians and to pray in them. The sages said (TB *Avodah Zarah* 52b) that even the Holy Temple did not become contaminated when they set up an idol there. In the liturgy for Chanukah (*v'al ha-nissim*), we state that the Greeks 'contaminated Your Sanctuary', yet when the Hasmonean *cohanim* re-consecrated the Temple, it was used as before. This provides an *a fortiori* argument: If a place possessing the great sanctity of the Temple does not lose its sanctity because of the severe sins committed there, a lesser sanctuary such as the synagogue obviously does not lose its sanctity even if grievous sins have been committed there. Do not suggest that, although idolatry is the more serious crime, homosexual intercourse is more despicable, thus rendering the place like a bathhouse, in which it is forbidden to pray. This is not the case, for idolatry is also despicable and is referred to in the Scriptures as 'excrement'. *Avodah Zarah* is no better than homosexuality or bestiality (*Teshuvot Rabbi Eliyahu Mizrachi*, no. 81 – cited in R. Kagan (1839–1933), *Mishnah Berurah*, *Bi'ur Halachah* on *Orach Chayim*, 151:1).

3 See Exodus 21:10; Maimonides, *Hilchot Ishut* 14:1–2; *Shulchan Aruch Orach Chaim*, 240:1; *Even HaEzer*, 25:2. Whilst it is true that in Judaism, the primary function of the sexual act is the *mitzvah* of procreation, it is also recognised that most men could not remain celibate and therefore the Torah provided mankind with a permissible 'sexual outlet' – through marriage. Even one who is unable to bear children or one who has already fulfilled the *mitzvah* of procreation, is advised to get married; a primary reason for this is that it is almost impossible for an ordinary person to remain single without violating his sanctity by transgressing the dictate of the Torah's sexual code. R. Meir Simchah of Dvinsk (1843–1926) in his *Meshech Chochmah* on Genesis 9:1 (s.v. *p'ru u'rvu*) writes: '… the Torah did not deprive sexual pleasure from any creature with the exception of Moses [who was, at a certain stage in his life obliged to abstain from conjugal relationships at all times, since he had to be constantly ready, and in a state of purity, to receive direct communication from God], who, due to his unique level, did not require this'. For any other individual this would constitute a 'burden that his body is not able to accommodate'. God's Torah, says R. Meir Simchah, is a Torah of 'pleasantness and peace' and would never demand the impossible.

In this context it is also noteworthy, that whilst by no means accepted by other halachic authorities, one prominent rabbinic authority – Rabbi Yaacov Emden – advocated the institution of *pilagshim* (concubines) as a deterrent against licentiousness and promiscuity. He wrote a lengthy responsum presenting halachic arguments which would endorse the reintroduction of a form of concubine marriage (*Teshuvot She'elat Yavetz* 2:15). This would have involved a couple agreeing to live together as sexual partners without any religious ceremony or marriage contract. The relationship could be dissolved without the need of a *get* (halachically acceptable Bill of Divorce), and thus, such an arrangement would not cause the problems of *mamzerim* (children born out of certain illegitimate relationships) in the event that the 'partnership' would break down. R. Emden supported his position with the argument that his ruling would help save the sanctity of the Jewish people who had been influenced by a promiscuous Gentile environment and the licentious practices of the Shabbatean sects. If more latitude could be granted for forging either pre-marital or extra-marital stable and healthy sexual partnerships, R. Emden argued, then people would be less likely to break the prohibitions of the Torah (and there would be more opportunities to increase the Jewish population). What is relevant in our context is that R. Emden emphasises the all too human need for sexual relationships which, he says, is the reason that prior to the ban on polygamy instituted by Rabbeinu Gershom, Jews were allowed – and in some Sephardi communities are still allowed – to have more than one wife. R. Emden is of the opinion that polygamy was endorsed by the Torah precisely because of its recognition of man's passionate desires, especially given the fact that if a man were only to have one partner, there would be significant time spans when he would not have any permissible sexual outlet, such as when his wife is in a state of ritual impurity after her menstrual flow, childbirth and the like.

R. Emden advocated that his view ought to be publicised and that it would be advantageous even for God-fearing Torah scholars to avail themselves of the option of concubinage, because 'he who is greater than his fellow, has a more passionate inclination than his fellow'. I reiterate that other authorities, both contemporary to him and later, did not support R. Emden's position by allowing such concubine partnerships, but his comments are most pertinent in this context, in terms of the appreciation by a great halachic authority of the nature of sexual drives and impulses, something which – probably his disputants would also agree with – the Torah realistically recognises and seeks to accommodate for within the parameters of *halachah*.

4 See TB *Yoma* 69b; *Sanhedrin* 64a.

5 Alternatively, there is the strange idea advanced by R. Kook, *Orot Ha-Kodesh*, vol. 3, p. 297 ('Perversions of the Natural Inclinations') – recently elaborated upon by R. Naor in his *Rav Kook on Homosexuality* – that the homosexual may be able to find relief for his homosexual desires in heterosexual anal intercourse! (See my comments below, chapter 7, note 31.)

6 See the position statement on 'Psychiatric Treatment and Sexual Orientation' issued by the American Psychiatric Association, 1998; Davison, 'Construction and Morality in Therapy for Homosexuality'; Drescher, 'I'm Your Handyman', pp. 19–42; Haldeman, 'The Practice and Ethics of Sexual Orientation Conversion Therapy', pp. 221–227.

7 In 1992, an organisation was founded in the USA called NARTH, 'National Association for Research and Therapy of Homosexuality', which is composed of a group of psychoanalysts, psychologists, social workers, behavioural scientists, 'as well as laymen in fields such as law, religion and education'. This organisation believes that some homosexuals are able to experience 'substantial healing'. Some of them may be able to 'reach a level' where they can live 'committed celibate lives' and some may have their homosexual feelings 'diminished greatly' after 'several years' of therapy fuelled with 'desire, persistence, and a willingness to investigate the conscious and unconscious conflicts from which the condition originated'. More recently, a 'Jewish Outreach Organisation established to assist men and women in working through unwanted same-sex attractions' was established by psychotherapist, social worker and Rabbi Sam Rosenberg under the name of JONAH, as an acronym for the phrase 'Jews Offering New Alternatives to Homosexuality'. Borrowing substantially from NARTH, JONAH patrons the ideas of Dr Joseph Nicolosi, executive director of NARTH and author of *Reparative Therapy of Male Homosexuality*, who believes that homosexuality is often a developmental problem associated with a faulty family constellation, particularly between a distant father and son, with an overly intrusive mother. These factors, coupled with poor peer-group relationships and/or sexual molestation, have the effect that the boy does not fully internalise male gender identity (similar theories are advanced for explaining the phenomenon of female homosexuality). Nicolosi has documented his theory in the above-mentioned book (and in a subsequent book entitled *Healing Homosexuality*, in which he reports 'case stories of reparative therapy'). However, even if we were to ignore the highly controversial nature of Nicolosi's ideas and methods, it ought to be noted that even Nicolosi does not believe that homosexuals can become heterosexuals.

Even Nicolosi believes that the underlying homosexual attractions felt by homosexuals rarely, if ever, disappear. Thus, reparative therapy is aimed at reducing their salience, encouraging heterosexual contacts and eventual marriage and children, with celibacy the supported action for those who do not find their heterosexual attraction reaching levels that would allow sexual contacts with women.

In *Reparative Therapy*, chapter 3 (page 22), Nicolosi writes as follows: 'In his final work, "Analysis: Terminable and Interminable", Freud concluded that analysis is essentially a lifetime process. This is true in the treatment of homosexuality, which – like many other therapeutic issues such as alcoholism or self-esteem problems – requires an ongoing growth process. Yet while there are no shortcuts to personal growth, how long it takes to reach a goal is not as important as the choice of direction. A sense of progress toward a committed value is what is important. The non-gay homosexual is on the road to unifying his sexuality with his masculine identity. That he can look back over the past months and see a realization of some of the goals to which he has committed – this is what gives hope.'

Elsewhere, Nicolosi writes: 'Usually some homosexual feelings will persist or reoccur during certain times in the life cycle. Therefore, rather than "cure", we refer to the goal of "change". As one married ex-gay man described it: "for many years I thought I was gay. I finally realised I was not a homosexual, but really a heterosexual man with a homosexual problem ... Now those homosexual fantasies are more like a gnat buzzing around my ear."'

8   See Berger, 'Orthodox Attitude to Homosexuality' (letter) in *Jewish Chronicle*, 30 June 1995, p. 31. See also his *Truth about Homosexuality*, where he advocates an extremely conservative attitude towards modern claims about homosexuality, but nevertheless acknowledges 'the truth of the matter' that, whilst some homosexuals may benefit from certain types of therapy (which will enable them to experience healthy heterosexual relationships), 'for a number of homosexuals, they may indeed have very little choice in terms of their orientation' (p. 93). See in greater detail his article 'The Psychotherapeutic Treatment of Male Homosexuality', pp. 251–261. See also R. Bulka, *One Man*, p. 35: 'Therapy only works if the patient really wants it, *and even then there is no guarantee.*'

9   Nicolosi, for example, acknowledges in *Reparative Therapy* that 'this treatment fits the majority of the homosexual clients *in my practice*. Some others *are inappropriate for reparative therapy because they show no signs of gender identity deficit and do not match our developmental model*' (p. 22). R. Bleich, *Judaism and Healing*, p. 72 (probably following R. Lamm in his *Judaism and the Modern Attitude to Homosexuality*, p. 201), for example, writes: '*it is estimated that as many as a third of all homosexuals may ultimately be cured*, and it is believed that with utilisation of psychiatric behaviour-control techniques the rate of success is even higher'.

10 In general, R. Feinstein, *Iggerot Moshe Yoreh De'ah*, vol. 2, no. 57, is extremely ambivalent about resorting to the professional help of 'non-believers' in the psychological sphere. He is particularly concerned that the therapist may introduce his client to ideas which go against Torah values, if not indoctrinating him with heretical beliefs. He therefore recommends that only God-fearing Jews should be sought for psychological and psychiatric treatment. In the event of a child or adolescent requiring psychological help, and no observant Jew being available for the purpose, R. Feinstein – somewhat reluctantly – suggests that the parents stipulate with the therapist that he will not in any way undermine the child's Torah-oriented value system.

In connection with therapy for people with a homosexual orientation, there are numerous additional problems. See, for example, Moshe Halevi Spero, 'The Halakhic status of *Hirhur Asur* in Psychotherapy', in his *Judaism and Psychology*, p. 145 ff. See also his 'Homosexuality: Clinical and Ethical Challenges', idem., p. 158 ff. Spero acknowledges that 'the treatment of homosexuality is as fraught with divergent theories as the issue of its development. Opinions range from pessimistic views that even early intervention can do no more than avert the development of more severe pathology to views which recognise that relief from anxiety, focal relief of homosexual symptoms, and even cure are possible with some homosexuals. Successful case studies have been reported by psychoanalytically oriented therapists and by behaviorists.' Insight-oriented psychotherapy (exploration of the 'defensive aspects of homo-sexual relationships') has sometimes helped to 'cure' homosexuals especially ones who are 'young and serious about change'. The definition of 'cure' in this context is 'cautiously defined as the achievement of the capacity to control homosexual urges or, at best, the abolition of overt homosexual responses and possibly the development of some heterosexual response'. Spero then proceeds to explore the problems incurred by behavioural therapies, which 'promise rapid, effective and economical programs of change'.

Spero outlines two methods of behavioural therapy used to help homosexuals change:

Based on the clinical evidence that heterosexual responsivity can be demonstrated in most homosexuals, despite their apparent lack of interest in and aversion to heterosexuality, two major approaches have been devised. One is the behavioral rehearsal of heterosexual activity with deconditioning of the heterosexual anxiety (a learned fear response to heterosexual stimuli). The second involves orgasmic reconditioning procedures using both the patient's own homosexual fantasies as well as erotic audiovisual material to slowly build up a response to fully heterosexual stimuli as well as to heterosexual relationships. The use of female surrogates in such therapies has not been unheard of (though Masters and Johnson and others have officially discontinued the use of surrogates in their sexual dysfunction and sexual deviance clinics). Masturbation to increasingly greater amounts of heterosexual stimuli, and initially to autoerotic stimuli, is generally a crucial aspect of both approaches' (p. 159).

Spero demonstrates convincingly that there are halachic complications in both psychoanalytic and behavioural treatment approaches to homosexuality. The first is the halachic prohibition against *hirhur arayot* (thoughts about illicit sexual relationships), which may be 'involved in talking of homosexual fantasies and wishes, incestuous feelings which underlie homosexual behaviour, or auto-erotic impulses'. Spero develops a rather complex approach to this issue, which he feels may facilitate the permissibility of *hirhur arayot*, in the context of therapy. He suggests that such adventures may represent part of the process of *viduy* (confession) and *teshuvah* (repentance): 'Repentance for any sin, whether of an interpersonal nature or between man and God, requires a full recognition of all aspects of the sin. The *viduy* must be both an internal and a verbal experience ... perhaps the modern tool of psychotherapy can be conceptualised halachically as following the models of *teshuvah* and *viduy*. This is not to say that merely reciting *al het* (the confessional prayer) can be equated with full psychotherapy when psychotherapy is what is indicated, but rather that psychotherapy is accepted into the halachic world *via* its meta-psychological form as *viduy*. If so, then all the halachic details of *viduy*, its goals and mechanics, would obtain with regard to the psychotherapeutic encounter as well. Thus, what was formerly construed as *hirhur assur* [forbidden thoughts] now becomes a halachic desideratum if it is therapeutically necessary for the successful modification of behaviour – if it is something which should rightfully be confronted and dealt with during *viduy*. That is, *qua* the experience of *viduy*, one deals with the affective nature of the thought/act divorced from its negative value, while, reflectively, one is aware that in other contexts the act has negative value ... practically speaking, it becomes halachically tenable to expect the religious patient to nondefensively probe, examine, and discuss the realm of *hirhurim*' (pp. 151–152).

Even if one were to accept Spero's theory that in certain circumstances the exploration of erotic thoughts and fantasies can be considered part of a rehabilitative, and consequently penitential, procedure, it would require an extremely God-fearing therapist to ensure that the 'confessional prayers' did not degenerate into the realm of forbidden thoughts, for as Spero himself writes, 'it becomes the responsibility of the therapist to ensure that the atmosphere of the therapeutic encounter remains consistent with the halakhic guidelines' (Spero, p. 152). In pragmatic terms, this would mean that only a therapist who is conversant with and committed to the observance of the 'halachic guidelines' – subtle as they are – would be able to serve as a therapist for an observant Jew, according to Spero.

With regard to the procedure of 'orgasmic reconditioning' involved in some behavioural models, Spero notes that there is a variety of problems (the use of female surrogates would be out of the question), since the prohibition against stimulating an erection to auto-erotic or forbidden sexual stimuli would impede the critical aspects of current trends in behavioural therapy for homosexuals. Spero does suggest an innovative idea whereby it could be argued that such stimuli would be permitted: 'the prohibitions referred to until now ... revolve around the sexual act and impulse solely as a function of *kiruv derekh hibah ve-nishuk be-derekh ta'avah*: acts of intimacy in the manner of *conscious desire for a forbidden relationship* or forbidden relationships in general. There should be a sense, then, in which the sexual act can be separated from the motive, if not from the biological mechanism of sexual arousal, so that one could conceive of a halachically appropriate manner in which the homosexual patient might be allowed to produce an erection to therapeutically introduced sexual arousal (stimuli of the type discussed in the preceding paragraph). Some examples reflect the differentiation I am suggesting' (pp. 161–162). After presenting what may constitute halachic precedent for such a premise, Spero, however, concludes that even if such a premise could be established, it would probably not be sufficient to justify the above-mentioned behavioural techniques from a halachic point of view. In Spero's own words: '... *Nevertheless, from the standpoint of the clinical requirement that the patient undergoing behavorial therapies experience these sexual sensations without anxiety and as desirable and pleasurable sexual responses, it is difficult to say that the psychological factors concomitant to the physical evidence of arousal are separable*' (pp. 162–163, italics for emphasis in the original). Thus, at the end of the day, Spero acquiesces that all forms of psychological therapy entail grave halachic problems which would result in the unfortunate conclusion that 'the halakhically observant professional has nothing to offer the homosexual patient save helping him to accept the halakhic status of *ones*, one compelled to be in one's condition' (p. 161). See also Steinberg, *Encyclopaedia* (note 5), p. 76. (As Morris writes in 'Challenge, Criticism and Compassion: Modern Jewish Responses to Jewish Homosexuals' (p. 287), the apparent upshot of Spero's writings on this issue is 'that the delicacy of Halakhah impedes the very kind of thorough treatment he recommends ... The most traditional psychological treatment is off limits to the most traditional Jew'.)

With regard to Nicolosi's models of treatment (note 6), the reader concerned with the halachic problems may wish to consider the following paragraph from *Reparative Therapy*:

> Heterosexual, sexual attractive male friendships *with men for whom the client feels an erotic attraction offer the greatest opportunity for healing.* Only through such associations can there be the transformation from erotic attraction to true friendship – that is, the demystifying of the distant male. While aesthetic appreciation for the man's good looks and masculine qualities may always be present, it will become increasingly evident that sexual fantasies do not fit within the mutually respectful friendship (pp. 199–200).

Nicolosi also writes (p. 193): 'Clients report that when they engage in vigorous physical activity ... they feel more masculine'. He suggests that homosexuals would benefit from 'going to the gym, a particularly "straight" gym where there are no distractions'. Nicolosi is apparently unaware of the fact that many homosexual men may find heterosexual athletes to be particularly attractive, or to paraphrase Nicolosi, 'distractive'.

I am not claiming that the above-mentioned problems are insurmountable – it is possible that there are halachically valid solutions to them. (The correspondence between R. Moshe Tarashchanskij and R. Berlin, published in the latter's *Teshuvot Meishiv Davar*, part 2, nos. 43–44, sheds some light on this issue. These authorities discuss the propriety of counselling a person to commit a lesser sin, in a situation where, were he not to do so, it is probable – or even inevitable – that he would not abstain from committing a more severe sin. Netziv concludes his discussion of this matter with the following statement: 'The following principle [is paramount]: great caution must be exercised before permitting a transgression in order to avoid [a more severe] transgression. The matter is analogous to physical surgical therapy: if a doctor detects a severe malaise in a person's hand, he may choose to amputate the hand in order to avoid the possible risk of the disease's spreading to the rest of the body and endangering the person's life. Conversely, he may decide that it is better for the patient to endure the pain so as not to lose the hand. Such decisions are only made after the careful deliberation of medical specialists, who take into account the dangers inherent in both options. In a similar vein, [concessions in halachic matters for the sake of] cure of the spiritually sick demands the cautious deliberation of people who are great in Torah ...' This subject and its many ramifications awaits a comprehensive study.) I merely seek to emphasise that those professionals who firmly believe in the advantages of psychological therapy for homosexuals have themselves acknowledged that the methods that are employed in such therapies involve components which may not allow a devout Jew to benefit from such procedures, without compromising on his own religious integrity. As Spero writes (ibid. p. 161) we still await 'a full treatment of the topic by recognised halakhic authorities'.

Parenthetically, R. Spero's position is somewhat unclear on this matter, since in a later article – 'Further examination of the halakhic status of homosexuality', p. 11 – he argues that those who think that homosexually orientated individuals are 'compelled' to remain in their 'present state' are in error. He writes: 'Of course, the viable treatment techniques are time-consuming and involve a level of commitment and participation from the patient that is not easy to maintain. Thus, many of the so-called 'unsuccessful techniques' or 'untreatable' cases of homosexuality, are in fact instances of incomplete or inadequate treatment. ... Precisely who are those homosexuals ... who 'cannot' change? Are they in fact homosexuals who bolted treatment when insight became too painful? Were they homosexuals who were misaligned with their particular psychotherapist, or who lost interest in change, following several unfortunate experiences with pseudo-therapeutic modalities? Or where they homosexuals who would have sought change, had their homosexuality caused them sufficient anguish and conflict …?'

In light of Spero's conclusion in his earlier article, one would have to assume that his latter argument about the feasibility of therapy was either based on a hypothetical situation, whereby 'recognised halakhic authorities' would sanction the halachically-controversial therapies, or entertain the unlikely notion that this argument was addressed to those who do not abide by the dictates of *halachah*.

Aside from the possible inconsistency in Spero's articles regarding the viability of therapy from a halachic perspective, I believe that there is an inherent flaw in his logical argumentation. When one speaks about the feasibility of change in sexual orientation, one must take into consideration the subjective conditions; particularly those of the person seeking change. There is no guarantee that people will be aligned with the 'ideal' psychotherapist, they do not ordinarily elect or regulate the degree of 'psychological anguish and conflict' that their condition causes them, nor do they have an infinite power of perseverance when exploring the dynamics of their inner psyche. Moreover, even those professionals in the psychological field who believe that therapy can modify homosexual orientation are in disagreement about what constitutes the correct techniques. Under such circumstances, how can the lay person ensure that the form of therapy he has chosen (or can afford) would not be considered as one of the 'pseudo-therapeutic modalities,' by other professionals? Thus, the fact that in prevalent conditions, Spero seems to acknowledge that many homosexuals have not found the effective therapy or therapist, means – in simple terms – that such people have not been *able* to change their orientation. Consequently, even if Spero's hypothesis is true, such homosexuals are still 'compelled' in their orientation until the arrival of the ideal set of circumstances.

11 The pitfalls of analogies are many. Notwithstanding these, I suggest that a comparison to marital therapy may be illustrative. A variety of therapies for the improvement, or even the 'salvation', of marriages has emerged from modern schools of psychology. Most people would agree that such therapies have enjoyed success as well as failure. However, I venture to say that few would advocate the notion that, since we are now blessed with a plethora of 'treatments' designed to restore harmony and meaningfulness to a relationship, there is never reason to consider divorce. With the best therapies in the world, some marriages are, unfortunately, irredeemable. The same may be true with regard to homosexuality. It may be possible that certain therapies may provide opportunities for *some* homosexuals in *certain* conditions to embark upon heterosexual relationships. Whether or not this is the case, and to what degree this is possible, is debatable. However, the claim that is unfortunately not unheard of, namely that there is no need for a religious guide for the confirmed homosexual, his family and community because 'given the right therapy' such a situation is only a temporary one, strikes me to be logically most unfounded.

12 It is worthwhile noting that a (rather poor) English rendition of R. Feinstein's responsum on this matter has already been produced by Moshe Goldberger, in his *A Treasury of Teshuvah Selections* (pp. 25–26), which was published with an approbation from – amongst others – R. Feinstein himself.

13 Leviticus 18:22; 20:13.

14 Cited in note 4 to this chapter.

15 TB *Yoma* 35b.

16 For details of the most awesome challenge confronted by Joseph, see *Yoma* (previous note).

17 See TB *Avodah Zarah* 26b. The Talmud there explains that although, generally speaking, people find the idea of eating insects and gnats most repulsive, it is possible for a person to develop a desire to taste 'the forbidden fruit'. Something which is forbidden automatically becomes tempting.

The Mishnah at the end of Tractate *Makkot* states 'Rabbi Chananya ben Akashya said: The Holy One, blessed be He, wanted to confirm merit upon Israel; He therefore gave them a copious Torah and an abundance of commandments; as it is said (Isaiah 42:21), God desired for the sake of [Israel's] righteousness to make the Torah great and glorious.' Rivan in his commentary on the Mishnah explains that this means that although people abstain from eating things like crawling creatures and carrion after their own accord, God made the abstention from consuming such foods a *mitzvah* – by commanding against eating them in the Torah – so as to bestow upon Israel reward for something they would do anyway.

R. Soloveitchik, *Derashot Bet HaLevi* 12th Discourse, explains, however, that the very fact that injunctions against eating such abominable things have been included in the Torah, causes the evil inclination to desire what the person would otherwise have found most repulsive.

18 Deuteronomy 32:16.

19 See *Rashi* on Deuteronomy (previous note), who explains the Hebrew term '*b'toe'vot*' as: 'with abominable acts such as male homosexuality and witchcraft, to which Scripture applies the term "abomination"'. (Witchcraft is referred to as an abomination in Deuteronomy 18:12.) R. Feinstein explains that witchcraft, like homosexual practices, is also a tool for encouraging sinful behaviour for the sole purpose of annoying God. He cites, in this context, the Gemara (TB *Sanhedrin* 67b), which interprets the biblical term for sorcery *keshafim* as an acronym for '*makchishin pamalya shel ma'alah*' – '[the sorcerers] undermine the Heavenly forces'. For the sorcerers can inflict death on people who – had they been left to the dictates of Divine Ordinance – would have lived. R. Feinstein explains that the sorcerers, through their witchcraft, cause people to rebel against God and do things to annoy Him. In this way, the sorcerer is (almost) as bad as the man who engages in homosexual congress, who also does so – according to R. Feinstein – for no other reason other than to annoy God!

20 R. Feinstein, *Iggerot Moshe Orach Chayim*, vol. 4, no. 115. It is noteworthy that in his discussion on lesbian practices (*Dibrot Moshe* on TB *Shabbat*, vol. 2, ch. 53, section 35), R. Feinstein does acknowledge the possibility of intense desire for lesbian relationships, although it seems evident that the idea of a women being of exclusive homosexual orientation was foreign to him. R. Feinstein writes that 'it is certain that women who have such passionate desires and lusts [for sexual relationships] would likewise have an enormous desire for [heterosexual] promiscuity, if they would only have the opportunity' (although, it is possible, he writes that a woman who indulges in lesbian pleasures may abstain from pre-marital intercourse with a man since heterosexual pre-marital intercourse is a more severe sin than lesbianism). R. Feinstein writes that it is possible that Rav Huna (TB *Yevamot* 76a) who declared that a woman who had engaged in lesbian activities is ineligible to marry a *cohen gadol* (according to the interpretation of Rashi TB *Shabbat* 65b) – did not consider the lesbian activities tantamount to 'harlotry' and therefore disqualify the woman as the Talmudic commentaries seem to suggest but he – did so on the grounds that a woman who allowed herself to indulge in lesbian activities must be possessed by such a powerful sexual drive, that it is reasonable to believe that she had engaged in (heterosexual) pre-marital relationships which would render her unsuitable for marriage with a High Priest who is only allowed to marry a *betulah* (virgin).

21 See, for example, the discussion in Tosafot on TB *Sanhedrin* 9b, *s.v. liretzono* – quoted extensively in chapter six of this book, note 26. (This problem has already been indicated by Steinberg, *Encyclopaedia*, vol. 4, p. 75, note 561.)

22 Maimonides *Hilchot Deot* 1:1–2.

23 R. M. Schneerson, '*Rights*' or Ills, p. 6.

24 R. Bleich, *Bioethical Dilemmas*, p. 134. Elsewhere R. Bleich writes: 'The homosexual act is a matter quite distinct from the state of homosexuality. The former is an act governed by free will, while the latter is a state of being. The former can be proscribed; the latter may well be beyond a person's control. It is the act, rather than the psychological state, which is the subject of the Torah's admonition.' (*Judaism and Healing: Halakhic Perspectives*, p. 71.)

Spero ('Further examination of the halakhic status of homosexuality', p. 110) dismisses this as 'halakhically inaccurate'. Firstly, Spero states: 'Rabbi Bleich is suggesting that homosexual *behavior* is reprehensible when it is not the result of *ones*, and that the homosexual *condition* is not reprehensible because it is not behavior!'. This is merely a fair paraphrasing of Bleich, but Spero considers this to be untenable. For, halachically, 'fantasy, the realism of *hirhur* [contemplating], is considered a basic tributary of behavior ... *hirhur* about content of illicit sexual nature (*hihur arayot*), such as homosexual fantasies, is considered an 'appurtenance of *arayot*' and is rabbinically if not biblically forbidden in its own right.' Concomitantly, Spero concludes, 'that homosexuality as a state of being, while not punishable according to the express biblical criterion, is no less subject to halakhic accountability ...'

Spero's argument is unconvincing. If one were to accept his line of reasoning one would, arguably, have to conclude that the heterosexual 'state of being' – the heterosexual 'condition'

– is likewise a sin for which one is accountable. This would mean that virtually all people are sinners by mere virtue of the fact that they are prone to sexual thoughts and experience sexual desires; this is obviously not the case. Indeed, *halachah* forbids wilful entertainment of any sexual thoughts outside the environment of marital intimacy. This does not mean that a human being is commanded to ensure that he is never visited by sexual thoughts and desires. As will be explained at greater length in chapter 3, the Torah recognises that the human mind and heart are open and vulnerable and thus subject to all sort of wants, including sexual ones. Such phenomena are not under the control of the human being and are thus not forbidden by the Torah (which does not demand the literally impossible). We are commanded, however, that when visited with illicit thoughts we should dismiss them by diverting our minds to different things – a commandment that human beings of any sexual orientation often find extremely difficult to abide by. Thus, both the homosexual and the heterosexual *acts* (including wilful indulgence in sexual fantasies) *are* proscribed by the Torah; and conversely both the homosexual and the heterosexual as *states of being* – namely people who are designed to experience desire – are *not* proscribed by the Torah. On this analysis, R. Bleich (who would undoubtedly acknowledge that indulging in homosexual fantasies is forbidden by the Torah) is correct in his assertion that it is the homosexual act – not condition – that is proscribed by the Torah.

25 All emphasis – in the quotation from R. Feldman – has been added by this author.
26 R. Feldman, *A Personal Correspondence*, p. 69.
27 See Maimonides, *Shemonah Perakim*, ch. 6.
28 R. Bleich (note 24), p. 135.
29 R. Bulka, in his work *One Man*, p. 31, writes: '… one must reject the idea that human types be divided along the lines of what they do in the bedroom. The dictates of modesty and the imperative to walk humbly with God make the labelling of anyone as homosexual, or heterosexual, for that matter, inappropriate.'

I am in full agreement with Rabbi Bulka that personal identity should not be defined by sexual practices ('what they do in the bedroom'), or, for that matter, by their sexual desires or emotional chemistry. Indeed, I believe that if society would veer away from the current tendency to categorise people – men or women – according to their sexual disposition, much of the unjustified discrimination towards those with a minority sexual disposition would be ameliorated. Yet, the term homosexual may still be used as an adjective to describe the emotional infrastructure of any given individual who is attracted only to members of the same sex. To be sure, using such adjectives as 'heterosexual' or 'homosexual', when discussing issues where this information is not relevant, would seem to infringe on the ethos of modesty. However, in the context of a study such as ours, which concerns itself with the challenges confronted by the individual (and his environment) precisely because of his or her sexuality, I see no reason why such adjectives should not be employed.

30 R. Freundel, *Homosexuality and Judaism*.
31 R. Freundel (previous note), p. 79.
32 R. Freundel (note 30), p. 80.
33 See Midrash Shemot Rabbah 34:1; Bemidbar Rabbah 12:3.

3 THE FORMIDABLE CHALLENGE

1 See Maimonides, *Hilchot Teshuvah* 5:1–2.
2 See TB *Makkot* 23b; Maimonides, Introduction to *Mishneh Torah* (end).
3 See Maimonides (note 1), 5:4: 'If God were to decree that an individual would be righteous or wicked or that there would be a quality which draws a person by his essential nature to any particular path [of behaviour], set of ideals, attributes or deeds, as imagined by many of the fools [who believe] in astrology – then how could He command us through [the words of] the prophets to: "Do this", "Improve your behaviour", or "Do not follow after your wickedness"? … What place would there be for the entire Torah?'
4 This constitutes Maimonides' eleventh Principle of Faith. See Maimonides in his commentary to the Mishnah, *Sanhedrin*, ch. 10: 'God grants a generous reward to those who observe the commandments of the Torah, and punishes those who transgress its prohibitions. The

ultimate reward is the World to Come, and the ultimate punishment is *karet* (excision).' See also, at length, Maimonides, *Shemonah Perakim*, ch. 8.

5   See Maimonides (note 3): 'Were God to decree that an individual would be righteous or wicked ... according to which sense of justice would retribution be administered to the wicked or reward to the righteous – shall the Judge of the entire world not act justly?'

6   TB *Berachot* 33a.

7   Maimonides, *Guide for the Perplexed*, part 3 ch. 49 writes: 'if a man becomes sexually excited without having intended it, he is obliged to direct his mind to some other thought and to reflect on something else until this sexual excitement passes away'. R. Schneur Zalman of Liady, *Likkutei Amarim – Tanya*, ch. 12, explains: '... For this is how man is created from birth, that each person may, with the will-power in his brain, restrain himself and control the drive of lust that is in his heart, preventing his heart's desires from expressing themselves in action, word or thought, and divert his attention altogether from the craving of his heart toward the completely opposite direction particularly in the direction of holiness ... even in the mind alone, in so far as sinful thoughts are concerned, evil has no power to compel the mind's volition to entertain willingly, God forbid, any wicked thought rising of its own accord from the heart to the brain ... no sooner does it reach there than he thrusts it out with both hands and diverts his mind from it the instant he reminds himself that it is an evil thought, refusing to accept it willingly, even to let his thoughts play on it willingly; how much more so to entertain any idea of putting it into effect ...'

See also R. Schneur Zalman, *idem*, ch. 14, that the task of man is 'to "turn away from evil and do good", in actual practice – in deed, speech or thought, wherein the choice, ability and freedom are given to every man that he may act, speak and think even what is contrary to the desire of his heart and diametrically opposed to it. Even when the heart craves and desires a material pleasure ... he can steel himself and divert his attention from it altogether ...'

8   See *Pirke Avot* 2:3: 'Do not be sure of yourself until the day you die.' See also R. Schneur Zalman, *Likkutei Amarim*, ch. 27, where he speaks of those who experience sadness as a result of the thoughts and desires that enter their minds, and explains that there is no logical basis for such a feeling. The service of man to God involves a repetitive procedure whereby man is called upon 'to subdue the evil impulse and thought rising from the heart to the brain, and completely to avert the mind therefrom, thrusting the temptation away with both hands ...'

Moreover, R. Schneur Zalman writes, there is cause for joy inasmuch as the intruding thoughts give him occasion to fulfil a *mitzvah* and therefore, 'he should, on the contrary, be happy in his portion in that, though they enter his mind, he averts his mind from them in order to fulfil the injunction, "That ye seek not after your own heart and your own eyes, after which ye goest astray" ... Indeed, the rabbis, of blessed memory, have said [TB *Kiddushin* 39b], "He who has passively abstained from committing a sin, receives a reward as though he had performed a *mitzvah*".' R. Schneur Zalman concludes with the following statement: 'therefore, no person should feel depressed, nor should his heart become exceedingly troubled, even though he be engaged all his days in this conflict, for perhaps because of this was he created and this is his service – constantly to subjugate the *sitra achra* [the forces of impurity].'

9   See Maimonides, *Hilchot Deot* 1:1. Maimonides, *Shemonah Perakim* (note 4), elaborates: '... It is, however, possible for a person to be born with a tendency to ... one of the shortcomings – i.e., conduct [representative of this trait] will come easier to him than other types of conduct. ... If the person who is by nature coarse and phlegmatic applies himself to study and conceptual activity, he will be able to learn and comprehend, albeit with greater difficulty and after expending more effort. Similarly, there are those, whose nature is more heated than the norm, who will be inclined to boldness. If [such a person] habituates himself to this form of conduct, it will come more readily to him. Conversely, a person whose nature is more cold-hearted than the norm will be inclined towards timidity and fear. If he habituates himself to these traits, he will acquire them faster, and it is only with great difficulty that he will be able to incline his conduct towards boldness. But if he trains himself in this direction, he will acquire this trait without a doubt.'

10   See TB *Shabbat* 88b–89a.

11   R. Meir Simchah of Dvinsk (1843–1926), *Mesech Chochmah* on Genesis 9:1 (8d) *s.v. p'ru*

u'rvu. See, in greater detail, chapter 2, note 3.

12 R. Emden, *Siddur Bet Ya'akov, Hanhagat Leil Shabbat, Mitot Kesef,* 7:1: '... When sperm is "surplus", nature prepares to discharge it, like other surpluses that are to be discharged. If, therefore, when the reproductive organs are ready to expel it but it gathers up inside, this is harmful and intercourse is necessary. Moreover, for one overcome by depression or insanity, *intercourse is beneficial, for it dissipates melancholy, calms bad temper, and gladdens the soul.* Also, a healthy man ... who becomes sexually aroused involuntarily and feels a heaviness in his loins, yet does not cohabit ... his sperm gathers ... and creates bad vapours which may affect the heart, brain and stomach, damaging his health and causing possibly fatal illnesses. So it happened with some who were accustomed to sexual release and then refrained for a long time; they died suddenly[!] Therefore, coitus is good for such a one; it cleanses the body of its fullness, lightens heavy-headedness and brightens his eyes ... but in moderation, coitus is good and beneficial in the ways stated ... *Just as proper and disciplined eating preserves life and sustains strength and health, so proper sexual expression is a source of pleasure and benefit to body and soul.*' (See also the ideas of R. Emden quoted in Chapter 2, note 3.)

   With regard to the physical benefits of sexual intercourse as a praiseworthy motivation to engage in such, see also R. Avraham Ibn Ezra, in his commentary to Leviticus 18:20 and Nachmanides, ibid., 18:19. In this context, it is worthwhile noting that Rabbi Yitzchak Aboab (fifteenth century), *Menorat HaMa'or, Ner Shlishi, Klal Shishi* (pp. 372–3), paraphrasing the list of commendable motives for sexual intercourse as outlined by Rabbi Avraham Ben David of Posquières (c.1120 – c.1197) in his famous formulation of a 'hierarchy' of praiseworthy reasons for engaging in intercourse, *Ba'alei HaNefesh, Sha'ar HaKedushah* (paraphrased in *Tur, Orach Chayim,* ch. 240 and *Even HaEzer,* ch. 25), includes an additional facet to the fourth motive of the Ravad. The Ravad states that the husband's intention is a meritorious one if he engages in intercourse in order to avoid 'sinful thoughts'. R. Aboab interpolates into this category the teaching of Maimonides (*Hilchot De'ot* 4:10) to the effect that sexual intercourse for the purpose of relief from physical pressures is healthy and morally appropriate.

13 See TB *Yevamot,* 62b ff. and commentaries thereon. See also the text of the seventh 'Marriage Blessing' in TB *Ketubot* 8a. The misery of not being able to marry is also possibly depicted in the talmudic narrative (TJ *Yevamot* 8:1; *Shabbat* 19:2) that an amoraic sage, who had a son who would not be able to marry in accordance with Jewish Law, prayed that his son should die!

14 See *Midrash Shemot Rabbah* 34:1; *Bemidbar Rabbah* 12:3; TB *Ketubot* 67a; *Sotah* 13b.

15 Dorff, *Matters of Life and Death,* p. 145. See also Conservative Rabbi Michael Gold, *Does God belong in the Bedroom?,* p. 148: '... To see halakhah in black-or-white, permitted-or-forbidden terms is to give a gay Jew a choice of either heterosexual marriage or a life of celibacy. A heterosexual marriage for a gay Jew would lead to a life of sexual frustration, unhappiness, and incompleteness, and it would be unfair for the spouse to be trapped in a marriage without hope of sexual fulfilment. On the other hand, *a life of celibacy is a tragedy in Jewish tradition. God created humans as sexual creatures; to deny one's sexuality for a lifetime is to frustrate God's design*' (emphasis added).

16 Indeed, we are commanded to emulate the attributes with which God is described (Deuteronomy 28:9; 11:22, as explained in *Sifrei* ibid.; Maimonides, *Sefer HaMitzvot* positive commandment no. 8; *Hilchot De'ot* 1:6): 'Just as the Holy One, Blessed be He, is called 'merciful', you, too, be merciful; just as He is called 'gracious', you, too, be gracious; just as He is called 'righteous', you, too, be righteous ...'. See also TB *Sotah* 14a (cited in *Sefer HaMitzvot,* ibid.).

17 See Deuteronomy 23:2: 'A man with crushed testicles or a severed organ shall not enter the congregation of the Lord'. For the details of this injunction, see Maimonides, *Hilchot Issurei Biah* 16:1–3; *Shulchan Aruch Even HaEzer* 5:1–2.

18 See Deuteronomy 23:3: 'A *mamzer* shall not enter the congregation of the Lord, even his tenth generation shall not enter the congregation of the Lord'. See Maimonides *Hilchot Issurei Biah,* ch. 15; *Shulchan Aruch Even HaEzer,* ch. 4.

19 There is an inclination amongst many halachic authorities that it is not a good idea to cause *mamzerim* to proliferate, something which would almost inevitably happen should *mamzerim* marry each other or converts. [See R. Babad (c.1800–1874), *Minchat Chinuch,* Mitzvah, no. 1, section 22, p. 6, that the proliferation of *mamzerim* would go against the

ethos of the Torah, whose 'ways are the ways of pleasantness', cf. R. Yosef Te'omim (c.1727–1792), *Peri Megadim, Mishbetzot Zahav Orach Chayim*, ch. 140:1; R. Landau (1713–1793), *Teshuvot Noda Be'Yehudah, Mahadura Tinyana, Yoreh De'ah*, no. 182; R. Emden, *Teshuvot She'ei'lat Ya'avetz*, vol. 2, no. 97.] Also, there is an understandable reluctance to advise a convert to marry a *mamzer*, given that the convert is a perfectly suitable match for a Jew who does not suffer any illegitimacy and could therefore sire untainted children (see, for example, R. Henkin, *Teshuvot Bnei Banim*, vol. 2, no. 39). There is possibly another solution (for a male *mamzer* only) to marry in a manner that he could bear children who would ultimately become fully fledged, legitimate Jews; see TB *Kiddushin* 69a; Maimonides *Hilchot Issurei Bi'ah* 15:4; *Shulchan Aruch Even HaEzer* 4:20. However, there are many legal, technical and pragmatic problems involved in such a procedure. Also, contemporary halachic authorities are very much divided on this issue, which makes its implementation – even if it were desirable – fraught with ever more problems. See R. Weiss (1902–1989), *Teshuvot Minchat Yitzchak*, vol. 5, no. 47; R. Breisch (1895–1976), *Teshuvot Chelkat Ya'akov*, vol. 3, no. 91. The reader interested in pursuing this matter is referred to R. Katz, *The Mamzer and the Shifcha*, pp. 73–104.

20 See *Midrash Vayikra Rabbah* 32:8; *Kohelet Rabbah* 4:1 (commenting on the verse in *Kohelet* 4:1). See also R. Breisch (previous note) who expresses his dismay with the tendency, in certain rabbinic circles, to make extraordinary efforts to free *agunot*, but who do not seem to exercise equal endeavour to free someone from the plight of *mamzerut*. R. Breisch acknowledges that the unfortunate *mamzer* will almost inevitably sin, given that perpetual sexual celibacy is hardly a viable option. (Given that a confirmed homosexual is also consigned – albeit for very different reasons – to 'perpetual sexual celibacy', we have reason to believe that R. Breisch's compassionate attitudes would also extend to a homosexual in such a situation.)

21 It is noteworthy that, in addition to the prohibition against the *mamzer* 'entering into the congregation of the Lord', there are several other most painful experiences he is likely to endure as a result of Jewish laws and principles applying to his 'condition'. See TB *Yevamot* 78b; TJ *Yevamot* 8:3 and *Kiddushin* 4:1; Midrash *Vayikra Rabbah* 32:7; Midrash *Bemidbar Rabbah* 9:4; *Shulchan Aruch Yoreh De'ah* 265:5; commentary of R. David HaLevi (1586–1667), *Turei Zahav*, ibid., no. 8; R. Shabbtai HaCohen (1621–1663), *Siftei Cohen*, ibid., no. 9; R. Eliyahu of Vilna, *Bi'urei HaGra*, ibid., nos. 21–22. See also R. Bachya Ibn Pakudah (eleventh century), *Chovot HaLevavot, Sha'ar HaTeshuvah*, ch. 10 and R. Dovber of Lubavitch (1773–1827), *Sha'ar HaTeshuvah*, vol. 2, 42d, to the effect that when the adulterer – who brought the *mamzer* into being – repents properly, the *mamzer* will automatically die (thus leaving no tangible 'souvenir' of the adulterer's sin – see the commentary of Rashi on TB *Chagigah* 9a, s.v. *Veholid mamzer*).

22 See R. M. Schneerson, *Emunah u'Madda*, p. 122. See also *Torat Menachem – Hitva'aduyot* 5744, vol. 1, pp. 290–91.

23 *Pirke Avot* 4:15.

24 This is quite characteristic of Conservative theologians. See, in a similar vein, Matt, *A Call for Compassion*, pp. 430–32: 'The crucial question, however, is whether homosexuality in contemporary society is to be identified with what the Torah forbade – whether, that is, the ancient and modern significance and consequences of homosexuality are the same and whether homosexuality today is inherently idolatrous, immoral and destructive of Jewish existence. The answer to the question involves, once again, the issue of free choice: are homosexuals able to choose and to change? If they are, they should be considered in violation of the Torah's prohibition, which is still binding; if they are not, but except for the sexual identity of their made do live faithfully by traditional Jewish standards, they should be fully accepted and respected … Those of us … who insist that it is God's "right" to prescribe standards for human behavior in general and for Jewish behavior in particular, and who teach that heterosexual behavior is God's intended norm, must not be so presumptuous as to deny God's "right" to create or permit the "homosexual exceptions". Indeed, with regard to such "exceptions" we must strive to echo and to mediate God's full acceptance and approval.'

25 See above chapter 1, note 30.

26 TB *Menachot* 29b.

27 Isaiah 55:8.

28 Psalms 145:17.
29 R. Feldman, *A Personal Correspondence*, p. 69. (Parenthetically, I disagree with R. Feldman's contention that 'it is not necessary' for the homosexual to change his orientation 'if that is at all possible'. If it is possible, I believe that a homosexual ought to change for reasons that I have elaborated upon in Chapter 2. The real issue is that it is not necessarily possible to change. For many homosexuals it appears to be impossible.) R. Feldman continues (p. 70), '... The fact is that neither homosexual or heterosexual activity has the capacity to grant happiness to humans, as even a cursory glance at our unhappy world will demonstrate. The only activity which can give us happiness is striving toward reaching the true goals of life. Life is not meant to be an arena for material satisfaction. It is to be used to carry out God's Will by coming closer to Him and serving Him by keeping His commandments. Sexual activity, by which the family unit can be built, is only one of the activities with which one can serve God. But someone who does not have this capacity still has a whole life and unlimited opportunities to serve God. I have written at the outset that it is important for you to come to terms with your homosexuality. But to do so, it is vital to change your orientation away from the manner in which Western culture views life, and instead see sexuality in its proper perspective. How does Judaism look at the reason for someone having been born or becoming a homosexual? Life is meant to be a set of challenges by which we continuously grow spiritually. Any physical defect curtails the enjoyment of life, but on the other hand, meeting the challenge inherent in such a defect can be the greater source of joy and accomplishment. Challenges are what life is all about, and homosexuality is one of these challenges. It is difficult for us to understand why certain people were given certain shortcomings as their challenge in life and others were not. We cannot fathom God's ways, but we can be sure that there is a beneficence behind these handicaps. When these short-comings are met, they will grant us a greater satisfaction from our lives and a deeper devotion to God than if we were not given them.'
30 R. Bleich, *Bioethical Dilemmas*, p. 136.
31 Ibid.
32 On a practical level, ultra-Orthodox communities certainly provide for an extremely tight and rigid separation and segregation between the sexes in any activities and enterprises that are intended to serve the needs of single people.
33 See *Midrash Bemidbar Rabbah*, 17:6; *Midrash Tanchuma Parashat Shelach*, 31; Rashi on Numbers 15:39.
34 It is noteworthy that, whilst the halachic codes provide for a most detailed list of prohibitions – designed as precautionary measures – to prevent forbidden sexual stimulation and activity between men and women, the laws provide very little for precautionary measures against homosexual stimulation and activity. The reason for this is that homosexuality is considered rare, a 'minority interest', which, therefore, does not warrant the legislation of such pre-cautionary measures which – by definition – would apply universally. See *Shulchan Aruch, Even HaEzer* 24:1 (based on TB *Kiddushin* 82a and paraphrasing Maimonides *Hilchot Issurei Bi'ah* 22:2) who writes: 'Jewish people are not suspect of homosexual copulation or bestiality; therefore it is not forbidden to be in seclusion with them [other males and animals]. However, if a person abstains from being in seclusion with a fellow male or an animal, his conduct is praiseworthy. The great sages would distance themselves from an animal, so that they should not be in seclusion with it. In our generations, in which there has been an increase of lewd people, it is appropriate to distance oneself from being in seclusion with a fellow male.' R. Sirkes (c.1561–1640), *Bayit Chadash, Even HaEzer* ibid. is of the opinion that 'nowadays', there is no need for such precautionary measures. R. Sirkes argues that the *Shulchan Aruch* which advocates avoiding seclusion with a fellow male was not giving a universal ruling, rather he was suggesting that in an environment – such as that in which the author of the *Shulchan Aruch* lived – where people indulged in homosexual practices, extra precaution is warranted. However, 'in our countries where it is unheard of that people have behaved promiscuously, committing the sin of homosexual intercourse, there is no need to distance oneself' to such an extent. Nevertheless, even he concludes that one who does distance oneself in such a manner 'is praiseworthy'. R. Luria (c.1510–1573), *Yam shel Shlomoh,* on TB *Kiddushin* 4:23, goes even further and suggests that it is *inappropriate* to abstain from seclusion with a fellow male or an animal and he argues that it smacks of *yuhara* (religious

snobbery) to avoid seclusion with a fellow male or an animal, because Jewish people are beyond suspicion of engaging in sodomy or buggery. (Likewise, with regard to female homosexuality, Maimonides, *Hilchot Issurei Bi'ah*, 21:8, paraphrased by *Shulchan Aruch, Even HaEzer*, 20:2, cautions: 'a man should be particular with his wife concerning this matter and he should prevent women *who are known for their lesbian practices* from visiting his wife or from having her visit them'. The implication is that unless 'known for their lesbian practices', no precautionary measures need be taken.)

However, see the discussion in *Otzar HaPoskim, Even HaEzer*, ibid., section 2. See also R. Pallagi (1788–1869), *Ruach Chayim, Even HaEzer* ibid.; *Tochachat Chayim* on Genesis *(Parshat Vayetzei)* p. 125. See also R. Kook (1865–1935), *Teshuvot Da'at Cohen, Yoreh De'ah* no. 3, who expresses the view that, in the 'hot' eastern countries, people have a greater propensity to desire homosexual relationships. [Gentiles, on the other hand (in ancient times), were always considered suspect of homosexual abuse: See TB *Avodah Zarah* 15b; Maimonides, *Hilchot Issurei Bi'ah* 22:5. *Avadim Kena'aniyim* – gentile slaves, purchased and owned by Jews, who acquired 'quasi-Jewish' status (see Maimonides, *Hilchot Issurei Bi'ah*, 12:11) – were suspected of engaging in homosexual activity, even with children. See TB *Berachot* 45b and the commentary of Rashi thereon, *s.v. im ratzu ein mezamnin*; Maimonides, *Hilchot Berachot* 5:7; *Shulchan Aruch Orach Chayim* 199:6; *Shulchan Aruch HaRav*, ibid., section 7; *Mishnah Berurah* ibid. section 14 (with regard to the impropriety of Canaanite slaves joining children for *zimmun*); TB *Pesachim* 91a–b and the commentary of Rashi thereon (95b), *s.v. avadim*; Maimonides, *Hilchot Korban Pesach* 2:4 (with regard to the impropriety of grouping slaves together with children for partaking of the Paschal lamb). However, these slaves were also suspected of excessive licentious behaviour in relation to women, as is evident in the above-mentioned sources.]

The Mishnah (TB *Kiddushin* 82a) teaches: 'A bachelor should not accustom himself to be a teacher of small children'. Commenting on this teaching the Gemara (ibid.) asks what is the reason for this ruling '... if it be suggested [that it is] because bachelors are [to be suspected of committing homosexual acts with] the children, surely this cannot be, for it was taught in a *Baraita* that ... Jewish people are not suspected of homosexual acts or bestiality!' The Gemara therefore concludes that the reason for a bachelor's avoiding the position of teacher of young children is because such a position would bring him into regular exposure to the mothers of the children who bring their small children to school. In such a situation, the bachelor may have to confront undue challenges of sexual desire as a result of his contact with the mothers (see Maimonides *Hilchot Issurei Bi'ah* 22:13; *Shulchan Aruch, Even Ha'Ezer* 22:20 and commentaries; cf. R. Yekutiel Yehudah Teitelbaum (1808–1883), *Teshuvot Avnei Tzedek, Yoreh De'ah*, no. 76, who offers justification for the practice of employing bachelors as teachers. See also R. Klatzkin (1852–1932), *Teshuvot Devar Halachah* no. 36). The Mishnah (ibid.) also cites the ruling of R. Yehudah who says that a bachelor 'may not herd cattle [Tosafot ibid. *s.v. ve'lo* explained that a bachelor would have more desire for bestiality than a married man]; two bachelors may not sleep sharing one blanket [because they may be drawn into homosexual acts]'. The Mishnah concludes, however, that the sages permit these things. Once again, the reason is because – according to the sages – Jewish people are not, in general, suspect of homosexual acts or bestiality. Maimonides, *Hilchot Issurei Bi'ah* 22:11 rules in accordance with the opinion of the sages and his view is cited by later authorities. Nevertheless, some authorities do advocate adopting the stricture of men not sharing the same blanket as a universal precautionary measure even in places where homosexuality is not rife, see *Otzar HaPoskim*, ibid., section 2.

Another area of male conduct in which the assumption that Jewish males are beyond suspicion of homosexual practices is that of men using perfume. The Gemara, TB *Berachot* 43b, cites a *Baraita* which teaches that a Torah scholar 'should not go out to the street perfumed'. R. Yochanan then qualifies this ruling. He says that 'it pertains only to a locale where people are suspected of homosexuality' and (according to Rashi) would wear scent (on their garments) to entice other men to desire them for homosexual relationships. Maimonides *Hilchot De'ot* 5:9 codifies this ruling: 'A Torah sage ... should not go out in the street perfumed, or with perfumed clothes nor should he put perfume on his hair. However, he is permitted to rub perfume on his body if he does so in order to remove sweat ... all of these [restrictions were instituted] because of the possible suspicion [of immorality]'.

R. Avraham di Boton (1545–1588), *Lechem Mishneh* on Maimonides, makes note of the fact that Maimonides does not qualify his ruling, as does R. Yochanan in the Gemara, to refer only to a place where homosexual practices are common. Later authorities, however, when citing this Gemara, do mention the qualification of R. Yochanan and some assert that 'nowadays when people are not suspect of indulging in homosexual practices, it is permissible for a man to wear perfume'. (See also R. Ayash (d. 1760), *Lechem Yehudah*, on Maimonides ibid., who contends that Maimonides would also agree that the prohibition against men wearing perfume only applies in places where people are suspect of homosexual practices. Maimonides did not find it necessary to state this qualification because it is self-evident from the above-mentioned Mishnah in *Kiddushin* which is cited in Maimonides' *Hilchot Issurei Bi'ah* 22:13. Cf. R. Karkovsky (d. 1929), *Avodat HaMelech*, on Maimonides *Hilchot De'ot* ibid. See also R. Avraham HaLevi (d. 1684), *Gan HaMelech* (published in *Teshuvot Ginnat Veradim*) no. 61 cited in *Otzar HaPoskim, Even HaEzer*, ibid., section 3.)

Yet another area in which the presumption is made that Jewish males are not ordinarily suspect of homosexual tendencies is that of bathing. The *Gemara* (TB *Pesachim* 51a) teaches that (with few exceptions) even close relatives may bathe together in the same bathhouse (see also Rama, *Shulchan Aruch Even HaEzer* 23:6). Rashi, ibid., *s.v. rochatzin shnei achim k'echad*, explains that the Gemara means to say that such conduct is not considered improper. We do not consider the possibility that, since they live together and now see each other naked, they will be aroused to homosexual activity. Cf. R. Yeshayah di Trani (c.1180–c.1260), *Tosafot Rid* on *Pesachim* (*Mahadura Telita'ah*), ibid., *s.v. v'ha-tanya* (p. 106).

35 See above chapter 2, note 9.
36 18:25.

4 ATTITUDES TO THE PRACTISING HOMOSEXUAL

1 See, most recently, Grossman, 'The Gay Orthodox Underground'.
2 This argument is particularly relevant to those theologians who are affiliated with Progressive movements, who, whilst feeling quite free to reject many commandments of the Torah, suddenly become 'devout traditionalists', citing biblically prescribed penalties for homosexual congress etc. – an image which they apparently feel tallies with their harsh condemnation of homosexuals and homosexual activity.

In this context, it is noteworthy that, whilst many rabbinical authorities – who were, naturally, adamantly opposed to homosexual activities – were not prepared, even in earlier days of the epidemic, to describe AIDS as a punishment for indulgent homosexuals (see, for example, Lord Jakobovits, 'Halachic Perspectives on AIDS', p. 14), a newspaper columnist, Chaim Bermant (not known for his religious zeal or 'fundamentalism') seemed more ready to do so. In his article 'Depravity, not deprivation, is the cause of our ills', he speaks with dismay about how 'every university has its gay society', and expresses his horror about the proliferation of AIDS, which 'is by far the deadliest venereal disease'. Bermant concludes with the following observation: 'Morals, or at least sexual morals, have in recent years been consigned to philosophers, theologians and biblical exegists. They have now become a matter of life and death and may suggest the truth of Goethe's saying: *Alle schuld racht sich auf erder* – all guilt is punished on earth.' Note also the extremely condemnatory attitude of a Reform Jew, Dr. Lehrman, in his Homosexuality and Judaism: are they Compatible?' and his 'Homosexuality and Judaism' and esp. 'Homosexuality: A Political Mask for Promiscuity', in contrast to e.g. Conservative Rabbi, Gordon Tucker, 'Homosexuality and Halachic Judaism' p. 40 ff. For a critique of Dr. Lehrman's ideas, see R. Wurzberger, 'Preferences are not Practices'; Matt, 'A Call for Compassion' and Gordon, 'Letter to the editor' in *Tradition*, Winter 2000, p. 101 ff.
3 It has not taken long for the Reform movement to come full circle in its attitude towards the prohibition against homosexual practices. Just over 30 years ago, Reform Rabbi Solomon Freehof – described by Soloff in his 'Is there a Reform Response to Homosexuality?', p. 417, as 'the eminent Reform *posek*' – expressed an 'authoritative' view on this issue, which was relatively loyal to traditional Jewish teachings. By the year 2000, the Reform movement had discarded virtually all traditional Jewish teachings regarding homosexuality. Whilst the

Conservative movement has not made such radical changes as the Reform movement, it should be noted that, whereas Conservative leaders such as Robert Gordis was, relatively speaking, committed to traditional Jewish teachings on this matter (see his *Love and Sex*, p. 149 ff and his 'Homosexuality and Traditional Religion' p. 398), present-day Conservative rabbis are becoming increasingly more open to a total revision of Jewish law in this regard (see Artson, 'Judaism and Homosexuality', pp. 52–54; Dorff, *Matters of Life and Death*, p. 139 ff).

The inability on the part of Progressive movements to establish a consistent attitude to the Torah's teachings with regard to sexual morality is well illustrated in a recently published '*Teshuvah*' of the CCAR Responsa Committee, 'On Homosexual Marriage'. The Progressive authors of this lengthy study acknowledge that Reform Jews 'have long since done away with the [kosher] dietary laws as an obligatory element of our religious practice' (p. 11). They continue 'to abhor many of the sexual unions proscribed in Leviticus 18 and 20, but we do so *not so much* because the Torah finds them abhorrent, but because *we see them* as violations of *our* most cherished moral standards. We condemn incest, for example, because it inherently involves an abusive relationship ... one which inflicts deep emotional and psychological damage ...'

They acknowledge that they no longer abhor homosexual relationships, because 'we, unlike our ancestors, are aware of the possibility of committed, stable, monogamous and loving relationships between members of the same gender'; they emphasise that, for an act to be considered a *to'evah*, it 'must be abhorrent to *us*; it must strike *us* as a transgression against the most basic standards of *qedushah* that the Jewish people are called upon to uphold. And we no longer view homosexuality as such a transgression.' Nevertheless, after a lengthy explanation of why 'it no longer makes sense to classify homosexual behaviour as a sin ... given our contemporary understanding of the nature of human sexual orientation', the authors cannot bring themselves 'to endorse rabbinic officiating of same-sex "marriage" or commitment ceremonies'. In the reasoning they offer to substantiate their opposition to a homosexual marriage 'within the context of Judaism', they suddenly 'revive' the heretofore rejected concept of *to'evah*. They write:

> we do not accept the suggestion that the ritual category of *to'evah* is irrelevant to the question under discussion. While we Reform Jews have departed from traditional practice in many areas, we continue to 'abhor' virtually all the sexual prohibitions listed in Leviticus 18:20 as destructive of the Jewish conception of a life of holiness and morality. While it may be true that we as a community no longer look upon homosexual behaviour, as we once did, as a repulsive act, the fact remains that no Jewish community has ever gone so far as to sanctify as marriage a sexual relationship which the Torah defines as *ervah*. Not even we, with all our liberality, have ever done this before. To do so now would be a revolutionary step, one that would sunder us from all Jewish tradition, including our own, down to most recent times.

A presentation of the critique of the inherent dichotomies in the writings of the CCAR Responsa Committee is, I daresay, hardly necessary. However, a number of questions may be posed to the chroniclers of the above-mentioned article. Firstly, the authors have already made it amply clear that it is, in their opinion, *nonsensical* to classify homosexual relationships as abhorrent. Consequently, the fact that they continue to abhor other sexual prohibitions listed in Leviticus cannot be the basis for their objection to the 'Jewishness' of homosexual commitment ceremonies. For commitment ceremonies are designed to stabilise and enhance 'monogamous and loving relationships between members of the same gender' – something whose value the authors acknowledge – and partners in such relationships are 'active members of our synagogues, colleagues in the rabbinate, and creative contributors to our religious and intellectual life'. It is therefore clear that their abhorrence to other sexual acts proscribed in Leviticus is not based on the Pentateuchal ban, but – as the authors themselves assert – 'because *we* see them as violations of ... moral standards'. Therefore, once it has been acknowledged that homosexual relationships no longer offend *their* moral sensibilities, what reason is there to the claim that, because 'our ancestors' considered homosexual relationships abhorrent, and because – 'coincidentally' – the prohibition against such relationships is located in the same chapter of Leviticus as other proscribed sexual activities that *do* offend *our* moral sensitivities, we should not be willing to support the moral endeavours of contemporary homosexual partners who seek to sanctify and celebrate their relationships?

Secondly, it is simply not true that these two chapters in Leviticus enjoy a special status in Reform Jewry, in light of the fact that Progressive Jews – in the same way as they have 'done away with the dietary laws' – have 'done away' with the biblical prohibition against intercourse with a woman after she has experienced her menstrual flow – a prohibition stated explicitly in Leviticus 18:19 and located between the prohibitions against incest and adultery and repeated in Leviticus 20:18 – also located amongst proscribed incestuous relationships, still abhorred by the authors of the article. To be fair to the authors, they do acknowledge this problem in note 36 (p. 33), where they write that 'The prohibition against sex with a *nidah*, or menstruating woman ... *may be something of an exception*. Though we have never 'legalised' it, the subject is absent from virtually all discussions of sexual ethics in Reform Judaism. At any rate, the *halakhah* also distinguishes between the *nidah* and the other *arayot* in that *qiddushin* with the former, unlike with the latter, is recognised as valid.' I fail to see the cogency in this argument. If the laws of *niddah* 'may be something of an exception', why not have another exception?

The fact that Jewish law differentiates between *niddah* and other *arayot* is a rather lame basis for distinction, for (in addition to the fact that Progressive Jews do not consider themselves bound by *halachah*) the fact that only those parts of Leviticus chapters 18 and 20 dealing with prohibited partners which *halachah* declares cannot effect a marriage with each other (*kiddushin*) should remain sacrosanct is in itself incomprehensible. (It is also noteworthy that – whilst not contained in the above-mentioned chapters of Leviticus – the Bible (Deuteronomy 23:3) declares that 'a *mamzer* shall not enter the congregation of the Lord', and the *halachah* does not recognise the validity of *kiddushin* with the *mamzer*. This, however, has not prevented Progressive movements from ignoring, if not opposing, the 'stigmatisation' of a *mamzer* and the prohibition of marriage with a *mamzer*, all which offend their moral values.

Thirdly, the fact that 'no Jewish community has ever gone so far as so sanctify as marriage a sexual relationship which the Torah defines as *ervah*' could not serve as a reason to oppose officiation at lesbian 'marriages' – a relationship which the Torah does not define as *arayot* (as explained in chapter 1).

Finally, why should a Reform rabbinate which is committed to religious and moral 'progression' refuse to take a 'revolutionary step' and break away from Jewish Tradition, when surely such steps are the very hallmark of Progressive movements over the last couple of centuries?

The authors seem to concede that, since 'sexual orientation is both unalterable and irrelevant to the capacity of an individual to form a loving and stable relationship with another', gays and lesbians should be '*encouraged, like their heterosexual counterparts, to find partners and to form monogamous, stable, and hopefully permanent relationships*'. They acknowledge the fact that the traditional Jewish values of marriage and family – including the wedding ceremony, 'that moment of magical transformation when two individuals become a *bayit beyisrael*' – are applicable to homosexuals. Why then do they maintain that their responsibility as rabbis does not 'warrant officiation at weddings or wedding-like "commitment ceremonies" for gay and lesbian couples' just because they know of 'no form of "Jewish marriage" other than *qiddushin*' which they understand as an institution 'whose legal essence excludes homosexual relations'?

4 See TB *Avodah Zarah* 26b; *Chullin* 4a; Maimonides, *Hilchot Rotzeach* 4:10; 12; *Hilchot Teshuvah* 3:9 and commentaries thereon; and *Shulchan Aruch, Yoreh Deah* 2:4–5; *Choshen Mishpat* 425:5 and commentaries thereon.

5 See Maimonides, *Hilchot Rotzeach* (previous note); *Hilchot Gezeilah Va-Aveidah* 11:2; *Shulchan Aruch, Yoreh De'ah* 158:1–2; and *Choshen Mishpat* 266:2, 425:5 and commentaries thereon; R. Kagan, *Mishnah Berurah* 329:9 (and *Sha'ar HaTziyun*, thereon no. 8); *Ahavat Chesed* 3:2–3 (and *Netiv HaChesed*, thereon no. 2); *Hilchot Lashon HaRa, Klal Vav, Be'er Mayim Chayim*, no. 27. It must be emphasised that this 'exclusion' only applies to certain areas of *halachah*. Essentially, every Jew – even the heretic or idolater – remains a Jew as the Talmud (TB *Sanhedrin* 44a) states: 'a Jew, even though he has sinned, remains a Jew.' He is

simply not able to 'give up' his Judaism. The *mumar le-hachis* is, like any other Jew, obliged to fulfil all the *mitzvot* of the Torah. See Maimonides, *Iggeret Teiman*, wherein he states that the wicked and idolatrous Jeroboam ben Nevat would be held accountable for failing to fulfil any *mitzvah*. Moreover, unlike a gentile whose act of betrothal to a Jewish woman does not take effect, the betrothal of an apostate to a Jewish woman is legitimate in *halachah* and thus can only be severed by a bill of divorce. See TB *Yevamot* 47b; Maimonides, *Hilchot Issurei Bi'ah* 13:17; *Shulchan Aruch, Even HaEzer* 44:9; (*Yoreh De'ah* 268:12); and R. Landau (1713–1793), *Teshuvot Noda BiYehudah, Even HaEzer, Mahadura Kamma*, no. 162, cited in R. Eisenstadt (1813–1868), *Pitchei Teshuvah, Even HaEzer* 44:9. See also R. Boronstein (1839–1910), *Teshuvot Avnei Nezer, Yoreh De'ah*, no. 109.

6 See R. J. Schneerson (1880–1950), *Iggerot Kodesh*, vol. 2, p. 526, who argues that the majority of Jewish sinners nowadays (in the 1930s!) are to be considered sinners out of desire for forbidden indulgence and not as heretics and atheists (whatever the formal statement of their position may be).

7 Obviously this only applies to those homosexuals who may be described as 'deliberate sinners'. Arguably, nowadays, the vast majority of homosexuals do not come under this category – because they instead come under the category of *tinok shenishbah* and its far-reaching ramifications (which will be discussed in Chapter 6).

8 See, most recently, R. Tendler, 'Treife Sex' – a response to R. Boteach's article, 'Dr. Laura Misguided on Homosexuality': '... The Torah refers to homosexuality as 'an abomination' and Boteach, with the irreverence of one who left the fold, points out that this same pejorative is used for other sins of mankind ... But he well knows that it is *such an aberration because it incurs the death penalty*.' See also, R. Feinstein, *Iggerot Moshe, Orach Chayim*, vol. 4, no. 115 (s.v. *hinei*), where this authority makes the point that homosexual intercourse is punishable not merely by *karet* (excision) but also with *sekilah* (stoning) – see above, chapter 1, notes 2–4.

9 One who desecrates the Shabbat deliberately, publicly and brazenly (even if he does so out of lust rather than spite) *has* excluded himself from the Jewish People for many purposes. See TB *Eruvin* 69a; *Chullin* 5a; Maimonides, *Hilchot Shabbat* 30:15; *Hilchot Geirushin* 3:15; *Hilchot Shechitah* (note 4); *Shulchan Aruch, Orach Chayim* 385:3; *Yoreh De'ah* 2:5; *Even HaEzer* 123:2 and the commentaries thereon.

10 See Maimonides, *Hilchot Shabbat* 1:2; and *Hilchot Issurei Bi'ah* 1:1–2. It is noteworthy that certain forbidden relationships which are – strictly speaking – not forbidden for gentiles, such as intercourse with a daughter or daughter-in-law (see Maimonides, *Hilchot Melachim* 9:5; and *Hilchot Issurei Bi'ah* 14:10), are also capital crimes for Jews. See Maimonides, *Hilchot Issurei Bi'ah* 1:4–5 (cf. Tosafot, TB *Nazir* 23a s. v. *le-Lot*; TB *Sanhedrin* 57b s.v. *la na' arah*). This seems to undermine the claim that the reason why homosexual intercourse is a capital crime is because it is forbidden for all humanity; see chapter 1, 'Universal Responsibility' and the notes thereon.

11 See above, beginning of chapter 1 ('Male Homosexual Behaviour') for details of *giluy arayot* and its attendant stringency.

12 See the references in chapter 1, note 6. Cf. R. Krauser, *Devar HaMelech* on Maimonides, *Hilchot Issurei Bi'ah* 1:9 (p. 22).

13 See R. Yom Tov Ishbili – *Ritva* (fourteenth century), *Chiddushei haRitva* on TB *Pesachim* 25a; R. Caro, *Bet Yosef* (1488–1575), *Yoreh De'ah*, chapter 195 s.v. *ve'katav od biTerumat haDeshen*; R. Shabbtai HaCohen (1622–1663), *Siftei Cohen* on *Shulchan Aruch, Yoreh De'ah*, ibid., no. 20; R. Yaffe (c.1535–1612), *Levush*, ibid., no. 17; R. Kluger, *Chochmat Shlomoh* on *Yoreh De'ah*, chapter 157. See also the exhortation of the *Chafetz Chaim* in his *Sefer HaMitzvot HeKatzer*, Negative Commandment no. 123. (*Taharat Yisrael*, ch. 4; *Bet Yisrael* ch. 3; *Machane Yisrael, Ma'amarim* 16:2; *Dinim*, ch. 18; *Nidchei Yisrael* 41:23; *Geder Olam* ch. 9. See also *Mishnah Berurah* 75:17. See also R. Perlman (1835–1896), *Ohr Gadol*, no. 1 (8a); and R. Feinstein, *Teshuvot Iggerot Mosheh, Yoreh De'ah*, vol. 1, no. 55 (end). There are others who disagree: see *Sefer HaChinnuch*, Commandment no. 296; R. Yehoshua ben Yosef of Cracow (d. 1648), *Teshuvot P'nei Yehoshua*, vol. 2, no. 44; R. Boronstein, *Teshuvot Avnei Nezer, Yoreh De'ah*, no. 129, subsection 11; R. Weingarten (1847–1922), *Teshuvot Chelkat Yo'av, Yoreh De'ah*, no. 29, in the second footnote thereon; R. Engel (1859–1919), *Atvan De'Oraita*, section 21; R. Yosef Chaim of Baghdad, *Teshuvot Torah Lishmah*, no. 494. See

also R. Waldenberg, *Teshuovt Tzitz Eliezer*, vol. 16, no. 70 section 2; vol. 17, no. 32; vol. 20, no. 36.)

The *Chafetz Chaim* once spoke about the commandments against incestuous relations with one's sister and intercourse with one's wife whilst she is in a state of ritual impurity following her menstrual flow. Both these commandments, he said, are included in the same portion of Leviticus, which enumerates the sexual liaisons that are forbidden under the category of *giluy arayot*. Both these commandments, he observed, are punishable by *karet*. Yet, is it not incongruous, he asked, how shallowness and ignorance have led people to appreciate the severity of one crime whilst grossly underestimating the essentially equal severity of the other crime? The *Chafetz Chaim* said:

> Could you imagine what would happen in the Jewish community if someone decided to transgress the first prohibition and marry his sister? He would be considered a social outcast, ostracised even by members of his own family. He would be disenfranchised in the synagogue and would certainly not be honoured with any communal position. On the other hand, someone who violates the second transgression, who does not observe the laws of family purity, can – in our day and age – be considered a distinguished member of the community, can become a synagogue warden or a patron of Jewish charity organisations. His renown and popularity may even be increased if he is also financially affluent. In truth, however, what is the difference between the first transgression and the second? Both of them come from the same source, the punishment incurred for both of them is the same. Why the extreme difference in communal reaction to these two crimes? It is merely ignorance and the loss of Torah values that has caused people to differentiate between these two transgressions. If knowledge of the Torah and true fear of God would prevail, we would not draw any distinction between these two prohibitions, and we would fulfil the laws associated with *niddah* with the same degree of meticulousness with which we all observe the prohibition against incestuous relationships with one's sister. (*Chafetz Chaim al HaTorah*, pp. 156–7.)

14 The only *single* laws that a person who violates even *le-tei'avon* and, as a result, loses his status as a member of the 'Jewish fraternity' are *Shabbat* (see note 8) and *avodah zarah*: see TB *Chullin* 5a; Maimonides, *Hilchot Avodah Zarah* 2:5; *Shulchan Aruch Yoreh De'ah* 2:5 *Even HaEzer* 123:2 and commentaries thereon.

15 See above, chapter 1, 'Female Homosexuality' and notes 21 and 22.

16 See also R. Freundel, 'Homosexuality and Judaism', p. 72:

> If one were, in fact, to apply a halachic category to this individual it would be the general category of *mumar l'teiavon* (one whose desires put him in opposition to Torah law), specifically *mumar l'mishkav zachor* (one who because of his repeated involvement in homosexual activity is in opposition to Torah law). Such a category exists in halachic literature, is clearly defined, and places the homosexual on an equal footing with other *mumarim* who violate other laws.

17 See above, chapter 2, 'The Hard Line' and notes 12 ff.

18 R. Herring, *Jewish Ethics*, p. 185 – based on R. Feinstein, note 7.

19 See chapter 2 and note 21 therein. See also Rashi, TB *Sanhedrin* 26b s.v. *ba-al hana'ah*.

20 R. Bulka, *One Man*, p. 33. See also R. Freundel (note 16):

> Some might argue that homosexuals who are exclusively homosexual [in their sexual activity] are actually *Mumarim L'hachis* (following Rashi A.Z., ad. loc. s.v. *L'teiavon*). Although some militant homosexuals may come close to this definition, the emotional conflicts and extenuating circumstances involved make it difficult to describe most, if any, homosexuals as having actively chosen to reject permissible sexual relations for forbidden ones in the same way that Rashi describes the *Mumar L'hachis'* behavior regarding non-kosher meat.

Whilst R. Freundel evidently rejects the notion that contemporary homosexuals would be termed '*mumarim le-hachis*', it is somewhat curious that he even considers, albeit tentatively, the idea that 'homosexuals who are exclusively homosexual' in their behaviour ought particularly to be described as sinners out of spite. Surely, those who are 'exclusively homosexual' are less likely to be engaging in homosexual intercourse 'out of spite'. The fact that they only engage in homosexual intercourse is presumably because they are of exclusive homosexual orientation. Consequently, they certainly do not have a reasonable, 'alternative option' to homosexual activity.

21 See the sources and discussion in R. Stern, *Imrei Yaakov* on *Shulchan Aruch HaRav, Choshen Mishpat, Dinei Nizkei Guf VaNefesh*, no. 72 and the notes thereon. See also, ibid., *Bi'urim* s.v. *aveirah le'hachis*. [See also R. Shor (d. 1633), *Tevuot Shor* 2:17 and *Bechor Shor* on TB *Avodah Zarah* 26b, based on Maimonides, *Hilchot Teshuvah* 3:9.]

22 Chapter 7. See note 23 there also.

23 One practical application is in the laws of the priestly blessing (*birkat cohanim*). A *cohen* who publicly desecrates the Shabbat, for example, is ineligible to perform the *mitzvah* of *birkat cohanim*. In contrast, a *cohen* who is known to indulge in *giluy arayot* is, nevertheless, entitled to fulfil this *mitzvah* – unless he is involved in an illicit sexual relationship which is *specifically* forbidden for *cohanim*. See R. Schneur Zalman of Liady, *Shulchan Aruch HaRav, Orach Chayim* 128:52–53 and *Chafetz Chaim, Mishnah Berurah* 128:134, 143–144. See also below chapter 6.

24 See above, beginning of chapter 2, 'Contemporary Understanding of Sexual Orientation'.

25 Novak, 'AIDS: The Contemporary Jewish Perspective', p. 147.

26 See R. Shor, *Simlah Chadashah* 2:13, that one who fails to fulfil a positive commandment may also be deemed a *mumar le-hachis*. (See also Nachmanides on Deuteronomy 27:26.) Cf. R. Teumim (c.1727–1792), *Peri Megadim, Petichah Kollelet* to *Orach Chayim* part 4 section 1; *Orach Chayim, Eshel Avraham* 37:1; R. Ashkenazi (1660–1718), *Teshuvot Chacham Tzvi*, no. 100.

27 TB *Avodah Zarah* 26a.

28 Maimonides, *Hilchot Rotzeach* 4:11–12.

29 Novak (note 25) also refers – p. 154, note 26 – to *Hilchot Teshuvah* 3:9. However, even a cursory reading of this source would suffice to demonstrate that it does not support Novak's contention.

30 Tur and Bet Yosef, *Choshen Mishpat* 425:5.

31 Bet Yosef on Tur (previous note), s.v. *v'yesh le-dakdek*.

32 R. Falk, *Derishah, Chosen Mishpat* (note 30) no. 12; *Me'irat Enayim* no. 21.

33 R. M. Sofer, *Teshuvot Chatam Sofer*, vol. 6, no. 67; R. Avraham Shmuel Binyamin Sofer (1815–1872), *Teshuvot Ketav Sofer, Choshen Mishpat*, no. 20, section 3.

34 *Chazon Ish, Yoreh De'ah* 2:16.

35 See Maimonides, *Hilchot Teshuvah* 2:9; *Hilchot Rotze'ach* 4:9; and *Sefer HaChinnuch*, commandment 258. See also Maimonides, *Guide for the Perplexed*, 3:35, who clearly classifies illicit sexual relationships in the category of commandments that are *bein adam laMakom*.

Since no distinction is drawn in this regard, this categorisation is, evidently, also true of those illicit sexual relationships that are forbidden under the Noachide Code (listed in TB *Sanhedrin* 58a; Maimonides, *Hilchot Melachim* 9:5). This premise may also be supported by the thesis of R. Meir Simchah HaKohen of Dvinsk (1843–1926), *Ohr Sameach* on Maimonides, *Hilchot Melachim* 3:10. He advances the argument that Maimonides' ruling to the effect that a Jewish monarch was entitled use his discretion and execute sinners (Maimonides speaks explicitly only of murderers) based on the testimony of one trustworthy witness (not usually accepted by Jewish courts) applies only to those who sinned in matters of *bein adam la-chaveiro*. However, with regard to misdemeanours that are committed *bein adam laMakom* and hence do not have such an effect on the smooth running of the country, the king has no such rights. R. Meir Simchah then questions his own theory on the basis of TJ *Sanhedrin* 6:3, from where it emerges that King David would have had the authority to kill two individuals who were guilty – according to the account of a pious and trustworthy person – of cohabiting with a dog. R. Meir Simchah suggests a tentative solution to this problem, the details of which are irrelevant to our topic. Evidently, R. Meir Simchah was of the opinion that bestiality (forbidden also for gentiles) belongs – like other of illicit sexual relationships – to the category of *bein adam laMakom*. See also the comment of R. Berlin, *Ha'amek Davar* on Genesis 6:11 in relation to the 'generation of the flood' who were sexually sinful (particularly with regard to homosexuality). See above, chapter 2, note 2.

Adultery (with someone else's wife) is apparently an exception to the rule. See commentaries of Nachmanides and R. Avraham ben HaRambam (1186–1237) on Genesis 36:9. [See also *Ezekiel* 18:6; *Midrash Bemidbar Rabbah* 10:2; and *Sefer HaChinnuch*, commandment 35.] This is also evident from the fact that the prohibition against adultery is included in the second half of the decalogue (Exodus 20:13 and Deuteronomy 5:17) which contains those commandments that are between man and man; see R. Abarbanel (1437–1508), Exodus 20:1; R. Horowitz (c.1560–1630), *Sh'nei Luchot HaBrit*, *Masechet Shavuot* 190b.

36 See Tosafot, *Avodah Zarah* 26a, s.v. *ve-ha-ro'im*.
37 R. Shabbtai HaKohen (1622–1663), *Siftei Cohen*, *Yoreh De'ah* 158:3.
38 See TB *Rosh HaShanah* 19a.
39 Lamm, 'Judaism and the Modern Attitude to Homosexuality', pp. 194–205.
40 Lamm (previous note) p. 203.
41 Although in certain ancient cultures homosexual intercourse may have been almost always associated with pederasty: See Sussman, *Sex and Sexuality in History*: 'Sexual intimacy between men was widespread throughout ancient Greek civilization. The male homosexual act usually involved anal intercourse with a boy.' See also Greenberg, *On The Construction of Homosexuality*.
42 The difference between a person who transgresses the prohibition against homosexual intercourse with a 'consenting adult' and a predatory paedophile need hardly be spelt out. The former has committed a sin between man and God (see above note 35) whereas the latter has committed a horrific crime against his fellow man: even 'the seduction of a minor is tantamount to rape' (TB *Yevamot* 33b). This distinction is also manifest in the halachic ruling (TB *Sanhedrin* 73a; Maimonides, *Hilchot Rotzeach* 1:10; and *Shulchan Aruch Choshen Mishpat* 425:1) that one who is caught chasing another person in order to sodomise him, falls under the category of '*rodef*', and like one who is pursuing another in order to kill him, may be prevented from doing so even at the cost of the pursuer's life *if necessary*. See also R. Pallaggi (1788–1869), *Teshuvot Chikekei Lev*, *Yoreh De'ah*, no. 46, wherein he discusses the case of a male schoolteacher who was, allegedly, fondling his young students' private parts and possibly even sodomising them. R. Pallaggi writes (ibid., s.v. *ivra d'im*) that in addition to the severity of the prohibition against *mishkav zachar*, the additional crime of the harm he does to the innocent children must be taken into consideration (see also R. Weiss, *Teshuvot Vaya'an David*, vol. 3 *Yoreh De'ah*, no. 68). Elsewhere R. Pallaggi writes (*Ruach Chayim* on *Even HaEzer*, ch. 24):

> It is obvious that where we found that a certain person had succumbed to the temptation [of sodomy], and if he were a teacher or one of the other professions, then under no circumstances would one allow him a further opportunity to be alone with a male ... Is it not fitting that one who has succumbed to temptation in his professional life should not be allowed to return to his former post ... It seems that anyone who succumbed in such a situation, even though he made complete repentance, is nevertheless forbidden against seclusion with a male. He would need to take a solemn and binding oath that he will never allow himself to be alone with a male by day and even more by night. Only then will his repentance be sufficient [to reinstate him in his professional position]. Everything depends upon the view of the local dayanim ...

R. Lamm is not the only one who seemingly fails to draw the far-reaching distinction between homosexual and paedophiliac behaviour. Reform Rabbi Rodney Mariner, 'The Jewish Homosexual', p. 90, also does not seem able to draw this distinction in a 'reverse direction'. Mariner writes:

> Maimonides' paradigm [*Hilchot Teshuvah* 2:1] of perfect repentance is that of a man who has committed a sexual sin who, as a result of his repentance, is able to be with the same woman, in the same circumstances and, as a result of his repentance, is able to resist temptation. It would seem that while it might be possible to give the benefit of the doubt if a woman was the sex object, fear of ravishment by even a penitent sodomite was too much for a heterosexual male to be expected to risk.

Parenthetically, it goes without saying that Maimonides never suggested that a penitent sinner should expose himself to temptation in order to 'test' whether he has achieved 'perfect repentance'. On the contrary, Maimonides states (in the same chapter) that the true penitent would constantly 'separate himself from the subject of his sin'. [See also R. Lunshitz (d. 1619), *Olelot Ephrayim*, vol. 2, discourse no. 277; R. Landau, *Drushei HaTzlach* 4a; R. Schneur Zalman of Liady, *Ma'marei Admur HaZaken – Inyanim* p. 311.] Maimonides is merely asserting that the ideal penitent would be one who could restrain himself even if confronted with the same degree of temptation.

Moreover, R. Pallaggi is primarily discussing the case of a teacher who exploited his innocent students. Surely, a teacher – whether homosexual or heterosexual – who has sexually abused his students, can repent and nothing stands in the way of *teshuvah*. However, society still has an obligation to protect the vulnerable, and if there is the slightest doubt about the resolution and stamina of the penitent teacher, he would be best advised to pursue other professions rather than expose himself to temptation and children to possible danger. Why R. Mariner cannot draw the distinction between an 'ordinary' penitent and one who had abused his position of trust to rape young children or sodomise naïve teenagers, is beyond me.

43 Prager, 'Judaism, Homosexuality and Civilization'.
44 Bell and Weinberg, *Homosexualities*, p. 85.
45 Prager note 43, part II, p. 11. See also Bulka, *One Man*, p. 45. Even non-Orthodox writers who clearly support homosexual relationships have acknowledged this problem. See Greengross, *Jewish and Homosexual*, ch. 4, p. 21: '... homosexual relationships are sometimes more ephemeral than heterosexual ones'.
46 Prager (note 43) part IV, p. 21.
47 See R. Epstein, *Aruch HaShulchan, Even HaEzer* 1:1 (see also *Avot* 2:2).
48 Weinstein and Wolowelsky, 'Counselling Homosexual Students', p. 93, correctly observe: 'While the rabbi or counsellor has an obligation to protect the student's religious well-being, there is clearly a similar obligation to protect his physical health. A person who has already engaged in certain types of homosexual behavior should be considered at serious life-threatening risk for AIDS and needs immediate health counselling. While it may be necessary to say outright that some specific behavior is anti-halakhic, it is also necessary to make clear that counselling is a process that takes time. It is important for the student to be kept safe while the process continues and, although desirable, it is unrealistic simply to demand (or expect) that non-halakhic behavior cease immediately. The rabbi or counsellor has to make this clear, and providing proper health information, including how to protect oneself from disease, is part of this obligation. Similar considerations apply when counselling a promiscuous heterosexual student.'
49 See TB *Bava Kama* 28b.
50 R. Riskin, 'Homosexuality as a tragic mistake'. There is, admittedly, some ambiguity in R. Riskin's statement. Initially he seems to acquiesce that it is 'cruel' to deny exclusive homosexuals any expression of their natural sexual desires. In contrast his last sentence seems to imply that unless the homosexual 'is acting out of compulsion' [presumably this means that he is not able to control his physical actions] he is held culpable. If indeed this is what he means, how has he answered his original question: 'how can we deny a human being the expression of his physical and psychic being?' I am therefore inclined to believe that R. Riskin's words suggest the possibility that an exclusive homosexual orientation may be sufficiently 'compelling', and, therefore, the homosexual is excused for his homosexual acts.
51 R. Freundel, 'Homosexuality and Halachic Judaism', p. 43.
52 R. Amsel, 'Healing AIDS patients and endangering oneself', *The Jewish Encyclopaedia of Moral and Ethical Issues*, p. 95.
53 Lamm (note 39) p. 202. In this context, R. Lamm appears to be rather indecisive, thus leaving room for much ambiguity on the part of the reader. Lamm writes '... This rubric will now permit us to apply the notion of disease (and, from the halakhic point of view, of its opposite, moral culpability) to the various types of sodomy ... we are not asserting the formal halakhic definition of mental illness as mental incompetence ... the categorisation of a prohibited sex act as *ones* (duress) because of uncontrolled passions is valid, in a technical halakhic sense, only for a married woman who was ravished and who, in the course of the act became a willing participant ... the homosexual act may possibly lay claim to some mitigation by the

halakhah ... it is our contention that the aggadic principle must lead us to seek out the mitigating halakhic elements so as to guide us in our orientation to homosexuals who, by the standards of modern psychology, may be regarded as acting under compulsion ... to apply the halakhah strictly in this case is obviously impossible; to ignore it entirely is undesirable ... Admittedly, the method is not rigorous, and leaves room for varying interpretations as well as exegetical abuse, but it is the best we can do.'

54 Maimonides, *Hilchot Rotze'ach* 2:2.

55 See Maimonides, *Hilchot Evel* 1:11 and the commentaries thereon.

56 See Maimonides (previous note).

57 See Goldstein, *Suicide in Rabbinic Literature*, p. 27 ff.

58 See my remarks above, note 42.

59 I am not sure what Dr. Lamm wishes to suggest by highlighting this difference. If his intention is to imply that male to male intercourse is a more severe sin than committing suicide, he has failed to do so. For notwithstanding the fact that the prohibition against suicide is not stated *explicitly* in the Torah, it is considered – in Jewish law – as tantamount to murder which is a more severe sin than sexually forbidden acts (see Maimonides, *Hilchot Rotze'ach* 4:9). See R. Ganzfried (1804–1886), *Kitzur Shulchan Aruch* 201:1; R. Tykocinski (d. 1955), *Gesher HaChayim*, vol. 1, 25:1 and the sources cited there. Cf. R. Babad, *Minchat Chinuch* Commandment 35 and R. Posner (1729–1807), *Bet Meir* on *Yoreh De'ah* 115:5.

60 Genesis 9:5; TB *Baba Kamma* 91b; Maimonides, note 54.

61 Lamm, note 40.

62 See also Lamm 'The New Dispensation on Homosexuality', p. 14.

63 H Matt, 'Sin, Crime, Sickness or Alternative Life Style?', p. 17. See also Conservative Rabbi Robert Gordis, *Love and Sex*, p. 156.

64 See above, chapter 3: 'Unequal Trials'; 'The Unique Challenge of Homosexuality'.

65 R. Bleich, *Judaism and Healing*, p. 71.

66 See R. Zadok, *Tzidkat HaTzaddik,* ch. 43 (6c): 'Sometimes a person is confronted with such a great test that it is simply impossible for him not to sin ... In such circumstances, the person is considered to be the subject of duress and the All-Merciful exempts him. Sometimes the evil inclination is so strong that the temptation is literally irresistible and the person has no choice but to sin ...'. R. Zadok continues, however, to assert that no-one can claim with any degree of certainty that he was subject to such compelling temptation, for how does one know; 'perhaps he did have the ability to subjugate his desires' but simply did not exert his full strength and stamina in the battle with his passions.

67 R. Mordechai Yosef Leiner of Izbica (1800–1854), *Mei HaShiloach*, on *Parshat Pinchas* 54a. R. Zadok was a disciple of R. Leiner and his reference in *Tzidkat HaTzaddik* (previous note) to the novel interpretation he heard with regard to the Zimrei episode, is probably the one elaborated upon in *Mei HaShiloach*.

68 See R. Epstein, *Aruch HaShulchan Yoreh Deah* 345:5: 'The general rule with regard to suicide is that we attribute it to any [extraordinary] condition such as [overwhelming] fear, suffering or the loss of one's senses, or the [erroneous] assumption that it was a *mitzvah* to do so in order to avoid having to commit other sins, and so on. [This must be the case] since it is truly unlikely to suppose that a person would commit such a heinous act with a clear mind.'

69 Novak (note 25) p. 148.

70 R. Goldberg, 'Homosexuality: A Religious and Political Analysis', p. 30.

6 THE CHILD'S CRY

1 TB *Shabbat* 68b; *Shavuot* 5a.

2 Maimonides, *Hilchot Mamrim* 3:3. See also his *Perush HaMishnah, Chullin,* ch. 1 (and the parallel text in the Kafach Edition of the *Perush HaMishnah*); *Hilchot Shechitah* 4:16 as interpreted by R. Aboab (1610–1720), *Teshuvot Devar Shmuel, Yoreh De'ah,* no. 4; R. Schwadron (1835–1911), *Da'at Torah* on *Shulchan Aruch Yoreh De'ah* 2:5; *Chazon Ish* (cited below, note 7); R. Moshe Soloveitchik (1879–1941) in *HaPardes* (Cheshvan 5747), pp. 9–10; R. Hutner (1906–1980), *Pachad Yitzchak, Pesach,* third Discourse, part 3.

3 From the wording of Maimonides in this paragraph, it is evident that he considers the *tinok*

shenishbah to come under the category of *onnes*, namely one who does wrong as a result of compelling circumstances that are beyond his control. This is in contrast to the halachic category of *shogeg* ('the inadvertent sinner'), who is not considered culpable for his wrong-doing as is the *meizid* ('the deliberate sinner'), for, whilst he sinned unintentionally, there was some carelessness on his part (see Maimonides, *Hilchot Shegagot* 5:6, who explains that the reason a *shogeg* has to bring a sin-offering to atone for his inadvertent sin is because he should have been more cautious and meticulous in his behaviour 'for if he had examined matters carefully [before acting] and made careful enquiries, he would not have come to sin inadvertently').

[See, however, R. Moshe Schick (1807–1879), *Teshuvot Maharam Schick, Yoreh De'ah*, no. 132, who asks why Maimonides (in *Hilchot Mamrim*, previous note) classifies the *tinok shenishbah* as an *onnes*, when he himself rules (in *Hilchot Shegagot* 2:6) that one who was a *tinok shenishbah* has subsequently to bring a sin-offering for the transgressions which he committed in that state. This would seem to indicate that the *tinok shenishbah* does assume a certain degree of 'accountability' for his errors, for otherwise why would he require the atonement achieved by the sin-offering? This question was anticipated by R. Falk, *Pnei Yehoshua* on *Tosafot Shabbat* (note 1) *s.v. aval tinok*. *Pnei Yehoshua* explains that there is no greater *annus* than a *tinok shenishbah*, but, nevertheless, the halachically accepted view in the Talmud is that one sin-offering is still required in order to serve as a *kaparah* (atonement); evidently, the sins of the *tinok shenishbah* also require a 'minimal' degree of cleansing. For a different explanation as to why the *tinok shenishbah* is obliged to bring a sin-offering, although he is most definitely an *onnes gamur*, see R. Weingarten (1847–1922), *Chelkat Yoav*, vol. 1, *Dinei Onnes, Anaf Alef*.]

At any rate, from the wording of Maimonides and the subsequent authorities that cite him, it would appear that he considered the *tinok shenishbah* not to be a *shogeg*, but rather an *onnes* or at least a quasi-*onnes*: see the discussion in R. M. Sofer, *Teshuvot Chatam Sofer*, *Choshen Mishpat*, no. 22 *s.v. ve-zot sheinit* ff; and R. Spektor (1817–1896), *Teshuvot Eyn Yitzchak*, vol. 1, *Even HaEzer*, no. 70, section 4 sub-section 19 (p. 380); R. Feinstein, *Teshuvot Iggerot Moshe, Orach Chayim*, vol. 5, no. 13, section 9; R. Sternbuch, *Teshuvot Vehanhagot*, vol. 2 no. 207. (These sources provide a partial response for Spero ('Further Examination of the Halakhic Status of a Homosexual', note 59, p. 121), who is 'not even sure if the full halakhic status of the oft-cited category *tinok shenishbah* ... actually means to render the individual to whom it is applied an *ones gamur*'.)

For a variant reading of the paragraph in *Hilchot Mamrim* – according to which the 'inclusivist' nature of this teaching is somewhat modified – see R. Rosanes (1657–1727), *Mishneh L'Melech Hilchot Malveh v'Loveh* 5:2 (*s.v. od katav*); *Mabit*, vol. 1, no. 37. R. Rappaport, *LiTeshuvat HaShanah* on Maimonides *Hilchot Teshuvah* 3:6 (p. 215) reports that R. Yitzchak Ze'ev Soloveitchik (1886–1959) favoured this reading.

On the other hand R. Karelitz, 'BeGeder Tinok Shenishbah', p. 21, R. Becher and R. Newman, *Avotot Ahavah*, section 3, chapter 2, note 4 (p. 41) argue that even according to Nachmanides, *Chiddushei HaRamban* on TB *Bava Metzia* 71b (cited in R. Yosef Chaviva, *Nimmukei Yosef* (fifteenth century) and R. Caro (1488–1575), *Bet Yosef* on *Yoreh De'ah* ch. 159) who argues for a more limited definition of the *tinok shenishbah* than Maimonides, the average, present day, non-observant Jew would still be classified as a *tinok shenishbah*.

4 See the tentative ruling of R. Ettlinger, *Teshuvot Binyan Tziyon haChadashot*, no. 23; R. Schmelkes (1828–1906), *Teshuvot Bet Yitzchak, Yoreh De'ah* vol. 2 (in his *Kuntros Acharon*, no. 23) and *Even HaEzer*, vol. 2, no. 65; R. Schwadron (1835–1911), *Teshuvot Maharsham*, vol. 1, no. 121; and R. Yosef Sha'ul Nathanson (1810–1875), cited in R. Hoffman (1843–1921), *Teshuvot Melamed LeHo'il, Orach Chaim*, no. 23.

5 Even halachic authorities of the Hungarian-Satmar school have taken such a view: See R. Harfenes, *Teshuvot Nishmat Shabbat*, vol. 2, no. 497 (p. 393).

6 R. Weinfeld, *Responsa Lev Avraham*, vol. 1, no. 87. See also R. Weiss, *Teshuvot Va'Ya'an David*, vol. 2, *Choshen Mishpat*, no. 249: '... The *tinok shenishbah* does not come under the category of the *mumar*, even if he does not adhere to a single commandment of the Torah'. See also ibid., no. 262, section 3 (see further note 39).

7 See, for example, R. Kagan, *Kitvei Chafetz Chaim*, vol. 3, letter no. 65, who describes 'contemporary' sinners as people who are misled by others, 'they are literally like lost sheep

who do not know how to find their way home'; R. Karelitz, *Chazon Ish Yoreh Deah*, 1:6; 2:18 (and the footnote thereon, 8a); R. Teichtel (1885–1945), *Em HaBanim Semechah*, ch. 1 (pp. 72–3); ch. 2 (p. 110); ch. 3 (p. 185); R. Henkin (1891–1973), *Kitvei HaGrya Henkin*, vol. 2, no. 8, section 2 *s.v. uvedoreinu* ('... we treat them as *annusim* ...'); R. M. Schneerson, *Likkutei Sichot*, vol. 6, p. 273; vol. 26, p. 131; vol. 30, p. 213; R. Feinstein, *Iggerot Moshe, Orach Chayim*, vol. 3, no. 12; vol. 4, no. 91, section 6; 'A Time for Action', published in the *Jewish Observer*, June 1973 ('... many people who are far from a Torah life can be categorised as *Tinokos Shenishbu*, people held captive by Gentiles since infancy ...'). See also R. Klein, *Teshuvot Mishneh Halachot*, vol. 9, no. 407, *s.v. umikol makom*, and ibid., no. 228. (It is noteworthy that R. Klein applies the *tinok shenishbah* status and its attendant ramifications to a Jew who is guilty of murder and other horrendous crimes.)

   Recently, many Orthodox authorities have acknowledged that Progressive ministers may also be classified as *tinokot shenishbu*. See, for example, R. Frand, 'Where there is Rabbinic Will', p. 9, who discusses the writings of a 'female rabbi'. He says: 'I do not mean to mock this "rabbi"; she is in the category of a *tinok shenishba* – a captive child, brought up without benefit of exposure to Torah teachings and Torah values.'

8 R. S. Wasserman (d. 1992), *Reb Simcha Speaks*, p. 45. See also R. Sternbuch, *Teshuvot veHanhagot*, vol. 1, no. 477; *HaDerech LiTeshuvah* on Maimonides, *Hilchot Teshuvah* 3:7.
9 R. Herzog (1888–1959), *Pesakim u'Ketavim, Yoreh De'ah*, vol. 2, no. 146.
10 R. Z. Chajes (1805–1855), *Minchat Kena'ot*, published in *Kol Kitvei Maharatz Chayes*, vol. 2.
11 *Minchat Kena'ot* (previous note), p. 1013. With regard to contemporary Reformers R. Schwab writes (*Selected Speeches*, p. 155): 'We have before us 5.7 million Jews in America ..., of which maybe ten percent are *shomrei Torah umitzvos* [observant]. That leaves five million Jews, of which over half are absolutely ignorant of what it means to be Jewish; they are totally assimilated, not affiliated with any Jewish causes, and not even members of any synagogues or so-called temples. All of these five million Jewish souls, children of Jewish mothers, are ... "children that were held captive among the nations". *When they will stand before the Heavenly Tribunal they will be exonerated, for they are not to blame.* They know nothing about *Yiddishkeit*, since they have been fully excluded from all Jewish influence. The other half of these five million are associated with Reform and Conservative temples. With the exception of their leaders, or rather, misleaders, *they are equally innocent*. They are helpless victims, misled sheep who have lost their way. They are estranged from the *Ribono Shel Olam* [The Master of the Universe] and His Torah through no fault of their own. Their parents failed to receive a Jewish education since their grandparents had nobody to lead them to the truth of Torah when they came to America so many decades ago. They are our brothers and we have a responsibility for our brothers. We apply to them the rule that ... "although they have sinned, they are still part of our nation". We love them all. Don't let anyone say there is a polarisation of "our side" and "their side". They are all on our side, and we are on their side.' R. Bleich, 'Orthodoxy and the Non-Orthodox: Prospects of Unity', p. 100: 'If one were to inquire into the halakhic status of our separated brethren, whether they be Reform, Liberal, Progressive, Conservative, Reconstructionist, or of whatever ilk, stripe, or appellation, certainly those of our generation are as *tinokot she-nishbe'u bein ha-akum*, children who have been abducted by idolaters ... They are the products of their culture, of their education or lack thereof, and of the climate of opinion in which we live. They cannot be held responsible for what they are.'

   See also the sources cited in note 48. (The acceptance of this attitude is evident from remarks such as the following extract from the 'Editorial Statement' in the *Jewish Observer*, vol. 20, no. 4, May 1987, p. 21: 'we have no quarrel with the broad, unlearned masses of Conservative and Reform Jews. Tragically, they have never been exposed to our rich heritage of Torah and *mitzvos*, *emuna* and *bitachon* [faith and trust], and we have no right to expect an educated commitment from them. Their leaders, however, must bear culpability for the spiritual alienation of their followers.')
12 R. Schwab, 'Challenges Ahead: Setting Sights for New Horizons, Address to Agudah Convention, November 24 1988', in *Selected Speeches*, p. 156; 'The Shepherd and His Flock' in *Selected Writings*, p. 174. See also R. Halberstam (1904–1994), 'Mikivshonah Shel Kenesset Yisrael', p. 2.
13 See R. Newman and R. Becher, *Avotot Ahavah*, part 3 (p. 40 ff).

14 See R. Y. Y. Teitelbaum, *Teshuvot Avnei Tzedek, Yoreh De'ah*, no. 105. See also Maimonides, *Hilchot Melachim* 10:1–2, where he rules that a gentile is not culpable for transgressions that he committed (inadvertently, or) in circumstances that are beyond his control. The ramifications of this ruling with regard to gentile sinners and the question of the application of *tinok shenishbah* status to contemporary gentiles awaits a special study. See also R. Schmelkes (note 4).

15 However, no blanket ruling can be given on this matter. See R. Karelitz (note 7) that each individual must be assessed according to his personal, subjective conditions.

16 For example, author and broadcaster Lionel Blue, described as 'Convenor of the Religious Court of the Reform Synagogues of Great Britain', who speaks about his homosexual lifestyle in his *My Affair with Christianity*.

17 Even many of those who opposed the repeal of Section 28 in the British Parliament (in the year 2000) did so not so much as a result of their opposition to homosexual practices by confirmed adult homosexuals, but as a precautionary measure, lest the repeal have a negative effect on children otherwise capable of pursuing a heterosexual relationship and raising a family. It is noteworthy that the *Jewish Chronicle*, 28 January 2000, carried an editorial in which even the Chief Rabbi's opposition to the repealing of Clause 28 – on the grounds that it will encourage a 'promotion of a homosexual lifestyle' was criticised. The writer expresses concern about the effect that Clause 28 will have on 'individual gay and lesbian young people … especially … if, as Rabbi Sack's statement implies, schools … are directed to teach that homosexuality is a "wrong way to live"'.

18 Maimonides (note 2).

19 See R. A. Karelitz, *Chazon Ish Yoreh Deah* 2:16 (end).

20 F. Rosner, published in G. Freudenthal (ed.), *AIDS in Jewish Thought and Law*, p. 39 ff.

21 This ruling is based on R. Y. Grünwald (1845–1920), *Teshuvot Zichron Yehudah*, vol. 1, no. 45, cited also in R. Weinberg (1885–1966), *Teshuvot Seridei Esh*, vol. 2, no. 6, who argues that, since, by and large, people are not placed under ban of excommunication (*cherem*) nowadays, the criteria as to whether a person may be counted in a *minyan* or not can no longer be based on whether or not he has been excommunicated. Rather, if the person is worthy of being excommunicated (and would have been excommunicated in times bygone) as a result of his transgressions, he may not be counted as part of a *minyan* even though the excommunication can, for whatever reason, not be 'materialised'. R. Grünwald, followed by R. Weinberg, apply this argument to a Jew who has married out of the faith. In an era when excommunications were imposed, the authorities would excommunicate intermarried persons in order to assert the reprehensible nature of this transgression. Consequently, nowadays, even though excommunications are not generally served, the would-be 'outcast' ought not to be counted in a *minyan* or called up to the Torah. (However, some communities, nowadays, do call up such Jews and count them in a *minyan* in light of the fact that they are considered to be *tinokot shenishbu*. It ought to be noted that R. Grünwald, in his responsa, refers to someone who falls under the category of a *rasha mefursam*, a 'renowned sinner'.)

22 Based on *Mishnah Berurah* 53:22.

23 Based on *Shulchan Aruch Orach Chayim* 128:39 and *Mishnah Berurah* there 143.

24 Based on Maimonides, *Hilchot Nesiat Kappayim* 15:9.

25 Rosner's concerns revolve around the issue of *chanufah* and its ramifications as discussed by R. Feinstein, *Iggerot Moshe*, vol. 2, no. 51.

26 Rosner writes that 'support for this position can be found in the Talmudic commentary known as *Tosafot*, which quotes the passage stating that one who is suspected of adultery is nevertheless eligible as a witness'. He refers to the commentary of Tosafot to TB *Sanhedrin* 9b, s.v *liretzono*. However, this source is inadequate as a support for Rosner's contention that homosexuals who 'know what they are doing' be eligible as witnesses.

The comments of the Tosafists that Rosner refers to come against the following background. The Gemara (TB *Sanhedrin* ibid.) cites a ruling of Rav Yosef with regard to someone who testifies that a certain person had sodomised him. Rav Yosef ruled that if the alleged victim of the sodomy claims that the act of sodomy was performed against his will, his testimony is accepted together with the testimony of one other valid witness to confirm the authenticity of the claim (and have the culprit put to death). If, however, he says that he wilfully participated in the offence he can no longer serve as a witness for by his own testimony he is a sinner (*rasha*), and the Torah disqualifies him as a witness. Rava, however, disagrees and maintains that a person does not have the power – according to Jewish law – to disqualify himself as a witness by establishing himself as a sinner (through admitting that he was compliant in the act of sodomy). Therefore, the victim's words are only partially accepted (*palginan dibburei*). His statement that a certain person sodomised him is accepted (together with the testimony of another witness) whereas his statement that he was eager to participate in the forbidden union is disregarded.

The Tosafists (ibid., 9b; 26b *s.v. he-chashud*) and other mediaeval commentaries pose the following question. Later in the same tractate (*Sanhedrin* 26b) the Gemara records the teaching of Rav Nachman that 'one who is suspected of engaging in forbidden sexual relationships is [nevertheless] qualified to give testimony' in court. The Tosafists assume that even one who is known to have engaged in forbidden sexual practices retains his eligibility as a witness. For whilst a transgressor of other violations is rendered invalid as a witness, one who violates the sexual code is not disqualified. If so, the Tosafists ask, why would a wilful participant in homosexual congress be disqualified as a witness? Why should he be different than any other sinner in the realm of sexual intimacy?

The Tosafists suggest several alternative answers to this question. First, they suggest that, when Rav Nachman laid down the rule that 'one who is suspected of engaging in forbidden sexual relationships is qualified to give testimony', he was not referring to someone who – witnesses had confirmed – had *definitely* committed a sexual transgression; rather the reference was to someone whose general disregard for the halachic precautionary measures against licentiousness and overall 'loose' conduct would seem to indicate that he would indulge in forbidden sexual pleasures. If this is the meaning of Rav Nachman's statement it would have no bearing on one who was a confirmed transgressor of the prohibition against *mishkav zachar*.

Second, the Tosafists suggest, that – even if Rav Nachman was referring to a confirmed transgressor – his ruling would not apply to the participant in *mishkav zachar*. The reason that Rav Nachman treats the transgressor of the sexual code differently than other sinners (who lose their eligibility as witnesses if it has been confirmed that they have committed serious transgressions) is because violators of this code are driven by an extraordinary passion. Given the compelling force of the drive for sexual indulgence, they may not be considered 'willing sinners' to the extent that they are rendered ineligible for testimony in court. In contrast, however, one who commits the crime of sodomy is not subject to the same degree of forceful lust, for – the Tosafists argue – the desire for sodomy is not as strong as the desire for other forms of forbidden sexual unions. According to this answer of the Tosafot, there is also no basis or proof for Rosner's view.

Third, Tosafot propose that the desire for homosexual relationships is (like the desire for other forbidden sexual relationships) powerful enough to make us consider the sinner as one who succumbed to the compelling force of his lust – rather than a 'willing sinner' – and therefore not lose his eligibility as a witness. Nevertheless, his testimony that another person had committed the crime of *mishkav zachar* would not be accepted based on the principle that one who is suspect of committing a specific crime cannot serve as a witness with regard to *that particular crime*. Consequently, a person who admitted that he was a willing partici-pant in the sin of *mishkav zachar* can no longer serve as a witness to condemn another person for committing that very crime (unless we accept the view of Rava whereby we only give partial credibility to his words).

However, all this has no practical bearing on Rosner's hypothesis. Firstly, the law as codified by Maimonides (*Hilchot Eidut* 10:2; 12:1; see also *Hilchot Sanhedrin* 19:4), Tur (*Choshen Mishpat*, ch. 34), the *Bet Yosef* (ibid.), R. Isserles (the Rama, *Choshen Mishpat*, ibid. section 25) and other universally accepted authorities clearly dictates that one who is known for – rather than suspected of – engaging in forbidden sexual intercourse is unequivocally disqualified as a witness. Given the overwhelming consensus of opinion in this regard, the alternative interpretation of Rav Nachman that the Tosafists are ready to consider does not lend credibility to Rosner's contention.

Furthermore, the Tosafists themselves only suggest this interpretation (which, as mentioned, is not accepted as the normative ruling) as a possibility alongside two other interpretations which do not lend support to Rosner.

At any rate, Rosner's wording is misleading, for, whilst the Tosafists do employ the term *vechashuv k'annus* ('and he is considered like one who is compelled'), the Tosafists did not mean to suggest that anyone who engages in forbidden sexual practices is subject to the law that 'a person who sins under compulsion is divinely exempted from punishment'. As R. Ettlinger, *Aruch LaNer* on *Sanhedrin*, ibid., explains, the Tosafists could never have entertained such an idea, since it is undeniably the fact that some sexual transgressions involve capital punishment and the sexual transgressor is considered responsible and accountable for his actions like any other transgressor. (If this were not the case, but – as Rosner suggests – the sexual transgressor were considered an *onnes*, not only would he be an eligible witness, but he would also not be subject to many of the strictures that may apply to a wilful sinner and which Rosner therefore applies to the active homosexual.)

What the Tosafists were suggesting was that it is plausible to differentiate between sexual sins and other sins with regard to their respective effect on one's eligibility as a witness. Given the extreme force of sexual temptation and desire (which far surpasses the craving for other sins), it may be argued that whilst such transgressors are most definitely not 'exempt from punishment', they do not lose their legitimacy insofar as testifying in court is concerned.

27 Rosner's lenient recommendation in the case of a practising homosexual who had suffered for some time before his death –and probably experienced some degree of contrition and remorse for his sinful behaviour – is based on R. A. S. B. Sofer, *Responsa Ketav Sofer, Yoreh Deah* no. 171; (see also R. Moshe Sofer, *Yoreh De'ah*, no. 341, s.v. *uve-lav hachi nami*; R. Schick, *Teshuvot Maharam Schick, Orach Chayim* no. 140). His stringent ruling with regard to an AIDS patient who 'was a sinner' is based on Proverbs 10:7 'but the name of the wicked shall rot' as interpreted by the Gemara TB *Yoma* 38b 'to mean that rottenness enters their names in that none name their children after them'.

28 Quite aside from the legal issues in the narrow sense of the word, halachic authorities have advocated an approach to such questions that takes into consideration the effect that such sanctions may have upon the community. For example, R. Weinberg was of the opinion that, in principle, there is no halachic objection to giving an *aliyah* to a person who knowingly ignored the *mitzvah* of circumcising his son. However, he argued that whether or not such a person should be given an *aliyah* in practice depends on the assessment of the local rabbinic authority. If the rabbi is of the opinion that calling such a person up to the Torah would have a negative spiritual effect on people, then he should not be called up. If, however, calling up such a person is likely to achieve a more positive result than 'alienating' him, then he ought to be given the *aliyah*.

29 See TB *Chullin* 5a; *Eruvin* 69b; Maimonides, *Hilchot Shabbat* 30:15; *Shulchan Aruch Orach Chayim* 385:3.

30 See Maimonides, *Hilchot Avodah Zarah* 2:5; *Hilchot Mamrim* 4:2.

31 See *Mishnah Berurah* 126:2.

32 See *Mishnah Berurah* 128:143.

33 See Maimonides, *Hilchot Eidut* 11:10.

34 See Rama on *Shulchan Aruch Yoreh Deah* 264:1.

35 See Maimonides, *Hilchot Shechitah* 4:14; *Shulchan Aruch Yoreh Deah* 2:5; 117:7.

36 See *Shulchan Aruch Yoreh Deah* 240:18 and commentaries.

37 See *Shulchan Aruch Yoreh Deah* 340:5; 345:5 and commentaries.

38 See, for example, *Shulchan Aruch Yoreh Deah* 159:3 and commentaries.

39 See R. Weiss, *Teshuvot Minchat Yitzchak*, vol. 3, no. 65. R. Weiss' assertion – made in the 1960s – that all Jews appreciate the severity of intermarriage (Cf. R. Shlomo Zalman Auerbach (1910–1995), cited in R. Goldschmidt, *Teshuvot Zikaron BaSefer, Choshen Mishpat,* no. 5 s.v. *u-ve-eileh*), as is evidenced by the fact that the vast majority of Jews do not marry out, and therefore those who marry out cannot reasonably be qualified as *tinokot shenishbu*, does not reflect the reality of our day. As R. Rokowsky, 'It's Not My Problem', p. 23, writes: 'We are inundated with devastating statistics on intermarriage – it is well known that before 1960, less then 6% intermarried, meaning that more than 90% of Jews in America remained Jewish. Today, only 30 years later, the number of Jews who are marrying Jewish is barely 45%. We have become indifferent to the plague; somehow, we accept it fatalistically, as a fact of life. And that is a terrible mistake. There *is* something that we can do about it – and must – because it really is "my problem".'

40 See R. Weiss (previous note), vol. 4, no. 10.

41 See, most recently, R. Scheinberg, 'Birur b'da'at haGra b'din tinokot shenishbu bizmaneinu, ha'im mitztarfin l'minyan asarah', in *Yeshurun*, vol. 6, p. 392 ff and his conclusion on p. 395. See also, with regard to Progressives, R. Stern (1831–1903), *Teshuvot Zecher Yehosef*, *Orach Chayim*, no. 21 (and ibid. section 6, p. 84); R. Weiss, *Teshuvot Va'Ya'an David*, vol. 1, no. 12, section 1, *s.v. u'l'inyan*.

42 See, for example, *Teshuvot Seridei Esh* (note 21), no. 10, where R. Weinberg discusses the question of calling up uncircumcised Jews to the Torah. R. Weinberg argues that such decisions must be made by the local rabbi. In the event that honouring the uncircumcised Jews would, to his mind, have a positive effect on the 'deviants' – they would be encouraged by such 'inclusivism' to spiritual growth and the observance of the *mitzvot* – they should be called up to the Torah. If, however, the local rabbi is of the opinion that honouring such people would be counter-productive to spiritual growth, then he should forbid them from being called up to the Torah. (With regard to the question of calling up uncircumcised Jews to the Torah, see the discussion and variant views in R. Nathanson (1810–1875), *Teshuvot Shoel u'Meishiv*, second series, vol. 3, no. 64 and *Teshuvot Minchat Yitzchak* (note 40); R. Waldenberg, *Teshuvot Tzitz Eliezer*, vol. 11, no. 9; R. Horowitz (1844–1910), *Teshuvot Mateh Levi*, vol. 2, no. 4; R. Hoffmann (1843–1921), *Teshuvot Melamed Leho'il*, vol. 2, no. 79; the discussion and correspondence cited in R. Hildesheimer (1820–1899), *Teshuvot Rabbi Ezriel Hildesheimer*, vol. 1, no. 4; R. Feinstein, *Teshuvot Iggerot Moshe*, vol. 2, no. 33, section 3, p. 217.) (It is noteworthy that this teaching of the *Akeidat Yitzchak* has been adopted as a guiding principle by many halachic authorities. See, for example, R. Schwadron, *Da'at Torah*, on *Orach Chayim* 551:0; R. Moshe Tarashchanskij in his responsum – published in R. Berlin, *Teshuvot Meishiv Davar*, part 2, no. 43; R. Roller (early twentieth century), *Teshuvot Be'er Chayim Mordechai*, vol. 1, *Yoreh De'ah*, no. 40, *s.v. ulam;* vol. 2, *Yoreh De'ah*, no. 21, *s.v. u-mah she-tzided;* vol. 3, *Even HaEzer*, no. 49, *s.v. u-ve-chein;* R. Leiter (early nineteenth century), *Teshuvot Darkei Shalom*, vol. 1, no. 50, subsection 10.)

See also R. Schick, *Teshuvot Maharam Schick*, *Orach Chayim*, no. 304, writing in response to a rabbi who sought to completely ostracise the Reformers (who denied the belief in the Messianic redemption, etc.) and sought to forbid Orthodox *mohalim* from circumcising their sons! R. Schick – notwithstanding his zealous opposition to the Reformers (see, for example, ibid., no. 305) – writes that, even if the law of the land would allow the implementation of such a ban, he could not agree that it should be extended to a refusal to circumcise the children of the Reformers. The issue, he wrote, was whether or not such a measure would serve to strengthen Orthodoxy and observance, *lemigdar milta*. He argues that such a harsh attitude is unlikely to achieve its intended purpose: 'who knows whether indeed a "fire will descend from Heaven" and the name of the Holy One, Blessed is He, will be sanctified ... how can we override the certainty [the obligation of circumcision]' for such dubious goals. Further-more, such an attitude will appear to the masses as extremely peculiar and the suggested measures will be perceived as unwarranted cruelty. Even Orthodox and observant Jews would thus be led to speak disparagingly about the rabbis. Finally, he adds, it is not improbable that the Reformers are looking for the slightest excuse to refrain from circumcising their children, and if the suggested ban were imposed, we would only be playing into their hands and guilty of promulgating sin.

43 See the interesting exchange in R. Sternbuch, *Teshuvot veHanhagot*, vol. 1, no. 482, with a rabbi who suggested that a divorcee who is married to a *cohen* (in violation of a biblical injunction) should not be granted access to the *mikveh* in order to purify herself from her state of *niddah*. The anonymous interlocutor sought to support his stance from the fact that such regulations were instituted in Orthodox neighbourhoods in Israel. R. Sternbuch forcefully dismisses the comparison and argues that in all such matters the local circumstances must be taken into consideration. In an Orthodox community, such measures may be warranted, but in a community consisting primarily of non-observant Jews, such bans do not have any place. A woman who wishes to perform the *mitzvah* of going to *mikveh* should be supported in her quest for family purity, notwithstanding the fact that her marital union is forbidden on other grounds.

44 See Maimonides, *Hilchot Teshuvah* 3:2.

45 See TB *Bava Kamma* 28b.

46 See R. Schneur Zalman of Liady, *Torah Ohr*, on *Parashat Miketz*, 31c, who 'argues' that if

Nebuchadnezzar deserved reward for the relatively small gesture he made towards the Almighty, then *a fortiori*, there is not a single Jew who does not deserve all the good in the world (as a reward for the many good deeds he will almost inevitably have performed). See also Maimonides, *Iggeret haShmad*, ch. 3.

47 R. M. Schneerson, *Sefer haSichot 5751*, vol. 1, p. 228–29.

48 It is for this reason that, whilst halachic authorities have overwhelmingly encouraged an inclusivist attitude towards Jews who have affiliated themselves with Progressive Jewish movements (see R. Bamberger (1807–1878), *Teshuvot Yad HaLevi, Yoreh De'ah*, no. 129; R. Hirsch (1808–1888), *Teshuvot Shemesh Marpe*, no. 46; *The Collected Writings*, vol. 6, pp. 207, 297–8; R. Scheinberg, *Shoalim BiTeshuvah*, no. 14 (p. 20 ff); *Nishmat Shabbat* (note 5) no. 500, section 2, p. 408), they have been most adamant in their opposition to any activity which could be interpreted, if only erroneously, as an endorsement of the legitimacy or authenticity of Progressive movements (see the *Pesak Din* published in *HaPardes*, vol. 30, June 1956).

49 See R. Bleich, *Bioethical Dilemmas*, p. 133: 'One of the classical commentators, R. Isaac Arama [1420–1494], *Akeidat Yitzchak, Bereishit, sha'ar* 20, observes that the homosexual conduct of Sodom was punished much more severely than the homosexuality that was rampant in other cities. He asserts that the inhabitants of Sodom were singled out for censure and punishment because they had institutionalised the form of deviant sexual activity that has become associated with the very name of their city. As recorded in *Bereishit Rabbah* 50:10: "The people of Sodom agreed among themselves that any stranger entering the city would be subjected to homosexual intercourse." Sodomy was not unique to Sodom. But only in Sodom was it accepted as a matter of course; only in Sodom did it become *de rigeur*. In other societies such acts were forbidden by statute, although the law was honoured only in the breach. In Sodom, declares *Akedat Yitzchak*, not only was such conduct decriminalised but it was ritualised as well. Removal of the odium associated with a transgression is potentially more serious a matter than the transgression itself and it was for that reason that the people of Sodom were punished so severely.'

Parenthetically, there is an inaccuracy in R. Bleich's citation of R. Arama. It is true that R. Arama speaks about the Torah's particular abhorrence of the 'institutionalisation' of sin. (In this context, he chastises those Jewish communities who favoured the de facto acceptance of prostitution in the community and on occasion even harbouring them with food and shelter – with the argument that, in this way the prostitutes could be 'supervised' and this system would serve to contain and minimise the degree of sin and its ramifications in the community. R. Arama says that the establishment of such a system was in itself a grave perversity, for it meant that the community – whatever its motives were – would be providing a sanction for sin.)

R. Arama explains that the essential sin of the Sodomites for which they were doomed to destruction was their extreme self-centredness and their adamant opposition to hospitality and concern for others, even if no cost or inconvenience was involved. This sin assumed a colossal dimension when they institutionalised their evil ways by endorsing the practice of alienating wayfarers as official communal policy. It is for this reason that the Sodomites were subjected to a worse fate than other egocentric communities. R. Arama does not say that 'the inhabitants of Sodom were singled out for censure and punishment because they had institutionalised the form of deviant sexual activity that has become associated with the very name of their city' as R. Bleich suggests. On the contrary, he asserts that the immoral deeds of sodomy practised by the Sodomites were 'merely incidental' to their primary failing which was in the area of interpersonal relationships with strangers. The decision of the Sodomites to rape as well as rob every stranger who passed through the city – as stated in the above-mentioned Midrash – was designed to establish a reputation that would keep strangers away. The immorality of the Sodomites was essentially a tool to serve their needs of greedy possessiveness and perverse attitudes to the 'outsider'. According to the *Akedat Yitzchak*, it is for this reason that the prophet Ezekiel, when describing the iniquity of Sodom (Ezekiel 16:49), states: '... She and her daughters had pride, surfeit of bread and peaceful serenity, but she did not strengthen the hand of the poor and the needy'. Explicit reference is made only to the uncharitable characteristic of the Sodomites; their immoral sexual practices are not mentioned explicitly in the Scriptures. Why? Because it was their attitude to outsiders that was the quintessential crime of the Sodomites, and this is encapsulated in the phrase 'she did not strengthen the hand of the poor and the needy'. Their immorality was not intrinsic to their character – and could have been atoned for – but was performed in order to serve their primary goal of institutionalised alienation of strangers. It was this crime that sealed their fate. (Similarly, the Gemara, TB *Sanhedrin* 109a–b, lists numerous examples of the misdeeds of the Sodomites, all which possess the common factor of corrupt monetary judgements, and other socially perverted machinations and atrocities that prevailed there. This also indicates that it was the issue of attitudes to other people that was the crux of the Sodomite problem.)

50 See R. Y. Halberstam, *Teshuvot Divrei Yatziv*, vol. 3, *Yoreh De'ah*, no. 49, section 5, who argues that, in our relationship with a *meisit*, namely one who encourages and entices others to sin, the fact that the *meisit* may be a *tinok shenishbah* does not provide for an accommodating approach. Those who are responsible for leading others astray must be disenfranchised in the interest of the better good for society as a whole.

See Maimonides, *Hilchot Sanhedrin* 11:5, who writes, in connection with the *meisit*: '... that the harsh treatment of those who mislead the masses after the pursuit of vanity is [verily] an act of universal compassion'. The disenfranchisement and elimination of negative forces in the community, whilst it may appear at face value to be symptomatic of unfair or even cruel principles, is actually an expression of care and concern for the innocent victims of such forces. See also the discussion in R. M. Schneerson, *Likkutei Sichot*, vol. 8, pp. 163–5.

51 R. Bulka, *One Man*, pp. 117–18.

7 PROCREATION AND PARENTHOOD

1 *The Jewish Quarterly*, vol. 40, no. 3, Autumn 1993 ('Homosexuality, Jewishness and Judaism', p. 5 ff.).

2 Unterman, *Judaism and Homosexuality – Some Orthodox Perspectives*, p. 73. [Unterman, somewhat curiously, does not differentiate between men and women in this regard; see the references cited in note 12.] This also seems to be the implication of R. N. Lamm, as quoted by Nussbaum Cohen ('New Day for Orthodox Gays', in *The Jewish Week*, 3 November 2000, p. 13): 'The fact that a person has a predisposition to homosexuality is no reason to give in to it rather than try to live a straight life. I defy people who say it cannot be done. People should sublimate it.' Whilst R. Lamm's comments are somewhat ambiguous, he seems to assert that confirmed homosexuals can and should get married – 'live a straight life' – by 'sublimating' their homosexual orientation.

3 Genesis 1:28; 9:1; Mishnah *Yevamot* 61b; Maimonides, *Hilchot Ishut* 15:1; *Shulchan Aruch, Even Ha-Ezer* 1:1.

There is some discussion as to whether Gentiles are obliged to procreate: see TB *Sanhedrin* 59b; Tosafot on TB *Yevamot* 62a, s.v. *b'nei*; TB *Chagigah* 2b, s.v. *lo tohu*; and R. Rosanes, *Mishneh LaMelech*, on Maimonides, *Hilchot Melachim* 10:7.

4 See *Sefer HaChinnuch*, Commandment no. 1. (See also R. J. Schneerson, *Likkutei Dibburim*, vol. 4, 746a; *Sefer Ha-Sichot* 5701, p. 46.) *Sefer HaChinnuch* explains that the 'greatness' of this *mitzvah* lies in the fact that procreation – which produces new generations – 'brings about the fulfilment of all the commandments in the world, which were given to human beings rather than to angels'. See also R. Bachya ben Asher (d. c.1340), *Midrash Rabbeinu Bachya* on Genesis 1:28. See also TB *Shabbat* 31a, that one of the first questions that a person is asked when brought to judgement is 'did you engage in procreation?'

Maimonides, Rabbi Moshe of Coucy (early thirteenth century), and Rabbi Yitzchak of Corbeil (d. 1280), however, do not list procreation as the first of the commandments: see *Sefer HaMitzvot*, positive commandment 212; *Sefer Mitzvot Gadol (Semag)*, positive commandment 49; and *Sefer Mitzvot Katan (Semak)*, commandment 284.

5 *Even Ha-Ezer* (note 3).

6 TB *Yevamot* 63b.

7 See, for example, the essays 'Artificial Procreation'; 'Sperm Banking in Anticipation of Infertility'; 'Surrogate Motherhood', in R. Bleich, *Bio-Ethical Dilemmas*, pp. 203–68. See also Steinberg, *Encyclopaedia*, vol. 1, p. 154 ff. See also Rosner and R. Tendler, *Practical Medical Halachah*, p. 29: 'Artificial insemination using the semen of a donor other than the

husband (A.I.D.) is considered by most Rabbinic opinion to be strictly prohibited for a variety of reasons, including the possibility of incest, confused genealogy, and the problems of inheritance ...'.

8   TB *Niddah* 31a.

9   This is not to suggest that all parents are perfect. Unfortunately, we are only too well aware of dysfunctional family units and the phenomenon of child abuse by biological parents. Nevertheless, it should be self-understood that whatever the degree of prevalence of such aberrations, they must be viewed as symptomatic of psychological illness and other disorders. To refer, as some have done, to such cases in order to demonstrate the bankruptcy of the traditional family unit and advocate artificial alternatives is as absurd as the argument that we should only eat artificially manufactured food, because so many people have contracted food poisoning and other diseases *even* as a result of consuming natural food.

10 Numerous verses in the Scriptures, teachings in the Talmud and midrashim confirm the rectitude of this approach. See, for an example, TB *Kiddushin* 31a where different educational and parental roles are assigned to the mother and the father respectively. See also TB *Ketubot* 102b–103a; Maimonides, *Hilchot Ishut* 21:17; *Shulchan Aruch, Even HaEzer* 82:7 which provide the law that – in the case of divorce – children below the age of six must ordinarily be put in the custody of their mother, for they are mainly in need of the physical care and attention that mothers typically give children of that age group. Above the age of six boys must be with their father so that he can fulfil his obligation to teach his sons Torah, whilst girls must be with their mother so that she can instruct them and guide them in the ways of modesty. Clearly, parents of both genders have distinctive roles to play in the lives of their children and this further underscores the disservice that is done to children when they are placed – *ab initio* – in artificial and unnatural family structures which lack the equilibrium of father–mother input in the rearing of their children. *In the absence of any Divine commandment* to embark upon such endeavours, why 'create' disadvantaged children?

   [See R. Y.Z. Soloveitchik, *Chiddushei HaGriz al HaTorah, Parshat Toldot* (Genesis 25:22), from where it emerges that in the absence of a biblical mandate to procreate, considerations of the consequences of procreation ought to determine one's course of action. Cf. however, Halperin, 'Post-Mortem Sperm Retrieval' in *Assia: A Journal of Jewish Medical Ethics and Halacha*, vol. 4, no. 1, February 2001, p. 12. He cites Rabbi Zalman Nechemiah Goldberg to the effect that if a man gave explicit consent to post-mortem sperm retrieval, or if it is clearly known that he would have wanted the procedure done, it is permitted provided that 'there is strict supervision ensuring that there will be no mixing of sperm, and there is documentation of the child's paternity.']

   With regard to the importance and role of *biological* relationships, see Maimonides, *Guide for the Perplexed,* part 3, ch. 49, who rationalises the commandments of the Torah which insist on the traditional family nucleus as follows: '... for fraternal sentiments and mutual love and mutual help can be found in their perfect form only among those who are related by their ancestry ... and the attainment of these things is the greatest purpose of the Law. Hence, harlots are prohibited (Deuteronomy 23:18) because through them the lines of ancestry are destroyed. For a child born of them is a "stranger to the people" for no-one knows whom he "belongs to".'

   With regard to filial and parental obligations, it must be remembered that, according to Jewish law, these cannot be 'disowned' or 'acquired' by adoption (see R. Feinstein, *Iggerot Moshe Yoreh De'ah*, vol. 3, no. 138). Whilst parents of adopted children have obligations to their 'acquired' children and vice versa, Jewish law insists that certain obligations remain towards biological parents and children irrespective of adoption: with regard to the obligation for an adopted child to honour his biological parents, see R. A. S. B. Sofer, *Ketav Sofer al HaTorah* on Deuteronomy 5:16; R. Meir Simchah of Dvinsk, *Meshech Chochmah* on Deuteronomy ibid., who explain (how it is rooted in the Decalogue) that the *mitzvah* of honouring one's parents is not contingent upon his parents' having cared for him.

   It would be beyond the scope of this work to provide a summary of Jewish teachings that reflect the ideal of the family institution composed of biological male father, female mother, and child.

11 See R. M. Schneerson, *Iggerot Kodesh*, vol. 23, p. 24; R. Waldenberg, *Teshuvot Tzitz Eliezer*, vol. 6 (*Kuntres HaYichud*), no. 21; vol. 7, no. 44; R. Weiss, *Teshuvot Minchat Yitzchak*,

vol. 4, no. 49; vol. 9, no. 140; R. Wosner, *Teshuvot Shevet HaLevi*, vol. 5, no. 205; vol. 6, no. 196; R. Halberstam, *Teshuvot Divrei Yatziv, Even HaEzer*, no. 46.

12 Mishnah *Yevamot* 65b; Maimonides, *Hilchot Ishut* 15:2; *Hilchot Issurei Bi'ah*, 21:26; *Shulchan Aruch, Even HaEzer* 1:13. See, however, Maimonides, *Hilchot Ishut* ibid. and the gloss of R. Isserles, ibid.

There is a view (based on Tosafot TB *Gittin* 41b, s.v. *lo tohu*) that, whilst women are exempt from the commandment *p'ru u'rvu*, they are obliged to marry in order to fulfil the mandate of *lashevet* (which – in contradistinction to biblical *p'ru u'rvu* – may be fulfilled with the birth of *one* child, boy *or* girl); see particularly R. Shmuel Ben Uri Shraga Feivush (c.1640–c.1700), *Bet Shmuel* on *Even HaEzer* 1:2; R. Berlin (18th Century), *Atzei Arazim, Even HaEzer*, 5:9. See, however, R. Falk, *P'nei Yehoshua* on Tosafot, ibid.; R. Eiger (1761–1837), *Hagahot Rabbi Akiva Eiger* on *Shulchan Aruch Even HaEzer* 1:1 based on R. Nissim of Gerona (c.1290–c.1375), *Teshuvot HaRan*, no. 32 (see also R. Yom Tov Ishbili (fourteenth century), *Teshuvot HaRitva*, no. 43); R. Azulai, *Birkei Yosef, Even HaEzer* 1:16; R. Epstein, *Aruch HaShulchan Even HaEzer* 1:4; R. Schwadron, *Teshuvot Maharsham*, vol. 1, no. 180, s.v. *shuv ra-iti* (end). Cf. R. Kluger, *Teshuvot HaElef Lecha Shlomoh, Even HaEzer*, nos. 1 and 2; R. Babad, *Minchat Chinuch*, Mitzvah 1, no. 28; R. Ettlinger, *Teshuvot Binyan Zion*, vol. 1, no. 123; R. Schmelkes, *Teshuvot Bet Yitzchak, Even HaEzer*, vol. 1, no. 91, subsection 6 (end).

13 R. Meir Simchah sees this as part of an umbrella principle manifest in all the laws of the Torah, namely 'that the laws of God and His ways are "ways of pleasantness and all its [the Torah's] paths are peace" (Proverbs 3:17). Hence the Torah does not impose upon the Jew a burden that his body is not able to accommodate … It is for this reason that the Torah [namely, Biblical Law] does not command us to fast more than one day a year [Yom Kippur], and [even then] instructs us to prepare ourselves for the fast by eating on the day before. The Torah did not deprive sexual pleasure from any creature with the exception of Moses [who was, at a certain stage in his life, obliged to abstain from conjugal relationships at all times, since he had to be constantly ready, and in a state of purity, to receive direct communication from God], who, due to his unique level, did not require this.' (See our comments above in chapter 2, note 3.)

14 See TB *Yoma* 83a; 85a–b; Maimonides, *Hilchot Shabbat* 2:1; *Shulchan Aruch, Orach Chayim* 328:10.

15 R. Meir Simchah of Dvinsk, *Meshech Chochmah* on Genesis 9:1 (8d) s.v. *p'ru u'rvu*.

16 See the ruling of the Rama, *Shulchan Aruch, Orach Chayim* 656:1.

17 See *Magen Avraham, Orach Chayim*, 656:1, no. 7. See the discussion in R. Kagan, *Mishnah Berurah Orach Chayim*, ibid. no. 8 and *Bi'ur Halachah*, s.v. *yoter me'chomesh*.

18 See Rama, *Orach Chayim* (note 16); *Yoreh Deah* 157:1. See R. Eliyahu of Vilna, *Biurei HaGra Orach Chayim* (previous note), where he cites the Mishnah in TB *Shabbat* 121a as a source for the ruling that a person must be prepared to forfeit his entire fortune rather than transgress even a *rabbinical* commandment.

19 Of course, generally speaking, the option remains for people to do just that, if they are motivated to do so.

20 See, for example, R. Feinstein, *Iggerot Moshe, Orach Chayim*, vol. 1, no. 172 (as understood by R. Yosef, *Teshuvot Chazon Ovadiah*, part 1, vol. 2, no. 33, p. 630). Cf. R. Shlomoh HaCohen of Vilna (1828–1906), *Teshuvot Binyan Shlomoh*, vol. 1, no. 47, p. 328, s.v. *u-mihu ketsat*.

21 See TB *Yevamot* 64a, that one who (voluntarily) abstains from fulfilling the commandment to procreate is 'liable to death' (by the hands of Heaven). See, however, R. Sirkes, *Bayit Chadash*, on *Even HaEzer* ch. 1, s.v. *umah she'amar shekol mi she'eino osek* etc.

See also TB *Berachot* 10a, in the dialogue between Isaiah the prophet and Chizkiah the king, where it was decreed upon the latter that he would die as a punishment for deliberately abstaining from marriage in order not to sire children. (Chizkiah claimed that he had foreseen that he would bear unworthy offspring and this was the reason for his choosing to remain a bachelor. However, Isaiah told him that it was not within his prerogative to abstain from fulfilling God's commandment to procreate despite the fact that he was privy to 'God's secrets' and that his abstention was based on noble motives. Notwithstanding Isaiah's prediction that the decree that Chizkiah would die was irrevocable, Chizkiah relied on a tradition that he had received from his ancestors that a person should never refrain from prayer 'even if a sharp sword lies on his neck' and, therefore, Chizkiah then prayed to God to spare his life. God granted him an additional fifteen years of life, in the duration of which he got married and gave birth to Menasheh, the king who misled Israel for many years and under whose reign idolatry proliferated in Israel.)

It may also be noteworthy that the *halachah* also sanctions some otherwise forbidden enterprises in order to facilitate the fulfilment of the commandment to procreate. For example, one is allowed – in certain circumstances – to sell a *Sefer Torah* in order to secure the finances necessary for marriage (see TB *Megillah* 27a; Maimonides, *Hilchot Sefer Torah* 10:5; *Shulchan Aruch Even HaEzer* 1:2).

22 R. Auerbach, *Teshuvot Minchat Shlomoh*, vol. 3, no. 103 (p. 20). See also *Pitchei Teshuvah* on *Shulchan Aruch, Even HaEzer* 154:127, and R. Wahrmann of Buchach (c.1771–1840), *Ezer MiKodesh, Even HaEzer* 76:5 who cite with regard to the commandment of procreation the limits of financial expenditure mandated for this purpose as outlined in *Orach Chayim* (note 15). See, however, R. Sternbuch, *Teshuvot veHanhagot*, vol. 1, no. 890, *s.v. v'nireh*, who suggests that for such a great *mitzvah* as procreation, 'one ought' to spend what would amount to more than one-fifth of one's assets. (R. Bleich, *Bioethical Dilemmas*, p. 243, does not cite any of these authorities but takes it for granted that 'fulfilment of the commandment to be fruitful and multiply does not require assumption of a burden greater than that required for fulfilment of any other positive commandments'.)

According to the view that women are also obliged to marry on the grounds of *lashevet* (see note 12), the qualification and limitation of the *mitzvah* of *lashevet* as articulated by R. M. Sofer, *Teshuvot Chatam Sofer, Even HaEzer*, no. 20, s.v. *u-mah she-hikshah*, is most relevant in our context.

23 Bulka, *One Man*, p. 32, has the following to say: 'Most individuals who engage in homosexual acts are capable of heterosexual acts. Surveys show that two thirds of "homosexuals" have had heterosexual experience. They may feel more comfortable with same-sex partners, *but they can consummate a heterosexual union.* That they engage in homosex rather than heterosex is a matter of choice. However, there are some, very few to be sure, who are totally incapable of heterosex. Some men simply cannot function with a woman. Is this normal or pathological? The APA say it is not pathological, but many distinguished psychiatrists and psychologists say it is. Who is right? From the Judaic perspective, this argument is almost, though not quite, irrelevant. Homosex is wrong, whether engaged in by one who is capable of heterosex or by one who is unable. However, one who can achieve consummation with a member of the opposite sex but instead opts for a same-sex partner, has arguably committed a more serious breach, since such homosexual act comes at the expense of an available, achievable, and permissible alternative. In such instance, the homosexual act is simultaneously an act of rebellion against the Torah. *If there is such an entity as a homosexual, it would be a person who is simply not able to achieve an erection with a female but could do so with another male.*' [emphasis added]

This argument appears to me to be untenable. To suggest that a person of homosexual orientation (whether or not we are ready to accept this as a 'homosexual entity' is merely a question of semantics) who is 'able to achieve an erection with a female' has 'an available, achievable, and permissible alternative', is, in light of the prohibition of sex outside marriage, unrealistic. As we will yet demonstrate, the ability to go through the mechanics of heterosexual intercourse does not necessarily make such relationships available, achievable, or even permissible.

24 With 'emotional support', I refer also to the *mitzvah* of *onah*; see Exodus 21:10; Maimonides, *Hilchot Ishut* 14:1–2; *Shulchan Aruch Orach Chayim* 240:1; *Even HaEzer* 25:2. The duty of *onah* is presented in the Torah (primarily) as a negative commandment; one who does not fulfil his duties in this respect has not only 'abstained' from fulfilling a positive commandment, he has also 'transgressed' a negative commandment (*Mechilta* on Exodus, ibid.; TB *Ketubot* 47b; Maimonides, ibid., sections 7 and 15; *Shulchan Aruch Even HaEzer* 76:11; 77:1). See above (and note 17) for additional strictures attached to a negative commandment. These strictures are cited in connection with *onah* by R. Wahrmann (note 22).

Although the term *onah* is often rendered (somewhat freely) as 'conjugal visitation' (whereby the husband is obliged to honour, at the very least, a halachically prescribed minimum for engaging in physical intimacy with his wife), this term does not really serve to express the essence of the *mitzvah* of *onah*. The biblically mandated *onah* refers to the obligation that a husband has to 'gladden' his wife through physical intimacy (see TB *Pesachim* 72b). Consummation of the marital act *per se*, it need hardly be said, does not necessarily make a woman happy. The physical union in a marriage constitutes the fulfilment of the *mitzvah* of *onah* when it provides one's wife with the feeling of being loved, cherished as a person, and physically desired. The ideal moment of *onah* (to which a married couple should aspire) is one in which the husband showers his affection on his wife, and she responds with reciprocal expressions of love which culminates in husband and wife becoming united mentally, emotionally and physically. See the commentaries on TB *Nedarim* 20b: *Shittah Mekubetzet*, s.v. *amarti lo* and s.v. *ha bemilei detashmish* and s.v. *acharei levavchem*; *Tosafot Yeshanim* (ed. R. Halpern), no. 201 (p. 88), s.v. *lo kashya*; no. 207 (p. 89), s.v. *d'artzeyeh artzuyeh*. (See also TB *Shabbat* 152a where the cessation of sexual ability in old age is described as the cessation of the instrumentality of domestic peace (*shalom bayit*). See also *Midrash Kohelet Rabbah* 12:5.) See particularly *Iggeret HaKodesh* (attributed to Nachmanides) ch. 6 (pp. 207–8): '... Therefore engage her first in conversation that puts her heart and mind at ease and gladdens her. Thus your mind and your intent will be in harmony with hers. Speak words which arouse her to passion, union, love, desire and *eros* (*agavim*) – and words which elicit attitudes of reverence for God, piety and modesty ... win her over with words of graciousness and seductiveness ... hurry not to arouse passion until her mood is ready; begin in love; let her "semination" (orgasm?) take place first ....' (See also the discussion and the sources cited in R. Bulka, *Jewish Marriage*, p. 114 ff; R. F. Jacobs, *Family Purity*, ch. 11, p. 129 ff.)

In this context it is noteworthy that R. Feinstein (*Iggerot Moshe Even HaEzer* vol. 1, no. 102, s.v. *uvidvar she– eilatecha im koden ha-nissuin*) was asked by a prospective bridegroom whether the *mitzvah* of *onah* implies that he ought to study 'medical books' on how intercourse ought to be performed in a manner 'pleasing to his wife and conducive to domestic peace'. R. Feinstein answered in the affirmative, with the qualification that his interlocutor ought not to read such books until a few days before the wedding, when his mind is anyway preoccupied with concerns about physical intimacy in marriage. (At an earlier stage, sinful thoughts may be aroused.) In another responsa (*Teshuvot Iggerot Moshe, Even HaEzer*, vol. 3, no. 28) – also relevant to our discussion – R. Feinstein writes: 'As to the innovation of recent authorities that, nowadays, Torah Scholars should perform the mitzvah of *onah* twice a week I too support this view ... Because of the licentiousness of this generation and jealousy for another woman's lot, a woman feels desire and passion more often than once a week. Since the essence of the *mitzvah* of *onah* is to satisfy the woman's sexual needs, her husband is obligated [in this respect].'

25 Needless to say, if a person's homosexual orientation manifests itself in such a way that sexual intercourse with a woman is not even mechanically possible, there would be no obligation for such a person to marry (even if he found a spouse who was prepared to marry him whilst he is in such a condition). Even R. Bulka (note 23) acknowledges: 'From the Judaic perspective, one who is thoroughly incapable of heterosexual consummation and therefore refrains from all sexual activity is guilty of no offence'.

26 See *Sefer Chasidim*, no. 507. See R. Adler, *HaNissuin KeHilchatam*, part 1, ch. 3, p. 89 ff and footnotes.

27 There is a well known novel ruling of R. Feinstein that a woman who upon marriage discovers a severe defect in her husband does not require a *get*. According to R. Feinstein the marriage is null and void. It was an 'erroneous transaction' – a *mekach ta'ut*. (Whilst not unique to R. Feinstein's, his ruling is novel because a number of earlier and eminent halachic authorities had not been prepared to accept this notion – at least as an independent basis – to declare the marriage completely null and void – even on a rabbinical level (*mi-derabanan*); see R. Karelitz, *Chazon Ish Even HaEzer* 69:23; R. Spektor, *Teshuvot Eyn Yitzchak, Even HaEzer*, no. 24 (section 44); *Teshuvot Be'er Yitzchak*, no. 4, section 3; R. Grodzinski, *Teshuvot Achiezer*, vol. 1, no. 27. See the discussion in R. Bleich, *Kiddushei Ta'ut*, p. 99 ff.)

R. Feinstein applied this ruling in at least five cases: (a) a woman who discovered, after marriage, that her husband was sexually impotent (*Iggerot Moshe Even HaEzer*, vol. 1, no. 79) – sexual intercourse and gratification is an intrinsic and primary component of marriage, consequently no woman would agree to such a marriage; (b) a woman whose husband fled and she subsequently discovered that he had been suffering (and, as a result, institutionalised) before marriage from a mental illness (*Iggerot Moshe Even HaEzer*, ibid., no. 80); (c) a woman who discovered that her husband had converted to another religion prior to marriage (*Iggerot Moshe Even HaEzer*, vol. 4, no. 83); (d) a woman who discovered that her husband was vehemently opposed to having children and had even forced his wife to abort a foetus (*Iggerot Moshe Even HaEzer*, vol. 4, no. 13). The fifth case involved a woman who after having married discovered that her husband was a practising homosexual. R. Feinstein, *Iggerot Moshe Even HaEzer*, vol. 4, no. 113, *s.v. aval* ruled that since the woman entered the marriage without knowledge of the circumstances, the marriage-transaction was considered to be a *mekach ta'ut* (an erroneous transaction) which never took effect, and therefore there was no need for a *get* (provided that – as in all cases of *mekach ta'ut* – the woman left her husband as soon as she became aware of the defect). R. Feinstein argues that if the husband had engaged regularly in homosexual relations to the extent that it could be said 'that he enjoys homosexual relations more than heterosexual relationships' there are most definitely valid grounds for the annulment of the marriage, for which woman would want to enter a marriage with a person who prefers 'this despicable sexual union to sexual intercourse with his wife?'.

Furthermore, R. Feinstein says that even if one were to argue that the husband's pre-occupation with homosexuality came from a 'mental illness' (*shtut*) – for after all, the desire for homosexual relationships is totally unnatural, hence possibly a symptom of pathological disorder – it would still be in order to declare the marriage a *mekach ta'ut*. Since the husband was 'blemished' with this *shtut*, he would undoubtedly have the propensity to other forms of deranged behaviour ('*alul le'od shtutim*'). R. Feinstein concludes, however, by reiterating that in truth the drive for male homosexual congress comes not from any mental disorder but from *rishut* (wickedness). This is consistent with R. Feinstein's overall view on homo-sexuality as elaborated upon in *Iggerot Moshe, Orach Chayim*, vol. 4, no. 115 and *Yoreh De'ah*, vol. 3, no. 115, and discussed in chapters 1 and 2 of this book. See also the discussion in chapter 1, note 52.

(There does however seem to be an apparent inconsistency in R. Feinstein's writings. For in his responsa in *Orach Chayim* and *Yoreh De'ah* R. Feinstein argues that it is truly impossible for *any man* to have any intrinsic physical desire for homosexual congress. In his opinion in those *teshuvot all* people who engage in homosexual activities do so only in order to annoy God Almighty (*le-hachis*), whilst in *Iggerot Moshe Even HaEzer* he seems to acknowledge that it is conceivable that someone's 'evil inclination had overpowered him' to engage in homosexual intercourse and that one could even enjoy 'homosexual relations more than heterosexual relationships'. One possible way of reconciling this apparent discrepancy would be to surmise that R. Feinstein's reference in our context to a person who 'enjoys homosexual relations more than heterosexual relationships' – and the idea of a person being overpowered by his 'evil inclination' to engage in a one-off homosexual relationship – refers to someone who prefers and has a stronger 'desire' to 'annoy God' than to indulge in libidinal pleasure.)

R. Feinstein adds a final qualification to his ruling: only if the husband habitually engaged in homosexual congress – thus demonstrating 'that he enjoyed homosexual intercourse more than heterosexual intercourse' – could one assume that the marriage-transaction was a *mekach ta'ut*. If, however, he was not 'immersed' in homosexual practises but had indulged in a 'one-off' experience 'because his evil inclination had overpowered him' (even though one homosexual relationship is enough to categorise the husband as 'completely wicked' – a *rasha gamur*) one cannot consider the marriage to be null and void.

(R. Jachter, *Gray Matter*, p. 47, argues that R. Feinstein's ruling may not apply to contemporary homosexuals, since 'some homosexuals, with the help of psychotherapy, can lead a healthy married life'. I do not agree with this contention, because, even if we were to accept that opportunities for sexual reorientation through psychotherapy would change the 'presumption' ('*barur lan*') that a woman would not want to marry a homosexual, there is no evidence that psychotherapeutic techniques for sexual reorientation have become more available or effective since the year 1978 when R. Feinstein issued his ruling and 1981 when R. Feinstein published his ruling).

All this surely adds weight to our argument about the propriety of marriage for a confirmed homosexual. For whilst it is true that R. Feinstein addresses a case in which the husband was an active homosexual (which he says makes him most 'repulsive' and brings shame on 'the entire family'), and it was only in this case that he was prepared to say that the marriage-transaction was a *mekach ta'ut* (to 'nullify' a marriage we have to be absolutely sure that 'no woman in the world' would knowingly consent to such a marriage), it seems abundantly clear – and it is extremely pertinent to our discussion – that R. Feinstein would support the view that in the vast majority of circumstances a woman would not want to share her life with a confirmed homosexual even if he had never (yet) acted upon his disposition. For, after all, the basic argument obtains: which woman would want to enter a marriage with a person who prefers 'this despicable sexual union to sexual intercourse with his wife'! Consequently, a woman would ordinarily be best advised not to enter into a marriage with a man whose sexual preferences lie with members of his own gender.

28 This may fall under the rubric of removing a 'stumbling block' from before the blind; see the details in R. Kagan, *Chafetz Chaim, Hilchot Lashon HaRa* 4:11; *Hilchot Issurei Rechilut* 9:3–4. See also *HaNissuin KeHilchatam* (note 26), p. 91.

29 See the exhortation of R. J. Schneerson with regard to this, *Iggerot Kodesh*, vol. 6, p. 157.

30 It should also be emphasised that whilst a woman may forgo her 'conjugal rights', it may be her prerogative to change her mind at a later stage, at which point her husband is no longer exempt from his duties. See R. Abraham Di Boton (1545–1588), *Lechem Mishneh*, on *Hilchot Ishut* 15:1 (end); R. Eliyahu ben Chayim (c.1530–c.1610), *Teshuvot HaRanach, Mayim Amukim*, vol. 3, no. 44 and particularly, R. Schneur Zalman of Liady, *Shulchan Aruch HaRav, Choshen Mishpat, Hilchot Nizkei Guf VaNefeshi*, section 4. Cf. R. Orenstein (1775–1839), *Yeshuot Ya'akov, Even HaEzer* 1:1.

31 The Talmud (TB *Nedarim* 20b) and codes (Maimonides, *Hilchot Issurei Bi'ah* 21:12 ff; *Shulchan Aruch Orach Chayim* 240:2–3; *Even HaEzer* 25:8–10) mention a number of circumstances in which intercourse between husband and wife is forbidden, and is likely to have an extremely negative effect on the offspring that are conceived by such a relationship. One of them is '*b'nei temurah*', namely where the husband was thinking of another woman whilst cohabiting with his wife. As the commentaries and halachic authorities explain, marital intimacy must only be performed when the husband and wife are united – not only in body, but also in heart and mind. Consequently, if either husband or wife is mentally or emotionally detached from this union, even if this is not manifest physically, the relationship is deemed an unholy and unchaste performance. Suffice to say, this consideration may be particularly relevant for a homosexual or his potential wife when contemplating the prospect of marriage together.

See also Rashi on TB *Niddah* 17a, *s.v. onnes shinah* who writes that a man should not cohabit with his wife when overwhelmed by fatigue. In that state, he may not feel particularly desirous of his wife. He may be engaging in intimacy merely in order to fulfil his marital duty or to appease his wife. Viewing the relationship as a burden, he may even feel repelled by her and under such circumstances, the act would come under the category of the forbidden forms of intercourse mentioned above. See also R. Menachem HaMeiri on *Niddah* ibid., and the discussion in R. Pontremoli (eighteenth–nineteenth century), *Petach haDevir, Orach Chayim* 240:5 (p. 134 ff).

Recently, R. Bezalel Naor, *Rav Kook on Homosexuality*, has suggested that according to R. Kook (1865–1935), in *Orot ha-Kodesh*, vol. 3, p. 297 – 'Perversions of the Natural Inclinations' – the halachic 'concession' to allow anal intercourse with one's wife (see Maimonides, *Hilchot Issurei Bi'ah*, 21:9; R. Isserles, *Even HaEzer* 25:2 and commentaries) was made in order to provide homosexuals with an outlet for their desires. Rejecting another possible interpretation of R. Kook's words, R. Naor asserts that it is 'more reasonable to assume that while engaging in anal intercourse with his wife, the latent homosexual will act out a homosexual fantasy'.

However, in light of the unequivocal prohibition to entertain thoughts of another woman during intercourse with one's wife, I think that it is most unlikely that R. Kook would have suggested that it is permissible for a homosexual to 'act out a homosexual fantasy' whilst engaged in anal intercourse with his wife – even in the unlikely event that this were to provide some possible release for the homosexual's craving for male-to-male intercourse.

32 See, for example, R. Riskin, 'Homosexuality as a Tragic Mistake', who writes: 'It is not by

accident that the verse preceding the prohibition against homosexuality reads "And thou shalt not give any of thy seed to Moloch" (Leviticus 18:21). One sacrifices potential future generations through homosexuality ... And children do not bear only existential significance; in Judaism, later generations carry our names and genes, but more importantly they also bear our values, our moral code, our Torah traditions. Cutting oneself off from the possibility of having children and grandchildren is cutting oneself off from the fundamental theological experience in Judaism, the secret of the three generations, Abraham, Isaac and Jacob.' One wonders if R. Riskin would exhort infertile couples in the same manner. Would he also describe them as 'cutting themselves off' from the 'secret of the three generations'? Would he also compare them with those who sacrifice their children to the Moloch?

33 R. Feldman, *A Personal Correspondence*, p. 69.
34 See TB *Bava Kama* 28b.

Bibliography

All references in the text and endnotes to the Holy Scriptures, The Mishnah, The Jerusalem and Babylonian Talmud (including commentaries of Rashi and Tosafot),Tosefta, Midrashim: Sifra d'vei Rav (Torat Cohanim), Midrash Rabbah, Midrash Tanchuma, Yalkut Shimoni, Pirkei Rabbi Eliezer and Zohar are to the standard printed editions of these works.

Abarbanel, Rabbi Yitzchak, *Rosh Amanah*, Constantinople, 1506.
— *Abarbanel Al HaTorah*, Amsterdam, 1768.
Aboab, Rabbi Shmuel, *Teshuvot Devar Shmuel*, Jerusalem, 1983.
Abudraham, Rabbi David, *Abudraham HaShalem*, Jerusalem, 1959.
Abulafia, Rabbi Meir, *Yad Ramah on Sanhedrin*, Salonica, 1798.
Achai Ga'on, Rabbi, *She'iltot*, Mossad Harav Kook, Jerusalem, 1986.
Aderet, Rabbi Shlomoh, *Teshuvot HaRashba*, Machon Yerushalayim, Jerusalem, 1997.
Adler, Rabbi Binyamin, *HaNissuin KeHilchatam*, Jerusalem, 1988.
Aharon ben Avraham, Rabbi, *Korban Aharon on Sifrei d'vei Rav*, Venice, 1926.
Albo, Rabbi Yosef, *Sefer HaIkkarim* (ed. I. Husik), Philadelphia, 1926.
Alfasi, Rabbi Yitzchak (Rif), *Halachot*, in standard printed editions of Talmud Bavli.
Amsel, Rabbi Nachum, *The Jewish Encyclopedia of Moral and Ethical Issues*, Jason Aronson, New Jersey and London, 1994.
Angel, Rabbi Marc, et al, 'Homosexuality and the Orthodox Jewish Community', *Jewish Action* (Winter 1992).
Appleby, Amy (ed.), *Quentin Crisp's Book of Quotations: 1000 Observations on Life and Love by, for and about Gay Men and Women*, Macmillan, New York and London, 1989.
Arama, Rabbi Yitchak ben Moshe, *Akeidat Yitzchak*, Jerusalem, 1961.
Ariele, Rabbi Yitzchak, *Eynayim LaMishpat* on *Berachot*, Mossad Harav Kook, Jerusalem, 1947.

Artson, Bradley S., 'Judaism and Homosexuality', *Tikkun* 3/2 (March/April 1998), pp. 52–54.

Asher ben Yechiel, Rabbi, *Tosafot HaRosh HaShalem*, Israel, 1971.

Ashkenazi, Rabbi Betzalel, *Shittah Mekubetzet*, B'nei B'rak, 1988.

Ashkenazi, Rabbi Tzvi, *Teshuvot Chacham Tzvi*, Jerusalem, 1981.

Auerbach, Rabbi Shlomo Zalman, *Teshuvot Minchat Shlomoh*, vol. 3, Machon Otzrot Shlomoh, Jerusalem, 1999.

—— Avraham ben David of Posquières, Rabbi (Ra'avad), *Ba'alei HaNefesh*, Mossad Harav Kook, Jerusalem, 1964.

Hasagot HaRa'avad al Mishneh Torah, in standard printed editions of Maimonides' *Mishneh Torah*.

—— *Perush Ha Ra'avad* on *Sifra d'vei Rav*, Jerusalem 1959.

Avraham ben HaRambam, Rabbi, *Perush LeSefer Bereishit u-Shemot* (ed., S. D. Sassoon), London, 1958.

Avraham ben Mordechai, Rabbi, *Teshuvot Ginnat Veradim*, Yismach Lev-Torat Moshe, Jerusalem, 1991–2.

Avraham ibn Ezra, Rabbi, *Yesod Mora V'Yesod Torah*, Jerusalem, 1958.

—— *Commentary on the Torah*, Mossad Harav Kook, Jerusalem, 1977.

Azulai, Rabbi Chayim Yosef David, *Birkei Yosef on Shulchan Aruch*, Vienna, 1860.

—— *Eyn Zocher*, Livorno, 1793.

—— *Petach Eynayim*, Jerusalem, 1959.

—— *Teshuvot Chayim Sha'al*.

—— *Tov Ayin*, F. Kawalek, Husiatyn, 1904.

Babad, Rabbi Yosef, *Minchat Chinnuch*, Machon Yerushalayim, Jerusalem, 1992.

Bachya ben Asher, Rabbi, *Midrash Rabbeinu Bachya*, Mossad Harav Kook, Jerusalem, 1977.

—— *Kad HaKemach*, Constantinople, 1515.

Bachya ibn Pakuda, Rabbi, *Chovot Halevavot*, Mossad Harav Kook, Jerusalem 1949.

Bailey, J. M., Dunne, M. P., Martin, N. G., 'Genetic and Environmental Influences on Sexual Orientation and its Correlates in an Australian Twin Sample', *Journal of Personality of Social Psychology* 78 (March 2000).

—— and Pillard, Richard C., 'Genetics of Human Sexual Orientation', *Annual Review of Sex Research* VI (1995).

—— 'Biological Perspectives on Sexual Orientation', in D'Augelli, Anthony R., Patterson, Charlotte J. (eds), *Lesbian, Gay and Bisexual Identities over the Lifespan: Psychological Perspectives*, Oxford University Press, New York, 1995.

—— and Dawood, Khytam, 'Behavioural Genetics, Sexual Orientation, and the Family', in Patterson, Charlotte J., D'Augelli, Anthony R. (eds), *Lesbian, Gay and Bisexual Identities in Families: Psychological Perspectives*, Oxford University Press, New York, 1998.

Bamberger, Rabbi Yitzchak Dov HaLevi, *Teshuvot Yad HaLevi*, Jerusalem, 1965.

Bancroft, John, 'Homosexual Orientation: The Search for a Biological Basis', *British Journal of Psychiatry* 164 (April 1994).

Bar-Ilan, Rabbi Naftali, 'Choleh She-Yitzro Tokfo', *Assia* 49/50, Schlesinger Institute, Jerusalem, 1990.

Bayer, Ronal, *Homosexuality and American Psychiatry: The Politics of Diagnosis*, Basic Books, New York, 1981.

Becher, Rabbi Mordechai and Newman, Rabbi Moshe, *Avotot Ahavah*, Jerusalem, 1991.

—— *After the Return*, Feldheim, Jerusalem and New York, 1994.

Bell, Alan P. et al, *Sexual Preference: Its Development in Men and Women*, Indiana University Press, Bloomington, 1981.

Belmonti, Rabbi Yitzchak, *Sha'ar HaMelech al HaRambam*, Salonica, 1771.

Benveniste, Rabbi Chayim, *Keneset HaGedolah*, Izmir, 1731.

Berdugo, Rabbi Raphael, *Responsa Mishpatim Yesharim*, Druck von Josef Fischer, Cracow, 1891.

Berger, Dr Joseph, 'The Truth about Homosexuality', *The Jewish Action Reader* vol. 1, Mesorah Publications, Brooklyn, 1996.

—— 'Orthodox Attitude to Homosexuality', *Jewish Chronicle*, 30 June 1995, p. 31.

—— 'The Psychotherapeutic Treatment of Male Homosexuality', *American Journal of Psychotherapy* 48 (Spring 1994).

—— 'Letter to the Editor', *Tradition* 34/4 (Winter 2000).

Berlin, Rabbi Naftali T. Y., *Teshuvot Meishiv Davar*, Brooklyn, 1987.

—— *Meromei Sadeh*, Jerusalem, 1957.

—— *HaAmek Davar*, Jerusalem, 1975.

Berlin, Rabbi Noach Chayim Tzvi, *Atzei Arazim*, Fiorda, 1790.

Berman-Ashkenazi, Rabbi Yissachar Ber, *Mattenot Kehunah* on *Midrash Rabbah*, in standard printed editions of *Midrash Rabbah*.

Bermant, Chaim, 'Depravity, not Deprivation is the Cause of our Ills', *Jewish Chronicle*, 26 December 1986, p. 16.

Bindman, Rabbi Yirmeyahu, *The Seven Colors of the Rainbow*, Resource Publications, California, 1995.

Bleich, Rabbi J. David, *Judaism and Healing*, Ktav, New Jersey, 1981.

—— *Bioethical Dilemmas – A Jewish Perspective*, Ktav, New Jersey, 1998.

—— 'Kiddushei Ta'ut: Annulment as a Solution to the Agunah Problem', *Tradition* 33/1 (Fall 1998), pp. 90–128.

—— 'Orthodoxy and the Non-Orthodox: Prospects of Unity', in Sacks, Jonathan (ed.), *Orthodoxy Confronts Modernity*, Ktav, New Jersey, in association with Jews' College, London, 1991.

Blue, Lionel, *My Affair With Christianity*, Hodder & Stoughton, London, Sydney and Auckland, 1998.

Boronstein, Rabbi Avraham, *Teshuvot Avnei Nezer*, Tel Aviv, 1944.

Boteach, Rabbi Shmuley, 'Dr Laura Misguided on Homosexuality', *Jewish Week*, 26 May 2000.

—— 'Does Homosexuality Differ from Heterosexuality?', in *Moses of Oxford*, André Deutsch, London, 1994.

de Boton, Rabbi Avraham, *Lechem Mishneh*, in standard printed editions of Maimonides' *Mishneh Torah*.

Breisch, Rabbi Mordechai, *Teshuvot Chelkat Ya'akov*, vol. 2, London, 1959; vol. 3, B'nei B'rak, 1966.

Bresslau, Rabbi Aryeh Leib, *Teshuvot Pene Aryeh*, Amsterdam, 1790.

Brill, Norman Q., 'Is Homosexuality Normal?', *Journal of Psychiatry & Law* 26/2 (Summer 1998).

Broyde, Rabbi Michael, 'Bullets that Kill on the Rebound: Discrimination against Homosexuals and Orthodox Public Policy', *Jewish Action* 54/1.

Buber, Shlomoh, ed., *Midrash Tehillim (Shocher Tov)*, Vilna, 1891.

Bulka, Rabbi Reuven P., *One Man, One Woman, One Lifetime – An Argument for Moral Tradition*, Huntingdon House Publishers, Louisiana, 1995.

—— *Jewish Marriage: A Halakhic Ethic*, Ktav, New York, 1986.

Byrne, William and Parsons, Bruce, 'Theories of Sexual Orientation: A Reappraisal', *Archives of General Psychiatry* 51/5 (May 1994).

Cameron, P., Cameron, K. and Playfair, W. L., 'Does Homosexual Activity Shorten Life?', *Psychological Reports* 83 (December 1998).

Cardozo, Rabbi Dr Nathan Lopes, 'Religious and Secular Morality', in his forthcoming *Thoughts to Ponder*, Urim Publications, Jerusalem, 2001.

Caro, Rabbi Yosef, *Bet Yosef on Arba'ah Turim*, in standard printed editions of R. Ya'akov ben Asher's *Arba'ah Turim*.

—— *Kesef Mishneh al HaRambam*, in standard printed editions of Maimonides' *Mishneh Torah*.

—— *Shulchan Aruch*, Vilna, 1875.

Castro, Rabbi Ya'akov, *Erech Lechem*, Constantina, 1718.

Chajes, Rabbi Tzvi Hirsch, *Kol Kitvei Maharatz Chajes*, Jerusalem, 1958.

Chayim ben Attar, Rabbi, *Ohr HaChayim*, in many standard printed editions of The Pentateuch.

Chizkiah ben Manoach, Rabbi, *Chizkuni: Perushei HaTorah*, Mossad Harav Kook, Jerusalem, 1981.

Clorfene, Chaim, and Rogalsky, Yakov, *The Path of the Righteous Gentile: An Introduction to the Seven Laws of the Children of Noah*, Targum Press, Israel, 1987.

Cohen, Rabbi Dr Jeffrey, 'No Room for Wandering Souls', *Jewish Chronicle*, 18 August 2000, p. 19.

David ben Shmuel HaLevi, Rabbi, *Divrei Dovid (Turei Zahav) al Perush Rashi She'al HaTorah*, Mossad Harav Kook, Jerusalem, 1978.

—— *Turei Zahav on Shulchan Aruch*, in standard printed editions of R. Yosef Caro's *Shulchan Aruch*.

David ben Zimra, Rabbi, *Teshuvot HaRadbaz*, Israel, 1982.

De Cecco, J. P. and Parker, D. A., 'The Biology of Homosexuality: Sexual Orientation or Sexual Preference?', *The Journal of Homosexuality* 28/1 and 2 (1995).

Dorff, Elliott N., *Matters of Life and Death*, The Jewish Publication Society, Philadelphia and Jerusalem, 1998.

Drescher, J., 'I'm your Handyman: A History of Reparative Therapies', *Journal of Homosexuality* 36 (1998).

Duran, Rabbi Shlomoh, *Teshuvot HaRashbash*, Machon Yerushalayim, Jerusalem, 1998.

Eckert, Elke D. et al, 'Homosexuality in Mono-zygotic Twins Reared Apart', *British Journal of Psychiatry* 148 (April 1986).

Eger, Rabbi Akiva, *Teshuvot Rabbi Akiva Eger*, Vienna, 1889.

Eidels, Rabbi Shmuel Eliezer (Maharsha), *Chiddushei Agadot*, in standard printed editions of Talmud Bavli.

Eidensohn, Rabbi D. E., *Teshuvot Bayit Ne'eman – Ribbit*, New York, 1991.

Einhorn, Rabbi Ze'ev Wolf, *Perush Maharzav* on *Midrash Rabbah*, in standard printed editions of *Midrash Rabbah*.

Eisenstadt, Rabbi Avraham Tzvi Hirsch, *Pitchei Teshuvah* on *Shulchan Aruch Yoreh De'ah*, in standard printed editions of R. Yosef Caro's *Shulchan Aruch*.

Eliezer of Metz, Rabbi, *Sefer Ye're'im*, Vilna, 1892.

Eliyahu ben Chayim, Rabbi, *Teshuvot HaRanach, Mayim Amukim*, Jerusalem, 1984.

Eliyahu ben Shlomoh, Rabbi (Gaon of Vilna), *Bi'urei HaGra* on *Shulchan Aruch*, in standard printed editions of R. Yosef Caro's *Shulchan Aruch*.

Elyashiv, Rabbi Yosef Shalom, *Kovetz Teshuvot*, Jerusalem, 2000.

Emden, Rabbi Ya'akov, *Birat Migdal Oz*, Eshkol, Jerusalem, 1978.

—— *She'eilat Ya'avetz*, Lemberg, 1884.

—— *Siddur Bet Ya'akov*, Zhitomir, 1880.

Engel, Rabbi Yosef, *Otzrot Yosef*, Vienna, 1928.

—— *Gilyonei HaShas al Nashim u-Nezikin*, Vienna and Warsaw, 1937–8.

—— *Atvan D'Oraita*, B'nei B'rak, 1970.

Epstein, Rabbi Baruch HaLevi, *Torah Temimah*, Hebrew Publishing Company, New York, 1925.

Epstein, Louis M., *Sex Laws and Customs in Judaism*, Bloch Publishing Company, New York, 1948.

Epstein, Rabbi Moshe, *Bet Moshe*, Zamosch, 1848.

Epstein, Rabbi Yechiel Michel, *Aruch HaShulchan*, Jerusalem, 1974.

—— *Aruch HaShulchan HeAtid*, Mossad Harav Kook, Jerusalem, 1987.

Ettlinger, Rabbi Ya'akov, *Minchat Ani al HaTorah*, Frankfurt-am-Mein, 1925.

—— *Teshuvot Binyan Zion*, Jerusalem Academy of Jewish Studies, Jerusalem, 1989.

—— *Teshuvot Binyan Zion HaChadashot*, Jerusalem Academy of Jewish Studies, Jerusalem, 1989.

—— *Aruch LaNer*, Jerusalem, 1962.

Falk, Raabi Ya'akov Yehoshua, *P'nei Yehoshua*, Lemberg, 1809.

Feldman, Rabbi Aharon, 'A Personal Correspondence', *Jewish Action* 58/3 (Spring 5758/1998).

Feldman, Rabbi David M., 'Homosexuality and Jewish Law', *Judaism* 32/4 (1983).

Feinstein, Rabbi Moshe, *Iggerot Moshe, Even HaEzer*, vol. 1, New York 1961.

—— *Iggerot Moshe, Even HaEzer*, vol. 2, New York, 1963.

—— *Iggerot Moshe, Even HaEzer*, vol. 3, New York, 1971.

—— *Iggerot Moshe, Even HaEzer*, vol. 4, New York, 1973.

—— *Iggerot Moshe, Orach Chaim,* vol. 1, New York, 1959.

—— *Iggerot Moshe, Orach Chaim*, vol. 2, New York, 1963.

—— *Iggerot Moshe, Orach Chaim*, vol. 3, New York, 1973.

—— *Iggerot Moshe, Orach Chaim*, vol. 4, New York.

—— *Iggerot Moshe, Orach Chaim*, vol. 5, Jerusalem, 1996.

—— *Iggerot Moshe, Yoreh De'ah*, vol. 1, New York, 1959.

—— *Iggerot Moshe, Yoreh De'ah*, vol. 2, New York, 1973.

—— *Iggerot Moshe, Yoreh De'ah*, vol. 3, B'nei B'rak, 1981.

—— *Dibrot Moshe* on *Shabbat*, New York, 1971.

—— 'A Time for Action', *The Jewish Observer*, June 1973.

Frand, Rabbi Yissocher, 'Where There's a Rabbinic Will, there's a Halachic Way: Fact or Fiction?', *The Jewish Observer*, October 1990.

Freehof, Solomon B., *Current Reform Responsa*, vol. 3, Hebrew Union College Press, Cincinnati, 1969.

Freudenthal, Gad (ed.), *AIDS in Jewish Thought and Law*, Ktav, New Jersey, 1998.

Freundel, Rabbi Barry, 'Homosexuality and Judaism', *The Journal of Halachah and Contemporary Society* 11 (Spring 1986).

—— 'Homosexuality and Halachic Judaism', *Moment*, June 1993.

Friedman, Richard C., 'Homosexuality', *The New England Journal of Medicine* 331 (October 1994).

—— and Downey, J., 'Neurobiology and Sexual Orientation: Current Relation-ships', *Journal of Neuropsychiatry & Clinical Neurosciences* 5 (Spring 1993).

Gantz, Joe, *Whose Child Cries: Children of Gay Parents Talk About Their Lives*, Jalmar Press, California, 1983.

Ganzfried, Rabbi Shlomoh, *Kitzur Shulchan Aruch*, Leipzig, 1933.

Gerondi, Rabbi Yonah, *Sha'arei Teshuvah*, B'nei B'rak, 1986.

Gold, Rabbi Michael, *Does God Belong in the Bedroom?*, The Jewish Publication Society, Philadelphia and Jerusalem, 1992.

Goldberg, Hillel, 'Homosexuality: A Religious and Political Analysis', *Tradition* 27/3 (1993).

Goldberg, Rabbi Zalman Nechemiah, 'B'Din Mamzer Nosei Shifchah', *Yeshurun* 7, Machon Yeshurun, Israel, 2000.

Goldberger, Moshe, *A Treasury of Teshuvah Selections with the 20 step program to Perfect Teshuva, with Responsa by Rabbi Moshe Feinstein*, Gross Bros. Printing Co. Inc., Brooklyn, 1984.

Goldschmidt, Rabbi Pinchas, *Teshuvot Zikaron BaSefer*, Moscow, 1995.

Goldstein, Rabbi Sidney, *Suicide in Rabbinic Literature*, Ktav, New Jersey, 1989.

Gombiner, Rabbi Avraham Abale, *Magen Avraham*, in standard printed editions of R. Yosef Caro's *Shulchan Aruch*.

— *Zayit Ra'anan* on *Yalkut Shimoni*, Dessau, 1704.

Gordis, Robert, *Love and Sex*, McGraw-Hill Ryerson Ltd, Toronto, 1978.

— 'Homosexuality and Traditional Religion', *Judaism* 32/4.

Gordon, Muir, 'Sexual Orientation: Born or Bred?', *Journal of Psychology & Christianity* 15/4 (Winter 1996).

Gordon, Seth, 'Letter to the Editor', *Tradition* 34/4 (Winter 2000).

Gordon, Sol, 'Homosexuality: A Counselling Perspective', *Judaism* 32/4.

Green, Richard, *The "Sissy Boy Syndrome" and the Development of Homosexuality*, Yale University Press, New Haven and London, 1987.

Greenberg, David E., *The Construction of Homosexuality*, Chicago University Press, Chicago, 1988.

Greengross, Wendy, *Jewish and Homosexual*, The Reform Synagogues of Great Britain, London, 1982(?).

Greiniman, S. (ed.), *Chafetz Chaim al HaTorah*, B'nei B'rak (no date).

— *Chiddushim U-Biurim* on *Masechet Shabbat*, B'nei B'rak, 1980.

Grodzinsky, Rabbi Chayim O., *Teshuvot Achi'ezer*, Ma'or HaGalil, Israel, 1976.

Grossman, Naomi, 'The Gay Orthodox Underground', *Moment* 26/2 (April 2001).

Grünwald, Rabbi Yehudah, *Teshuvot Zichron Yehudah*, Budapest, 1923.

Guttel, Rabbi Neriah Moshe, *Hishtanut HaTivim Be-Halachah*, Machon Yachdav, Jerusalem, 1995.

Halberstam, Rabbi Yekutiel Yehudah, *Teshuvot Divrei Yatziv – Even HaEzer*, Machon Shefa Chayim, Jerusalem, 1999.

— 'Mikivshonah Shel Keneset Yisrael', in *Digleinu*, Israel, 1960.

Haldeman, D. C., 'The Practice and Ethics of Sexual Orientation Conversion Therapy', *Journal of Consulting and Clinical Psychology* 62 (April 1994).

Halperin, Mordechai, 'Post-mortem Sperm Retrieval', *Assia: A Journal of Jewish Medical Ethics and Halacha* IV/1 (February 2001).

Halpern, Rabbi Salomon Alter (ed.), *Tosafot Yeshanim al Masechet Nedarim*, London, 1965.

Halpert, Stephen C., '"If it ain't broke, don't fix it": Ethical Considerations Regarding Conversion Therapies', *International Journal of Sexuality & Gender Studies* 5 (January 2000).

Hamer, Dean H., and Copeland, Peter, *The Science of Desire: The Search for the Gay Gene and the Biology of Behaviour*, Simon & Schuster, New York, 1994.

Harfenes, Rabbi Yisroel David, *Teshuvot Nishmat Shabbat*, vol. 2, Jerusalem, 1996.

Hass, Rabbi Shlomoh, *Kerem Shlomoh*, Feldheim, Jerusalem, 1974.

Haynes, James D., 'A Critique of the Possibility of Genetic Inheritance of Homosexual Orientation', *Journal of Homosexuality* 28/1–2 (1995).

Heller, Rabbi Yom Tov Lipmann, *Tosafot Yom Tov* on the *Mishnah*, in standard printed editions of the *Mishnah*.

Henkin, Rabbi Yehudah Herzl, *Teshuvot B'nei Banim*, vols 1 and 2, Jerusalem, 1992.

Henkin, Rabbi Yosef Eliyahu, *Kitvei HaGrya Henkin*, vol. 1, Ezrat Torah, New York, 1980.

Herring, Basil F., *Jewish Ethics and Halakhah for our Time*, vol. 1, Ktav, New York, 1984.

Hershberger, Scott L., 'A Twin Registry Study of Male and Female Sexual Orientation', *Journal of Sex Research* 34/2 (1997).

Herzog, Rabbi Isaac, *Pesakim u'Ketavim, Yoreh De'ah*, Mossad Harav Kook, Jerusalem, 1990.

Hildesheimer, Rabbi Ezriel, *Teshuvot Rabbi Ezriel Hildesheimer*, vol. 1, Tel Aviv, 1969.

—— *Teshuvot Rabbi Ezriel Hildesheimer*, vol. 2, Tel Aviv, 1976.

Hillel ben Elyakim, Rabbi, *Perush al Sifra d'vei Rav*, Jerusalem 1961.

Hirsch, Rabbi Samson Raphael, *The Collected Writings of Rabbi Samson Raphael Hirsch*, Feldheim, New York, 1984.

—— *Teshuvot Shemesh Marpei*, Mesorah Publications, New York, 1992.

Hoffmann, Rabbi David, *Leviticus with a Commentary by David Hoffman*, vol. 2 (Hebrew Edition), Mossad Harav Kook, Jerusalem, 1963.

—— *Teshuvot Melammed LeHo'il*, Frankfurt, 1926–32.

—— (ed.) *Midrash Tana'im on Deuteronomy*, Berlin, 1907.

Horovitz, Rabbi Mordechai HaLevi, *Teshuvot Matteh Levi*, Devar Yerushalayim, Jerusalem, 1979.

Horowitz, Rabbi Yeshayah (Shelah), *Sh'nei Luchot HaBrit*, Mifal HaShelah, Haifa, 1992.

Hunsberger, Bruce, 'Religious Fundamentalism, Right-wing Authoritarianism, and Hostility towards Homosexuals in non-Christian Religious Groups', *International Journal for the Psychology of Religion* 6/1 (1996).

Hurwitz, Rabbi Pinchas HaLevi, *Sefer Hafla'ah*, Lemberg, 1816.
—— *Sefer HaMiknah*, Jerusalem, 1922.
Hutner, Rabbi Yitzchak, *Pachad Yitzchak: Sha'ar Chodesh Ha-Aviv*, Gur Aryeh, Brooklyn, 1970.
Isay, Richard A., 'The Development of Sexual Identity in Homosexual Men', in Greenspan, S. I. and Pollock, G. (eds), *The Course of Life*, vol. 4, International Universities Press, Madison, CT, 1991.
—— 'Heterosexually Married Homosexual Men: Clinical and Developmental Issues', *American Journal of Orthopsychiatry* 68 (July 1998).
Ishbili, Rabbi Yom Tov, *Sefer HaZikaron*, Mossad Harav Kook, Jerusalem, 1982.
—— *Chidushei HaRitva* on *Pesachim*, Mossad Harav Kook, Jerusalem, 1983.
—— *Teshuvot HaRitva*, Mossad Harav Kook, Jerusalem, 1959.
—— *Chidushei HaRitva* on *Yevamot*, vol. 2, Mossad Harav Kook, Jerusalem, 1992.
—— *Chidushei HaRitva* on *Shabbat*, Mossad Harav Kook, Jerusalem, 1990.
—— *Chidushei HaRitva* on *Niddah*, Mossad Harav Kook, Jerusalem, 1978.
Isserles, Rabbi Moshe, *Teshuvot HaRama*, Warsaw, 1883.
—— *Hagahot HaRama* on *Shulchan Aruch*, in standard printed editions of R. Yosef Caro's *Shulchan Aruch*.
Jachter, Rabbi Chaim, with Ezra Fraser, *Gray Matter: Discourses in Contemporary Halachah*, New Jersey, 2000.
Jacobs, Rabbi Fishel, *Family Purity: A Guide to Marital Fulfilment*, Campus Living and Learning, Vermont, 2000.
Jacobs, Louis, *A Jewish Theology*, Daton, Longman & Todd, London, 1973.
Jacobson, Rabbi Simon, *Toward a Meaningful Life: The Wisdom of the Rebbe, Menachem Mendel Schneerson*, Vaad Hanochos Hatmimim, Brooklyn, 1995.
Jaffe, Rabbi Mordechai, *Levush HaOrah*, Bresslau, 1860.
—— *Levush Malchut*, Zichron Aharon, Jerusalem, 2000.
Jakobovits, Rabbi Immanuel, 'Only a Moral Revolution can Contain this Scourge', *The Times* (London), 27 December 1986.
—— 'Memorandum on AIDS, Submitted by the Chief Rabbi to the Social Services Committee of the House of Commons [1987]', *Assia* 2/1 (January 1991).
Johnston, Michael W. and Bell, Alan P., 'Romantic Emotional Attachment: Additional Factors in the Development of the Sexual Orientation of Men', *Journal of Counselling & Development* 73/6 (Jul–Aug 1995).
Kagan, Rabbi Yisroel Meir (The Chafetz Chaim), *Chafetz Chayim Hilchot Issurei Lashon HaRa U'rechilut va'avak shelahen*, B'nei B'rak, 1991.
—— *Ahavat Chesed*, Warsaw, 1888.
—— *Nidchei Yisrael*, Warsaw, 1897.
—— *Machane Yisrael*, New York, 1943.

—— *Mishnah Berurah*, Pardes, Tel Aviv, 1954.

—— *Bet Yisrael*, Eshkol, Jerusalem, 1974.

—— *Geder Olam*, Eshkol, Jerusalem, 1974.

—— *Taharat Yisrael*, Eshkol, Jerusalem, 1974.

—— *Kitvei HeChafetz Chaim*, Z. Berman, Brooklyn, 1989.

—— *Sefer HaMitzvot HaKatzer*, Feldheim, Jerusalem, 1990.

Kalir, Rabbi Elazar, *Cheker Halachah*, Munkács, 1895.

Kaplan, Gisela and Rogers, Lesley J., 'Race and Gender Fallacies: The Paucity of Biological Determinist Explanations of Difference', in Tobach, Ethel and Rosoff, Betty (eds), *Challenging Racism and Sexism: Alternatives to Genetic Explanations*, New York, 1994.

Karelitz, Rabbi Avraham Y., *Chazon Ish: Yoreh De'ah and Even HaEzer*, B'nei B'rak, 1991.

Karelitz, Rabbi Nissim, 'BeGeder Tinok Shenishbah', in *Kovetz Zichron Mordechai Al Masechet Berachot*, Kollel Chazon Ish, B'nei B'rak, 1999.

Karkowsky, Rabbi Menachem, *Avodat Hamelech* on Maimomides' *Sefer HaMada*, Mossad Harav Kook, Jerusalem, 1971.

Kasar, Rabbi Yichya, *Perush Shem Tov al HaRambam*, Jerusalem, 1986.

Katz, Rabbi Yissachar Ber, *Matenot Kehunah HaShalem*, Jerusalem, 1985.

Kaufman, Rabbi Moshe, *Kuntres Mei Menuchah B'inyanei Shidduch*, B'nei B'rak, 1991.

Kirshner, Robert, 'Halakhah and Homosexuality: a Reappraisal', *Judaism* 37 (1988).

Klatzkin, Rabbi Eliyahu, *Teshuvot Imrei Shefer*, Munkács, 1913.

Klatzkin, Rabbi Yosef, *Devar Halachah*, Lublin, 1921.

Klein, Rabbi Menashe, *Teshuvot Mishneh Halachot*, Machon Mishneh Halachot Gedolot, New York, 1998.

Kluger, Jeffrey, 'Can Gays Switch Sides?', *Time Magazine*, 21 May 2001.

Kluger, Rabbi Shlomoh, *Chochmat Shlomoh on Shulchan Aruch*, in standard printed editions of R. Yosef Caro's *Shulchan Aruch*.

Kook, Rabbi Abraham Yitzchak HaCohen, *Teshuvot Da'at Cohen*, Mossad Harav Kook, Jerusalem, 1969.

—— *Teshuvot Mishpat Cohen*, Mossad Harav Kook: Jerusalem, 1985.

—— *Orot HaKodesh*, vol. 3, Mossad Harav Kook: Jerusalem, 1969.

Krauser, Rabbi Dov Meir, *Devar HaMelech*, vol. 1, Jerusalem, 1962.

Lamm, Rabbi Dr Norman, 'The New Dispensation on Homosexuality: A Jewish Reaction to a developing Christian Attitude', *Jewish Life* 35/3.

—— 'Judaism and the Modern Attitude to Homosexuality', *The Encyclopaedia Judaica Yearbook,* Keter, Jerusalem, 1974.

—— 'Judaism and the Modern Attitude to Homosexuality', *L'Eylah* 1/3 1977 (Spring 5737).

Landau, Rabbi Yechezkel, *Teshuvot Noda BiYehudah*, Jerusalem, 1969.

—— *Drushei Hatzlach*, Warsaw, 1899.

Lema, Rabbi Moshe, *Chelkat Mechokek on Even HaEzer,* in standard printed editions of R Yosef Caro's *Shulchan Aruch.*

Lehrman, Nathaniel S., 'Homosexuality: A Political Mask for Promiscuity: A Psychiatrist reviews the Data', *Tradition* 34/1.

—— 'Homosexuality and Judaism: Are they Compatible?', *Judaism* 32/4.

—— 'Response to letters' in *Tradition* 34/4 (Winter 2000).

Leiner, Rabbi Mordechai Yosef of Izbica, *Mei HaShiloach,* B'nei B'rak, 1994.

Leiter, Rabbi Yechiel Michel, *Teshuvot Darkei Shalom,* vol. 1, Vienna, 1932.

LeVay, Simon, *The Sexual Brain,* Massachusetts Institute of Technology Press, Massachusetts and London, 1993.

—— *Queer Science: The Use and Abuse of Research into Homosexuality,* MIT Press, Massachussetts, 1996.

Levenberg, Rabbi Yehudah Heshel, *Imrei Chein al HaRambam Hilchot Mamrim,* Brooklyn, 1989.

Levi ben Gershon, Rabbi, *Perushei Ralbag al HaTorah, Sefer Vayikra,* Mossad Harav Kook, Jerusalem, 1997.

Levi ibn Chabib, Rabbi, *Teshuvot Rabbi Levi ibn Chabib,* Lemberg, 1865.

Levi, Rabbi Leo, *Modern Liberation – A Torah Perspective on Contemporary Lifestyles,* Hemed Books, New York, 1998.

Lifschutz, Rabbi Shlomoh, *Teshuvot Chemdat Shlomoh,* Warsaw, 1836.

Lipschütz, Rabbi Yisroel, *Tif'eret Yisrael on the Mishnah,* Berlin, 1862.

Loew, Rabbi Yehudah Leib (Maharal of Prague), *Chumash Gur Aryeh,* Machon Yerushalayim, Jerusalem, 1989.

—— *Netivot Olam,* New York, 1969.

Lunshitz, Rabbi Ephraim, *Olelot Ephrayim,* Jerusalem, 1988.

Luria, Rabbi Shlomoh, *Yam Shel Shlomoh,* Machon Even Yisrael, Jerusalem, 1999.

Maggid, Barry, 'Is Biology Destiny after all? Three Clinical Conundrums: Homosexuality, Alcoholism and Obesity', *Journal of Psychotherapy Practice and Research* 4/1 (Winter 1995).

Magonet, Jonathan (ed.), *Jewish Explorations of Sexuality,* Berghahn Books, Providence and Oxford, 1995.

Maimonides Rabbi Moshe (Rambam), *Moreh HaNevuchim,* Mossad Harav Kook, Jerusalem, 1977.

—— *Shemonah Perakim,* Mossad Harav Kook, Jerusalem, 1961.

—— *Mishneh Torah – Yad HaChazakah,* Otzar HaSefarim, New York, 1956.

—— *Sefer HaMitzvot,* Lemberg, 1860.

—— *Perush HaMishnah,* Mossad Harav Kook, Jerusalem, 1963.

Matt, Hershel J., 'Sin, Crime, Sickness or Alternative Life Style? A Jewish Approach to Homosexuality', *Judaism* 27/1 (1978).

—— 'Homosexual Rabbis?', *Conservative Judaism* 39/3 (Spring 1987).

—— 'A Call for Compassion', *Judaism* 32/4 (1983).

Matzner-Bekerman, Shoshana, *The Jewish Child: Halakhic Perspectives*, Ktav, New York, 1984.

McConaghy, Nathaniel, 'Biologic Theories of Sexual Orientation', *Archives of General Psychiatry* 51/5 (May 1994).

McGuire, Terry R., 'Is Homosexuality Genetic? A Critical Review and some Suggestions', *Journal of Homosexuality* 28/1–2 (1995).

Meier, Rabbi Levi (ed.), *Jewish Values in Health and Medicine*, University Press of America, Inc., 1991.

Meir HaKohen, Rabbi, *Hagahot Maimoni*, in standard printed editions of Maimonides' *Mishneh Torah*.

Meir Leib ben Yechiel Michel, Rabbi (Malbim), *Perush HaTorah VeHaMitzvah*, Vilna, 1922.

Meir Simchah HaKohen, Rabbi, *Ohr Sameach*, Jerusalem, 1993.

— *Meshech Chochmah* (ed., A. Abraham), Israel, 1972.

Meiri, Rabbi Menachem, *Bet HaBechirah* on *Sanhedrin*, Jerusalem, 1965.

— *Bet HaBechirah* on *Shabbat*, Jerusalem, 1968

— *Bet HaBechirah* on *Yevamot*, Jerusalem, 1962.

Meyer-Bahlburg, Heino F., 'Can Homosexuality in Adolescence be "Treated" by Sex Hormones?', *Journal of Child and Adolescent Psychopharmocology* 1/3 (1991).

Meyuchas ben Eliyahu, Rabbi, *Commentary on Leviticus*, Yeshiva University Press, New York, 1996.

Miller, E. M., 'Homosexuality, Birth Order and Evolution: Toward an Equilibrium Reproductive Economics of Homosexuality', *The Archives of Sexual Behaviour* 29/1 (February 2000).

Mizrachi, Rabbi Eliyahu, *Teshuvot Rabbi Eliyahu Mizrachi*, Jerusalem, 1937.

Mohr, Richard D., *Gay Ideas: Outing & Other Controversies*, Beacon Press, Boston, 1992.

Morris, Bonnie J., 'Challenge, Criticism and Compassion: Modern Jewish Responses to Jewish Homosexuals', *Jewish Social Studies* XLIX/3–4 (Summer–Fall 1987).

Moshe ben Ya'akov, Rabbi, *Sefer Mitzvot Gadol*, Machon Yerushalayim, Jerusalem, 1993.

Munk, Rabbi Elie, *The Call of the Torah: An Anthology of Interpretation and Commentary on the Five Books of Moses*, Mesorah Publications, New York, 1992.

Nachmanides, Rabbi Moses, *Kitvei HaRamban* (ed., B. Chavel), Mossad Harav Kook, Jerusalem, 1962.

— *Iggeret HaKodesh* (attributed to Nachmanides) (ed. Ephraim Ariel Buchwald), B'nei B'rak, 1990.

— *Perush Al HaTorah* (ed., B. Chavel), Mossad Harav Kook, Jerusalem, 1960.

—— *Hasagot HaRamban LeSefer HaMitzvot*, Mossad Harav Kook, Jerusalem, 1981.

—— *Chidushei HaRamban* on *Yevamot*, Machon HaTalmud HaYisraeli HaShalem, Jerusalem, 1987.

—— *Chidushei HaRamban* on *Shabbat*, Machon HaTalmud HaYisraeli HaShalem, Jerusalem, 1973.

—— *Chidushei HaRamban* on *Sanhedrin* and *Yevamot*, Machon HaTalmud HaYisraeli HaShalem, Jerusalem, 1970.

Naor, Rabbi Bezalel, 'Rav Kook on Homosexuality', in *Orot.com*, 1998.

Nathanson, Rabbi Yosef Shaul, *Teshuvot Sho'el U'Meishiv*, Lemberg, 1865–1890.

Navon, Rabbi Yehudah, *Kiryat Melech Rav*, Kustandina, 1750.

Nicolosi, Joseph, *Healing Homosexuality, Case Stories of Reparative Therapy*, Jason Aronson Inc., New Jersey, 1993.

—— *Reparative Therapy of Male Homosexuality – A New Clinical Approach*, Jason Aronson Inc., New Jersey and London, 1991.

Nissim of Gerona, Rabbi, *Chidushei HaRan al HaShas*, B'nei B'rak, 1981.

—— *Perush HaRan al Masechet Nedarim*, in standard printed editions of the Talmud Bavli.

—— *Teshuvot HaRan*, Warsaw, 1907.

—— *Commentary on Alfasi's Sefer Halachot*, in standard printed editions of the Talmud Bavli.

Novak, David, 'AIDS: The Contemporary Jewish Perspective', in Katz, S. T. (ed.), *Frontiers of Jewish Thought*, B'nai B'rith Books, Washington, 1992.

Olyan, Saul M. and Nussbaum, Martha C. (eds), *Sexual Orientation & Human Rights in American Religious Discourse*, Oxford University Press, New York, 1998.

Orenstein, Rabbi Ya'akov Meshullam, *Yeshuot Ya'akov*, Lemberg, 1863.

Ovadiah of Bertinoro, Rabbi, *Amar Nekei* on *Perush Rashi al HaTorah*, Czernowitz, 1857.

—— *Commentary on the Mishnah*, in standard printed editions of the Mishnah.

Pallaggi, Rabbi Chaim, *Ruach Chayim Commentary on Shulchan Aruch Even HaEzer*, Izmir, 1876.

—— *Chayim B'yad* (Responsa on Yoreh Deah), Izmir, 1877.

—— *Tochachat Chayim Al HaTorah*, Jerusalem, 1978.

—— *Chikekei Lev*, vol. 1, no. 47, Jerusalem, 1979.

Pardo, Rabbi David Shmuel, *Chasdei David* on *Tosefta*, Jerusalem, 1969.

Parker, William, *Homosexuality Bibliography: Supplement*, Scarecrow Press, New Jersey, 1977.

Paul, Geoffrey, 'Troubled times for Orthodox homosexuals', *Jewish Chronicle*, 9 June 1995.

Perlman, Rabbi Yerucham Yehudah Leib, *Ohr Gadol*, Machon Yerushalayim, Jerusalem, 1986.

Perlow, Rabbi Yerucham Fishel, *Commentary on Sefer HaMitzvot LeRabbeinu Sa'adiah Ga'on*, Jerusalem, 1973.

Pillard, R. C. and Bailey, J. M., 'A Biologic Perspective on Sexual Orientation', *Psychiatric Clinics of North America* 18 (March 1995).

—— 'Human Sexual Orientation has a Heritable Component', *Human Biology* 70 (April 1998).

Plotzki, Rabbi Meir Don, *Klei Chemdah al HaTorah*, Pietrikov, 1927.

Poczanowski, Rabbi Yosef, *Pardes Yosef Al HaTorah*, New York, 1986.

Podhoretz, Norman, 'How the Gay Rights Movement Won', *Commentary* (November 1996).

Pontremoli, Rabbi Chayim Binyamin, *Petach HaDevir*, Jerusalem, 1978.

Posner, Rabbi Meir, *Bet Meir on Shulchan Aruch*, Jerusalem, 1972.

Prager, Dennis, 'Judaism, Homosexuality and Civilization', *Ultimate Issues* 6/2 (April–June 1990).

Primoratz, Igor, *Ethics and Sex*, Routledge, London, 1999.

Rakeffet-Rothkoff, Rabbi Aaron, *The Rav – The World of Rabbi Joseph B Soloveitchik*, Ktav, New Jersey, 1999.

Rappaport, Rabbi Yisroel Yosef, *LiTeshuvat HaShanah*, B'nei B'rak, 1986.

Riskin, Rabbi Shlomo, 'Homosexuality as a Tragic Mistake', *The Jerusalem Post*, 30 April 1993.

Rokeach, Rabbi Elazar of Worms, *Commentary on the Torah*, London, 1959.

Rokowsky, Rabbi Yisroel, 'It's Not My Problem...Or Is It?', *The Jewish Observer*, Summer 1993.

Roll, W., 'Homosexual Inmates in the Buchenwald Concentration Camp', *Journal of Homosexuality* 31 (1996).

Roller, Rabbi Chayim Mordechai, *Teshuvot Be'er Chayim Mordechai*, Weinstein & Friedman, Cluj, 1924–36.

Roper, W. G., 'The Aetiology of Male Homosexuality', *Medical Hypotheses* 46/2 (February 1996).

Rosanes, Rabbi Yehudah, *Parashat Derachim*, Makkor Publications, Jerusalem, 1961.

—— *Mishnah LaMelech al HaRambam*, in standard printed editions of Maimonides' *Mishneh Torah*.

Rosen, Rabbi Yosef, *Tzofnat Pa'aneach* on *Sanhedrin*, Machon Tzofnat Pa'aneach, Jerusalem and New York, 1963.

—— *Teshuvot Tzofnat Pa'aneach*, Machon Tzofnat Pa'aneach, Jerusalem, 1965.

—— *Teshuvot Tzofnat Pa'aneach*, Warsaw, 1935–6.

—— *Teshuvot Tzofnat Pa'aneach*, Dvinsk, 1931.

Rosenberg, Kenneth Paul, 'Biology and Homosexuality', *Journal of Sex & Marital Therapy* 20/2 (Summer 1994).

Rosner, F., *Pioneers in Jewish Medical Ethics*, Jason Aronson, New Jersey and Jerusalem, 1997.

—— 'AIDS: A Jewish View', in Freudenthal, Gad (ed.), *AIDS in Jewish Thought and Law*, Ktav, New Jersey, 1998.

—— and Tendler, Harav Moshe, *Practical Medical Halachah* (3rd revised edition), Ktav, New Jersey, 1990.

Rozovski, Rabbi Shmuel, *Zichron Shmuel*, Israel, 1985.

Ruse, Michael, 'Nature/Nurture: Reflections on Approaches to the Study of Homosexuality', *Journal of Homosexuality* 10/3 and 4 (Winter 1984).

—— *Homosexuality: A Philosophical Inquiry.*

Sa'adiah Ga'on, Rabbi, *Sefer HaEmunot veHaDe'ot*, Mossad Harav Kook, Jerusalem, 1993.

—— *Perush Rasag Al HaTorah* (ed., Y. Kafach), Mossad Harav Kook, Jerusalem, 1962.

—— *Perush Rasag on Genesis*, Jewish Theological Seminary, Jerusalem, 1984.

Sacks, Chief Rabbi Dr Jonathan, *Tradition in an Untraditional Age: Essays on Modern Jewish Thought*, Valentine Mitchell, 1991.

Sassoon, S. D. (ed.), *Moshav Zekeinim – Kovetz Perushei Rabboteinu Ba'alei Tosafot Al HaTorah*, London, 1959.

Scheinberg, Rabbi Chaim Pinchas, *Shoalim BiTeshuvah*, Association for Jewish Outreach Professionals, New Jersey, 1991.

—— 'Birur b'da'at haGra b'din tinokot shenishbu bizmaneinu, ha'im mitztarfin l'minyan asarah', *Yeshurun* 6, Machon Yeshurun, Israel, 1999.

Schick, Rabbi Shlomoh, *Teshuvot Maharam Schick*, Jerusalem, 1972.

Schlesinger, Rabbi Eliyahu, 'Kiddushin b'Ed Echad Kasher v'Ed Ecahd Passul', in *Divrei Mishpat, Me'asef Torani b'inyanei Even HaEzer v'Choshen HaMishpat*, Machon Divrei Mishpat, vol. 1, Tel Aviv, 1996.

Schlesinger, Yaffa and Appell, Victor, 'Jewish Responses to AIDS', *Journal of Homosexuality* 33/1 (1997).

Schmelkes, Rabbi Yitzchak, *Teshuvot Bet Yitzchak*, Premszl, 1875.

Schneerson, Rabbi Dovber, *Sha'ar HaTeshuvah*, Kehot Publication Society, Brooklyn, 1975.

Schneerson, Rabbi Joseph Isaac, *Likutei Dibburim*, vol. 4, Kehot Publication Society, Brooklyn, 1954.

—— *Sefer HaSichot 5701*, Kehot Publication Society, Brooklyn, 1976.

—— *Iggerot Kodesh*, vol. 2, Kehot Publication Society, Brooklyn, 1985.

Schneerson, Rabbi Menachem Mendel, *Emunah u'Madda*, Machon Lubavitch, Kefar Chabad, 1977.

—— *Rights or Ills*, Sichos in English, Brooklyn, 1986.

—— *Torat Menachem – Hitva'aduyot 5744*, vol.1; 5746, vol.2, Kehot Publication Society, Brooklyn, 1990.

—— *Sha'arei Halachah U'minhag*, 4 vols, Heichal Menachem, Jerusalem, 1994.

—— *Likkutei Sichot*, vols 1–38, Kehot Publication Society, Brooklyn, 1999.

—— *Likkutei Sichot*, vol. 39, Kehot Publication Society, Brooklyn, 2000.

—— *Gidran Shel Mitzvot – Chukim u'Mishpatim*, Kehot Publication Society, Brooklyn, 1994.

—— *Iggerot Kodesh*, vol. 6, Kehot Publication Society, Brooklyn, 1988.

—— *Iggerot Kodesh*, vol. 23, Kehot Publication Society, Brooklyn, 1994.

—— *Sefer HaSichot 5751*, vol. 1, Kehot Publication Society, Brooklyn, 1992.

Schneur Zalman of Liady, Rabbi, *Likkutei Amarim – Tanya*, Kehot Publication Society, Brooklyn, 1973.

—— *Iggeret HaTeshuvah*, Kehot Publication Society, Brooklyn, 1973.

—— *Shulchan Aruch HaRav*, Kehot Publication Society, Brooklyn, 1960.

—— *Ma'amarei Admur HaZaken – Inyanim*, Kehot Publication Society, Brooklyn, 1983.

—— *Torah Ohr*, Kehot Publication Society, Brooklyn, 1996.

Schneur Zalman of Lublin, Rabbi, *Teshuvot Torat Chesed*, Jerusalem, 1909.

Schochet, Rabbi Ezra, 'Boteach is the One who is Misguided', *The Jewish Press*, 14 July 2000.

Schwab, Rabbi Shimon, *Selected Writings*, CIS Publications, New Jersey, 1988.

—— *Selected Speeches*, CIS Publications, New York, London and Jerusalem, 1991.

Schwadron, Rabbi Shalom Mordechai, *Teshuvot Maharsham*, Machon Da'at Torah, Jerusalem, 1988–92.

—— *Da'at Torah al Shulchan Aruch Yoreh De'ah*, Machon Da'at Torah, Jerusalem, 1988.

Sforno, Rabbi Ovadiah, *Perush Sforno Al HaTorah*, Jerusalem, 1992.

Shabtai HaKohen, Rabbi, *Siftei Kohen on Shulchan Aruch,* in standard printed editions of R. Yosef Caro's *Shulchan Aruch.*

Shallenberger, David, *Reclaiming the Spirit: Gay Men and Lesbians Come to Terms with Religion*, Rutgers University Press, New Jersey, 1998.

Shapira, Rabbi Chaim Elazar, *Teshuvot Minchat Elazar*, Brooklyn, 1991.

Shlomoh ben Aderet, Rabbi, *Teshuvot HaRashba*, Machon Yerushalayim, Jerusalem, 1997.

Shlomoh ben Yitzchak, Rabbi (Rashi), *Commentary on the Holy Scriptures and the Talmud Bavli*, in standard printed editions of these works.

Shlomoh HaKohen of Vilna, Rabbi, *Teshuvot Binyan Shlomoh*, Jerusalem, 1992.

Shmuel ben Shraga Feivush, Rabbi, *Bet Shmuel on Shulchan Aruch*, in standard printed editions of R. Yosef Caro's *Shulchan Aruch*.

Shokeid, Moshe, *A Gay Synagogue in New York*, Columbia University Press, New York, 1995.

Shor, Rabbi Alexander Sender, *Simlah Chadashah* with *Tevuot Shor*, Zhitomir, 1868.

—— *Bechor Shor* (published with *Simlah Chadashah* and *Tevuot Shor*), Zhitomir, 1868.

Shor, Rabbi Avraham Chaim, *Torat Chayim*, Jerusalem, 1969.

Sirkes, Rabbi Yo'el, *Bayit Chadash on Arba'ah Turim*, in standard printed editions of R. Ya'akov ben Asher's *Arba'ah Turim*.

Sofer, Rabbi Avraham Chaim Binyamin, *Teshuvot Ketav Sofer*, Machon Chatam Sofer, Jerusalem, 1986.

—— *Ketav Sofer al HaTorah*, Pressburg, 1889.

Sofer, Rabbi Moshe, *Commentary on Ketubot*, Brooklyn 1955.

—— *Teshuvot Chatam Sofer*, Vienna, 1855.

—— *Hagahot Chatam Sofer al HaShas*, in standard printed editions of the Talmud Bavli.

Soloff, Rabbi A., 'Is there a Reform Response to Homosexuality?', *Judaism* 32/4.

Solomon, Mark, 'A Strange Conjunction', *Jewish Explorations of Sexuality*, Berghahn Books, Providence and Oxford, 1995.

Soloveitchik, Rabbi Aharon, 'Kiddushei Shamranim', in *HaPardes* (Cheshvan 5747), New York, 1986.

Soloveitchik, Rabbi Yitzchak Ze'ev, *Chiddushei HaGriz al HaTorah*, Jerusalem, 1963.

Soloveitchik, Rabbi Yosef Dov Ber, *Bet HaLevi al HaTorah*, New York, 1973.

—— *Bet HaLevi – Derashot* (published with *Teshuvot Bet HaLevi*, vol. 2), Warsaw, 1874.

—— *Reshimot Shiurim – al Masechtot Shavuot uNedarim* vol. 1, H. Reichman, Brooklyn, 1993.

Sorotzkin, Rabbi Yitzchak, *Gevurat Yitzchak al Hilchot Teshuvah*, Brooklyn, 1989.

Spektor, Rabbi Yitzchak Elchanan, *Teshuvot Eyn Yitzchak*, New York, 1965.

—— *Teshuvot Be'er Yitzchak*, New York, 1948.

Spero, Rabbi Moshe HaLevi, 'Homosexuality: Clinical and Ethical Challenges', in *Judaism and Psychology: Halakhic Perspectives*, Ktav, New York, 1980.

—— 'Further Examination of the Halakhic Status of Homosexuality: Female Homosexual Behavior, and Homosexuality as *Ones*', *Proceedings of the Associations of Orthodox Jewish Scientists* 7 (1983).

—— 'The Didactic-Psychological Function of Three Rabbinic Blessings', *Proceedings of the Associations of Orthodox Jewish Scientists* 8 (1987).

Steif, Rabbi Yehonatan, *Limmudei HaShem on Genesis*, Budapest, 1927.

—— *Sefer Mitzvot HaShem – Kuntres Dinei B'nei Noach*, unpublished work.

Stein, Terry S., 'Deconstructioning Sexual Orientation: Understanding the Phenomena of Sexual Orientation', *Journal of Homosexuality* 34/1 (1997).

Steinberg, Rabbi Dr Abraham, 'AIDS – Hebetim Refu'iyim, Musariyim va-Hilkhatiyim' [AIDS – Medical, Moral and Halakhic Perspectives], in Halperin M. (ed.), *Sefer Assia* 7 (1993). Originally published in *Assia* 47–48 (vol. 12, nos. 3–4) (Kislev, 5750/1990).

—— *Encyclopaedia of Jewish Medical Ethics*, vol. 4, Falk-Schlesinger Institute, Jerusalem, 1988–96.

—— 'AIDS: Jewish Perspectives', in Rosner, F. (ed.), *Medicine and Jewish Law*, vol. 2. English translation of a slightly modified text of Steinberg, 'AIDS – Hebetim Refu'iyim, Musariyim va-Hilkhatiyim'.

Stern, Rabbi Ya'akov Meir, *Imrei Ya'akov – Al Dinei Choshen Mishpat*, B'nei B'rak, 2000.

Stern, Rabbi Yosef Zechariah, *Teshuvot Zecher Yehosef*, Jerusalem, 1967.

Sternbuch, Rabbi Moshe, *Teshuvot VeHanhagot*, vol. 3, Jerusalem, 1997.

—— *Teshuvot VeHanhagot*, vol. 2, Jerusalem, 1994.

—— *Teshuvot VeHanhagot*, vol. 1, Jerusalem, 1992.

—— *HaDerech LiTeshuvah* on Maimonides' *Hilchot Teshuvah*, B'nei B'rak, 1978.

Sullivan, Andrew (ed.), *Same-sex Marriage, Pro and Con: A Reader*, Vintage Books, New York, 1997.

Sussman, Norman, ' Sex and Sexuality in History' in Sadock, Kaplan and Freedman (eds), *The Sexual Experience*, Williams & Wilkins, Baltimore, 1976.

Tanenbaum, Rabbi Malkiel, *Teshuvot Divrei Malkiel*, Vilna, 1901.

Teichtel, Rabbi Yissachar Shlomoh, *Em HaBanim Semechah*, Machon P'ri Ha'Aretz, Jerusalem, 1983.

Teitelbaum, Rabbi Yekutiel Yehudah, *Teshuvot Avnei Tzedek*, Jerusalem, 1992.

Teitelbaum, Rabbi Yoel, *Teshuvot Divrei Yoel*, vol. 2, Brooklyn, 1983.

Tendler, Rabbi Moshe David, 'Treife Sex', *Jewish Week*, 2 June, 2000.

Te'umim, Rabbi Joseph, *Tevat Gome*, Nehedar Publications, Tel Aviv, 1966.

—— *Peri Megadim*, in standard printed editions of R. Yosef Caro's *Shulchan Aruch*.

Thomas, Lawrence, *Sexual Orientation and Human Rights*, Rowman & Littlefield, Lanham, 1999.

Trani, Rabbi Moshe, *Kiryat Sefer*, New York, 1985.

—— *Bet Elokim*, Warsaw, 1872.

Tuvya ben Eliezer, Rabbi, *Midrash Lekach Tov*, Vilna, 1884.

Tykocinski, Rabbi Yechiel Michel, *Gesher HaChayim*, Jerusalem, 1960.

Tziyoni, Rabbi Menachem, *Perush al HaTorah*, Jerusalem, 1964.

Unterman, Dr Alan, 'Judaism and Homosexuality, Some Orthodox Perspectives', *Jewish Quarterly* 30/3 (Autumn 1993). Also in *Jewish Explorations of Sexuality*, Berghahn Books, Providence and Oxford 1995.

Vidal of Tolosa, Rabbi, *Maggid Mishneh al HaRambam*, in standard printed editions of Maimonides' *Mishneh Torah*.

Vital, Rabbi Chayim, *Sha'ar HaGilgulim*, Jerusalem, 1912.

Wahrmann, Rabbi Avraham David of Buczacz, *Ezer MiKodesh*, in standard printed editions of R. Yosef Caro's *Shulchan Aruch*.

Waldenburg, Rabbi Eliezer Yehudah, *Teshuvot Tzitz Eliezer*, Jerusalem, 1985.

—— *Teshuvot Tzitz Eliezer*, vol. 16, Jerusalem, 1990.

—— *Teshuvot Tzitz Eliezer*, vol. 17, Jerusalem, 1990.

—— *Teshuvot Tzitz Eliezer*, vol. 20, Jerusalem, 1990.

Washofsky, Mark et al (CCAR Responsa Committee), 'On Homosexual Marriage', *CCAR Journal, A Reform Jewish Quarterly* (Winter 1998).

Wasserman, Rabbi Elchanan Bunim, *Kovetz Ma'amarim*, Jerusalem, 1963.

—— *Kovetz He'arot* on *Yevamot*, Tel Aviv, 1967.

Wasserman, Rabbi Simchah, *Reb Simchah Speaks*, Mesorah Publications in conjunction with Yeshiva Ohr Elchanan, Jerusalem and New York, 1994.

Weinberg, Rabbi Yechiel Ya'akov, *Teshuvot Seridei Esh*, Mossad Harav Kook, Jerusalem, 1977.

Weinberger, Rabbi Moshe, *Jewish Outreach: Halakhic Perspectives*, Ktav, New York, 1990.

Weinfeld, Rabbi Abraham, *Teshuvot Lev Avraham*, Brooklyn, 1977.

Weingarten, Rabbi Yoav Yehoshua, *Chelkat Yo'av*, Israel, 1977.

Weishut, D. J., 'Attitudes Towards Homosexuality: An Overview', *Israel Journal of Psychiatry & Related Sciences* 37 (2000).

Weiss, Rabbi Chayim Yosef David, *Teshuvot Va'Ya'an David*, vols. 1 and 2, Jerusalem, 1993; vol. 3, Jerusalem, 1996.

Weiss, Rabbi Yitzchak Ya'akov, *Teshuvot Minchat Yitzchak*, vol. 3, London, 1962.

—— *Teshuvot Minchat Yitzchak*, vol. 4, London, 1967.

—— *Teshuvot Minchat Yitzchak*, vol. 5, Jerusalem, 1978.

Wolowelsky, Joel B. and Weinstein, Bernard L., 'Initial Religious Counselling for a Male Orthodox Adolescent Homosexual', *Tradition* 29/2 (1995).

—— 'Counselling Homosexual Students', *Tradition* 29/4 (1995).

Wood, Mary E., 'How We Got This Way: The Sciences of Homosexuality and the Christian Right', *Journal of Homosexuality* 38/3 (2000).

Wosner, Rabbi Shmuel HaLevi, *Teshuvot Shevet HaLevi*, vol. 5, B'nei B'rak, 1984.

—— *Teshuvot Shevet HaLevi*, vol. 6, B'nei B'rak, 1988.

Wurzburger, Walter S., 'Preferences are not Practices', *Judaism* 32/4 (1983).

Ya'akov ben Asher, Rabbi, *Arba'ah Turim*.

—— *Perush Ba'al HaTurim al HaTorah*, B'nei B'rak, 1971.

Yehoshua ben Yosef of Cracow, Rabbi, *Teshuvot Penei Yehoshua*, Lemberg, 1860.

Yehoshua Falk HaKohen (Katz), Rabbi, *Derishah and Perishah on Arba'ah Turim*, in standard printed editions of R. Ya'akov ben Asher's *Arba'ah Turim*.

—— *Sefer Me'irat Eynayim on Shulchan Aruch Choshen Mishpat,* in standard printed editions of R. Yosef Caro's *Shulchan Aruch.*

Yehudah HeChasid, Rabbi, *Sefer Chasidim,* Mossad Harav Kook, Jerusalem, 1957.

—— *Perushei HaTorah LeRabbi Yehudah HeChasid* (ed., I. S. Lange), Israel, 1975.

Yeshayah di Trani, Rabbi, *Tosafot Rid,* Yerid HaSefarim, Jerusalem, 1995.

Yitzchak of Corbeil, Rabbi, *Sefer Mitzvot Katan,* Jerusalem, 1979.

Yosef ben Moshe, Rabbi, *Leket Yosher* (ed., J. Freimann) Berlin, 1903.

Yosef Chaim ben Eliyahu of Baghdad, Rabbi, *Teshuvot Rav Pe'alim,* Jerusalem, 1901.

—— *Teshuvot Torah Lishmah*,* Jerusalem, 1973.

—— *Ben Yehoyada al Aggadot HaShas,* Jerusalem, 1962.

Yossef, Rabbi Ovadiah, *Teshuvot Chazon Ovadiah,* part 1, vol. 2, Jerusalem, 1991.

Zadok HaCohen, Rabbi, *Tzidkat HaTzaddik,* B'nei B'rak, 1973.

Zion, William P., 'AIDS and Homosexuality: Some Jewish and Christian Responses', in William Closson James (ed.), *AIDS in Religious Perspective,* Queen's Theological College, Kingston, Ontario, 1987.

Zilberberg, Rabbi Moshe, 'Edut shel Tinok Shenishbah', in *Divrei Mishpat, Me'asef Torani b'inyanei Even HaEzer v'Choshen HaMishpat,* Machon Divrei Mishpat, vol. 3, Tel Aviv, 1997.

---

* NB: Rabbi Eliezer Portman, in the rabbinical journal *Moriah* (Ellul, 1978, p. 103), disputes the widely accepted attribution of this work to Rabbi Yosef Chayim of Baghdad.

Subject Index

Please note that references to notes have an 'n' after the page number, followed by note number

Index of Names

Please note that references to notes are denoted by page number, followed by 'n' and number of note. Where the reference or note extends to more than one page, the note details are in brackets.